SUMMER PLACE
A Golf Professional's Memoir

PATRICK LITTLE
CANADIAN PGA, LIFETIME MEMBER

One Printers Way
Altona, MB R0G 0B0
Canada

www.friesenpress.com

Copyright © 2023 by Patrick Little
First Edition — 2023

Cover illustration: Jordan Weiss

Based on a true story.

All rights reserved.

No part of this publication may be reproduced in any form, or by any means, electronic or mechanical, including photocopying, recording, or any information browsing, storage, or retrieval system, without permission in writing from FriesenPress.

ISBN
978-1-03-917330-9 (Hardcover)
978-1-03-917329-3 (Paperback)
978-1-03-917331-6 (eBook)

1. BIOGRAPHY & AUTOBIOGRAPHY, AVIATION & NAUTICAL

Distributed to the trade by The Ingram Book Company

For
Jackie, Robert, and Janine
"For the hours of leisure you gave up."

Contents

Acknowledgments	vii
Preface	xi
Chapter One ... Spring (Journal Entries 1 through 35)	1
Chapter Two ... Summer (Journal Entries 36 through 200)	35
Chapter Three ... Autumn (Journal Entries 201 through 331)	173
Chapter Four ... Winter (Journal Entries 332 through 399)	299
Epilogue	369
Summer Place Jukebox	371
Author's Blurbs	381

Acknowledgments

To   Joanna Cockerline for early encouragement, and Barbie Lefevre for corrections and inspiration.

To   Jackie for being an honest, non judgmental listener, and James Dow for patience over telephone recitals.

To   Every legitimate golf course architect whose land art endures, every musician, composer and lyricist whose music influenced me, and every politician who sought to avoid conflict.

To   Johnathan Heckbert who saved my draft and Jordan Weiss who created the cover.

To   The endless sources for whom I sought accuracy and advice as well as my dad … who took me to that first **Summer Place**.

As is so often said,
hard work is never so hard, when it is done with love.

—Audrey Hepburn

People will come, Ray.
They'll come to Iowa for reasons they can't even fathom.
They'll turn up your driveway, not knowing for sure why they're doing it.
They'll arrive at your door as innocent as children … longing for the past.

.

.

.

Then they'll walk off to the bleachers …
and sit in their shirtsleeves on a perfect afternoon.

.

.

.

Where they sat when they were children and cheered their heroes …
and they'll watch the game …
and it will be as if they dipped themselves in magic waters.
The memories will be so thick …
they'll have to brush them away from their faces.
People will come, Ray.

—W. P. Kinsella

Preface

Dedicated to *Larry Gavelin*

Writing a book wasn't easy and I didn't just sit down one day and decide to do it. For me, it was consequential.

In 2004, my wife Jackie and I invested in a golf course.

Golf had been my passion. And speculating our financial assets toward that passion seemed like my best shot. I don't mean the kind used to swing at someone or the magic of finesse. I meant the kind that business visionaries undertook when bankrolling themselves. To me, those were the **legitimate** best shots. Even among the professional golfers described within, there are few I believe who could have put up and played against their entire fortunes. I imagine the likes of Lee Trevino, Ben Hogan, or Tom Watson might have ... but few others ... and surely none of the new brand of pro golfers subsidized by the sovereign wealth fund of Saudi Arabia ... LIV Golf.

Consequently, when Jackie and I invested in the Hollies Golf Course in Port Alberni, British Columbia, we too joined those lonesome and sometimes forgotten entrepreneurs.

Then the Great Recession arrived!

In 2008, the global marketplace vomited. Suddenly we had to make serious survival decisions. Changes that forced us to lay off virtually every course employee. During the following years we became austere. Rolling up our sleeves, we were determined to survive and not go under as many did. Whether it was cutting greens, changing holes, bartending, monkey-wrenching, or teaching, we became solo employees, almost literally. It wouldn't have taken much then to ramble that same route Anthony Bourdain travelled when ending life. Thankfully I didn't. But those who've never taken those particular best shots, will ever know how threats of bankruptcy can be influencing. Alternatively though, I saw myself succumbing to burnout. I sought outlets or I'd have ended up like that infamous chef.

One black Port Alberni evening, staring into endless rain, I punched out an essay about what I knew best: golf. While hardly literary genius, it did relieve pressure. It fertilized another essay until eventually daily drafted efforts began delving into what shepherded my career, leaving me later examining where it vanished. As days became months and eventually years, rewrites became numerous. Living with uncertainties of ever publishing, there were no false expectations of being an Atwood or Hemingway, even after exhausting one Mac computer.

It amplified my moderate thinking liberalism. As one who appreciates social values like freedom and dignity, I grew to believe certain things could also survive change. Among them for instance, selective music, governance before Trump, and … golf! I wanted to hopefully, yet humbly, reflect that opinion in my work. Other elements evolved from the writing as well. Similarities between golf and life were reaffirmed. The challenges we face on golf courses, particularly links, when compared to life experiences. I also paid tribute to the many who shaped my career. Throughout, I dedicated this work to them in gratitude for the enjoyment I took away each day, on and off every course I played.

Finally golf has provided me indelible memories that included watching the best person in my life do one of the things she was so good at. Consequently, I wanted to paste some of those memories in print along with rationalizing the plight of golf's embattled artisan. The purist, if you want. **The one who still finds it fun playing original golf! The one who walks when playing, does it under four hours, keeps accurate score, plays by rules … and all while understanding why!** It's what I was nourished on and remained faithful to from the onset … golf's past. A past where perhaps even Holden Caulfield might have ranted, "Certain things they should stay the way they are."

Thank you for reading.

Summer Place

Summer Place is any place where golf is played. Where my soul and where Tom Morris, Arnold Palmer, and the spirit were all conceived.

Every golfer in the world has played there ... from Crail, Fife to Fletcher's Field, Québec. But to some of us, it's unseasonal, where a way of life endures and where earlier, possibilities of ending conflict between people existed.

And to borrow from the ideology of James Baldwin ... this work's an expression of that place. What remains is for readers to discern their own meaning from, when golfing there.

Chapter One

Spring

(Journal Entries 1 through 35)

Beginnings. Sam Snead.
Letter from Gary Player.
Golf's greatest shot.
Provincial Junior Champion.
Junior America's Cup. First time I see Jackie.
First lesson.

What follows, all happened, but only in the mind of the writer

Journal Entry #1: The Old Course (Part 1)
Dedicated to *Jackie*

St. Andrews, Scotland abides by the ocean in County Fife, on the countries' eastern shores. As site of one of the oldest universities in the English-speaking world, she's more mystically recognized as the home of golf. Knowing that, I was harnessed by the silence of anticipation when I first arrived there as a teenager.

That day began hours earlier in Perth under grim grey skies that eventually yielded to brilliant blue. I'd hitch-hiked all over the British Isles within previous months, and the smell from my boots confirmed the extent of those travels. To get to St. Andrews, a lorry driver with a rear flatbed had given me a lift. As we neared my destination, he pointed out a road sign that read *Royal Borough of St. Andrews*. The sight that followed telegraphed a distant community shaded in the colours of bone. Yet, the faded browns and medieval grays seemed ironically energized by mystic flows of vitality. He dropped me at what appeared its main intersection where I offered him my thanks. There, on a sullen building corner, I was immediately drawn to a sign which read, *Golf Place*. I knew this was where I was meant to be!

Beyond the placard, I felt a baptism awaiting as sunshine pacified the infamous St. Andrews clubhouse. A place known globally as, the Royal and Ancient. Flag posts next to that shrine dignified it as I ambled the short distance toward it along the narrow road with its perpetual traffic.

Let me explain to the reader about my life's round with golf. One, which later may become clearer. Golf has been not only like a kind matriarch to me, but a devout protectorate restraining me from exploring her inner realm. And yet, while confined to those fringes, over years I became an ironic clairvoyant who saw more than most who had good fortune to get onto her green, so to speak. And so it was disappointing having travelled so far, only to find **the Old Course** closed that time of year. There were five courses under direction of the Royal and Ancient then. I was welcome to play them all, but not the original. So I took my vengeance out on the New Course. And while some claim her superior, its predecessor was grander … chiseled by history, romance, and mystique as no other golf links in the world.

I played quickly before visiting other local haunts, like the grave sites of old and young Tom Morris as well as Allan Robertson, golf's first professional. I walked the town's distant stone pier which timelessly resisted ocean pulses. Like a lonely pathway leading toward unknown ends, it earlier abled locals to ship off toward North Berwick for hard-fought golf matches.

Later that afternoon, after removing myself from the bustle of Laurie Aucterlonie's golf shop, I returned to the Old Course where I was permitted to walk. Near the eleventh green, among dunes and gorse, gentle ocean breezes shifted fescue and marram, while warm sunshine beamed on me. There I slept.

In a sense, it felt the way my wife Jackie hugs our grandchildren. A loving embrace, not easily explained.

Journal Entry #2: The Education of a Golfer

Dedicated to *George Abric*

As a young teenager, the only great golfers or touring pros I'd seen were on television. But on a chilly 1960s May morning, I was fortunate to see golfing legend Sam Snead live when he visited my home town Edmonton.

Snead wasn't my golf hero. Regardless his book, **The Education of a Golfer**, was the first of instruction I read. Humorous and entertaining, his upbringing in Ashwood, Virginia where he was shaped into a professional golfer from a down-home boy, in a way was reminiscent of my own upbringing.

On that overcast spring morning, Alberta's grass remained brown at the Mayfair, a private club where the clinic was scheduled. A place where I later apprenticed. There on the driving range, I saw Snead dressed in a cardinal sweater and signature straw hat next to his red and white, larger-than-life

Wilson bag. It was when he began warming up I became a draftee of the golf swing. During the executions, he'd describe various shot outcomes with amazing accuracy. "Here's a high hook," he'd twang in Virginian, lofting a ball left, beyond the clouds. Next he'd claim, "And this is what a low fade looks like." It too, as if on command, shot off above ground level curving right. But the most persuasive aspect of the demonstration was Snead's persistent precision. Every shot was different, yet each swing appeared consistent.

Later as I grew, I sensed Snead was misunderstood among his peers. However, there was no misinterpreting that exhibition. I'd witnessed my first authentic golf swing, part of the mysterious game I sought to understand during the decades ahead.

Journal Entry #3: The Hawk (Keep Searchin')

Dedicated to *Bernie Parent*

I was introduced to the golf industry inadvertently ... before I played golf. I only discovered the game when my father recruited us to look for lost balls to sell (or hawk) at the local course.

Some people did it for that monetary gain. Others, like me however, found the hunting unexplainably gratifying.

Looking for golf balls might have appeared unusual and even deviant, but strangely it became a relaxing past time. One didn't hawk when golfing either. It was a separate outing and in a way unconnected to the game.

The place we hunted was on an air force base in Cold Lake, Alberta, at a course unaptly named Palm Springs. But while questionably named for one so far north, she was a haven for hawking. When I wasn't golfing, I hunted and friends joined too, sharing the experience. I became proficient at it, finding so many, I never had to buy. The favourites were *Wilson Staffs*. Cheap *Flyrite Campbells* were the most abundant, while the definite losers were made in Japan *Winners*. I found them imbedded in muskeg, nestled in blueberry bushes, lodged in trees, littering swamp bottoms and tapestried within beaver dams. They were everywhere.

Sometimes we weren't popular with golfers. Once, during the Airmen's Club Championship, old man Turnbull screamed at us so threateningly, I was certain he was in pursuit. We ran to escape, faster than a duck hook. At one point in that imaginary flight, I tripped on a hidden, barbed wire fence. Its rusted, jagged teeth ripped deep gashes of flesh out above both knees. Crusted with blood and dust, I limped the mile home to where my mother bathed those legs for weeks.

Those scars remain visible memories ... physical souvenirs of that subtle happiness I took from youth, searching for lost balls.

Journal Entry #4: Summer Place[1]
Dedicated to *Pete Burns*

During pre-teen years, my parents bought me a junior membership at that wilderness course. A place surrounded by what was called ... the woods.

And it was there most of my free time was spent. Whether scouting or building tree forts, I was among its descendants. I knew every hiding place there, including a seclusion among pines near the club. It was there I built my own course.

As a youngster creating a place to play, there weren't earth movers, shapers, or machinery to minimize work. It was only me. The soil was sandy and the trees were scrubby. The clearing was oval and the ground was lumpy. The geography however, accommodated two golfing holes among coniferous obstacles. One hundred and fifty yards of sand, made it virtually one massive bunker. At each end I cleared a tee and green adjacent each other. Tee boxes were the most level areas I found, while greens were where I could putt best. Hand-dug holes poked by branches for flagsticks finished the product. That was my layout. On days I couldn't play the airmen's course, I retreated there. Playing back and forth nine times, totalled eighteen holes. I patronized it every morning, walking the mile home for lunch, commandeering it again during afternoons. I've wondered many

---

1 "Summer Place:" Composition by Max Steiner, performed by Percy Faith.

times since why bears, cougars, or mosquitoes never challenged me then. My focus was only scoring lower than previous rounds.

Now retired, I occasionally remember back to that place where both greens and fairways weren't grass and the environment was stress free. A place where in solitude I dreamt of greatness while lingering indefinitely between shots. A **summer place** that was possibly the best golf course ever.

Journal Entry #5: Cherish
Dedicated to *Scotty Macgregor*

Scotty Macgregor was a cheerful mystery. She was a Palm Spring's member, and like the men, employed at the air base.

Originally, she was from Scotscraig, Scotland, a wee bit more than a brassie shot from St. Andrews. How she ended up in northern Alberta, I never knew. But I've met few people who possessed her knowledge and love for the game. Scotty might have held a PhD on the subject if offered. Even Sir Michael Bonallack, the Royal and Ancient's famous patriarch, might've had his hands full debating her.

Chubby, short, and round, I wouldn't say she was physically attractive. Yet, she radiated a casual, pleasant demeanour. Her washboard laughter, frizzy hair, and Gaelic way saying, "Cheerio" when departing, left everyone endeared to her.

Scotty wasn't someone you crossed though. Her guiding senses of right and wrong continually slapped my wrists during on course teenage miscues.

Scotty seemed comfortable playing to a mid-handicap level. Much later, when I turned pro, I remembered thinking back to how she swung a golf club, rotating about her thick core. Were all Scots born that way, or just byproducts of secretly brewed malt whiskeys? More probably, they were bred from playing responses to harsh North Atlantic winds which terrorized Scottish links!

When Scotty retired home, I invited her back to visit us and play. She accepted and stayed weeks, sharing herself with my family. After she returned, I lost track of her in Scotscraig. I heard she volunteered for the Open at St. Andrews during John Daly's win there, but no one knew where she finished her last round. Before we lost each other though, she needlepointed a Ben Hogan picture for me with a title embroidered: *The secret ... is in the dirt!*

I read that Hogan once claimed, "Listening is more important than talking." And had I known that as a youngster, I might have found Scotty was anything but mysterious.

Journal Entry #6: The Way They Were (Part 1)

Dedicated to *Tony Buchanan*

Golf courses attract distinctive clienteles. Memberships can look like an ingredients list from the book *The Joy of Cooking,* or like Ray Liotta's character impressions in Martin Scorsese's film, *Goodfellas*.

The Palm Springs course wasn't any different, except its golfers were airmen. Support staff for pilots in Canada's air defense system. They too were goodfellas, but a different species.

There was little Tony, who coincidentally was Italian. Short and tanned, he could have easily been cast in that same gangster flick. He walked with a wiggle and could play, although not quite well enough. Then there was Hank, the group's elder. He should have been a mentor, but you dared not take your eyes off him on the course. With an extremely narrow and closed stance, a nose shaped like a hawk, and Croatian facials, he was a force and a favourite but not a popular one. Danny was a southpaw whose Mediterranean tan convicted him sweaty. The unpredictable player nervously tapped the ground with his toes before swinging, like the irritating waggles of Spaniard Sergio Garcia.

Andy and Bozak were the club's long bombers. We juniors lobbied who drove it further. Big men with wide shoulders, they each owned physical professional wrestling traits. Andy had Gene Kiniski's crewcut while Bozak could have been Hulk Hogan's twin. Both were advanced players, always trying to bust the ball. Andy taught me to always bring a jacket when golfing, claiming: "If you bring it and have to wear it, you can ... but not if you didn't." Simple logic! Forty years later he showed up at our golf course and strangely, wasn't big anymore.

Finally, there was Pete and George. Often inseparable, they were pals like the comic characters, Bert and Ernie. Popular and talented fixtures at the course, they owned expensive Wilson clubs which were kept immaculate. Both had been stationed overseas and golfed St. Andrews. It was their Old Course stories that continually rippled my imagination. Their presence as scorekeepers in our tournaments, inspired my own work later with juniors. Forty years later I reunited with George one sunny afternoon at his home course in Comox, British Columbia. But I never saw Pete again.

Good recipes are usually coveted. And like the Worcester sauce that seasons any properly made Caesar, memberships add flavour and diversity to golf courses.

Journal Entry #7: Time of the Season
Dedicated to *the Littles*

In the late 1960s, a tobacco company sponsored Canadian professional tour events, through marketing a cigarette named *Peter Jackson*. The product, which enjoyed a measure of publicity, was sold at many courses.

One of the lures of golf is its companionship with temptation. The unseen force flirts with every golfer from advanced to beginners. It's often due to each golfer's unwillingness to berate their built-in egos. A similar beckoning taunts youngsters to smoke that first cigarette.

I was an example of that in the summer of '68.

One sunny evening I found a full pack of Jacksons left on a bench by the second tee. After a quick survey accompanied by dark thoughts, I smuggled them into my bag.

Subsequent early mornings of solitary practise became a laboratory experimenting with that first and only fling with the fag. I disliked it immediately! First it failed any appealing test. Second, while addressing the ball, smoke annoyingly penetrated my nostrils, stinging eyes and diverting concentration. Third, was the persistent guilt of the misdemeanour. Consequently, I justified the exercise. I read tour golfers like Charlie

Sifford used the cigarette's mouth position to visually determine head movement when swinging ... a fundamental error. That didn't work either. And as I walked the fairways, macho feelings emerged when clasping the joint between my teeth like Canadian George Knudson did. That illegitimate maturity was also short-lived after a scrimmage with common sense. I determined smoking wasn't anything good.

Today, smart phones dispense undeniable information about the cancer stick, yet deniability prevails ... even despite tastes more than marginally below disgusting. Occasionally since, I've been gifted Cuban cigars and the inventory's grown as I rarely smoke them. However once in a while, after rare disputes with my wife, I've unwrapped the odd one and strolled onto the course for a light up. There the condemning campaign continues.

Journal Entry #8: Minds, Drugs, and Archery

Dedicated to *Uncle Art*

In the winter of '77, a single-engine Cessna piloted by my Uncle Art, supposedly disappeared during a storm over the Straits of Georgia! The mystery remains unsolved.

My uncle was extraordinary. British, he was short and a legitimate genius. A flamethrower in the army during World War II, he'd talked his way into recruitment at age fifteen. After immigrating to Canada, he applied for and was awarded a job operating heavy equipment in northern Alberta, persuasively claiming experience with none. Later, he settled on Vancouver Island where he became an expert archer, manufacturing bows which I've heard are collector's items.

The last time I saw him was during the late '60s; when he suggested a training method for golf, which I later used for students. In university the technique was called functional overload, a way of developing performance muscles.

He thought I could beef up my calves for golf by walking eighteen holes daily in snow. Today, that might be considered absurd. But truthfully, a golfer's lower limbs are probably the most underrated part of their equipment. His idea was to develop them in difficult conditions, enabling more specific motor skills. Since then, I've witnessed comparable results from athletes in various sports using the technique. Professional golfer Gary Player swung a bar bell feigning a golf club. The infamous Russian Red Army hockey squad skated with each other on their shoulders in practise. And the equally famous Montréal Canadian hockey star, Yvan Cournoyer too. He strengthened his hands for stick-handling using salmon cans of molten lead that simulated heavy pucks.

Later, after turning professional, I taught that overload technique along with goals and fundamentals. Even today, I use a weighted club on days before playing.

Later, my uncle unfortunately turned his brilliant mind toward pursuits of lesser value. He was recruited by the shady to design and assemble a capsule-making machine, of which he was capable. That door led my mother's brother into a world of narcotics, specifically the manufacture of MDMA. While too smart to ever indulge, he more than glimpsed its murky depths. My wife and I once visited one of his haunts, a mushroom laboratory, sophisticatedly equipped with two-way cameras, electron microscopes, and ingenious escape routes … a secret location for those dark interests. Eventually he was indicted by the provincial justice system which led to his bizarre disappearance.

Whatever happened to my uncle on that mysterious trip, we may never know. But he was an outstanding pilot and flying below radar wasn't limiting.

For over forty years as a golf pro, I've listened to most of the world's best teachers and while my uncle never golfed, his suggestions to improve stamina and technique were simplistically visionary. Unfortunately they fail to solve the lingering puzzle why those with incredible minds continue entertaining questionable life choices.

Journal Entry #9: See You in September
Dedicated to *Jim Dolan*

I've felt the human electricity pulsating the air among olive trees at Valderrama during the Ryder Cup Matches in Spain. I embraced the nostalgia competing against Arnold Palmer for the Canadian PGA championship. And I survived the tension from the 1978 Alberta Women's Amateur watching my wife sink a winning putt. An electric shot dethroning a Canadian icon and igniting an extraordinary amateur career.

But to me, the best golf tournament took place when I was a teenager at the air base. It framed many future golf memories which continue hanging from the walls of my mind.

During September of my first golf year, a lady member suggested I play in the Junior Club Championship. A week later, with a dozen others, I teed off in the eighteen-hole event amid bitterly cold conditions. Conditions which worsened as the day progressed. Rain followed, soaking everyone. A harsh and chilling arctic wind joined in, perforating us. The fact we all finished with sincere smiles, was inspiring. That it was occasion for acquiring my first trophy was irrelevant. It was the warmth engulfing numbed golf bodies huddling before a river-rock fireplace as nearby radiators warmed saturated clothing. Where juniors, scorekeepers, cups of chocolate, marshmallows, hotdogs and trophies mingled within the sheltering amber of that quaint log clubhouse.

I thought it was the best tournament ever.

As it's been said, "Less is more!"

Journal Entry #10: Downtown
Dedicated to *Geoff Collier*

Today, it's hard to believe parents would allow eleven-year-olds to hitchhike two hundred and fifty kilometres to big-city golf tournaments … fending for themselves. That was my first experience playing in an event far from home. My greatest fear however, had little to do with hitchhiking predators or child molesters. Instead, it was the tournament: the Edmonton Junior. I entered, claiming only a Junior Club Championship as experience.

After long rides and endless walks, I made it to the capital from the air base. There I was dropped off at the **downtown** hotel my parents had arranged for me. Finding the course next day was another matter.

In my search, I was accompanied by a shoddy pea-green bag, seven rusty clubs, and a parched local map. I began walking from the city core among urban smells from bustling vehicles, pedestrians, and dust. Hours later I arrived above the river valley to my destination ... the Highlands Golf Course. I hadn't even played before my blistered feet and throbbing shoulders forecasted the outcome.

I was unaware of my tee time when the tournament starter, an ogre named Gray, snarled at me for missing the appointment. While insensitive, he did allow me to participate at the draw's end, where I scored a disappointing 91.

Somewhere on the course though, my map vanished, forcing a return without directions. Fortunately back then, Edmonton's own CN Tower had become a new metro landmark. Looking west into the far distance, I saw its faint outline above ground covers of suburban rooftops and smog. I followed that structure into darkness, taking dead aim at its remote lights, all while nursing fatigue. After many hours I successfully returned, testifying to an early resourceful ability.

Journal Entry #11: I'll be Doggone!

Dedicated to *Geezy*

One sunny evening during a casual round, I saw my wife sink her tee shot for the first of five career holes-in-one. At Augusta National Golf Club, I saw the inventor of the sand wedge, Gene Sarazen hole a sand shot. As for myself, executing a subtle chip from behind the tenth green at Monterey's Cypress Point Club, where time actually seemed restrained, was a memory I kept forever.

And during the Masters, golfers everywhere witnessed the undeniable finesse of Tiger Woods. From behind Augusta's sixteenth green, he chipped in so delicately, it left even him mesmerized. But none of those qualified as golf's greatest shot. That was struck during 1968 at a modest nine-hole sand course in St. Paul, Alberta.

It happened during the town's annual Men's Open, where over twenty-seven holes on a hot and searing afternoon, a new suit awaited the winner. A prize I desperately wanted.

The man who struck it was named Geezy, short for Giesbrecht. Entering from Lloydminster, Alberta, he was a lanky bartender whose head shape cited dill pickle images.

I was fifteen years old then, competing against northern Alberta farmers and rednecks. With four holes left, I remained three strokes behind Geezy. I gained two back as we teed up on the second last hole, a one hundred and seventy-five yard blind shot over a gorge of tall poplars. Beyond it, the ground sloped toward a pancaked sand green. I struck a four iron nicely over the forest knowing it was close. Geezy followed with his worst. He pull-hooked (a curving, dive shot) far left into dense woods. After a long five minutes, we found it, but let descriptions guide a reader's opinion.

The ball was hidden among a thick grove of twenty-foot high saplings. Tall grass and waist-high brush added to the despair. From its location the fairway was invisible and at least twenty yards away. Worse, his ball wedged itself between the ground and an angled tree trunk. Geezy had two options, hit the prisoner or declare it unplayable. He decided on the former! In a bartender's mix of one-shot brilliance and an another sheer lunacy, he turned his iron sideways and used the clubhead's toe. Further, he swung left-handed due to the tree and tangles of brush. Making contact alone would have been achieving. The bartender took a lifetime assuming a crude, awkward squat before finally swinging. He struck it solidly! We all watched in amazement as it missed every branch and leaf impediment scoping a fairway. Flaring from the foliage, it then accepted ground slope momentum, scooting onward toward the distant green, as greyhounds do rounding bends. Unbelievably, its journey settled ten feet from the hole!

Geezy's putt finalized a par for the millennium. It would have been criminal had I made mine. With the bartender remaining one up, he went on to win.

Over five decades have passed since and during those times; I've occasionally seen Geezy. And while he's long outgrown the suit, golf's greatest shot has continued its legacy in our minds.

Journal Entry #12: Mini Ha Ha and the Rats

Dedicated to *Ken Hitchcock*

As a developing teen, at some point I had to compare myself to Alberta's best young golfers. It was at that first provincial championship, held at Edmonton's Derrick, where I met Mini Ha Ha.

I hitchhiked to the Alberta capital from the air base, and after a series of bus connections, found the south side course. There playing a practise round, I followed four other juniors. Eventually they invited me to join them. They were members of a city run course called Riverside and their nickname was ... the rats. More specifically, Riverside Rats. Breezy and fun, they went about their business playing for birdies. Brent and Donny were easy-going, yet serious about their golf. Jan was the son of a golf pro who'd been murdered in a sensational scandal that earlier clung to local papers. Finally, there was Mini Ha Ha, as they called him.

Mini, who was extremely overweight for a teenager, waddled the fairways wearing a pork pie hat and carrying his clubs. I knew course superintendents who flinched knowing Mini was playing because of the greens he compressed when treading them. Mini treated me as one of the boys, and I was always surprised how well he played considering the physical disadvantage. Yet he owned a self-assurance that silently ignored it.

Outside golf, he worked at a local bicycle shop, later etching his name historically as a renowned coach in Canadian Junior hockey circles.

I've read his nickname now is Hitch, and Ken Hitchcock evolved into a legendary National Hockey League coach. One with a Stanley Cup ring on his finger. Watching him now though, I can't help but admire his greatest win might have been earlier during those formative years as Mini Ha Ha.

Journal Entry #13: Gary Player (Part 1)
Dedicated to *Gary Player*

In idolatry, sometimes individuals are placed on life's pedestal, and like former US President Trump, perhaps not always for the better. That was confirmed in golf too, when fans suddenly craved the glitz of pro John Daly.

And so I claim cautiously, the South African **Gary Player** was my first golf hero.

As a golf hungry teen, I emulated him acknowledging our short characteristics and wills to succeed. He practised tirelessly, leading me to believe that attribute alone produced positive results. During the '60s he was a force in golf's major championships: the British Open, Masters, PGA, and US Open. During those events, I was hypnotically drawn to the television, watching him dressed in black tackling bigger, brawnier opponents.

I purchased his book *Positive Golf* and still own it today. From it, I extracted a series of values including diet, exercise and work ethics, which have remained with me.

Player's routines included weight lifting and running. I ran too, jogging daily. My route began from our military living quarters to nearby hangars housing CF-104 Starfighter jets. It was a five-kilometre journey where I ran so often, airmen regularly acknowledged me. That was early each morning before walking the kilometre to school and back. As a result, my legs became strong.

Player's training methods were legendary. He'd practise in sand traps until holing shots, improving both focus and technique.

Later as a golf professional, I shared that ideology in my teaching methods. It taught me the reality that everyone's capable of producing more than they believe. It also flavoured a developing opinion that success in life was rooted in dedication and discipline.

And within that frame of thought, nutrients of balance, harmony, perspective and proportion emerged, nourishing other outlooks in life … such as picking icons I chose to emulate.

Journal Entry #14: Riders on the Storm

Dedicated to *Andy Anderson*

Terrible Tommy was a nickname assigned the '50s PGA tour star, Tommy Bolt. A flamboyant player in a vintage era, he competed against legends like Arnold Palmer, Ben Hogan, and Sam Snead. In 1958, Bolt won the US Open. Unfortunately, he's instead been remembered for a rebellious temper.

Golf and tempers have lived together like quarrelling siblings since the game began. While not every golfer possesses one, there are enough to justify the claim. As one of the guilty, I swore with the best, threw clubs further than ball players, and choked trees with that same equipment.

Unfortunately, there were too many moments after rounds, when I felt shame and embarrassment. When thinking of the companions I disturbed with that anger, the remorse is a powerful depressant.

And while there was no justification for those actions, there was a footnote.

As a youngster, I was dialled into golf and there was no temper. But like the silence of cancer, it progressed proportionally to my practise efforts. I worked longer and harder than even PGA tour stars. As a small raging bull on driving ranges, I laboured endlessly trusting it would produce positive results. Hitting a thousand practise balls daily wasn't unusual. My hands bled regularly and I could accurately forecast stages of pain and blister recovery. But my efforts outpaced progress. Frustration rooted rage resulting in disgraceful acts of course behaviour.

Unlike my career peers though, I laboured that way without the benefit of professional instruction. I was fate's trial-and-error victim too many times … its punching bag. It wasn't an anger manager I needed, but a competent instructor.

Many years later, the father of one of my staff noticed, and gently offered me the benefit of his Peace Corps wisdom. He said: "You know, when you lose your temper, you lose control of those around you." That suggestion was transforming and as a businessman, I couldn't afford to dismiss it.

I only wish in hindsight he'd been there when I threw that first golf club!

Journal Entry #15: Soul Coaxing
Dedicated to *Jim Turnbull*

Occasionally, the word par is used loosely in phrases unrelated to golf. For instance, in Keith Richard's memoir, *Life*, he acknowledges going cold turkey from Jamaican dope as, "par for the course." And interestingly, as a golf pro, one of the most often asked questions was, "What's a par?"

Wikipedia suggests it's "A term in golf used to denote the pre-determined number of strokes that a scratch [or 0 handicap] golfer should require to complete a hole." That always seemed vague to me. Regardless of how it's decoded, shooting par or breaking it, can be inspiring and transforming. It can be rooted in the symbolism, "not giving up, going forward, and staying positive." Potent fuel for any career whether it be golf ... or life.

And while goal setting's important, par's measuring stick in golf varies. During my on course development, definitions of it followed. Initially my goal was to break forty over our nine-hole course followed by shooting par on that same nine. After that, I aimed to break eighty and eventually par over eighteen holes followed by breaking seventy on the same. And later retired, I saved the best for last, opening champagne after shooting my age. Only then did understand golf was the game of a lifetime.

All of those successes were memorable. However, the most empowering was breaking par over eighteen holes. For on that day, I faced a sharp, downhill thirty-footer on the final hole to achieve that goal. The fact it fell was irrelevant. By making that putt when needed, my soul was coaxed into believing anything in life was subsequently possible! Even weeks later, when scoring a blistering sixty-seven, it failed to duplicate that earlier seventy-first stroke.

I've saved each of those balls as testimony to par's power of inspiration.

Journal Entry #16: The Rain, the Park, and Other Things

Dedicated to *Darwin Sturko*

After my first provincial championship, I was ready for a second chance. The event was in Calgary, six hundred kilometres away. I was still hitchhiking across the prairies to tournaments, but that trip was longer. With only money for entry fees and food, I had to find accommodation once there.

The event was at Calgary's Country Club, a private parkland in the city's heart. With the course only bus rides away, camping at the local zoo and prehistoric park seemed a good idea.

Returning from competition each night, gigantic looming dinosaur shadows silhouetted urban background lights. But they were no comparison to the savage mosquitos that infested St. Georges Park. I chose a bushy area near the Bow River, where my clubs would be safe while sleeping out. Wrong choice!

Despite horrendous insect bites, I took away two wonderful tournament memories. First, after two rounds I was in second place, prompting competitors to query who I was. We played in near hurricane conditions, where mature poplars were uprooted and branches littered the course. Accompanying the rain, wind speeds were recorded over seventy kilometres per hour! I played spectacular scoring seventy-four, but by day's end, the southern Alberta favourites hadn't. With the field nearly finished, officials cancelled the round … along with my exceptional play.

The second event took place during my practise round.

Calgary's Country Club was home then to three famous amateurs who'd earned international prominence. Keith Alexander, Doug Silverberg, and Bob Wylie, were certified legends. On the tenth tee near the concession stand, was a prominent display of scorecards from their extensive travels. Places with names like St. Cloud, Royal Melbourne, and Cypress Point inspired my imagination. And in that spiritual moment, I ordained myself a global golfer.

I didn't win that tournament, but from my cancelled round, saw for the first time golf and life weren't always going to play fair and, later still, that legitimate passions survive forever.

Journal Entry #17: Dream

Dedicated to *John Cherniwchan*

> So dream, when the day is through
> Dream, and they might come true.
>
> —Roy Orbison

In school, I never flirted with outstanding grades. I was a dreamer, accounting for poor academic performances. School was a place with three potential outcomes: excelling toward university, digressing into trades, or dropping out.

In eleventh grade, I was heading toward choice two, relearning addition and subtraction ... steps away from choice three. One day, I deterred that with an original thought that depended on the provincial math program. The idea, if successful, would assure my entry into two advanced math classes. Passing them would make university possible. First though, I had to master logarithms and the slide rule. I came home excited, announcing the plan to my mother, who in turn, visited the school's vice principal, Mr. Harris. Later, he summoned me to his office trying to convince me the idea was meritless. Fortunately, he didn't have final say and that summer I registered in correspondence school.

Forcing myself to understand logarithms and the slide rule, I succeeded. The result allowed me to attend both math classes.

Focused on that goal, and guided by my kind teacher Mr. Cherniwchan, I kept the flame from flickering out, passing his courses of calculus, probability and trigonometry. A year earlier, those subjects were only a **dream** as I went on toward a university education.

It's been more than fifty years since my experience with those educators. But that lesson astonished me. If you have an idea based on **fact,**

accompanied by common sense, strong convictions, and perseverance, dreams can come true.

Much later during the Great Recession, one of the fallouts was a serious lack of golfers at the small course we owned. Possessing strong beliefs in what I was doing then, helped avoid bankruptcy in that crisis.

Journal Entry #18: Out of Time
Dedicated to *Ken Matson*

In the autumn of '69, we moved to the Edmonton suburb Sherwood Park. Relocation to private life was difficult for my father who was without skills and me as a teenager in an unfamiliar school. Our family struggled emotionally and financially, which impacted my golf as memberships were unaffordable. And without golf, life became lonely.

Within close walking distance from our home though, was a public course named Broadmoor. The urge to play was overwhelming and in desperation I found a solution. Property around the course was developing and a new street backed onto it. The course was laid out in ways I could enter from that road, undetected by the pro shop. I justified my actions, deluding I could walk in rain without getting wet.

Of course, the day arrived when I ran **out of time** … and got soaked. That was when I was confronted by head pro Ken Matson, a clone of '60s pop idol Dion DiMucci.

In my confession, I offered to pay back the misdemeanour by helping out in his shop. While he overlooked the offense, he didn't allow me to settle the score.

Years later, as a head professional myself, it became an ironic duty dealing with similar perpetrators. During those apprehensions though, I always tried maintaining an empathetic perspective.

Journal Entry #19: Shell's Wonderful World of Golf

Dedicated to *Gene Sarazen and Jimmy Demaret*

During the cold winter that followed, our family suffered intense emotional turmoil when my parents continually argued over incomes. We siblings were a nervous bunch, uncertain of outcomes should they divorce.

Those tension filled months were soothed Saturday afternoons watching the televised program, **Shell's Wonderful World of Golf.** Any Canadian who's enjoyed hockey, probably recalls CBC television's famous opening refrain to *Hockey Night in Canada.* Shell's program too, had an equally popular theme.

The telecast featured two legendary hosts. The charismatic Jimmy Demaret and his infamous partner Gene Sarazen. Each program focused on matches between two prominent pros in knock out formats, playing the world's most famous courses. Accented by those informative hosts, producers lasered in on the venues, locations, and cultures, nourishing my imagination and luring me to them later in life.

My parents never divorced and stayed together sixty years. And while we siblings aren't close, there are slender threads connecting us. I became in debt to that show, for not only fuelling my passions, but suturing those severed emotions during that sullen, harsh season.

Journal Entry #20: Ten Pound Note

Dedicated to *Peter Cushner*

During that unbearable tension at home, I ran away twice. I never got far though.

That's when I realized the agony didn't exist on golf courses. Further, as my academic peers were caught within crosshairs of drug abuse, hitting golf balls was my high. The following spring, my parents somehow purchased me a junior membership at Broadmoor.

There I plugged into a group of teens who all assumed the roles of PGA tour stars.

John was fair-haired and freckled. Lean and wiry, he enjoyed good but silly humour. We called him Chi Chi, after Chi Chi Rodriquez, the effervescent Puerto Rican star. He even emulated the Caribbean's ceremonial cup stabbings using his putter. Greg was fair-haired, lanky, and tall. He was my main opponent in the Club Championship. He had a lumbering swing and coincidentally made the forest industry his career. The controversial Frank Beard was his hero.

Mike was tall and dark-haired with a rangy swing reminiscent of the balloon man. Later, we reconnected frequently in the golf industry. He was Tom Weiskopf, fittingly as the temperamental PGA enigma was Mike's emotional equal.

Peter appeared Mediterranean and muscular. Like me, he loved golf and became a Canadian touring pro. Later, he settled as the popular head man in Lloydminster Alberta, succumbing eventually to an early passing. On course, he could be always counted on to bring up the subject of women's breasts. Canadian George Knudson was his icon.

Finally, there was me … the gang's short, hard-working, and passionate golfer. I had no idea what I swung like. And fittingly I was Gary Player, future golf pro and course owner.

They were the ones I played with regularly. Descendants who in my final junior year shared a pre-adult innocence. The one's whose steel spiked shoes clacked on pavement walking home nightly after fifty-four holes of golf. The one's I think about now when hearing Steel River's vocal harmony in **Ten Pound Note**.

Journal Entry #21: Gary Player (Part 2)

Dedicated to *Mike O'Reilly*

In the spring of 1970, I wrote a letter. Uncertain of the address, I was naive enough to believe mail always reached its intended destination. I sent it to my inspiration of the day, **Gary Player**. In the correspondence, among other things, I described what he and the sport meant to me.

One sunny afternoon weeks later, a letter arrived back. I trembled ripping open the envelope whose return address was Davis, Kirby, and Player Inc.

In it, hand written on stationary, were words from the South African himself. He thanked me, advising I get Masters tickets quickly. While I had no money for such fantasy, it didn't matter. Gary Player actually took time to correspond with me! Alone in my room later, I absorbed his most memorable sentence: "If you work hard in life you will <u>always</u> succeed," underlining always. He ended by expressing wishes to meet me one day.

The words, while inspirational, remained somewhat ethereal.

Journal Entry #22: I Go to Pieces

Dedicated to *Brick Miller*

After two rounds of the Edmonton Amateur I was in the hunt. As a junior, I found my golf at times remarkable, although inconsistent. After sinking a long putt on the thirty-sixth hole, I headed to the finals at Highlands, where this time I was up against the cities' best. I didn't anticipate crowds though.

People never followed me before and self consciousness began jellying within.

After my front nine, the spectators trickled away. I fell to pieces when my good scores did the same. On the back however I pulled it together finishing third, my first hint of success in a competition of substance.

Later, I saw another dimension to self-consciousness from the droll of Bob King, father of Canadian Olympic hockey coach, Dave King. Bob lampooned self conscious victims with the question: "When you're watching a football game, do you ever wonder if the players in the huddle are talking about you?"

I borrowed that line frequently later when teaching new golfers about the self-consciousness of first tee jitters.

Journal Entry #23: Alexander the Great (Part 1)

Dedicated to *Keith Alexander*

As a result of that Amateur showing, I was selected to participate in the intercity matches against Calgary's best. The series was played at Calgary's Canyon Meadows where I was overwhelmed learning my first game was against Canadian legend, Keith Alexander!

When I began golfing, I read articles about the Calgarian, published by our Royal Canadian Golf Association (now Golf Canada). His numerous achievements added fuel to my imagination. He'd won our national amateur, represented Canada at the Worlds, and played in the Masters.

Suddenly in team competition, I found myself paired against this same icon. A young teenager against one of earth's finest amateurs. I was awestruck in his presence. He wasn't physically big either, but pleasant to golf with. He called his attractive, red-haired girl friend Peaches and courted a silky smooth putting stroke. On one occasion, he played an errant shot and I followed it with mine. "Same dog bit you." He said, in his first direct comment to me.

My partner was a prominent Edmontonian playboy, who while slick, wasn't in Alexander's class. I sensed his subtle frustration with my inconsistency when in one situation, he coached me on a shot through a mature deciduous. He reasoned there was 80 percent air amongst its branches and I should "blast my way through." I winced when it failed, seeing his facial veins compete with the part in his jet-black hair.

We lost to Alexander, but like osmosis I absorbed all I could from him. It's a fact golf can be intimidating. But by forcing ourselves to play with others more advanced ... in golf or other endeavours ... we improve through learning naturally!

The question will always remain though, whether new-comers will rise to the occasion? Will they welcome opportunity and place ego aside? Later, when teaching beginner students, I explained that aspect with the analogy, "It's no different than the speech you hated reciting during English class in school." Invariably, improvement comes down to one thing ... how much one **truthfully** wants success!

Journal Entry #24: 15 Minutes (Part 1)

Dedicated to *John O'Brien*

Pop artist Andy Warhol reportedly claimed, "Everyone in life gets fifteen minutes of fame."

Mine came at Edmonton's Windermere during the 1970 Alberta Junior Championship ... my final year as a young amateur.

Preparing for it, I found my golf swing in shambles.

Golf swings are like picture puzzles families piece together during holidays. Various part's are integral to the whole. Golfers too, spend their time searching for their own total pictures. Often, when one swing part's found, another fades away and like life, the search ventures on. And sometimes without reason, seemingly small irrelevant swing changes produce enormous sweeps in performance. Even golf's finest instructors often fail diagnosing them. It was that kind of change before the tournament, that aired my destiny.

After a dismal practise round, I found myself unhappier. Consequently, late that day I was motivated to play an extra nine before next morning's start. Mini Ha Ha joined me and together, we headed out. While I don't recall what altered, it happened on the fifth tee, where something just clicked. The results while immediate, weren't spectacular. However, a scent of difference prevailed.

The two over par I shot that evening failed to forecast the outcome ahead.

Journal Entry #25: Snowbird

Dedicated to *Garry Meyers*

Sometimes memories are suppressed and then unexpectedly aroused through a sensual prompt. For instance, flashbacks mobilized by aromas of a previous time. One of my favourites is freshly mown golf course grass. And it's not only restricted to smell. It might be a popular song for instance.

During the first round, I scored seventy-four. I was happy with that, leaving me only strokes behind tournament leaders. The strange visceral feeling that emerged from the night before, had remained within me. They call it the zone, a place in the mind rarely visited and a sensation athletes crave to own. A site where owners can seemingly accomplish whatever they will their mind toward. I didn't understand it, but like a comforting friend, it hung around me those three days. And while it's never returned, I'm reminded of it when occasionally hearing the song, ***Snowbird*** written and performed by the Maritime duo Gene MacLellan and Anne Murray. I heard it everywhere I went that tournament.

Journal Entry #26: 15 Minutes (Part 2)

Dedicated to *Brent Bailey*

Blue, sunny skies and windless conditions monopolized the second day. I was paired with Brent, one of the Riverside Rats. My round began with astonishing approaches on two of the first six holes. There, I took advantage of tap-in birdies to finish my front nine two under.

That set up a round of seventy-one and a thirty-six-hole score of 145, tying me for second behind leader, Medicine Hat Don. Don was the province's premier junior. He'd overwhelmed the field a year earlier at Calgary's Country Club. With a slender, Mediterranean build, he was a defender with a serious disposition.

I was tied with a young up-and-comer from Red Deer named Mike. He'd been well coached by his highly respected club pro. One I later modelled myself after. Mike had all the shots.

While not in possession of his game, mine was regardlessly working. A local sports writer labeled me the "Cinderfella Kid," considering I came from nowhere.

On the eve of my final round, I slept soundly … accountable only to whoever was pushing the buttons of fate.

Journal Entry #27: 15 Minutes (Part 3)

Dedicated to *Darrell Meyer*

The gentleman of adventure, author Ernest Kellogg Gann, titled his novel, *Fate is the Hunter*.

The tournament's last day was another perfect one. I was in the second last group, approaching the fifth green when Broadmoor friends reported the woes of Medicine Hat Don. Fortunately, I wasn't smart enough to get my hopes up. A one over thirty-six on the front confirmed my relaxed nature.

As my back nine played out however, evidence confirmed the leader faltering as crowds began following me. My performance stayed steady and strangely consistent. I was hitting long par-four's in two with woods into small greens. It continued at the uphill, dogleg left final hole. There, after two putting for another thirty-six and a seventy-two, I signed my card and retired.

I was reclining on the clubhouse steps in shade, cautiously wondering what was happening, when suddenly everyone was in and I'd won by a stroke!

I dreamt of moments like that but after numerous failures, never believed it could happen. As a naive eighteen year-old with no tutoring, I succeeded with only primitive instincts and hitting more practise shots in seven years than most hit in lifetimes! Plus being absent social skills, I was ignorant of thank-you speeches or appreciating laurels extended me.

I suspected then, the almighty CEO simply took pity and reluctantly conceded me the fifteen minutes. Fate found its victim.

Journal Entry #28: A Horse With No Name

Dedicated to *Earl Keeley*

When writing this, a talented, young pro from Northern Ireland named Rory McIlroy ended a relationship with his agent. It was an aftershock following McIlroy's stunning US Open win and typical how his life became renovated. I too encountered change after capturing that Alberta Championship.

Winning the provincials however, could never be confused with a US Open victory, nor was I Rory McIlroy. Regardless, to an innocent teenager, that win altered my life. The question was whether I could identify and navigate the differences?

Changes arrived in various forms. I was fitted for uniforms, part of a national team representing Canada in Los Angeles. I was featured on radio, television, and written up in newspapers. People I never met became new best friends … long-lost pals. Others I knew from distances became closer. People acted different too, following and watching me in tournaments. But it didn't last because fate stepped in once again.

From those new relationships, needs to perform grew like weeds. Until then, I simply loved golf and lusted for improvement through practise. I savoured the experience of swinging golf clubs without pressure. I was like the great lady professional Mickey Wright, who enjoyed that aspect above all else. After my victory however, situations arose where I was incapable of reproducing shots newly found admirers were expecting. I became **a horse with no name**, and the inconsistency became persistent.

That's what faced me, preparing for the upcoming Junior Americas Cup.

Journal Entry #29: California Dreamin'

Dedicated to *Babe McAvoy*

The Junior America's Cup was an international event, alternately hosted by Canada, Mexico, and the States. That year it was held in Los Angeles, California where six players from each country competed in Ryder Cup formats. There in suffocating swelter and smog, I was introduced to the Southern Californian Golf Association, a legitimate powerhouse of young talents such as Craig Stadler and Corey Pavin.

My fear, however, wasn't aroused by any future Master's or US Open champion, but instead by a muscular local Greek, who had earlier dethroned a giant in American junior golf. Aly Trompas defeated Eddie Pearce, to become the reigning US Junior Champion. Hailed by sports writers as America's *"next great golfer,"* Trompas was our first round match! He wasn't overly tall, but brawny with lengthy tee shots matched by an explosive temper. For unknown reasons that week, I became the boss of-the moss and Trompas acknowledged it, claiming me one of the best putters he'd ever seen. I owned a cheap Bullseye wannabe putter then … light in the head with a snaky shaft. And for only cryptic reasons, Trompas coveted it. It was a good thing too, as my long game was lost that week. We triumphed though, as my partner kept us on the fairways while I purged the putts.

Trompas later played scholarship golf at Stanford University. The same institution Tiger Woods and Tom Watson excelled as amateurs. I never heard from him again! In the end, our Canadian team won in my first international competitive outing.

Journal Entry #30: Reflections of My Life

Dedicated to *Jay Lilge*

After the Junior Americas Cup, we flew to Halifax, Nova Scotia. There we crossed a long suspension bridge to Dartmouth and played the Canadian Junior Championships. Brightwood Country Club was a short, tricky course with rocky perimeters.

Our team's competition were Canada's other nine provinces, British Columbia the favourite.

The captain of BC's squad was Doug Roxburgh. Already a legend, he'd narrowly missed winning the nationals several times. It was there I first met him, but instead of admiration, found myself jealous of his golf schooling. A product of Vancouver's competitive Marine Drive, he'd been well coached and exposed to seasoned contests … environments I yearned for. In Roxburgh, I saw an all round gifted athlete appearing in complete control as he dominated the field. It was all amplified for me observing from the sidelines after missing the cut. Golf had been a rewarding pleasure, which somehow lured me into an abyss where suddenly there wasn't light. There was only the feeling of being sacrificed … by a game I so loved.

Summer was soon over. A surprising tournament win had turned sour. I couldn't afford lessons, so my choices were confined to continue schooling or find work. I was at the crossroads reflecting life and whichever direction I chose, faceless senses of immaturity and uncertainty clung to me like offensive odours.

Journal Entry #31: In My Father's Footsteps

Dedicated to *Dad*

It's doubtful this would have been written had I followed my mind rather than my heart during the winter of 1970.

Then, I discussed two potential careers with my father, computers and the golf industry. He thought little of either, claiming one unknown and the other a fine line toward success.

Regardless, I chose computer programming at Edmonton's Northern Alberta Institute of Technology. There that fall, I captained the golf team to victory over every provincial college and university. I began on the ground floor studying futuristic Cobol and Fortran theory. Long icy bus rides into town, were mournfully compensated mapping out flow charts. Although my grades failed justifying it, I became reasonably proficient. I knew it was the future, but could anyone then have predicted an iPhone revolution?

Like high school, however, I wasn't able to focus there either. Not with a heart passionately attracted to golf. Consequently, a day after the holidays, I kept my game alive by attending the winter golf school of Alex Olynyk's.

Journal Entry #32: Pipeline (105 Street and Jasper Avenue)

Dedicated to *Gordon McHattie*

Alex Olynyk was a popular local pro who owned and operated a golf school at 105 Street and Jasper Avenue. Bespectacled, squat, and balding, he summoned images of Pablo Picasso as he waddled the netted stalls tutoring golfers. He considered himself a ladies' man, and while women were often there taking his instruction, I was challenged understanding the attraction. In summer, he was head pro at the Windermere, where I won that previous season. During winters, he ran the school.

Alex never took to me personally, probably because I wasn't polished or a high revenue customer. His assistants however were kinder, possibly because I was the reigning provincial champion. Alex's right hand was a young, personable Scottish immigrant named Gordon McHattie. He gave numerous lessons and I was drawn to his golf stories told in stylish Gaelic accents. His sidekick was Ron Salter, a seasoned Welshman blessed with laughter and life and whose bald-head and flaming sideburns aroused Ronald McDonald images.

I used my lunch money there for practise balls while evading the drudgery of computer programming. And in that colonization, delinquency not only became complete, but a **pipeline** toward my first golf lesson.

Journal Entry #33: Crystal Blue Persuasion

Dedicated to *Walter Milenchuk*

Teachers once held high positions in society. Somewhere along histories' trajectory however, they lost their place among professional scientists and engineers. They wandered off, finding comfort instead among blue-collar orbits. Authentic teachers, like gifted surgeons, have rare skills. They not only impart knowledge, but extract life meanings by identifying blueprints for success within their flocks.

I never knew what McHattie or Salter thought of me as a pupil, but from my raging practise sessions, complicated probably entered their minds. When business slowed they'd rein me in, tempting me persuasively with changes that threatened to improve my swing. Coddled in that friendship, they revealed my worst swing fault, a delinquent left wrist position at the top of my backswing (the author's right-handed).

For consistency in a golf swing, harmony must exist between the grip and clubface angles among other things. This is true at the start of swings, and especially during them. I didn't have that relationship. When swinging the club back, my left wrist bent out-of-position collapsing. Consequently it altered my clubface angle at impact. No wonder I was inconsistent.

And unfortunately, by age eighteen, I'd hit too many delinquent golf shots. Consequently it was extremely difficult learning new hand positions.

To change a golf swing, students must understand three facts. First when swinging … what's **seen** and **felt** aren't alike. Subsequently golfers must trust competent instructors to identify and remedy what students can't. Second, remedies must be learned slowly. Slowly because it's assumed learning's rapid, but swing speeds impede that. Third, practising the remedy. It took weeks renovating the new grip, let alone memorizing it.

Unknowingly though, both instructors gifted me with more than a wrist change. Unwittingly, they introduced me to my future.

Journal Entry #34: Moon River

Dedicated to *Ron Salter*

Gordon and Ron took turns working on my left wrist. But Ron went further, mimicking my overall performance. Claiming elements of showmanship, he comically referred to me as the Broadmoor Swan. A name confirming where I golfed while attempting to look pretty when swinging. It was his way saying, I had no balance.

A golf swing is just that … a swing … not a hit! The former produces accuracy and distance. The latter … eternal suffering. I was an experimental witness to that. Before a student can learn to swing a golf club, there has to be balance. Especially during impact where a golfer's **forward** foot and particularly its heel must be firmly planted below the buttock. In other words, beneath the bodies' centre of gravity. It stabilizes the swing, and like the act of walking … is heel first, toe second … heel-toe, heel-toe. My swing emphasized toes first. Consequently, when transferring weight for distance, I was unsteady.

That second lesson improved my equilibrium, removing the Broadmoor Swan stigma. It was also when I was introduced to that distinction between **swinging clubs** and **hitting balls.** And where I innocently entered the mouth of a long river, exploring the difference.

Journal Entry #35: Pretty Lady
Dedicated to *Denzil and Mary Davies*

As a regular at Alex's, I became aware of his frequent customers.

One day, an older man and young woman walked down stairs from the outside cold. The man was short and well dressed, a mirror image of cartoon character Mr. Magoo. I assumed she was his daughter. Pausing on the landing, they surveyed below for vacant nets to hit balls into. There was something about the teenager's essence though which was difficult ignoring. Delicate and small, she was shy yet charismatic. Dark eyes and long brunette hair completed what appeared a teenage rendition of actress Audrey Hepburn.

Gordon said the dad brought her there frequently to practise. Not long after, spring arrived and local courses began opening. It would be a while again before I saw her.

Chapter Two

Summer

(Journal Entries 36 through 200)

Assistant professional. Glendale.
Neil Murray, Jimmy and the judge.
British travels. Jackie and me. University life. Learning the
golf swing. Encounter with Jim Lefevre. St. Andrews.
Canadian PGA. Mayfair. Courtship and marriage.
Meeting Arnold Palmer. Fatherhood.
Playing with Gary Player.

Journal Entry #36: My World is Empty
Dedicated to *Bob Milbrath*

Sometimes when our goals aren't being nursed, life nudges us along anyway.

I was past the point of no return studying computer technology. Binary codes and flow charts weren't in my blood and my world seemed empty. I had to find a career and lack of confidence compounded it.

McHattie helped with my swing, but had never charged me. I was grateful and in repayment assisted him replacing golf club handles. It wasn't easy then. Older cork and rubber grips were firmly cemented onto metal shafts demanding thirty stubborn minutes of removal by knife scraping before replacements could be reinstalled. I was dispatched to the back alley where temperatures loitered below zero. There among downtown dumpsters, I began a career in golf. During those primitive surgeries there were no comforts of gloves nor stabilizing vices for the work. Inventing ways in slush and snow was challenging. After exorcising each club's past reminders, Gordon delivered more. Then the Scot revealed the art of installing slide-on varieties and the spiralling technique demanded when wrapping leather grips.

I wasn't thinking it would lead to a career until McHattie informed me of a local course needing help. The Glendale Golf and Country Club was a new family facility located outside city limits. Their pro was looking for an assistant.

Journal Entry #37: Angel Baby
Dedicated to *Dick Afaganis*

When Gordon told me of the pro needing an assistant, the conversation while inviting, seemed only wishful thinking.

A week later though, rifling through *Edmonton Journal* classifieds, I saw the advert. A year earlier I competed at Glendale and remembered its beckoning wilderness appeal. Intimidation lured me to the phone where I hesitantly introduced myself. The man on the line was aware of my previous provincial win and suggested an interview. I met him there soon after, on one of those brilliant Alberta April mornings. Ones where snow continued lingering on the surrounding forested hills outside Edmonton's northwest corner.

The pro's name was Donny Buchkan. Olive-skinned with dark hair slicked back in Brylcreem, he relived **Angel Baby** memories of Sal Mineo, a silver screen heartthrob of earlier times. The interview was brief and afterwards the job was mine. It paid $350 a month including golf and range balls. In addition he added meal and pro shop discounts. I grabbed the position in a heartbeat, innocently bypassing my career compass.

The job began two weeks later May 1, 1971.

Journal Entry #38: Odds and Ends

Dedicated to *John Milner*

Most things change, but negotiating life's necessities seem timeless. Like when first entering the work force and making ends meet.

In my eighteenth year, I found a career … as a golf pro. However I had limited funds, no vehicle, and nowhere to live.

Scouring places to rent, I found a modest basement apartment near the winter golf school. For transportation, I owned a single speed bike that I cycled to and from the course. The distance was sixteen kilometres pedalling into westerly winds. My first pay cheque was fourteen days after work began and I had exactly that many dollars to see me through. Relying on that rigid budget and the club's discount menu, I ordered the same meal daily. I embraced the indifference though because I loved being there.

I made it through the fortnight, disciplined by that meagre money management. Others would have asked for advances, but it seemed an unfair request of a new employer. My expenses were food, rent, medical, play money, and career accessories. I purchased one tool per paycheque thinking my future was golf. I've kept some of that very equipment today. Anything leftover was banked for the unforeseen.

At the end of the day, financial stability is a powerful sedative. It revolves around the elementary principle … **never** allowing expenses to exceed revenues. As simple as it sounds, that recurring abuse anchors the prime reason why global economies constantly appear bleak. I learned quickly back then to put my ego aside and allocate earnings objectively.

With accommodation, transportation and my first paycheque in hand, I turned to what I enjoyed doing most … golfing. It was joined by learning a new craft which began by meeting the members and staff who were to soon influence the new adventure.

Journal Entry #39: Band on the Run

Dedicated to *Bryan Murray*

Basically a golf course is comprised of two groups. Those paying for golf services and others providing them. The former are green fee customers or members while the latter are primary staff consisting of managers, professionals, and course superintendents. In 1971, Glendale's staff introduced me to that industry, involuntarily becoming my earliest mentors.

Donny was in his forties, easygoing, and a throwback to the '50s. He always dressed neatly, often with light-blue sweaters and black-patent leathers. Single, he was always on the make with young bar servers who jokingly considered him seasoned. Donny was an accomplished golfer, originating from Edmonton's Riverside. Even though he possessed Glendale's then-course-record sixty-six, Donny failed to embody the traditional pro image. That was more like his first assistant.

Neil was his righthand man. A talented instructor, he was also a candidate for the planet's premier playboy, and equally its poorest. Originally from Vancouver, he was tall, attractive, and engaging. Everyone gravitated to his magnetic charm. With Neil there was daily debauchery, quick quips, and dark humour. Given to moments of depression, he was always loyal to Donny and me, his lowly working accomplice and new assistant.

Lockie Shaw, short for Lachlan, was known as the Earl of Shaw. Short, blond and charismatic, he was the course superintendent. He was so proficient in agronomy; he might have been able to grow moon grass. A fiery type with a persistent snap hook, he wasn't someone you crossed, yet ironically he was likable.

Finally there was Glendale's manager, Steady Eddie. Not tall either, Eddie's bald head was flanked by curly leftovers. And as an Englishman, he used British diction advantageously against opponents.

I rounded out the group. Everyone fussed over me realizing my naivety and yet how hard I laboured.

We were the **Band on the Run**, meeting early mornings, often with Neil's brother Bryan, the Edmonton Country Club assistant. Sometimes we met at Glendale or java shops along the Yellowhead Trail west of Edmonton. It was there, I began morning affairs with coffee, the modest vice of most pros.

Journal Entry #40: Par 27
Dedicated to *Bob Nebloch*

In the golf industry there are two kinds of pros. The traditional **golf professional** and the **professional golfer.** The former work in pro shops, servicing needs of golfers everywhere. Some say they're the pastime's backbone. The others play for a living in competitions, often in the media.

Professional golfers possesses different mindsets than golf professionals. That was apparent during a televised series filmed in Edmonton when I turned pro. The program was called *Par 27*.

It was a round-robin knockout show featuring the province's best golfers, hosted by the CBC's charismatic Ernie Afaganis. As the reigning provincial junior champion, producers felt my inclusion completed the field.

They called it *Par 27* because three different tee areas were used, and each player took three shots per tee box. Using three as par, the math came out to twenty-seven. For camera effects, we played from the regular tee, another fifty yards closer, and then finally within a greenside bunker.

The location was Edmonton's Country Club which had an amazing collection of short holes (par-threes). Filming took place on what I thought was its best, the eighteenth. It was a spectacular forced carry, where the green and tee were linked by a suspension bridge, a trestle where the club's chef in earlier times supposedly hanged himself!

In the series, I lost by a shot (twenty-eight to twenty-seven), but I can honestly say, "If it hadn't been for those cameras!"

Journal Entry #41: Sunny Afternoon
Dedicated to *Dr. Tony Pasternak*

One of the first members I befriended at Glendale was the Nak, a slight muscular genius named Tony Pasternak … hence the Nak. Several years my senior, he was an engineering graduate student at the University of Alberta. Tony, aware my Broadmoor friends called me Gary (after Gary Player), did the same. He was Nak, I was Gary.

During that first month, we golfed eighteen holes on **sunny afternoons** finishing with sand-trap competitions. Using our sand wedges, we'd challenge each other to see who could land a ball past the pin and spin it backwards, closer to the hole. We did that swinging the club head's sole close to the bottom of the ball as it laid in sand. I liked his company because he was academic. There was always something to be learned and I was like a sponge.

Tony achieved an early PhD and supposedly went on to specialize in the frontier of laser technology.

Later, I became friendlier with his younger brother, while Tony eventually vanished. But his early friendship broke the ice of a timid teenager exploring a new career.

Journal Entry #42: Mr. Bojangles
Dedicated to *Gordon Hayward*

To golfers, their clubs are almost as needy as spouses. There were fourteen clubs in a normal golfer's bag then and most owners took pride in them. They liked their clubface grooves free of dirt and handles replaced when crusted from sweat.

My initial responsibility was to supervise and maintain those clubs. Hundreds of members paid Donny an annual fee to have their sets stored, polished after golf, and ready for play when arriving next. When that happened, I had to be prompt in those deliveries. Most private courses back then had storage rooms for the like. Usually for convenience, it was located at ground-level near the shop. Glendale's however, was in a basement, accessed by a long, out-of-the-way cement ramp, probably the worst of its kind. Like Bojangles, I danced up and down that concrete over the next seven years, retrieving and replacing sets.

Additionally I answered phones, assisted in club repair, and occasionally offered lessons.

Today, I own several sets and maintain them all with that same care from those early career days.

Journal Entry #43: One Fine Morning

Dedicated to *Ernie Afaganis*

One of Glendale's founding members was CBC's famous, longtime sports commentator, Ernie Afaganis.

One morning soon after I joined Glendale's staff, he and Donny invited me out for a game. It was my first time playing with a personality. Afaganis enjoyed a prominent position with Canadian television. His international face was always recognizable when reporting CFL football, golf, or the Olympics. A friendly, genuine sports voice was complemented by debonair Greek looks along with knowledge and memory for names. Plus he was absent the arrogance so often contaminating celebrities. Afaganis couldn't play often because of extensive work commitments, but maintained a single digit handicap when he did.

During the round, Afaganis shared how tour pros played their basic shot patterns. How they faded (right handers curving a ball slightly right), or drew them naturally (slightly left).

His mild comments were my first soulful insights toward the legitimate shots forged by golf's finest players on the world's professional circuits.

Journal Entry #44: The Trans-Siberian Sandbagger

Dedicated to *Freddie Peters*

I first heard the term sandbagger mentioned in casual conversations before joining Glendale. But its definition received more traction when settling into my new position. It was an unsavory reference to golfers who sought competitive advantage by subtly manipulating their handicaps.

In golf's handicap system, regular participants are assigned numbers from their scores, designating their ability. A lower digit suggests a more advanced player. In competition, differences in those numbers equalize games. And just as there will always be cheats in card games, there inevitably will be golfers artificially inflating their handicaps to win, especially when cash is the prize.

Supposedly, Glendale's sandbagger was Freddie. Freddie was a husky middle aged Russian with a Brillo pad growth of hair. He was always smiling with a twinkle in his eye complimenting a subtle Slavic accent. It may have been only a facade.

Freddie was a carpet layer. He became that after escaping the Soviet Union and lumbering across Siberian tundra to eventual freedom. Immigrating to Canada, he made his way to Edmonton and began a new life, which included golf. His sandbagging reputation was likely precipitation from those survival postscripts.

Every golf course has a Freddie or two. If there were disclaimers on membership application forms, they might read, "Caution: Sandbagging is hazardous to your wallet," or, as they might claim in courtrooms, "Let the golfer beware!"

Journal Entry #45: Tapestry

Dedicated to *Rosemary Kirsch*

My life has been a tapestry of rich and royal hue
An everlasting vision of the ever changing view

> A wondrous woven magic in bits of blue and gold
> A tapestry to feel and see, impossible to hold!
>
> —Carole King

If there were ever words symbolizing my relationship to golf, they might be found in the above lines written by Carole King from her album "**Tapestry**." Within the nuance of that poetry, an unexplainable parallel to my passion for the game seemed to exist.

By coincidence, the album was released in the summer of that first year. A time when emerald fairways and cascading forest shadows shared themselves with me on setting Glendale twilights. There, chasing my future, I swung at endless golf balls, thought of girl friends, and other Carole King songs like "So Far Away" and "It's Too Late."

But it wasn't ... it was just beginning.

Journal Entry #46: One Toke Over the Line

Dedicated to *Bill MacBeth*

Occasionally, everyone does something rash, especially in developing years.

One day we finished work early due to rain, which closed the course. Neil invited several club members, bar servers, and me to his apartment, where we watched the televised NHL playoffs.

One of the servers was named Lindsay. She was a young, effervescent woman from Northern Ireland with a matching accent. She and I were glued to the game while others began lighting marijuana joints. Eventually it evolved into a party with the users becoming high. I'd never seen marijuana before and couldn't resist eyeing it. Insulated within a transparent plastic bag, it appeared relaxed ... like its users.

When the hockey finished, the celebration went into overtime. However with morning work shifts, Lindsay and I left early. On my way out though, I glanced once more at the bag and ignorantly ... took it! My juvenile sense of humour anticipated the next day's shop banter. In taking it however, I didn't foresee the penalty had we been stopped by authorities. I kept the bag for days, even rolling my own to uncover what the fuss was about. But it proved not unlike my aborted cigarette affair.

Then I made another mistake. Unsure what to do with the cargo and naive of the consequences, I mailed it back to Neil! Days later, I heard the stunned commentary among shop regulars, querying who sent the hash. Of course I kept my mouth shut. Fortunately, it blew over. But not without realizing life occasionally doles out well-learned lessons minus the punishment. However, only fools would make habits of it!

Journal Entry #47: Tiny Dancer

Dedicated to *Ed Cancilla*

As second assistant, my responsibilities also included helping juniors and occasionally offering lessons. As a result, I was partner to a life-changing conversation that first season.

A member named Denzil Davies saw my profile in the club newsletter and sought me out. I was still getting to know our members then, but he was more familiar. Davies was a short Welshman who dressed neatly in blazers and tie, often dusted in dandruff. His bald head was haloed by neatly combed silvery hair, like the comic character Mr. Magoo. But it was his hooked nose that distinguished him. He was the father with the daughter I noticed at the winter golf school.

At that morning meeting over coffee, Denzil introduced himself with a proposal. Reaching over, he discreetly handed me a fold of twenty-dollar bills, saying in the same breath, "I'd like you to teach my daughter to golf!"

I didn't remember how much he handed me, but it implicated television crime. Was that what the golf profession was about? I remembered his daughter was special though. What I didn't know, was how that meeting would influence my future!

Journal Entry #48: Concrete and Clay

Dedicated to *Dave Peterson*

It was only by coincidence Denzil Davies and his family were Glendale members.

As his daughter's newly appointed personal instructor, it was important I get to know her. Her name was Jackie, short for Jacqueline. Characterized by small stature, quiet disposition, and youthful essence, her confident eyes suggested more was within. From the beginning we became distant friends and for reasons not obvious then, she seemed at ease around me.

Jackie's golf companions were her parents. A close family friend named Eric who was like another father to her, occasionally joined too. One could set a clock to their nightly routine. It was always after supper, about the time I was preparing to close. That's when I heard the sounds outside the shop ... metal spikes clacking in unison on the **concrete and clay**. Articulations the Davies had arrived. The translation was I'd be working longer than I wanted.

The evenings were like soap operas. They'd all tee off down the first fairway into a squinting, setting sun. But by the sixth hole, Jackie would return to the shop alone, usually in tears. She'd been arguing with her dad about golf.

Each of those nights however were the whispers of what laid ahead in her extraordinary amateur career.

Journal Entry #49: Elusive Butterfly

Dedicated to *the Harveys*

Jackie Davies and I began a series of lessons that began at the driving range, progressed to the course, and then eventually playing lessons.

From our first session, she was approachable. I'd ask her to do this or try that and she'd work diligently at it. That set her apart from others, especially today. With lives suspended around computers and smart phones, I've sensed many students feel learning's entitled and to be delivered nano speed. Back then however, it was evident learning golf, unlike other sports, was similar to raising children. It was an **elusive butterfly** resisting intimidation or haste.

One of our sessions was near Glendale's eighteenth green. There, working on bunker techniques, I was unaware how much sand we were exploding onto the green. When course superintentent Lockie happened by, he too exploded, but it wasn't sand.

The short game practise area, now located adjacent Glendale's clubhouse is an indirect result of that lesson decades ago. It encouraged bunker practising there … rather than on course.

Journal Entry #50: Duke of Earl
Dedicated to *Lockie Shaw*

Guided by the science of agronomy, course superintendents are responsible for maintaining each course's playing conditions. The position may be one of life's more underrated professions. Consider average homeowners who complain about trimming their modest patches of lawn. Then think of the complexities mowing, maintaining, and managing over one hundred and fifty acres. Maximizing its beauty at the same time, testifies to that skill.

Lachlan Earl Shaw, aka the Earl of Shaw, was among golf's best. Nicknamed Lockie, he was so talented, Calgary's distinguished Country Club later headhunted him away to oversee their pristine facility.

Canadian assistants were usually employed over summer months. During winter they had to find alternate work to make ends meet. Neil asked Lockie then to hire me off-season to supplement my income. I began in fall when Lockie broke me in gently with manual labour. Then he showed me the walk behind greens mower, whose machine did what its name implied. Operators followed the self propelling engine as it sheared grass. One crisp October morning, after a heavy frost, I began cutting greens with it.

In our industry, mowing grass in frosty conditions kills grass plants (as well as one's job)! That morning I looked for evidence of ice crystals.

Seeing moisture instead, I began. The other staff disagreed and like vultures stalking prey, ring-sided the green where I was cutting. My sinking feelings were confirmed when above the motor's roar, I heard Lockie's car careen into the parking lot. It was followed by his profile streaking past the clubhouse toward us. His blond hair contrasted by purple facials confirmed the extent of my situation.

In the end, there was no damage and I'd been right, but we both agreed my introduction to grounds-keeping was premature. I went back to work in the pro shop.

Journal Entry #51: Lido Shuffle
Dedicated to *Neil Murray*

Neil was my first industry mentor. He could have been *Playboy* magazine founder, Hugh Hefner's too. Readers enjoying laughs over that could be forgiven poor judgment. If they've seen the made for television series *Californication* and the protagonist's role, portrayed by actor David Duchovny, they might understand Murray better. Substitute the role of writer for golf professional.

When I met Neil, he was living daily on life's edge. As an assistant he spent years in the company of peers who shared the good life. Among those pursuits were women and they in turn flocked to his seductive personality. He dressed appropriately for a pro, personifying himself lavishly and using vocabulary Hefner himself might have appreciated. His slacks were "strides," while his shoes were "kicks."

Neil could be forgiven introducing me to the bubbly beverage cider. Most days since, I've enjoyed my own pint-a-day, and admitting I owed that to Neil wouldn't be fair either. I was as guilty as the next emulating him. The fact Glendale's bar never inventoried cider until Neil began working there, implicated them as well. That being written, Neil gave me direction. He badgered me repeatedly about health habits, how to dress, and manners becoming a professional.

While Neil lived life to its fullest, he also had another side ... integrity. During those early industry years, Donny came under scrutiny from

Glendale's board of directors. Experiences I'd endure decades later myself. Given Neil's popularity, a subversive group of members there wanted Donny ousted and replaced with the charismatic assistant … a pro shop *coup d'etat*. Neil arose above the temptation however, remaining faithful to his employer.

He may not have been the best professional, but those who courted him could have cared less. Mentors vary, but I believe ultimately, they're framed by principle, virtue, and devotions to do good.

Journal Entry #52: The Donald
Dedicated to *Don Buchkan*

It would be untrue writing Donny was my mentor, but not unfair either.

Donny was a good man, but known for a secretive nature and strange habits. Single and without a father, he lived with his mother and sister. While Donny was clean and neat, he nevertheless had a sense of humour bordering smut.

Donny often played the ponies and hung out with bookies, unlike most pros are stereotyped. Consequently, prominent amateurs and local pros visiting Glendale, frequently treated Donny in ways I wouldn't have. Once in particular, Canadian Hall of Famer Al Balding played and treated Donny shamefully. I felt bad, but he took it, never saying anything because Balding was famous. Donny wasn't always that way though.

He too, once had a mentor. As a junior, Donny was one of the local Riverside Rats. The head pro there was Frank Willey. Willey was popular in Edmonton then and took a liking to Donny. He taught him, peeled him out of a shell and eventually made him an assistant. They became like father and son. During winter, Donny travelled and caddied for Frank in tournaments on the PGA tour's western swing. It was vitalizing for Donny, but tragically ended soon after.

In April 1962, Frank was phoned at work by a customer requesting a set of ladies' clubs as a gift. Willey disappeared delivering them and his body was never found! Murderous evidence at a house under construction was discovered, resulting in convictions against two men. Speculation claimed Willey's body was buried in a shallow grave, near Looma, south of Edmonton. Donny was left devastated.

Those I saw, who acted indiscriminately toward him though, probably weren't aware of his grief. While he wasn't my mentor, he was a man I empathized with. One I came to love for how he managed his loneliness when losing Willey.

Journal Entry #53: Shave, Shite, and Shampoo

Dedicated to *Jim and Doris Grant*

Golf was evolving into more than just a game to me.

As my new career began jetting off, the learning curve seemed endless. Take for instance the simplest and most basic of swing fundamentals ... the address position, comprised of grip, balance, aim, and posture. Each a cornerstone to the swing itself!

The business was equally vast. I was introduced to customer relations, overseeing equipment, staffing, inventories, maintaining a pro shop, merchandising, club repairs, starting play, hand and power cart repairs, plus organizing tournaments. And they were only glimpses into the distance.

Consequently, as a career-forging teenager, it was a challenge sifting through it. But as the season flew on, what emerged instead was an awareness of what appeared the irrelevant. They included in no particular order:

1. Doing laundry (regularly).
2. Paying bills (timely).
3. Being cautious with what I put into my body.
4. Cleaning that body properly (including unexposed areas).
5. Being reciprocal in relationships.
6. Avoiding late nights when rising early.
7. Dodging discussions with customers about politics and religion.

8. Budgeting money carefully, and somewhat miserly.
9. Thinking before speaking.
10. Remembering names.
11. Avoiding alcohol in excess.
12. Treating everyone in ways, I too wished to be treated.

And it became surreal when acknowledging the extent their influence had on both my game and career! Especially when I remained committed to them.

Journal Entry #54: Best in Show
Dedicated to *Jim Phelan*

The golf show came to Edmonton each fall. It was scheduled during the off-season providing pros optimistic outlooks for the upcoming year. They called them shows because manufacturing agents showed their latest gadgets to sell … all in one location. There, pros viewed product lines and based on retail forecasts, ordered merchandise for spring delivery.

In my first year it was held at the Edmonton Inn, where I was introduced to the industrial sales force. There I met Jim Phelan, sales representative for Campbell Golf Equipment. Phelan arranged for my first professional contract, an agreement where I received a set of clubs, balls, and staff bag (complete with my name embossed). In return, Donny was obligated to purchase an agreed amount of equipment. In essence, I became another rep, promoting their wares. It happens similarly on the PGA Tour; except those players are more handsomely compensated.

I visited every corporate booth there, awed not only by the colourful, fresh merchandise, but the energizing camaraderie existing between agents and pros. A flavour that's remained historically intact, furthering golf's participation within the free capitalistic world.

Journal Entry #55: Steady Eddie
Dedicated to *Ed Orritt*

In the following years, I went on to work with many club managers. The first was **Steady Eddie** … as we called him. Eddie ran Glendale like a business and fit in with staff like a glove. Married with a family though, his life was different from Neil's adventurous nights or Donny's horse racing preferences. He always tried looking dapper with dark blazers competing with bright bell-bottomed slacks. Followers of haute couture might have suggested, "That isn't working Eddie." But he was always pleasant, rarely allowing problems to interfere with routine. Plus at times, Eddie was humorous when challenged about baldness, dress, or short stature. His rebuttals were weaponized in the form of subtle British diction thatstalled most comments in their tracks.

Before immigrating to Canada, Eddie managed a British pub and possessed no authentic golf background. Compared to club pros and superintendents, club managers often originated from work places other than the sport. And as such, I always felt that muddied the industries' direction.

At the end of my first year, Eddie suggested I live in the clubhouse over winter. It was an opportunity to protect it from vandalism while helping me out financially.

I took him up on his offer, becoming Edmonton's most eligible bachelor, with the cities' biggest pad.

Journal Entry #56: You've Got a Friend
Dedicated to *Dorothy Banks*

That winter, I became the unpaid clubhouse custodian. The bar, coffee shop, dining room, junior lounge, kitchen, locker rooms, offices, pro shop, and spike bar became my responsibility.

I settled into the comfortably furnished administration offices where I could detect unusual activity easiest.

The club hosted Christmas parties where I assisted bartenders and kitchen staff. Thankfully too, as often it was quiet during ice crystal nights. Nights when interior building beams might suddenly cry out from arctic temperatures. Awakened by the sharp cracks, I'd patrol the darkness with a three-iron, prepared for perpetrators.

During days I avoided boredom with routines which began mornings in the junior lounge. There I chipped into laundry baskets, never leaving until specific numbers found their target. Hogan did that, demonstrating for troops during World War II. After I moved upstairs, working on full swings under the dining room's higher roofline. Finally I'd practise putting on the carpets.

I also continued with my exercising. I'd jog from Glendale to the Yellowhead Trail on frozen roads in severe temperatures. Returning to the clubhouse and its lonely interior, I'd switch on the sound system to the soothing vocal harmonies of James Taylor's rendition of, "**You've Got a Friend**."

Journal Entry #57: Raindrops

Dedicated to *Jim Matheson*

In spring of my sophomore year, Neil returned from Vancouver where he learned of my off-season clubhouse life.

He encouraged a local journalist to write a story about it. The human interest article which included my picture, featured a teenager forging a career in golf. At the same time my Campbell clubs arrived accompanied by a large staff bag scripted with my name. One looking not unlike Sam Snead's.

Deep down however, it all felt illegitimate. **Raindrops** of flattery and materialism fell upon the glamour of being called … professional. Was I gaining without earning?

Regardless, five years later that article overshadowed all the accolades and promotions.

Journal Entry #58: Softly, As I Leave You

Dedicated to *Bernie Durward*

The article described my admiration for Gary Player, desires to play the world's great courses, and one day attend the Masters tournament in Augusta, Georgia.

After it was published, I was asked out for coffee by another member named Bernie. Bernie was loved by everyone at Glendale. She had a contagious smile that was complimented by silvery-grey hair, brushed in rolling waves. And anyone she met was greeted by her bouncy and lively, energetic gait.

As we sat across from each other that day, she passed me a silver dollar and began talking about it: "I read that article how you wanted to go the Masters." She said. "Years ago, when Bob and I were first married, he went off to war. But before he left, I gave him a silver dollar for luck so he'd return alive. I brought that here today because now I want you to have it. I hope you get to Augusta!"

It was hard describing how that made me feel. Suddenly there was meaning behind that phrase "taking one's breath away"! That's because my chest felt like an inflated balloon and it hurt breathing.

I kept that silver dollar and years later was invited to Augusta. Before playing there though, I hack-sawed her coin into three triangles. I discreetly threw one into the azaleas behind its famous twelfth green. I gave Bernie the second, while I kept the last.

And each year she and I continue watching the Masters, even though she's long left me and passed on.

Journal Entry #59: Rainy Days and Mondays

Dedicated to *Mike Sturko, Jr.*

One of Glendale's assistants from earlier times once reminisced of a par-five he scored on the tenth hole … from inside the pro shop!

To appreciate that, one has to envision the tenth tee geography relative to the clubhouse then. The golf shop's door faced the tee, one surrounded by dense, young poplars. The doorway was fifty yards below with a concrete balcony suspended above. If a spirited person used the appropriately lofted iron and made solid contact, a ball could be hit through the door and below the overhang. To reach the tenth fairway however, the poplars still had to be scaled. I knew it was possible, providing a gambler had stomach to brave smashing the glass panes bordering the single doorframe.

Rainy days and Mondays then were quiet at Glendale. On one of them, I worked up courage from a dare and played the contentious hole. I struck my seven-iron first shot perfect. I never saw it pierce the opening or ascend the trees. I knew if I flinched, the glass might explode. The young members initiating the taunt followed me as I located my ball above and next to the fairway. I then tore into my second, a three wood which hooked left around the dogleg corner. From before a large sand trap, short of the green, I then bulleted an eight-iron twelve inches from the flag. I made the birdie four ... from inside the shop!

It didn't take a genius to know when to quit.

Journal Entry #60: Rocky Mountain Highs

Dedicated to *Stanley Thompson*

Around the world, Canadians are considered humble, a characteristic I'm content being part of. However sometimes our outstanding accomplishments in business, entertainment, politics or sports, aren't awarded the weight they deserve. Shamefully worse ... by ourselves. And in the world of golf course design that opinion's valid. For even Canadians rarely recognize the genius of Stanley Thompson, one of our contributions to course architecture from golf's golden era.

Another passion arising from my industry introduction was course design. And two courses I played early in my apprenticeship stimulated that sentiment. The Banff Springs Golf Course and Jasper Park Lodge were among the enduring gifts left us by Thompson. I was immediately attracted to both. And while each were uniquely independent, there was no mistaking their originality.

At Jasper, buffalo plains were a foreground to distant alpine peaks. At Banff however, the Rockies intimidated golfing audiences. Appearing in-your-face, they jaggedly pierced the skies at right angles from ground up. Often at both, Thompson used summits to align his tee boxes, along with sensual stimuli. For instance at Jasper's ninth, one of the worlds great par-threes, he shared an erotic side, shaping the putting surface and green approach to accentuate life's effeminacy.

In more recent times however, Banff's routing was disappointingly altered. Extra holes were squeezed in, aborting Thompson's flavour. To me, one of Canada's iconic landmarks was maligned. Fortunately Jasper was designated a UNESCO World Heritage Site and retained its essence.

My hope remains that one day golfers visit Canada specifically to see and play Thompson's work among others. But for that to happen, desecration of his inspirations—by our very own—must end.

Journal Entry #61: The Verdict (Part 1)

Dedicated to *Rod McIntyre*

Glendale Bob was a judge and a southpaw.

As a left hander, he drove Donny crazy.

One job of head pros then was selling clubs to members. Donny took them in on trade, not unlike car dealerships. But Bob would order the most expensive, exotic ones he could find. He had the money and researched his preferences. That wasn't unusual. What was, were the numerous times in a calendar year he repeated the transaction. Consequently Donny became custodian to growing inventories of used, expensive, left-handed clubs. Equipment no one could particularly afford or want.

But the learned magistrate was also sympathetic to Donny, whose job at times was tenuous. Sometimes professionals had to bite-the-bullet and accept growing inventories of unsaleable merchandise were better than inconveniences of unemployment.

The judge's obsessions originated from tragic family losses. One's greater than should be allotted. And golf preserved Bob's sanity, which was why he practised as much as he played.

The judge developed his golf game with unique improvement methods. One I passed on to students over the years. In golf swings, the leading arm should always be extended at impact. The judge cut ends off one litre milk containers, washed them out, and slid them up that arm when practising. It reminded him to keep that elbow straight when swinging.

The judge drank litres of milk.

Journal Entry #62: The Verdict (Part 2)

Dedicated to *Justice Bob and Betty Spevakow*

Bob was also one of the club's more dictatorial members.

When I first faced him formally, it wasn't on the course but in his work place. I was contemplating a British golf trip and needed a notary for my passport. Donny, suggested I ask Bob. The adjudicator was accommodating and asked me to be in court next morning.

I'd never been in the rooms of justice before. I was mesmerized by the potpourri of those awaiting his say and decision on their misconduct. Did that many regularly break the law? Eventually, above chorused mumbles echoing off marbled walls, the magistrate called me to the bench.

As I advanced though, he motioned me up behind the high desk, rather than in front. There was a feeling I was being treated discriminately, as all eyes below followed my ascendence. There, he signed my book and chatted casually about my upcoming journey. Years later, I realized the moment was personal for him too. For Bob's days weren't always fulfilling. Unlike my career, he dwelt in drudgery. Drudgery dealing with the constant flow of those subverting the scales of justice.

Journal Entry #63: The Burma Road
Dedicated to *Aunt Beat*

Some golf courses, like people, are recognized by nicknames. For instance in Canada, Hamilton's Golf and Country Club is occasionally called "Ancaster." In England, the Royal Liverpool's known as "Hoylake." And so, Wentworth's west course outside London, England, is **the "Burma Road."** It's where I first experienced playing one of earth's great layouts outside Canada. The occasion was the beginning of a memorable excursion after my second year. That winter, most of my peers holidayed in California. I chose Britain instead, seeing opportunities to combine playing with a golf education, one scouring the origins of my new career.

I was like many youthful travellers then. Scruffy with long hair and bankrupt. But unlike them, I carried golf clubs rather than backpacks.

Thanks to the forward nature of my great Aunt Beatrice, I was able to play Wentworth at the start of that trip. She served tea at the famous heathland course, home to the World Match Play Championship. Among those she pampered was Wentworth's club captain, war hero, and golf writer … Mindy Blake. Through her, a game was arranged for me with the author.

Unfortunately, I was too immature. Meeting Bernard Gallagher seemed far more interesting. The charismatic English star, and future Ryder Cup captain was Wentworth's pro then. My curiosity was also aroused by the enormous brick mansions on the course's perimeter, whose owners, it was explained, were Elton John and Beatle George Harrison. And of course there was the layout itself. Lengthy and rugged, the woodland test was carved from umbrella pines roofing blankets of lavender heather.

Consequently, I didn't appreciate the extent of my windfall.

As a budding professional, one searching golf's past, I was in the company of an extremely knowledgeable author and innovator. Blake had taken golf swings apart from the science of physics and written exclusively about them in his book, *The Golf Swing of the Future*. In his spare time, he patented swing aids. As guests go I was as lame as a ball washer. And it didn't stop there!

After playing, I waited for Blake outside the clubhouse, chatting with his caddie. Caddies are like a golfer's support system. Support beyond just carrying clubs. I watched him during the round with his tie, tam, and soiled tweed sports jacket. Old, thin and unshaven, I dismissed him for what he appeared, a down and out rubby. As I was leaving though, he shared his life as a professional caddie, extolling an amazing resume of past clients including legends like six-time Open champion Harry Vardon, immortal amateur Bobby Jones, and the effervescent Walter Hagen! Stunned, I smuggled what I could from him before leaving. It's one thing reading about history, but transformational discussing actual events with participants.

I left the Burma Road with my first real journey around one of the planets more demanding tests. But it was accompanied by hollow feelings. One's affirming shamefully poor manners, regrets what I'd missed, and neglect of mission. I had squandered an early opportunity unlikely to come my way again.

Journal Entry #64: Sandwich (Royal St. Georges)

Dedicated to *Rob Whyte*

I love all golf courses, but if given choices, I'd always play links golf first.

A links is a course found among coastal sand dunes between oceans and encroaching farmlands, naturally carved by chisels of wind and time. Earlier, I wrote about my first visit to St. Andrews, Scotland, but that wasn't where I was enticed. That first seduction was at **Royal St. Georges** in **Sandwich**, a village on England's southeast coast.

During my trip off North America's continent, kind relatives in the London suburb Hounslow, accommodated me. I bought a bike and from there set out to discover the origins of golf. My other assets were a suitcase, golf clubs, and a passionate soul. I mapped out four separate journeys across the British Isles and that first destination then was St. Georges.

To begin my search, I left Hounslow toward Kent, alternating between busy motorways (which was illegal) and tranquil rural roads. I biked next to apple orchards en route to Folkstone and the White Cliffs of Dover. I glided past places like Canterbury and Sevenoaks where I golfed, slept out in cool winter evenings, and toured more religious shrines than I remember. Eventually after days of pedalling, the ocean appeared. I followed it until arriving at my first location, the Cinque Port of Sandwich.

Sandwich was one of five historic trade ports located on the coasts of Kent and Sussex counties. Its ocean proximity was central to its role in Britain's early economy. It was also home to one of golf's great links, Royal St. Georges. I had no idea where she was, so I solicited my instincts. On the town's narrow main road, I snaked my way through a Dickensian essence of brick and Tudor. As I cycled, lorries passed so close that the resulting breezes were frightening and exhausts suffocating.

Uneventfully, I found myself outside the hamlet with no course yet in sight. Then on the road's ocean side, while still cycling, I looked south and saw dunes decorated by tall grass bending from wind. Sounds of surf and sea gulls added to the optimism. Although still invisible, I inherently knew she was there. In later years, no matter where I travelled the world, I instinctively sensed where golf courses were located. Seeing those particular dunes then was the first of those experiences. It was late and light was fading fast as I continued pedalling. Unexpectedly among the mounds, fragments of fairway began unveiling themselves. And in ways a young man on a date senses what might be impending ... I found St. Georges.

Journal Entry #65: Walter Hagen

Dedicated to *Walter Hagen*

I never met **Walter Hagen**. The flamboyant player, who dominated professional golf between World War I and 1930, passed away when I turned pro.

From what I'd read though, we were opposites. He was outgoing, I'm shy. He was a world-class professional; I was a modest club pro. He was well dressed; I'm comfortable in my own clothing. He sipped extravagant beverages; I drank cheap bubbly. But we both love(d) golf. I know that because we shared one day few have known.

We played the three links at Sandwich and Deal … all fifty-four holes in one day … golfing from one to another … along the beach!

The distance between Sandwich and Deal is over six kilometres. They're home to a trio of renowned links, which all hosted the British Open. The Open (as it's known) is only played on links courses. It's never contested inland as wind's considered a factor determining champions.

After finding Royal St. Georges, I realized Princes Golf Club was literally next door. The links at Deal was further up the beach.

That day, I rose early and played St. Georges. Then, curiosity led me over the bordering fence to explore Prince's too. With both rounds completed by noon, the local pro directed me toward Deal. However, ideas of backtracking, retrieving my bike, cycling into town, out to the highway, plus another six kilometres seemed ridiculous. Re-strategizing, I instead golfed up the beach toward Deal.

It was a long hike, but in Gary Player's book, he wrote about striking clean iron shots off South African shores. The impact's margin of error was so close, golfers developed **crisp** feedback. Eventually I arrived at Royal Cinque Ports, camouflaged by her twelve-foot-high pebble dyke. As I skirted it, my shoulders ached from the weight of clubs. Miniature brick garrisons dotted her dunes, remnants of World War II. Afterward, with night approaching, I left her and played back toward Sandwich's distant lights, adjacent that same ocean.

I passed the famous Guilford Hotel, which appeared like a sentry peering south toward France.

Later, I read Hagen's biography where he reminisced of his stay there when winning the Open at St. Georges. He described practise rounds played on the three links, up the beach and back in one day.

So, even though Hagen and I were different, when sharing that particular day in our lives, there was no denying the mutual passion for golf that synchronized us.

Journal Entry #66: Little Things

Dedicated to *Gladys and George Quinn*

Professional golfers like Darren Clarke or Justin Rose must have found it frustrating travelling the European tour. They couldn't afford the extravagance, privileges, or luxuries that were lavished upon me during my 1972 British venture.

For instance, I joined the tony Youth Hostels Association. From its vast list of hostels to choose from, I had my picks where to travel to and stay for princely sums of a pence per night. I'd check in late afternoon, stay a night and finalize the occupation with an assigned morning chore before setting out again.

Often the accommodations were opulent. For example, cycling through county Hampshire, the city of Winchester was en route. There, I toured its famous cathedral and golfed Royal Winchester before checking in.

The hostel had been a pioneering flour mill. Built in the 1500s, it continued boasting its original water wheel. The showering system was strictly for the discerning and cultivated. Preferred guests like me, filled immense wooden buckets with water on the main floor. Next, lifting a trap door, I'd step below by ladder carefully. Carefully, because the porcelain shower basin below was slick and the fast flowing River Itchen, which ran through Winchester then, passed only centimetres away. Once balanced, I'd courageously pull a rope releasing the bucket's icy contents. Unfortunately I never experienced the exhilaration of slipping into the river's spirited current.

For supper, I dined exquisitely on prepared smash and ox tail soup. Smash was a powdery potato mix purchased for pennies. When added to water, it created instant mashed potatoes. By heating the canned soup and pouring it over my mix, I had a food critic's delight of hearty stew. During evenings in the common room, I was popular. I had golf clubs rather than hiking gear, making me the conversational go-to. In mornings, chores might include buffing biffys or furbishing floors. If that pleased hostel managers, I was free to search out my next round of golf.

So, as any reader might realize, Darren Clarke or Justin Rose couldn't possibly have afforded the sophistication golfers like me were extended.

But, as they say in Britain, "Pity!"

Journal Entry #67: Land of Make Believe
Dedicated to *Regine Leblanc*

Years later, as a club professional, I taught advanced course management. In one analogy, I described two philosophic approaches called the Greg Norman and Lee Trevino ways. Both golfers were legendary pros with different outlooks toward winning major tournaments. The former enjoyed success with his go-for-broke strategies which embellished his nickname *the White Shark*. Trevino, on the other hand, succeeded with more modest approaches. I always admired the latter. Sometimes though, I found it entertaining using Norman's style, which I exploited at Land's End.

In my travels, hostellers asked if I intended to visit Land's End in Cornwall. They described it as Europe's farthest western village. That led to my fantasy of teeing up a ball there and launching a massive drive. One my imagination saw spanning the entire ocean and landing in North America.

For clarity, it's not possible! Regardless, mystic elements have always partnered golf. Elements which have lured the curious for centuries. And it was that which beckoned me to Land's End, where by chance a hostel availed itself on the Penwith Peninsula.

On the afternoon of my arrival, I found the perfect location for my attempt … a level grassy area high above rocky outcrops and an angry Atlantic. There, with the orange sun gravitating in the far west … I teed my ball up. And in that surreal moment … I swung, watching my effort flee toward Newfoundland's horizon. I left content, knowing I'd given her my best … as only the white shark would have.

Journal Entry #68: Vincent
Dedicated to *Tanner and Marg Staples*

During nearly sixty years playing golf, I was the beneficiary of three unexplained, surreal experiences.

The first took place in Gloucester, England after golfing in the southern Welsh village Porthcawl.

Royal Porthcawl was a hidden gem. It had hosted prominent tournaments and reportedly then was the best course in Wales. There, I met their head pro and his assistant, who were genuinely interested in my travels. After my round, they fed me in their clubhouse before directing me to the main road. Earlier I sold my bike to make ends meet, and continued by hitchhiking. Eventually I arrived at a hostel in the nearby village Chepstow. It was always advisable reserving ahead when staying in hostels. That day I forgot and was foiled by a hostile host. "You Americans are all alike," he barked. "Well, not this time!" He slammed the door in my face, while failing to recognize my nationality. By then it was past ten o'clock at night.

At that time the village was quiet, courting needs to clear out. The longer I lumbered carrying suitcase and clubs, the lonelier it became. A few cars passed, but no one picked up strangers in darkness. After midnight, a car full of the creepy offered a lift, which appeared like an awaiting accident. Little else came my way that starry night. A night Welsh poet Dylan Thomas might have savoured. A night of soul searching, talking to myself, and sourcing heavens.

The distance to Gloucester was more than thirty kilometres, so en route I rested on farm fences.

Early next morning, after endless kilometres, a Gloucester patrol car lifted and abandoned me within the nearby city. Exhausted and dazed, I wandered about, eventually seeking refuge near a colossal cathedral. I nestled by its concrete base, sleeping until daybreak with only my gear and fatigue as companions.

Above on the cathedral window and unknown to me, was a stained-glass figure famous in golf. Reportedly built between the years 1340 and 1350, it's believed to be the world's earliest pictorial of a golfer swinging a club.

I could have ended up sleeping anywhere around Gloucester but, for only esoteric reasons, found my way there.

Journal Entry #69: Sunningdale
Dedicated to *Arthur Lees*

I first played **Sunningdale** on Christmas Eve and because it was the holidays, I was permitted to play her all day long.

There at that inland course south of London, my curiosity of design grew further. It was to continue as a long-lasting amateur relationship, where I became an outside admirer looking in.

Sunningdale appeared different from other courses. Its polar elements of exquisite turf grooming and rugged wilderness seemed to coexist in harmony. As a teenager, I was too young to understand the architectural significance of minimalism. However, for that Sunningdale visit I'll always be grateful to Arthur Lees.

Lees was remembered from the 1950s as one of Britain's finest European tour stars. A three-time Ryder Cupper, he was their head professional when I suddenly materialized before him, hoping to play. As if clairvoyant though, he let me golf, despite my long hair and inappropriate attire. At day's end, I left Sunningdale fulfilled, vanishing within the glitter of holiday lights. Years later, I realized Lees had inadvertently blessed me with a timeless holiday gift. An everlasting appreciation of a distinct type of golf course design.

Journal Entry #70: Coronation Street
Dedicated to *Bernie and Theo Gagnon*

It's a safe bet most golfers, amateur or professional, wouldn't know the name Jimmy Adams.

It was near dark on Christmas Eve in the London suburb of Sunningdale. I felt exhilarated from playing the historic heathland course, but tired from walking its thirty-six holes. Leaning against my clubs outside the course's entry gate, I began my usual hitchhiking routine. My destination was Staines, six kilometres away. Thumbing for rides then were waiting games. When dark, waits were longer and during holiday season longer still. Many cars passed that night, when finally an older blue station wagon emerged from the club's entrance. Its elderly occupant took pity, offering me a lift. A British cap, glasses and long overcoat claimed him a refugee from Britain's iconic television show, **Coronation Street.**

Then unexpectedly, his Gaelic accent swirled on about golf.

He peppered me with simple questions like: "Where are ye frum? What de ya play tu? What de ye think a tha coorse?" Weary, I was only capable of bland, one-word responses. At that youthful age … and even now, the craft of chat wasn't my strongest attribute. Nearing Staines though, I reluctantly gave in to the prods when he introduced himself as Jimmy Adams. Nearing the roundabout where we'd soon separate, my fingers were groping the door handle when he reminisced of his four times nearly championing the Open and being a five-time Ryder Cup member.

With last-minute shoppers swooshing past, traffic at the roundabout was hectic when we parted. Before I realized it, another opportunity had passed me as he disappeared into the slipstream of taillights! My inability to communicate had prevented me discovering more about him.

Since then, I've spent decades correcting that flaw, poorly finessing my way through most conversations. And frankly, I've remained unsuccessful. It's been my most challenging obstacle, largely due to shyness. Regardless, I've learned if there is one skill everyone—and particularly golf pros—should acquire, it's oratory prowess. Over time I've grasped some of the more vital qualities such as eye contact and how dialogue pivots around veiled forms of balance. Mutual exchanges, neither one-sided nor dominant. So now when asked, "How I am?" I can respond by looking back properly and politely returning words. However, even now in retirement, listening continues as a formidable challenge. Another reminder from that ride with Jimmy Adams, so long ago.

Journal Entry #71: Hi Tide Chipping
Dedicated to *Bob Kuspira*

During that British sabbatical, normal expenses bit into my quest. To finance it, I found a dream job in London. One which not only paid me under-the-table cash, but food and flexibility to travel and work as needed.

The Hi Tide Fish and Chip shop provided me that lease.

The restaurant was located near London, in Earl's Court. There I worked late shifts after catching the underground from Hounslow. My job was prepping for the evening's main trade by peeling and cutting potatoes into ritual rectangles. After, I manned the front counter, selling usuals of haddock, cod, or halibut. Traditional requests also included fries with a gherkin, swaddled in newspaper.

I worked with those whose names Halim and Malik implied Egyptian illegal. Together, we toiled past midnight when the pubs released their delinquents. We even served the famous, such as actor Sean Connery. In the early morning hours, I'd retrace my route back to Hounslow.

The shop owner, who was also a golfer, paid me weekly to subsidize my dwindling bank account.

That routine continued throughout winter, as I patiently awaited spring in Edmonton and the reopening of another golf season.

Journal Entry #72: Mersey Beat (Hoylake)
Dedicated to *Bill King*

There have been places I wanted to golf more than others but they were usually accompanied by reasons. There weren't any at Hoylake.

In 1967, the Argentinean professional, Roberto De Vicenzo won the Open there. A calendar year later, Dr. Martin Luther King, Jr. was assassinated in Memphis. Riots followed, consuming American cities. It was then, near the previous Open's anniversary, when I felt that need to play **Hoylake**, aka the Royal Liverpool links.

Five years later, I yielded to that yearn. To reach Hoylake from London, I hiked up the eastern Welsh border via route A49. I made my way to Liverpool, home of England's emissaries, the Beatles. There, I literally walked through the entire city with my gear. Try that when diets fail! After visiting the Cavern Club, the nightclub that made The Fab Four, I ferried across the Mersey. It was there, on the Wirral peninsula where the village of Hoylake was, the home of Royal Liverpool Golf Club.

I arrived finding rain so severe the skies seemed enraged, raining silver bullets. The pro shop staff said simply, "gofar it meight!" I was the only golfer in her embrace all day. I wore glasses then, straining to see each saturated shot, while the handles of my clubs seemed anointed in Vaseline. Twisting in my hands during impact, they often flew away helplessly. Consequently, I lost numerous balls that round, finishing at the clubhouse without ammunition. Undoubtedly, it was among the most torrid weather conditions I ever encountered. Interestingly, I found Royal Liverpool similar to Sunningdale, except the former was a links. She had that same bizarre blend of savagery and sanity. For example, the par-three thirteenth alongside the Irish Sea, had but a green and a tee box. Accessorized by only seaside dunes and marram, her sole strategy screamed "all or nothing!"

After my round, I doused myself for hours within the clubhouse's gigantic porcelain showers, awaiting dry clothes. There I pondered what had lured me. More than fifty years have passed since and I'm still searching.

Journal Entry #73: Bradshaw's Balls (Portmarnock)

Dedicated to *Joe and Rose Kay*

After that turbulent storm days earlier, my journey continued toward North Wales, over the Irish Sea and eventually to Dublin, Ireland. It was another sample of culture which included sipping Guinness ale and seeing Trinity College. Then I began assaulting the Emerald Isle courses. I started at Royal Dublin where I met legendary Irish star Christy O'Connor. From there, I continued on toward the nearby links at **Portmarnock**.

To find her, I left Dublin via the Coast Road. Portmarnock was located near the Howth peninsula on dunes that crept into the Atlantic. Weary foot soldiers found her constant beckoning from across the inlet enticing.

Portmarnock became one of my favourite links. After arriving there, I met her custodial Irish professional Harry Bradshaw, who wore a tam while manning the shop. He'd won the Irish Open ten times, but his ink was really measured during the 1949 Open at St. Georges. There, he lost a playoff to South African great, Bobby Locke. During one round, Bradshaw's ball found its way into a broken beer bottle. The veteran foolishly elected playing it, which ultimately cost him the claret jug. I wisely kept that to myself as ammunition for when showing up there, I had to beg Bradshaw for balls, owing to my Hoylake odyssey. In the golf industry then, it wasn't cool for one pro to beg equipment from another, especially when the other was the dry-witted Bradshaw.

Journal Entry #74: On the Border

Dedicated to *Tom Megan*

From Dublin I ventured north, exploring more of the planet's great links. Doing so, I tested the insanity of Northern Ireland. It began with a ride offered by a catholic priest who attempted vindicating the violence. Numerous bomb sites en route though, failed to mitigate his case. Nearing the border town Newry, his description of casualties only authenticated the distress, desensitizing my natural curiosity. He let me out in the tense town centre, where I made my way nervously toward its perimeter. There I found the perfect place to resume hiking, naive of my proximity to South Armagh, the epicentre for the Irish Republican Army. Appearances were deceptive, as I waited hours with no hints of a ride. As evening drew dark though, a white windowless van unexpectedly pulled over. The driver, querying my destination, furtively nodded me inside.

Four others sat in the sterile cab, spread-eagled on the panelled metal floor. Trying as their overalls implied, the men in their late thirties seemed more white-collar than mechanical. Short beards, toques, and shadows obscured faces. It wasn't until we moved that I sniffed the stiff air of no conversation; commodities hikers count on. For the next twenty minutes, uneasy desperation filtered the silence until I was deposited with relief near my destination ... Newcastle. There, I had reservations at a hostel close to the famous links, Royal County Down. I found my accommodations further up a lonely road which split Northern Ireland's dark, dew-drenched countryside. With thoughts riveted on golfing next day at County Down; I dismissed the strange ride.

Weeks later in London however, the bombing of a movie theatre—in the town where the van had released me—was in the news. Authorities were seeking a similar vehicle allegedly linked to the IRA.

Common sense insists terrorists don't pick up hikers and yet, over time, I came to trust the integrity of those impressions, dispensing thoughts it wasn't a ride with evil.

Journal Entry #75: Royal County Down

Dedicated to *Ian Ross*

Most of us indulge in hobbies. Mine include playing the world's most interesting golf courses, ones where I could spend eternity in peace. Ironically amid the violence, **Royal County Down** was one.

Walking the few kilometres from my hostel to Newcastle, I found County Down, basking by the Mourne mountains. Her rugged dunes, glittered in gorse, were punctuated by tee boxes of geometric dimensions. Their meticulously mown squares and rectangles perpetuated thoughts about one of golf's more sacred principles. That being, each tee box is handmade and once golfers play away, all gloves are off. In other words, a player should never touch a ball once in play, accepting any result good or bad. A parallel to challenges in life.

Leaving Newcastle, I found my way to Belfast. There, I met shock when witness to more barbaric evidence of a country in strife. Row houses, scarred and blistered by bricked-up doors and windows, recollected horrific terrors. Storefronts were garrisoned by obese orange drums, while yellow concrete humps repelled reams of city vehicles. Coils of razor wire crowded downtown cores like tangles of irate spectators. Collectively, they decreed a city impregnated by conflict.

Walking warily to the bus depot, I was searched endlessly by British armies in combat fatigues. Fears my golf bag harboured more than clubs, oranges, and stale bread dilated their doubt. I sensed weariness in their eyes, graduates of desperation. It was all accompanied by insane beliefs the grey rain, which fell that day, might extinguish flames from bombs threatening ignition anytime … anywhere! The depot itself seemed on life support. Its ticket office remained intact, surrounded only by horizontal beams dripping charcoal stalactites. Blasts from the past! In fear, I boarded a bus to the suburb Holywood, home to the Royal Belfast Golf Club.

And there on quiet parkland, I found a course pleading to convalesce. Like an elder seeking immunity from warring injustice, Royal Belfast seemed but only another casualty of an electrified city circuited by atrocity.

Journal Entry #76: Royal Portrush

Dedicated to *Nestor Fedoruk*

Leaving Belfast, I beelined coastward toward the infamous **Royal Portrush** links. On a detour off the famed Antrim Road, I climbed high on twisted routes, snaked between overgrown stonewalls. If other vehicles approached, there were no alternatives. One backed up, permitting others to pass. As I reached the apex in stunning sunshine, I was blown away by magnificent views. Mountainous meadows stretching north toward a vast Atlantic. Its sights were so paralyzing, had I peered long enough, I envisioned seeing Iceland in the dazzling distance. There I sensed differences between Northern Ireland and its southern cousin. The former, while frayed by war, was clean and void of advertising … less Americanized.

The lofty panorama continued as I eventually descended, weaving past Devil's Causeway, near Portrush.

Portrush had been the only Irish course then to have hosted the Open. In 2019, after sixty-eight years though, it was welcomed back. And who could blame visionary marketers? It was inevitable after the unprecedented success of Irish prodigies Darren Clarke, Padraig Harrington, Graeme

McDowell and Rory McIlroy. Time only would dictate its success, but golfs governing body, the Royal and Ancient, should be credited. Administrating a championship of such magnitude under equally skeptical circumstances might have been like performing heart surgery handcuffed.

Ireland's own Shane Lowry fittingly won that Open. With relentless accuracy and creativity, he out-survived the dense long grasses, rugged mounds, and the North Atlantic's tempestuous winds.

My own particular time ended abruptly at the fourteenth, a treacherous par-three locals call Calamity Corner. My stubborn attempts failed to satisfy her seductive green with its frontal crater. Exhausting my ball supply yet again, it seemed Portrush's way of implying, "She was too tired!"

Journal Entry #77: Royal Birkdale
Dedicated to *Gerry Schiele*

Before Glendale hired Donny, their club pro was a Brit named Nick Melvin. Melvin was a true career man, and from the beginning, a warm addition with his Blighty accent and charisma. Homesick however, he returned to England, leaving a vacancy which resulted in Donny's appointment.

I sought Melvin out at his Yorkshire home course, where I shared my travel plans. He suggested I visit his father, a retired pro living in Southport Lancashire … near another Open venue, **Royal Birkdale**.

From Melvin's midland home, I trekked across England once more to where the elder took me in. For days, he coached me in medieval methods adopted by early British instructors. I was his student in my own private golf school. After, he dropped me off at the famous Birkdale links.

A year earlier, she was the Open site where Mexican Lee Trevino fended off a persistent Taiwanese, affectionately known as Mr Lu. Lu engaged every golfer's imagination as the consummate gentleman. His charm and magical short game continually tempted fate. There, romanced by their encounter, I practised among the intimidating fairways and indiscriminate dunes, haunting places the Mexican and Asian duelled each other. And in that surround of solitude and salty ocean breezes, I dared my own imagination.

Journal Entry #78: Royal Lytham and St. Annes

Dedicated to *Norm Ursulak*

The links at **Royal Lytham and St. Annes** was different from others. Incarcerated from the ocean by housing and rail lines, she was one of the rare courses anywhere boasting a par-three opening hole.

Playing there on a cranky day, I came to the turn of her dogleg par-four seventeenth. There, within the left-hand bunkers, I found my tee shot's final demise. Preparing my next stroke, I noticed a plaque imbedded within the hazard's slope. A commemorate of a famous shot there in 1926 by legendary amateur Bobby Jones. A shot propelling him on to win the Open. It precipitated conversation with Lytham's pro. A giant of a man, he explained the very club Jones used back then was displayed in the upstairs gentlemen's games room. Naturally I had to see it, but the clubhouse was off-limits without blazer and tie.

Sensing my disappointment, the burly pro disappeared into the shop, returning with his own sports jacket. Unfortunately, it was gigantic and I still had no tie. Using his imagination though, the big man borrowed a narrow strap used when attaching golf bags to hand carts. Wrapping it around my sweaty shirt, he fabricated a crude Windsor knot. Returning my collar down, he finalized the rehearsal by placing his enormous cloak upon me. I followed his directions upstairs, all the while feeling like a Texan clown. With each lumbering step up I took, the garment's weight plunged me down. Eventually I found the room where the members took delight in my bizarre appearance and invited me to join them for billiards. There I marvelled at Jone's mashie, mounted in glass near large bays overlooking Lytham's eighteenth green.

Years later in the final round of the '74 Open, Gary Player, fabricated a left-handed putt from the flower bed directly beneath those very windows. When he played that televised shot, eventually winning, I recalled that Texan clown with affable amusement.

Journal Entry #79: Prestwick
Dedicated to *Robbie Jamieson*

A biopsy of golf wasn't complete without examining Scotland's west coast origins.

While St. Andrews remains globally acknowledged as golf's historical birthplace, it wasn't the only ancestral links. Golf became equally eminent in the Ayrshire village of **Prestwick** when Tom Morris, Sr. was hired to lay out her original course. And there, as keeper-of-the-links, he hosted the first Open. The championship remained there another dozen years before St. Andrews eventually acceded. Now unfortunately, Prestwick's fairways are too short for modern-day golf gorillas.

Prestwick lives on the Atlantic, bordered in-land and adjacent Glasgow's South Western Railway. There, wooden ties were necessities for train tracks. Morris used their discards as bulwarks when combatting erosion. Erosion that shifted dunes from frantic Atlantic winds. Even now they remain as bulkheads in primitive horizontal and vertical formations supporting sand banks and greens.

A classic example being her par-four, seventeenth. Approaches there were met by a camouflaging mountainous dune. Adding insult to misery was a latent cavernous bunker, supported by such ties. Other peaks at Prestwick were equally gripping. Morris bestowed names upon them such as the Alps and Himalayas. Descriptions that subpoenaed scales of size.

Prior to my arrival however, another had visited Prestwick. One who fell career witness to those wild land formations. An American who later introduced radical flavours of design which powerfully influenced course architecture. From that sojourn, he imported Morris' rail-tie theme which became the recognized trademark for insurance agent turned designer, Pete Dye!

Journal Entry #80: Troon

Dedicated to *Robert Cairns*

Britain's most difficult links on the Open rotation might be **Troon**. She's now known as Royal Troon Golf Club. In the summer of '73, the championship was hosted there.

When I arrived earlier with hopes of playing, workers were unloading scaffolds around her clubhouse. I assumed they were upgrading for the coming event. I introduced myself to the receptionist who stated the year's biggest tournament was scheduled that day and I couldn't play. But other than lorry drivers and equipment, the entire facility was eerie quiet. Wandering the clubhouse interior, I noticed a display of antique clubs. It was my first time seeing collections of such vintage. Known as the Troon Clubs, they were thought to be the sport's rarest, dating back to the seventeenth century. I was immediately attracted to their upkeep, mystic shapes, and mythical origins. Near the exhibit was that day's tournament draw. Eight golfers ... two foursomes! The year's big championship wasn't the Open but an outing of past notables.

I left the building and looked reflectively toward the nearby ocean. It seemed sad. A vacant course for only eight golfers? On the other hand, I'd flown six thousand kilometres just to be with her. I thought about the soles of my worn boots, which had slogged over much of Britain by then. I reaffirmed a commitment made years earlier at Calgary's Country Club ... one proclaiming myself a golfer of the world. As I continued staring at the Atlantic, the state of my footwear wasn't guaranteeing I'd ever be back. Consequently, I did what most purists might.

Examining Troon's scorecard, I conceived the lay of her land. Carrying my clubs, I drifted toward the beach, where her first hole paralleled the ocean. Continuing, I ascended a mound camouflaging her second tee and began playing. Commandeering a course wasn't within the scope of PGA bylaws. Nevertheless, I knew my presence was more privilege than rite, so I carried on. When I reached the famous eighth hole with her postage-stamp green, the grounds crew even photographed me. Eventually, after hours of joy in her company, I reached the final tee.

Initially, it seemed appropriate to exit discreetly; via the beach in the same covert way I'd entered. Seduced by needs to play in though, I abandoned the strategy and charged up her eighteenth fairway. If the secretary escorted me off … so be it. No one minded, however. Later that year, I watched Open winner Tom Weiskopf golf up that same fairway. I relived that moment, but as a different world golfer.

Journal Entry #81: Killing Me Softly (Carnoustie)

Dedicated to *Flo Brien*

Hitchhiking in Scotland was different from England. In the latter, drivers were generous and accommodating, while above the border I waited. My only recourse was walking … often gruelling distances. Begging for lifts on motorways was illegal, so golfers like me kept to secondary roads where traffic was less and the rides lesser. From West Caledonia to the East wasn't far in kilometres, but lugging a suitcase and clubs became wearisome. Consequently reaching my **Carnoustie** destination seemed a pilgrimage.

Lonely stone-walled kilometres were trekked listening to a pocket-sized transistor radio, whose batteries unexplainably resisted exhaustion. Each hour, the BBC played the newly released single "**Killing Me Softly**" by Roberta Flack. She became my companion as I rambled on toward the links near Dundee.

Player had won the Open there four years earlier. But instead, I was tuned to 1953 when Hogan championed there in his only attempt. The tournament was a close contest between him and South American, Antonio Cerda. Stories of their match were described like blow-by-blow prizefights. I felt an aftermath witness to it when reaching the par-five, sixth. Locals called it *Hogan's Alley* because "The Wee Ice Mon" found the tightly confined driving area during each round. One which continually rewarded his approaches.

After finishing, I set off in darkness toward Edinburgh again, resuming my reconnaissance for rides. I was growing weary by then, having walked endlessly about the isles. And the only rhythm maintaining that momentum emanated from desires to understand the game, links golf, and seek comfort from Roberta Flack. Decades later, an interpretation of Flack's endearing effort was recaptured in the movie *About a Boy.* An interpretation that renewed a misplaced affection for Scottish countrysides.

Journal Entry #82: C Moon (Gleneagles)

Dedicated to *Tom Zaleski*

With only days left in my career journey, I found my way to Scotland's cosmopolitan city Edinburgh. Nearby was the parkland resort **Gleneagles**, designed by five-time Open champion James Braid. Braid's architectural genius was overshadowed by his playing accomplishments.

Setting out to find Gleneagles that morning, I believed my hiking havocs had changed. A sympathetic businessman picked me up, claiming he knew where the course was. "Aweel ye'r in luck lawddie," he said excitedly. "Aye, ah'ament gaun thare, but ah kin drap ye a wee cloasr' n ye'll be thare in na tame!" We drove for a while, eventually moving off the main highway into country where we stopped on a lonely rural road. There he turned and said: "Okey lawddie, this is whaur we pairt, bit the coorse is juist ower thare," pointing toward some firs lining the road. "Juist ower thare," turned out being more than twelve kilometres!

That was the first surprise. My second was finding the streets deserted. Over the next six hours, only two cars passed as I aimlessly plodded the Perthshire hills. Sometimes at crossroads, I chose wrongly until redirected to the vital turnoff.

Eventually that afternoon in the distance, I saw an immense cloudy building sprouting chimneys. A Buckingham Palace in the forest. Gleneagles, that time of day was quiet and her golfers retired. She was mine to play, but there was little time remaining in the fading light. My arms were so weary; the act of swinging seemed an achievement. Gleneagle's maternal essence braided forests of pine with sensually vibrant land shapes reminiscent of Jasper back home. I played as fast as my legs moved before sunset, but not before wishing my stay could have been longer.

I left in darkness, again traipsing muted country routes, uncertain how to expedite myself back to Edinburgh. As always, I was guided by local signs, inquiries, and light from the **C Moon.**

Journal Entry #83: Mrs. Foreman's Pub

Dedicated to *Belle Harris*

Wherever golf is played, there is usually a watering hole, a place where golfers gather, imbibe, and talk the game. Also known as the nineteenth hole, it often has an energizing vibe distinguishing the sport.

St. Andrews and Prestwick were villages where early Opens were contested. However, there was a third locality, possibly more spiritual than either. Musselburgh's links were the oldest on an original site anywhere. Play began there in the thirteenth century. Then, laypersons and royalty golfed side by side before class stigmatized the sport. Only kilometres from Edinburgh, she became not only legendary for hosting the Open six times, but popularized by **Mrs. Forman's pub**.

George Foreman built the tavern in 1820, conspicuously close to Musselburgh's fifth tee. It became the go-to for locals seeking refreshment during rounds. Foreman's son took over until he died at age forty-one. Subsequently, his wife and eight children ran the residuary, calling it Mrs. Foreman's. During those years, many Open competitors spent hours there served by the family.

Decades later, I arrived there disillusioned. I found only an empty bar accompanied outside by an abandoned, wasted links. Reluctantly recognizable, she appeared victimized and desolate. I made out her fifth green a short distance from the public house. Withered, she was populated by long grass, worm castings, and a leaning stick with tattered cloth. Declarations of dwindled golf. Imprisoned within an equally hobbled oval race track, her unexpected appearance was foreign and faded. It was the same place Bobby Jones was photographed decades earlier, beaming with a beverage. My eyes were left with vestiges of a vacated, sacred golf temple. At first, I sensed fraud. But how many Mrs. Foreman's pubs could there be?

Nuzzling her grounds gently with my five-iron, I fired at the flimsy flags, angrily querying why history had been so punitive?

It was at Mrs. Foreman's pub, long ago, where the diameter and shape of a gutter downspout was fashioned by a local blacksmith into a template for golf's first hole-cutting device when changing cups on greens. Its dimensions of four-and -one-quarter-inch diameters are now found at each hole, on every green, at endless world courses.

Fortunately Musselburgh survived, persevering until 1982 when restoration was completed by a concerned group. The revitalization however, failed to include Mrs. Foreman's pub, which ceased operating in 2016. The golf links remain open though and anyone in the world can join her.

Often, the best moments at courses are shared after golf at the nineteenth. There players swap amusing tales, embodying Mrs. Foreman's station as golf's original pub.

Journal Entry #84: Muirfield

Dedicated to *Norm Witten*

On my last day in Britain, I hitched a ride past Musselburgh to Gullane. The pilgrimage concluded at the world's oldest golfing club, the Honourable Company of Edinburgh Golfers ... known more prudently as **Muirfield**! While Musselburgh was golf's oldest course on a continuous site, Muirfield was the earliest documented group to advance golf's first rules ... from their original site, Leith.

I arrived there finding contrasts to other Open venues. Muirfield had no professional, pro shop, or even a course par.

Entering the main clubhouse, I met the receptionist to inquire about playing when she bluntly told me to wait. Minutes later, she returned accompanied by a seasoned naval officer. Unknowingly, I was about to meet the infamous Captain PWT Paddy Hanmer. Years later I read about his steely hand, administering Muirfield with iron fists. He once denied Jack Nicklaus golfing privileges for insufficient notice. He berated Ben Crenshaw and Tom Watson late one evening for playing extra holes, after the latter's Open win there.

The captain herded me through the clubhouse toward his private domain where hardwood walls and floors echoed uncertainty. Commandingly, he ordered me to sit. Without wasting time he disapproved of my attire, failing to realize I'd circuited Britain's isles during the previous months. Hanmer followed by quizzing and answering the subject of my hair length for a pro. He stated pointedly: "You should be aware, it will be me, and only me deciding if you play here today!" My back recoiled responsively against the shivery correctional chair I sat in. I felt condemned in a school principal's office, detained like young Ebenezer in the movie *Scrooge*.

But as the dissection continued, I noted a developing curiosity in the Canadian flag crudely sown into my light-blue windbreaker. In a subtle change, the officer then confided his daughter had relocated to Montréal. He continued, querying in Gaelic tact whether she and I had ever met. I never thought myself a swift thinker, but like lightening I replied, "I'm not sure, but I'll look her up, if you'd like?"Appearing satisfied, he passed me her name and Québec phone number. Hanmer then personally escorted me to the first tee where I was promptly abandoned.

The escape was electric, although not because of Hanmer. It was during the Open at Muirfield the previous summer, Lee Trevino chipped-in twice during the final round, denying Jack Nicklaus victory. A moment golf history misapprehended.

The Professional Golfer's Association had staged their premier event in February a year earlier, rather than traditionally in August. Nicklaus won that event. The following year, he captured the Masters and US Open. Consequently he needed only the British to simultaneously own all four majors. When Trevino nudged him out, he deprived the Golden Bear that distinction.

My time in Britain was up! During the trip of a lifetime, I had not only unearthed the gold of golf's origins, but feasted at the tables of my chosen career. I returned home resuming my third season at Glendale.

Journal Entry #85: Admiral Halsey (Campbelltown)

Dedicated to *Eric Callicott*

Arriving back to Alberta, I had to find fresh accommodations.

Previously I was Glendale's live-in caretaker, but that couldn't last forever, especially during season. However, the club's chef made me an offer impossible to refuse.

He too coincidentally, originated from the air base and asked me to lease a home with him only minutes from Glendale.

It became my living quarters over the following years. The arrangement provided me two bedrooms, a living area, plus a bathroom and kitchen, all for thirty-five dollars a month! How could I go wrong?

The home owners were named Campbell. Paul McCartney recorded "**Admiral Halsey**" then, his first post-Beatles number-one single while living near Campbelltown, Scotland. A place where Tom Morris, Sr. built the magnificent Machrihanish links. Consequently, I named my new home **Campbelltown**.

Journal Entry #86: Dunrobin's Gone

Dedicated to *Billy Morris*

Following my sophomore year, Neil returned to Vancouver permanently. Donny then had to fill the vacancy for a right hand man. Among fantasies, I imagined he'd consider me. Despite an ego tugging at reality, I was eager and enthusiastic, although unqualified. My developing maturity however, came to a screeching halt learning his replacement had no industry experience! It was my first letdown in a business I was passionate about. It wouldn't have bothered me had the successor been qualified.

Instead, Donny chose an NHL athlete searching for an alternative career. My ego was bruised by a defensive check when Donny hired KayKay.

KayKay (as they called him) was a husky blue-liner with unflattering NHL credentials who'd been traded to Edmonton. The changes were immediate! During my previous years, Neil oversaw and shaped my career professionally. He was the big brother I never had. Working with KayKay was different.

Later, navigating course politics, I saw him as a logical successor. With Donny's job always in peril then, it made sense choosing a candidate the membership might promotionally identify with. One who could straddle pro shop problems with swagger. In Canada, an NHL jock on staff might be considered a bonus, even if unaccountable. It temporarily worked for Donny, seeing how members initially migrated toward those three persuasive letters ... NHL.

The workplace wasn't what it was though. I couldn't understand why in the midst of career change, a new recruit would spend hours newspaper leering and counter lounging. I'm sure he worked hard ... but I never saw it. In addition, Neil and I shared equal work shifts. He'd toil until two in the afternoon, when I took over. KayKay on the other hand, golfed daily and if that time extended into mine, it didn't matter. I was abandoned regularly, restricted to the shop covering for him. The situation became awkward because a younger man lacking maturity, confronting an elder about work ethics was tricky. And professional hockey players could do no wrong. I was smart enough to understand outspoken conduct would be viewed as spurns of a jealous assistant. It was the start of change, for as they say, "The honeymoon was over." But it's also been said, "When one door shuts, another opens," and through it walked James Dow.

Journal Entry #87: Daniel

Dedicated to *Jim Dow*

As if on fate's cue, a member named Jim Dow became a surrogate brother and new mentor to me.

An architectural consultant, Jimmy was also an art and design professor at the University of Alberta. Originally from Mainland China, he spent his childhood there prior to the country's 1949 Communist siege. The political winds influenced his families' refuge to neighbouring Hong Kong. Later, inspired by his great grandfather, he left for America pursuing a physics

PhD at a famous Boston institute. He became one of the Young Lions, a select group of visionary thinkers who travelled the world, creating solutions for global issues.

Settling in Edmonton, Jimmy became intrigued by the complexities of golf. He became a Glendale member, recognizing the subtle design that encouraged golfer's to think. Most members weren't aware of Jimmy's intellect. He never campaigned to hit balls far, like most men aspire. Nor was he interested in trapping trophies. Jimmy's time instead, was spent developing his swing and studying golf course design. Problems and solutions were his specialty. During my following years in the industry, if I had concerns of any nature, I usually turned to him for advice. And often there were answers. In my attempts to understand golf and life, I adopted his philosophic approach based on logic. Simply put ... obtain all relevant facts, weigh them ... and make decisions accordingly.

Journal Entry #88: Hoganomics

Dedicated to *Brian Dansereau*

When I wrote this, the global financial arena was recovering from the Great Recession. For many in the capitalist world, moments were fuelled by anxiety. At the beginning of my pro career, the experience of acquiring my first automobile influenced not only my business, but future management of capital during that uncertain time.

In those early years without a vehicle, I depended on cycling and the charity of fellow golfers to chauffeur me.

Eventually, I saved enough and invested in an honest, used machine. A boyhood friend whose passion was cars, helped. We haunted Edmonton car lots then ... lifting hoods, examining interiors and viewing underneath chassis, noting things I knew little of.

Eventually, we found a blue, 1967 Rambler at a south side dealership. The next step was negotiating with the salesman, whose name was Hogan ... no relation to golf's legend. I was naive in haggling then, which was apparent when he began toying with me. Earlier when prepping for the purchase however, I had withdrawn my budget of $1,100 cash. During the bargaining, I inadvertently exposed the thick wad. When his eyeballs leered at it, his demeanour suddenly changed and we had a deal faster than a linoleum putting green.

While Hogan's lesson might have been to treat customers with more respect, mine was … cash talked! I detected the value currency extolled in transactions and how absences of credit could litigate purchasing. And I saw how people naturally spent if opportunity existed. Subsequently, I acquired a purchasing philosophy I've rarely deviated from. I made the act of buying difficult, encouraging needs to make the freedom justified. I not only became discerning when acquiring anything, but sorted the differences between needing and wanting. It may be one reason I later became one of the few pros financially able to own a course, albeit a small one. But more importantly, why that modest facility financially survived in 2008, when so many others collapsed in bankruptcy.

Journal Entry #89: Dr. John (Part 1)

Dedicated to *Dr. John and Barb Pasternak*

One of the staff we hired to clean member's clubs then was John. He was the younger brother of Nak who befriended me earlier. Both were naturally inquisitive, pleasant being around, and dedicated golfers.

The Alberta Open came to Edmonton every other year. I used one occasion to take Glendale's juniors to watch the tour players in action. John became obsessed by one in particular … long-hitting Bob Panasik. Panasik teed his ball up several inches above ground level at heights meant to drive it from the stratosphere.

John copied Panasik's style, adding the unusual twist of tilting the ball far forward. Everyone thought it looked strange, but John claimed angling it backwards instead created a negative mental image. Unwittingly, he demonstrated how psychology impacts the golf swing, interpreting what Bobby Jones once claimed: "Golf is played mainly on a five-and-one-half-inch course … the space between one's ears."

John later entered University and graduated to become a respected physician.

Journal Entry #90: Moe Norman (Part 1)

Dedicated to *Wayne and Randy Kay*

One method I used to develop junior skills was what I termed seeing-and-mimicking. It was a simple technique matching young body builds to corresponding PGA tour physiques. Once I paired them, I encouraged juniors to imitate their style.

One of the teens was a freckled auburn named Glendale Red. A naturally cocky and provocative gambler, he practised endlessly, developing potential to contend nationally. I saw hints of Canadian legend **Moe Norman** in the young man and took him to the Open to watch the enigmatic ball striker. My hope was that by witnessing Norman's talent, the junior might capture his essence.

We arrived at the Highlands to find Norman at the fourth hole, a downhill par-four with a pancake green shaded by trees. A series of bunkers protected its front.

I'd never seen Norman live, but was solicited by accounts of his amazing accuracy. From behind the putting surface, we saw his conspicuous profile perched high above on the distant tee. I made out his wide foot stance and extended legs, as if a stick man below waist. He completed the image bending slightly at the hips, lasering a full arm extension toward the ball. There was no mistaking that address position.

Red and I both hesitated, caged by anticipation. We watched Moe move mechanically into his backswing to where he unleashed a drive that perished into the afternoon blue sky. Norman's ball fell silently and then suddenly reappeared, not unlike a scud missile. Instead though, it plopped apologetically with only an obligatory bounce or two. In one razor shot, he finished feet from the flag on the par four!

I can't claim that introduction to the infamous Canadian transformed Red, but it had lasting affects on me.

Journal Entry #91: Beyond the Clouds
Dedicated to *Twiggy*

Let your conscience be your guide?

Ricardo was considered by many, Glendale's most contemptible member. He was the first person I saw on my interview day, leaving me initially apprehensive. Naturally caustic and intimidating, his tall, chunky image was cursed by a boorish machine gun laugh. He'd been left a fortune, consequently Ricardo was financially independent and didn't work. Young and physically able, he was even considered an accomplished golfer, despite a swing any pipe fitter could have plumbed together. Yet despite the maverick's fortuity, he was a crude complainer, perpetual whiner, and flamboyant know-it-all. He even frequently and flagrantly cheated on his devoted wife.

During those early career years, Ricardo owned a distinct position among Glendale's crowd. One smearing him with rank within the club's hierarchy. No matter how he chiseled others, the narcissist had followers who acknowledged his actions as normal. In other times, they'd have been part of Donald Trump's base. It left me pondering, "What was I missing?"

As a youngster, I was exposed to a variety of sports. But after discovering golf, found it unique from the others. Golf was a game, which refreshingly encouraged players to act civil toward each other, unlike hockey for instance. In golf, there were self-regulated penalties for miscues that suggested **always** do the right thing! It was also a vocation where sincere kindness to one's opponent seemed just. But Ricardo mocked those observations. So at some point, it was reasonable to query how he successfully maintained that impetuous popularity. It taunted Trump's theory that winning in life was the only thing! Later, I sensed Trump himself, a slanted version of Ricardo.

Eventually though, and without reason, my inner voice pestered me, claiming Ricardo's contaminating bluster wasn't to be emulated. I rose above the glitter, migrating toward kinder behaviour. Snake-oil salesmen, con artists, and career criminals would have labelled it a losing choice, but fortunately I realized it wasn't what life was about. In those impressionable years, witness to Ricardo's ways, I was grateful to see **beyond the clouds**. I learned it was better to adhere to one's conscience and always do the right thing.

Journal Entry #92: The Mentor (Part 1)
Dedicated to *Jim Lefevre*

In my third season, the Edmonton Open was played at the private Mayfair. The event was one of several pros could participate in, so to assure a place in the field, I entered.

It was routine then to play practise rounds before tournaments. Consequently, days prior, I was assigned an early morning time. Upon arriving, the assistant informed me, no more than nine holes could be played. Opening with a drive that plunged me into the river valley, I fell under the spell of Stanley Thompson's subtle greens and articulate sand traps. Putting out on the triple tiered ninth green, I noticed she wasn't overly busy. Captivated by the classic design, I carried on, naively finishing my round.

It was customary after playing another's facility to thank the host. Subsequently I entered the shop, unprepared for the reception.

There, I saw the assistant at the centre counter accompanied by an elder in suit. An uncomfortable atmosphere, like unsaleable merchandise, hung about. The suit took over and I instinctively sensed trouble for taking the extra nine holes. Taller, with wavy red hair, a fair complexion and glasses he demanded knowing why I disobeyed pro shop instructions. Then with a bold Scottish accent, he **tore** into me. He drilled me sharply about professional conduct, obligation, and responsibility as his face turned crimson with each direct edict. He threatened decisive action curtailing my future play there should it happen again! I was in the presence of Mayfair's club manager, who owned undisputed authority over the shop staff.

I left dizzy, disheveled, and unquestionably aware future decisions could never again be taken for granted. I'd met James Russell Lefevre, unaware he would later become another mentor.

Journal Entry #93: Yesterday Once More

Dedicated to *Jack and Ester Ondrack*

In school, I didn't grasp the theory of history. Later, it became evident after reading quotes of a reputable Toronto businessman who claimed: "If you want to know what will happen tomorrow, you need to understand what took place yesterday!"

Steady Eddie asked me to respond to a letter from New Jersey requesting a club memento for his collection.

The sender was a member of an organization called the *Golf Collectors' Society*, one I was unfamiliar with. Soon after, a personal letter arrived from their president asking my opinion on some antique club's an Edmontonian was selling.

They were reminiscent of the rare equipment I saw earlier at Troon. After gathering the information, I forwarded it to the president.

As a result, I was invited to join the Collectors. They had more members than our own PGA and I became the first Canadian.

When the president declined buying the clubs ... I purchased them instead. Unknowingly, that seedling investment in golf history sprouted a deeper interest in contemporary equipment.

Journal Entry #94: Superstar

Dedicated to *Lois Payne*

After a series of lessons, I shifted my time with Jackie Davies toward on course instruction at tournament sites. I'd pick her up in my Rambler and we'd travel to courses dissecting her play. Soon after, she entered her first tournament.

Her Edmonton Junior debut at Riverside became the genesis of an amateur career seldom duplicated. During the next four years, her progress was eye-opening.

Professional golfers plan their annual tournament schedules. At her youthful age, Jackie too did the same. She began with the Club

Championship along with the City Junior. Soon after, she added the provincial and nationals to that list.

After her sophomore season, she competed in her first provincial at Edmonton's Country Club. There, Jackie finished fourth behind Alberta's premier player, Calgary's Carin McBean. Little did Jackie know, McBean would make a startling reappearance into her personal life forty years later. That same season, Jackie enjoyed her first success at the municipal Victoria, winning Edmonton's Junior by eight shots. The following year, she defended, while nearly capturing the provincials at Calgary. She also competed in her first Ladies Amateur against Edmonton's finest women (not juniors). There, she trailed Canadian legend Betty Cole by only strokes. The persistence paid off at rain drenched Red Deer where she won Alberta's Junior and Juvenile crowns. That year, she also took the City Championships for a third consecutive season … by an unprecedented thirteen shots.

Despite those accomplishments, it was her performance during the Canadian Junior at Highlands where she attracted authentic attention. We all waited, anxiously awaiting the outcome. The final was tight, as she was narrowly clipped by her arch competitor, Toronto's Stacey West.

Only eighty pounds, Jackie stood four feet and nine inches tall. She was seen as an oddity by spectators who often commented on the mighty figure dwarfed by bag and cart.

And as each season progressed, it became clear her game was advancing toward levels which were challenging mine too. At the pace she was winning, little doubt remained I'd have difficulty keeping up.

Journal Entry #95: Doctor My Eyes

Dedicated to *Chuck Taylor*

Pro-ams were golf tournaments where a professional and team of amateurs competed against others. The pros also played for cash prizes among themselves. The concept was a vehicle for promoting golf, while allowing pros personal interaction with group members. Charitable components accompanied it, resulting in donations.

Early in my career I didn't understand the concept. My learning curve came by way of a front row vision forcing me to peer into pro shop politics.

A local optometrist and new member became friendly with me as a pro-am teammate. Two problems arose from that brief partnership. One was my ignorance of team relationships and the doctor entered handicaps which I felt were inferior.

After several poor showings, I tried politely suggesting we re-examine his handicap. That's when I learned about diplomacy ... when my partner swiftly replied back by never golfing with me again, shunning me forever after. As one might expect, it became awkward later when we intersected at club events.

I couldn't blame him. He gave me a taste of my own medicine. It was my first experience diving into the waters of shop politics. Looking back, I should have waded in and gone with the flow. I saw then how empathy affected relationships on and off golf courses.

Journal Entry #96: Bob Wylie (Part 1)

Dedicated to *Bob Wylie*

The Alberta Assistants' Championship was contested at Calgary's Country Club. I'd played there earlier as a junior in horrific storms. This time however, the tournament was a pro-am and my partner was famed amateur, **Bob Wylie**.

Wylie's accomplishments are too extensive listing, but he was a multiple national champion and represented Canada internationally on numerous occasions.

Ironically, it was his demeanour which left a lasting impression upon me. Often talented sport figures possess egos too enormous to stomach. Wylie wasn't like that however, perpetually apologizing for his course misplays in sincere, unpatronizing ways. And Wylie, as an amateur, not only taught me proper pro-am etiquette, but also how to be nicer. The answer, of course, was treating others as they would want to be treated. He was also astute. Sensing my interest in course design, he detailed how each tree there had been historically hand planted. My education broadened watching him swing.

Calgary's tenth was a short, uphill par-four, doglegging right. Dog legs are fairway angles analogizing an animal's bent limb. There, Wylie attempted cutting his tee shot up and around its corner toward the green. That meant he curved his shot **gently** left to right, to follow the fairway's bend (he was right handed). Those shots land soft with little roll. On that effort, his bodies' movement through impact clearly guided the ball's curvature in air. It inspired needs within me to understand more about shotmaking ... the art of influencing ball flight trajectories through swing motion. As an assistant, I had some developed skills, but not like Wylie.

To play fifty-four holes with the veteran, watch a master at play with a golf club, as well as correcting my absentee behaviour, proved a wise career investment.

Journal Entry #97: The Verdict (Part 3)

Dedicated to *Jimmy Clarke*

The judge was also an original founder of Glendale. A short man of Jewish descent, he held strong opinions on subjects portraying him dominant and overbearing. When challenged though, he was usually proven right, suggesting a vast mind. His personal life however, was tragic, qualifying that phrase, "Life isn't always fair." One Halloween, he became another life-long friend.

That year, when he asked me to golf on that date, I thought it was his way of ending another season. One when robins left, green grass turned brown, snowflakes interrupted shots and firm autumn ground extended the length of our drives. But it was more. He was type who wouldn't share his reasons, but I knew it helped him deal with his tragedy.

Journal Entry #98: Educating Rita
Dedicated to *Tom Huggon*

As my friendship with Jim Dow grew and aware of my devotion to golf, he became a conduit for that passion, sharing principles of architecture with me. He was also a student of the golf swing. We'd dissect it for hours, regardless of season, swinging clubs in the living room of his Edwardian home. He'd challenge me to find the relationships between body positions and clubface angles during the swing.

But his subtleties extended beyond the sport to include compassion.

Once, he invited me to a party at his home where I was introduced to his business acquaintances and campus colleagues. Unaware it was a night of wall-to-wall people, my shyness exposed itself and I made an emotional exit. I relived that moment years later, watching the movie **Educating Rita**, starring Julie Walters and Michael Caine. There, Rita suffered the same impairment at a similar sophisticated soiree.

After fleeing Jimmy's party, I sought refuge in my own comfort zone … the golf course. And when I approached the second green that night, a lone figure with clubs, drove off the first tee to catch up. It was Jimmy. He abandoned his home and friends attending to my selfish mood. That compassion cemented our friendship, resulting in him becoming my next mentor.

In his life's search for truth he claimed then, shyness, despite its flaws, remains not only an act of honesty, but a characteristic unworthy of dismissal.

Journal Entry #99: Torrey Pines
Dedicated to *Val Gant*

Jackie Davies rapidly evolved into Glendale's most successful junior golfer. After early successes, she was selected to participate in the World Juniors at **Torrey Pines** in San Diego.

The list of entries there included future tour pros, Phil Blackmar, John Cook, Billy Mayfair, Nick Price, Jim Renner, and Mark Wiebe, along with Lori Garbacz, Heather Farr, and Kris Tschetter. Jackie was among talent.

It was her first taste of global competition where she finished second in the international field.

While there, competing in the Lengfeld Matches for girls, she golfed on the Monterey Peninsula's iconic courses, Cypress Point and Pebble Beach. After, she returned home and won her fourth consecutive City Championship by a whopping twenty shots! Her Torrey Pines encounter demonstrated to me then how performances are dramatically influenced when exposed to advanced competition.

Journal Entry #100: The Golden Bear

Dedicated to *John Robbins*

During my fifth season, I wrote the Canadian PGA Class "A" examination. Prior to that, I apprenticed as an entry-level "B."

Weeks later, I was awarded passing grades, promoting my status to "A."

The entire process however felt gratuitous, like gaining equity without earning it. Besides on site work and occasional seminars, how really qualified was I? Many pros then … and even currently, lived comfortably within those guidelines. But I couldn't.

Consequently, I registered at the University of Alberta's Faculty of Physical Education. If I was to teach the sport seriously and get paid, more genuine needs compelled me to learn more.

Before enrolling however, preliminaries dictated surviving two introductory interviews. The first was a generic one-on-one with Faculty Dean, Dr. Maury Van Vliet. The second was with senior advisor, Dr. Steve Mendryk.

Mendryk was an active member of the local Derrick Golf Club and one of his questions probed my enrolling intent. I replied, "Because I want to improve my teaching." Pausing, he smugly said: "You know, we've never had a golf professional in our program before. You'd be the first!" That's when I became a U of A Golden Bear.

And for the record, arguably golf's finest player ever, Jack Nicklaus, was never a Golden Bear.

Journal Entry #101: Night Moves
Dedicated to *Collette Clarke*

I began studying in a four-year athletic performance program for coaching, training, and conditioning.

To pay tuition, I needed another job. Johnny Aitken was head pro at Edmonton's bustling Victoria course. He also supervised the cities' robust Parks and Recreation program. When an instructor's job availed itself, he interviewed and awarded me the position.

There were three of us on staff. Besides Johnny and I, there was Ron Salter, the Welsh pro from the indoor school. He kept us loose with humour and his engendering image of Ronald McDonald. Arriving at gymnasiums, we'd unload our equipment of clubs, floor mats, and whiffle balls. The room was divided into practise areas where six days per week, we taught three evening classes with eight students per group.

There, over the next four years, I filled primitive teaching gaps with in-the-trench instructing experiences, introducing endless people to golf. They in turn fuelled and fertilized my fermenting skills.

Days became routine. University classes began at dawn continuing into afternoons when I then closed shop. From there, I crossed town and instructed, finishing nights amid flashes of studying. After thousands of students, my swing knowledge, public speaking, and coaching capabilities improved dramatically.

Those **night moves** paid my tuition.

Journal Entry #102: Whiter Shade of Pale
Dedicated to *John Shwets*

My time on campus was not only educational, but social. Attractive women were distractions as I fantasized endlessly about the brunette in front of me, the blonde two rows down, or redheads passing in libraries. It was a challenge to concentrate, lending credibility to skeptics claiming university values were questionable.

Most of my classes pertained to administration and sciences. Ironically however, my most memorable lesson, was delivered by a lady in English humanities, one considerably older than the younger one's I admired daily.

Growing up, it seemed fashionable in conversation to use vocabulary sounding cool, rather than clear. Consequently my words were often misinterpreted. I attempted resolving that one day in literature class, embarrassing myself within a room of art students.

That day, my professor was dissecting an essay focusing on the word lust. Seizing the opportunity, I raised my hand, querying its definition. In the ensuing seconds, the elderly spinster's answer was sudden paralysis. With her face, a **whiter shade of pale**, she spurted out, "Well … it's … it's … it's sexual in nature." My complexion changed colour too. The snickers that followed, spread throughout the semi-circle theatre like virus' penetrating a hard drive.

It seems trivial now extolling the best from four years of higher learning was vocabulary use. Regardless, while swallowing humble pie that day, I realized the influencing capability words possess in everyday communicating.

Journal Entry #103: Dr. John (Part 2)

Dedicated to *Bob Lister*

During my career, I often benefited in times of need from the knowledge of others. For instance, at university I had Dr. John.

John and I enrolled in college at the same time, attending movies, playing racquetball, and canvassing campus pubs. He was part of an academically gifted family. His father was an architect, his older brother an electrical engineer, and his younger sister an award winning filmmaker. John meanwhile followed his older sister into medicine..

John's curriculum of subjects was almost entirely science based. Among my sciences were anatomy, biochemistry, and physiology. Unfortunately my grades in them made mediocrity look good. Consequently, John became my source for dealing with science's sorcery. For instance, if I needed answers to a physics question, he was always available to translate its language.

Later, he became one of my groomsmen and we remained long time distant friends.

Journal Entry #104: I Saw the Light

Dedicated to *Don and Winnie Moore*

I stole secrets from a bank while attending university. I was never caught, prosecuted, nor incarcerated. I've remained undetected since, living with an intact conscience.

As a college sophomore, my bank account was constantly depleted. I had winter employment teaching golf, but it wasn't enough.

A janitorial job eased the problem. The work became essential as its schedule meshed with studying and teaching demands. One of my contracts was at a local bank, where duties included floor cleaning.

The hours extended into early mornings when occasionally I broke for rest. During those moments, I'd feign swinging golf clubs with my mop on the tiled floors … stretching and balancing career muscles toward imaginary targets. I'd position my feet along floor lines insuring my toes were glued to them. Eventually I noticed the mop's weight forced my ankles to roll, one of Jack Grout's earliest tips to his student, Jack Nicklaus. And from the mop's length I began thinking about swing planes and the centrifugal role hands played when centering with the body. From that, returning the clubhead's heel before of the toe when approached the ball, became relevant!

It all seemed innocent and unearth shattering, yet each fundamental I stole then became significant as I continued exploring golf's swing mysteries. Simple, original thoughts later authenticated at seminars conducted by golf's most knowledgeable teachers.

Journal Entry #105: The Science of Golf

Dedicated to *Dr. Howie Wenger*

In anatomy, we dissected rhesus monkey cadavers. Beneath their skin, we examined the overwhelming strength of musculature. When Tiger Woods suffered ACL and Achilles tendon damage later in his career, and knowing the resilience of that tissue, it appeared to me he misused it. I realized how humans could terrorize their bodies in other ways besides narcotics and foul food.

In organic chemistry, I learned cellular reproduction was limited in cooler climates. Cellular development was considered significant when golfers deferred to muscle memory. That may have been why Hogan avoided practising in colder temperatures.

These were among the interpretations I gathered from the entertaining physiology lectures of Dr. Howie Wenger.

In biochemistry, we memorized amino acid formulas, the backbone of body protein synthesis. That led to adrenal level studies when comparing golfing performances to other athletes. The challenge was discovering why specific competitors benefited from reflexive movements and enhancing responses that golfers didn't. Hormones were factors … byproducts from continual motion. For instance in golf, the ball remained still until struck. Because of that, golfers appeared deprived of adrenaline benefit. And while my search was unsuccessful, it became relevant later in practise theory.

I also learned golf could be improved through the hierarchy of broad sciences. For instance, physic's natural forces influenced chemical cell changes. They in turn supported biology's affect on circulatory, digestive, and nervous systems. Systems impacting physical and psychological performances.

As an assistant nearing the end of my degree, I was able to afford Canadian PGA seminars. But disappointingly, their roster of topics seemed redundant with subjects like club repairing, merchandising and teaching. I found myself questioning why North American pros rarely included sciences within those agendas. Particularly in golf swing development, the bread-and-butter of most pros.

Journal Entry #106: Marine Drive

Dedicated to *Hugh Burgess*

In my sixth season, I qualified for the Canadian Assistants' Championship at Vancouver's Marine Drive Golf Club. I never forgot the generosity of members raising funds for me to attend.

Marine Drive was a hotbed of Canada's finest golfers with national and international legacies. Her legion read like a Canadian golf who's who: Stan Leonard, Marilyn O'Connor, Doug Roxburgh, and later Jim Nelford and Richard Zokol—all Canadian Hall of Famers. It was imbedded within me to understand how Marine Drive cultivated that talent.

Marine Drive was a dignified, well-maintained private course near the Pacific on the Fraser River's north arm. My first impressions were answerless, concluding Glendale an equal test. Golf balls didn't travel as far on west coasts because barometrically the air was heavier. Their professional, the late Alvie Thompson had been a former touring pro, but his shop didn't appear any more polished than Donny's. They had a positive junior program, a hallmark history, and a thriving range that encouraged practise. But while the reasons remained mute, they suggested the answer was deeper within.

I determined it stemmed from the design of A. V. Macan. One featuring deceptive lengths psychologically conning golfers into believing every hole there could be birdied. Being open twelve months a year and having legendary Stan Leonard court her, surely embellished that reputation.

That inquest however, ironically routed me along a path where I began critiquing my own workplace. Unwittingly, it was the beginning of my end at Glendale.

Journal Entry #107: Alone in the Ring

Dedicated to *Sid and Lou Hamdon*

Returning from Marine Drive, I began seeing my future at Glendale waning. Donny seemed reluctant promoting me and despite what I'd learned about my golf game, it too wasn't progressive. I sensed an impending career change.

Jim Dow and I examined my competing on a professional tour. An idea intended to provoke fate. New careers however, demanded realistic answers to sobering questions. Was my game ready? "No!" Did I need the change? "Yes!" Did I have energy to make change? "Yes!" Did I have abilities to face challenges of change? "Yes!" Consequently we looked at qualifying on the European Tour. I leaned there because playing in Canada meant being **alone in the ring,** tolerating local naysayers.

The movie *Cool Hand Luke* was released then. The protagonist, actor Paul Newman, was roused into fights he couldn't win. Always thrashed, he never gave up. Returning to his feet constantly, Newman won when opponents finally quit in disgust.

I saw myself like that when weighing this imminent career change. In real life, I'm not cool nor Paul Newman, but I always persevered despite perpetual failure.

With belief in myself, no fear of change, and an unconfident golf swing, I began a quest for the European Tour. It would be my last season at Glendale.

Journal Entry #108: The Houston Cougar

Dedicated to *Ron Campbell*

In my final university year, change flirted with the spring air.

During those last weeks while preparing for qualifying school, I stumbled upon a campus library article which influenced my future teaching. It was a practise program written for a student by Dave Williams from the University of Houston.

Williams appears unknown in the golf industry. Yet, he was the most successful NCAA coach in history, leading his campus Cougars to unprecedented championships. His graduates included major champions: Fred Couples, Steve Elkington, John Mahaffey, and Fuzzy Zoeller. Williams' system was divided into chipping, pitching, putting, plus field and recovery shots. He set goals in each area for this player, encouraging him to meet those standards. Williams then calibrated the program incrementally like weight trainers, when muscle building. From that approach, he established a dynasty of astonishing records with reportedly minimal swing knowledge. It was a method that appeared credible and tailored for me. I saw it not only as a way to develop playing in the zone, but where I could blend swing fundamentals into customized practise programs for future students. I used it from then on in my own instructing.

With a conceived practise plan, I began training for qualifying school in England that fall.

Journal Entry #109: If You Could Read my Mind

Dedicated to *Dr. Roger Hackett*

I knew that excelling in life required studying hard and working harder. And as a young pro, through trial and error, I found golf development required more than just pounding range balls. There had to be smarter and more reliable practise ways to improve my play and that of others.

Nearing the end of my Glendale apprenticeship, inspired by William's methodology, I settled into my own teaching system. If you could have read my mind then, it jelled into the following.

I began by acknowledging three simple knowns which initially made hitting balls seem daunting. First, clubface dimensions were small, compared for instance to tennis rackets. Second, a club's control point … the grip … was a considerable distance from the clubface. The farther that clubface was from the control point, the greater chance of error … again compared to tennis rackets. And finally, a swing beginning from zero kilometres per hour to over one hundred, took only seconds. During most of those moments, the ball remained inanimately still.

Using those truths, I found a broad recipe for successful shots. It consisted of whole-heartedly seeing and feeling each effort before executing, acquiring proven fundamentals for those executions, and finally … through reliable practise, committing those fundamentals to muscle memory. And when developing that last detail, I tapped into adrenaline.

Adrenaline was useful to athletes because of its influence on performance or playing in the zone. In sports like hockey or baseball, where play was constantly in-motion, it seemed a natural byproduct. Golf was hindered though because the ball remained still until struck. Adrenaline wasn't factoring, so I instead found it useful when practising.

Practise began by focusing on a specific swing fundamental. For instance, the grip, a swing thought, or a lesson remedy (whatever I was working on then). And I only concentrated on that single fundamental. Second, I had to have a mission accompanied by commitments to accomplish it. For example, chipping: After choosing the appropriate club and technique, I set a rigid goal of chipping one ball into the hole. I'd remain there until that task was complete. During the assignment I was riveted on both that fundamental **and** chipping the ball into the hole! I resisted judging individual mistakes, assigning remedies for only patterns of poor shots. If time ran out, I resumed the task during my next session. Again, the mission's goal was seeing it through to completion.

The method's selling feature was adding or subtracting increments accordingly, like body builders. For instance, in the above example, as my chipping improved, I'd increase loads by chipping in two balls rather than one, or advancing to longer shots. This aroused my adrenal levels resulting in confidence-building practise sessions. I introduced the same approach to other game components like long shots, bunker shots, putting, etc. Shots, future students and I could potentially face in everyday play.

Now you've read my mind. Here's a summary …

Muscle memory can be developed in practise through technique and goal setting. They work in harmony like words and music. Patience is mandatory though as the downside is commitment to time, which often may be lengthy and frustrating. For me, it was productive. Having written that, I remained motivated keeping all practise fun.

Journal Entry #110: These Eyes

Dedicated to *Dr. Max Wyman*

Every golf course I knew had a member who quietly stood out. One naturally gifted in solutions to societal problems. A human beacon for betterment. A cornerstone and a rock. An individual few challenged regarding common sense, decency, and moral integrity. This was especially so when wills of the unjust appeared prevailing. During Donald Trump's presidency, that person was Justice Ruth Bader Ginsburg. Glendale had Dr. Max Wyman.

From my first days of work there, I knew Dr. Wyman was different. His roles as Dean of Mathematics at the U of A, and later its president, were characterized by vast intellect and compassion.

And Glendale was his sanctuary. When free to golf, he'd phone Donny who made sure I had the doctor's butterscotch coloured cart and Wilson clubs available in a flash. All he had to do was drive away and tee off. Quiet and almost ghostly, he preferred the solitude to assimilate his thoughts. Even then, he wore the scholarly dress of tailored shirt and bow tie.

When Donny experienced trouble from rogue board members, it was Dr. Wyman who plead on his behalf.

Similar burdens are born of presidents at golf clubs or those running countries. But most leaders don't possess the human qualities Dr. Wyman owned … as was obvious following the 2016 American election. So in the absence of such principles and ethics, every organization needs these incorruptible compasses.

Board members at golf clubs, for the most part, are voted into position from desires to better those facilities. Sometimes however, their intentions parallel personal agendas. When one or more of those types seize power, it can be the birthplace of crippling events stifling a club's or even a nation's progress. That's when the Justice Ginsburgs and Dr. Wymans are needed.

Dr. Wyman was far too busy to be my mentor, yet I silently admired his humble presence. I saw him instead as my moral blueprint.

Journal Entry #111: Philadelphia Morning

Dedicated to *Craig Moon*

In the spring of '77 I completed university and celebrated paying off my varsity loan balance. I'd worked three jobs the previous four years and the restitution comforted me with financial independence for a while after.

I began practising for the upcoming tour qualifying, working reclusively on each aspect of my training schedule. At the famous North Carolina Pinehurst Resort, they have a driving range known as Maniac Hill. I wouldn't have blamed anyone thinking me a refugee from it. The practise never ended. I placed small objects on the range at varying distances, never daring to leave until successfully hitting them. I went through a thousand range balls daily.

At that same time, the motion picture *Rocky*, written by and starring actor Sylvester Stallone, was released. The well-known story of a nobody having a shot at the World's Heavyweight Boxing Championship became a mantra. Its musical theme featuring Rocky running through Philadelphia streets, constantly led me to the range or putting green. Despite owning an inadequate golf swing, I genuinely believed I could qualify. Even now watching that film, I think of the range balls hit that summer and how my hands suffered.

Journal Entry #112: The Year of the Cat

Dedicated to *Bill and Julia Blazuk*

That season, I literally became obsessed with the golf swing.

By then I knew the fundamentals of addressing the ball which included grip, stance, aiming, and body posture. I was aware of hand positions in the backswing, and clubface relationships to them. I understood why swings originated from the ground up, along with the virtues of balance, planes, and head presence. But there were missing parts enslaving a young pro venturing toward uncertainty. And while rummaging about for those clues, a Scottish musician named Al Stewart recorded a popular song—one that led me further along that route shared by golf and life.

Like many young men, I too was interested in the opposite sex. When **"The Year of the Cat"** was released, I found comfort among its seductive lyrics. I saw a parallel between those of us seeking companionship and those obsessed with practising golf.

Stewart's refrain, arguably one of music's more popular, reminds me of those hours spent in driving-range asylum all while assessing a future with or without someone special.

It might have appeared delusional, but I was a dreamer … a romantic believing in what was coming. Only it wasn't what I expected!

Journal Entry #113: Girl Don't Come

Dedicated to *Cheryl Campbell*

Glendale's junior program, while modest, was rich in talent. Many of its young women finished prominently in city and provincial championships. Jackie Davies, though, was different. She wasn't just a standout at Glendale, but in Edmonton … and Alberta.

Jackie won her fourth consecutive Edmonton Junior by twenty shots. A year later, she did it again, increasing the margin by three. She then won her second provincial by similar numbers!

But like most teens, she underwent growing pains, uncharacteristically finishing fifth during her final years at the Canadians. While her life was changing, she was nonetheless developing into a superb amateur among world-class competitors. For instance at the Canadians, she was paired with Carole Semple Thompson, the recently crowned British and US Ladies Champion.

And during that same time frame, subtle changes began re-moulding our own student-teacher relationship.

Unknowingly we were advancing toward the next stage of our lives.

Journal Entry #114: Dr. John (Part 3)
Dedicated to *Brad Liptak*

The summer of '77 flew by, unlike my golf development. Even given the exhaustive work I put in, only slivers of confidence replied back! Regardless, I continued practising. During that time, Dr. John and I took a break and visited the air base where I discovered golf.

My sister was being married soon and during that trip, the topic of my date arose. Privately, I had somebody in mind. At one point in our conversation though, as if discovering a secret serum, the doctor blurted out, "What about Jackie Davies?" Exactly who I had in mind!

Journal Entry #115: Summer of '77
Dedicated to *Derrick Hawes*

Soon after, the Alberta Assistants' Championship was played in Red Deer.

After all my practise, a disappointing eighty during the first round was all I could manage. I wasn't pleasant company that evening. My friend amongst the assistants then was Derrick Hawes, a short blond-haired Englishman, who'd recently relocated to Red Deer.

That night, he invited me for supper, where in rhythms of conversation we discussed our rounds. Eventually when the topic of Jackie Davies arose, I confessed my awkwardness in asking her out. However, under the influence of Hawe's curly persuasive accent and the clout of Kahlúa, I phoned.

With nerves bouncing like pinballs, I stumbled on about the wedding, poorly putting my best foot forward. Her reply thankfully, was a quick and simple, "Yes!"

Journal Entry #116: Heaven Must Have Sent You

Dedicated to *Blackie Dionne*

Red Deer's first hole never bothered me before. It was a straightaway par-five, with a green pinched behind stunted poplars. Nevertheless, I began my final round there with a double bogey. It felt like salt on a bleeding wound, despite my high from the previous night's phone call.

But on the next hole my game suddenly changed, as it mysteriously can. I finished the remaining holes four under par, scoring seventy.

I returned to my hotel and began packing when Neil called claiming I was in a sudden death playoff. Three of us had tied for first.

It would be pleasant summarizing my win, but I exited on the first hole. One of Glendale's members, Blackie Dionne caddied for me and I couldn't have asked for anyone better. It didn't matter though. Finishing first along with my impending date atoned for the loss.

Journal Entry #117: First Date

Dedicated to *Wendy MacKenzie*

Back then the uncertainties of courting seemed endless. Relationships were like peering into the unknown.

The awkwardness of our first date though, quickly vanished which had much to do with Jackie. She was reserved, yet calm and mature beyond years. Following the wedding we went out again. This time to a theatre where we saw the sci-fi film, *Star Wars*. There were drinks after and the male server, noting her youthful essence, eye-balled me and asked for Jackie's identification.

On that second date, we both sensed the relationship deeper than either suspected. She furnished the five-year-old newspaper clipping of my budding career ... pocketing it the entire time. We saw each other over the next seven days and committed to a spring wedding date during Masters week. April and Augusta!

Journal Entry #118: The Lovin' Sound

Dedicated to *Bill and Helen Trusdale*

Most remember the happiest moment in their lives. A marriage, birth, meeting someone special, accomplishing a goal, or visiting memorable places. Mine was during a golf tournament soon after we became engaged. That's not suggesting our marriage or offspring were anticlimactic either.

Also, after setting the wedding date, I abandoned intentions of tour qualifying. In the end, I had to brave reality. I didn't yet own a dependable swing for high-level competition. I decided then to continue my career as a club professional. The intent of going on tour however, accomplished its goal … to provoke fate. And, as Oprah has been known to say, "It was life changing."

While I lost the provincial playoff, that performance rewarded me with another berth into the nationals, played then at the magnificent Stanley Thompson Mayfair.

Jackie watched me play wearing her grey, crushed velvet, junior executive suit which hugged her perfectly. Her presence there, in the surrounds of that captivating course continues as my life's happiest time.

Journal Entry #119: The Way They Were (Part 2)

Dedicated to *Lou Podersky*

Glendale's male membership was a fusion of Jewish golfers, sprinkled with migrants from Edmonton public courses.

Among them was Father Megan … who wasn't cleric. Bulky and silver-haired, the Irishman's grunting laugh was accentuated by mischievous twinkles in his eye. Over coffee, he'd reminisce of golfing in fierce Atlantic winds which terrorized the links of his origin. His pinkish face implied an inbred love of lager when engaging golfers in post tournament ballads. Jack, could have been mistaken for a bush pilot with his pipe and aviators.

The blond Harvard graduate spent many evenings in the shop with me unearthing the appeal of antique golf clubs,

Norm was Glendale's legal guide. The high profile lawyer's intimidating glare were accompanied by wings which could never be clipped. Ralph was a tall, slender judge who smoked extraordinarily long Panatelas. Tidier than Mr. Clean, he never had a hair out of place. Perversions of his honour on the bench with Havanas however, distorted more flattering opinions. Art also romanced the cigar as his Humphrey Bogart charm bankrolled his station as a grizzled car peddler.

Dunc had retired from the Canadian Football League. With his crimson temper, the heavy crewcut could snap golf shafts like toothpicks. Billy was another athlete, although more youthful and effervescent. A hockey pro with New York's Long Island Ducks, he'd cruise to the club in his Triumph while his tangle of locks danced to the wind. Genuine and pleasing, he was a jock without ego. Eddie was the godfather, but his sculptured Greek look was where the endorsement ended. Ironically, the confirmed bachelor was guided by a kind, humble, and avuncular soul. Gene was equally endearing. An energetic Ukrainian educator, he turned to politics becoming a decorated minister of various portfolios.

Glendale wouldn't have been Glendale without its inseparable twosomes. For instance John and Sonny were the club gamblers who played the horses with Donny while Jake and Dade played the Jewish odd couple, golfing daily in their emerald, three-wheeled power cart.

Finally there was Glendale's granddaddy, old Lou. A retired furniture retailer with sagging jowls, he and his son Danny financially anchored the club during its emergence. Every time I saw the elder though, I swore he was chomping that same two inch stogie.

Journal Entry #120: The Way They Were (Part 3)

Dedicated to *Donna Watson*

A golf memoir wouldn't be complete if reminisced only among shadows of man. During my apprenticeship, golf wasn't immune from gender discrimination. I was birthed into the business when Glendale's women were incarcerated by restricted weekend tee times. Despite that subservience, I admired, loved, and respected them. Those I served were as distinct as their gender counterparts.

Regine talked as fast as she drove her golf cart. Elderly, frantic and French, the retired educator's account of hitting a golf ball, made more sense to me than many pros. Her wispy continental accent reduced the swing to a, "Twist, slide, and turn." Another close friend was Lois. An original founder, committed to faith, she was one of several over time who tried converting me. One of the most impressionable was the judge's wife, Betty. She passed away prematurely which was a loss for him, their family, and Glendale. A privilege to serve, she had a determined, yet compassionate identity, symbolized by shirt pleats casually folded over sweater sleeves worn that day.

Olive was Glendale's most accomplished senior. Unfortunately she struggled with happiness, always sniping at someone or something. Freda was another Jewish elder who puffed more than anyone I knew. We once partnered successfully in a club function, putting miraculously through her veils of haze. Wendy was a nurse with a sad disposition who never smoked, yet ironically lost a courageous battle with cancer. Fran volunteered endlessly at Glendale, later becoming Alberta Golf's first woman governor. Julia's allure vacuumed every male's attention. Yet the gifted teacher had a finessing way of advocating women's rights around the opposite sex.

Finally, there was Mary, my first political acquaintance. She carried herself in stylish ways remembering names. As Minister of Culture within the Conservative Lougheed government, she was named Companion to the Order of Canada. In the end, she too insulated herself with the same veneer most legislator's eventually do.

Journal Entry #121: Seve

Dedicated to *Severiano Ballesteros*

Qualifying school was held in Surrey at Fox Hills Golf Course. Still possessing my travel fare, I revisited Britain to formally withdraw before the wedding. Other hopefuls in the field then included future Master champions Ian Woosnam and Sandy Lyle, along with world-famous instructor David Leadbetter.

Coincidentally, the World Match Play Championship was being contested then at Wentworth. I took in the tournament seeing for the first time the world's finest on one stage. Among them was a young Spaniard named Severiano Ballesteros. A teenage sensation, he nearly captured the Open a year earlier. Effervescent and fresh, he appeared like a new age Arnold Palmer. Palmer had the charisma, game, and looks within his resume. Ballesteros appeared the same, but with Spanish sparks instead. His shots bore trajectories of galactic heights. Then transitioning, they'd surrender, parachuting effortlessly toward each green. **Seve** was greatness packaged in youth.

There, I also saw Tom Watson, my next inspiration. And while my eyes took turns observing him and the others, they continually returned to the Pedrena profit whose ground divots hypnotized me, remaining air-born long **after he'd finished swinging.** Was it fate signalling the next differentiating clue between hitting balls and swinging clubs?

Journal Entry #122: Wheatsheaf Inn

Dedicated to *Hon. Gene "the Machine" Zwozdesky*

In an earlier journal entry, I wrote of a surreal experience in Gloucester. Another took place one sunny afternoon, six years later near Wentworth.

Wentworth was close to the **Wheatsheaf Inn**. A place whose electric pub was a post-tournament attraction for caddies, players, and spectators. Leaving the excitement, I wandered outside to the parking lot awaiting my ride.

There, coerced by some mysterious unknown, I was lured to the nearby road. I walked alongside ongoing traffic when a lake shimmering through trees stole my attention. The deviation continued, guiding my curiosity toward the water. There, in a setting sun, a still lagoon with gliding swans monopolized me. The unfamiliar force persuaded me to sit, breath-in the serenity, and take a picture before returning.

SUMMER PLACE

Years later, I read about one of golf's earliest and most famous rounds ever played ... a score of sixty-six. It was recorded at nearby Sunningdale in 1926 by the great amateur Bobby Jones. The story documented his legendary thirty-three field shots and putts, qualifying him for the British Amateur.

But it also described Jone's day prior to that round. He was staying at the Wheatsheaf when he suffered food poisoning. Stepping out for fresh air, he discovered that same paradise from the same roadway. A peacefulness which kindled the hot round he fired next day.

I kept that picture.

--Little

Journal Entry #123: Ground Control to Major Tom

Dedicated to *Dr. Archie and Terry MacPherson*

Growing up, Gary Player had been my golfing idol. Later, I included Tom Watson. During the 1977 Open, I admired not only how the Kansas kid defeated Nicklaus in what was then described history's finest sporting match, but how he let his club's talk rather than his mouth.

That admiration was amplified when writing this, thirty-seven years later during the 2014 Ryder Cup! An event where the American media and US team members publicly condemned Watson and his old-school methods for their loss. And during that prosecution Watson, like the captain and man he was, accepted sole responsibility, stating America was simply outplayed. The manner in which he manifested that mutiny and verbal whipping, claimed it was an honourable way to live.

Captain Tom did lead the US to victory. But it wasn't in Scotland, nor in 2014. It was 1993 in England when his team beat Europe, a victory conveniently forgotten by those critics.

But 2014 was different! It was a time America's golf fraternity redirected blame and failed accountability. A time undesirable behaviours spawned by social media began clutching a new America. Behaviours that nourished and endorsed an incoming renegade president.

Einstein supposedly wrote: "Great souls will encounter violent opposition from mediocre minds."

Journal Entry #124: Summer Wine

Dedicated to *Tom Watson*

I never believed Watson was credited for a swing which accomplicated his eight major championship victories. The photo of him which follows is possibly one of golf's great stop actions. The picture's timing appears so flawless, Watson's next movement is visually predictable.

Watson had a full shoulder turn with parallel shaft position to ground. It explained his long distances for a person not overly stout. His left ankle rolled, insinuating proper core rotation. Wrinkles in his right pant leg reveal knee readiness when initiating timely downswings. His spine appears straight suggesting simplicity in turn while his right hand seems correctly positioned under the club's shaft. One can assume he aims parallel to targets by physical alignment vectors, while his head remains anchored, yet relaxed. If I dared pick a flaw, it might be the subtle closed clubface insinuating he either swung **closed-to-open** or was victim to rebellious driving.

Regardless, rarely is there time when seeing this photo, I'm uninspired to practise.

--Anonymous

Journal Entry #125: The Old Course (Part 2)

Dedicated to *Ken Shergold*

Six years earlier, when visiting St. Andrews, I found **the Old Course** closed for that month. As a result, I returned to play her, as any purist might.

I arrived in darkness, checking into room sixteen of the downtown Ardgowan Hotel. There, over dinner, I found an appreciation for Alberta's renowned beef after spending a small fortune on a Scottish variety. I should have stayed with fish and chips.

Rising early and carrying my clubs, I headed toward Golf Place. There, I once again descended toward the grey-stone mansion. Teeing off solo, I was the day's first golfer, finishing with a birdie. It afforded me time again to immerse myself within the cities' vital culture. Late that afternoon I retraced my steps and replayed the Old Course as the day's final occupant. First out … last in.

Many times since I've ended my day's golf in fading light. There was a reason. Golf pros were usually extended perks of courtesy green fees. Grateful for that privilege, I always avoided intruding on a course's primary revenue times. Instead I asked for early or late openings, unless given alternatives. As a result, it often became ritualistic approaching the final hole near dusk, backdropped by a clubhouse. And there inside, the illuminated silhouettes of that day's golfers seemed to summarize the day's play.

St. Andrews then, was the first time I noticed those silhouettes.

Journal Entry #126: Harry Vardon

Dedicated to *Harry Vardon*

North of London in County Herefordshire is the town of Totteridge. There, appearing sedate and secluded is the famous parkland course, South Herts. A place where one of earths greatest professionals consummated an esteemed career.

Harry Vardon was the preeminent pro of his day. He'd won the Open an unprecedented six times and the American once. As a young pro, I felt urges to visit South Herts and see where Vardon completed his life's pursuit.

After my round, I saw the clubhouse tribute to Vardon, a brass relief of his hands decorating the foyer wall. A grip, which in golf circles came to be known as the *Vardon* or *Overlap*. One depicting the lower hand's baby finger overlapping the first knuckle of the opposite.

That grip today continues as the most popular taught by pros. But while a proper grip is obviously essential, it can still frustrate a golfer who hasn't been taught its relationship to clubface angle.

Journal Entry #127: Stoney End

Dedicated to *Jim Hallam*

Songwriter Laura Nyro wrote the words and music for the composition, "**Stoney End.**" Lyrics supposedly questioning gender uncertainty.

While elements of one's intimate preferences—compared to another's golf career—could never be confused, I too found myself harassed by inner demons when leaving Glendale. Demons interrogating my career choices with questions like: "How might my destiny been influenced if exposed to early golf instruction, especially when gifted passionate work ethics?" or "Did I make the right decision becoming a club pro rather than venturing out on tour?"

Despite what's been said of regret, my commitments to marriage and the club profession were right for me. Had I chosen the route of tour player, I might not have met Jackie! I wouldn't have been privileged to a life with her, our offspring, and eventually grandchildren. Nor would I have met the thousands I eventually taught and served in business.

Regardless, over years those same demons revisit and heckle me. And after witnessing Jackie becoming a competitive legend, I'd be lying if I failed admitting occasional slivers of envy. Fortunately reality always annuls the regret, rescuing me with reminders of my good fortune.

To me, in a roundabout way, it's not unlike learning the most important shot in golf … **the next one**!

Journal Entry #128: Exodus

Dedicated to *Marvin Dower*

Glendale was born in 1959 when Edmonton's Jewish community found challenges seeking memberships at local clubs. I learned that from one of the founders who became a personal friend.

Religion is a sensitive subject, energizing highly charged debates within society. As a result, I learned early to steer clear of membership discussions involving it. And during that mission, I remained faithful.

Now retired and agnostic, I'm no closer in understanding why the subject engulfs so many of us. To me, religious recruitment appears similar to marketing golf balls. There were two hundred and seventy worldly denominations at the time I wrote this and all sold faith claiming divine answers. Golf ball manufacturers market another version of faith. Which denomination or ball is right?

Regardless, I'm left challenged by two remaining questions about faith. Does some unexplained force somewhere or someplace navigate our universe? And why has religion failed the needy throughout history?

I have no answers, except what appears a single certainty. Had the Jewish sect not developed Glendale, would any of this have been written?

Journal Entry #129: Funeral for a Friend
Dedicated to *Norman Woods*

I never appreciated Glendale while working there. I was guilty of looking, but not seeing.

Canadian course architect Norman Woods designed Glendale, sculpturing her from thick blends of poplar and fir. Accented by a series of insurgent hills, Woods skillfully and subtly, threaded his inspiration around them in ways never comprehended until she matured. Fairways and greens were positioned harmonizing two concepts ... minimal earth movement and strategy, especially when approaching pin positions. An example, her short par-four sixth. There, golfers whose tee shots hugged the left fairway side, were rewarded by receptive angles to her green. Shots opposite couldn't hold her putting surface.

Over time though, Glendale succumbed to the infidelity of rotating course politics. Her virginity was ravaged by subsequent architects whose contours failed to match Wood's imitation of nature.

A common observation of the Old Course at St. Andrews, is her diversity. Glendale too, originally enjoyed a similar integrity and may have been Western Canada's most underrated challenge.

Regardless, my first seven seasons with her were passionately memorable as I plodded onward toward my golf degree. It was a pleasant place in time and my departure was a **funeral for a friend.**

Journal Entry #130: Strange Magic

Dedicated to *Mike Tomash*

Jesse was Mayfair's assistant. He had a laidback personality, not unlike pro Fred Couples. With a puppy-dog face and sauntering stroll, he never hurried for anyone. Talented, he came from Calgary and became immediately popular.

Like most assistants though, Jesse too aspired to become his own boss. That day arrived when he was appointed head pro at Sturgeon Valley, north of town. That left a vacancy for a new Mayfair assistant. That winter, Jackie and I discussed the opportunity. Consequently, I crafted a concise, yet detailed resume for the job.

While the content was important, what followed its delivery, may have been the **strange magic** that tipped the scales.

Coincidentally, Jackie worked as a bookkeeper at Mayfair, where each morning I chauffeured her to and from work. One day, KayKay was lurking in Gibby's pro shop. Derek Gibson was Mayfair's esteemed head professional, while KayKay was the NHL jock Donny hired over me years earlier. He still worked for Donny, and I assumed nothing after seeing him once or twice. But when the flirtations continued, I knew he was brown-nosing for the same position. As a result, I chose an alternative strategy of avoiding Gibby altogether. I'd let my resume act as its own sales device, hoping the veteran would see through the wheedling. I didn't hold my breath though. I knew of athletes and celebrities who could be high on themselves and low on commitment. Often employers and entrepreneurs either exploited that or resigned themselves to the impairments that followed.

I became like an aircraft in a holding pattern … patient within fate's clutch.

Journal Entry #131: Jackie Wilson Said

Dedicated to *Audrey Walker*

During the last days of 1977, Johnny Aitken retired. I took over his Parks and Recreation position and overhauled it, but my pro-shop future appeared dim.

Then, one grey Sunday afternoon, while teaching at O'Leary High School, that changed. I finished the first of three classes when I saw Jackie in the hallway motioning to me excitedly. Gibby had telephoned, wanting me to return his call. The afternoon refused to move fast enough.

I rarely spoke to Gibby as he and I didn't travel the same circles. As president of Alberta's PGA then, he was the type who wore striped suits to conferences, appearing competent, dignified, and assured. So, when I phoned later and he offered me the position, I was stunned! It was another moment measured only by a hand-written Gary Player letter, my first job, and that date with Jackie.

Derek and I spent moments reminiscing about seminars and other industry matters; but he primarily wanted me to visit and discuss the offer.

Journal Entry #132: A Summer Song

Dedicated to *Ed Thomas*

Gibby lived in an affluent neighbourhood on Edmonton's south side. While his home was modest, it was tastefully decorated with living room pictures hung low. "It's so the eyes appreciate art from sitting positions," he explained. My new boss revelled in popularity. An outgoing man's man, his athletic build had post-prime quarterback written upon him. A pleasant laugh and friendly smile complimented a natural attraction to others. His Québec wife Irene was platinum blonde absent the French accent. She too had an effervescence, embroidered with style. They complimented each other often competing to see who was more engaging.

Derek offered me an attractive salary; one I didn't see a point negotiating. While his offer was substantial, so too were the commitments. At

Glendale, I worked eight hour shifts, six days per week while keeping my lesson revenues. Gibby however, gave me ten-hour shifts and retained my teaching income. Meals were included and I had purchases at cost. A reduction in leisure time was the down-side.

We shook hands, agreeing on a March 1 start date, a month prior to the wedding.

Journal Entry #133: Where Have All the Flowers Gone?

Dedicated to *Jack Johnson*

The little house I'd lived in near Glendale had served its purpose. I moved out and into the basement of the Davies' city bungalow. Days leading up to our wedding and the new job were spent teaching nightly and studying golf swings.

We celebrated the New Year at Glendale with superintendent Lockie. There we planned the seating arrangements for our own big day, which Glendale would host.

During that night however, the groundskeeper leaned over, whispering he wouldn't be returning to Glendale! He'd been silently recruited to takeover the head job at Calgary's exclusive Country Club. I returned his look, sharing what had taken place regarding Mayfair.

We locked eyes, reminiscing of the numerous nights we'd laboured together at Glendale. While I closed shop, he'd be irrigating the course among the bats.

With our good days behind, we were being thrust into the throws of destiny.

Journal Entry #134: Gypsy
Dedicated to *Sam Vine*

As my career shifted toward an exciting future at a distinguished private club, it also meant coming to terms with my past employer. Primarily because of guilt.

Most who leave their jobs today, go on without regret. I wasn't like that, however. There was no exoneration leaving Donny, especially knowing his time was near. Donny never felt comfortable promoting me, yet he'd been fair. And while it was clear his days there were numbered, a feeling of deserting ship persisted. Regardless, he would have wanted me to advance. On that last day, he wasn't there when I removed my belongings, but I left him a note expressing my thanks and best wishes. Head professionals aren't unlike doctors, in a sense. They're perceived as confident and reassuring, not troubled or helpless. But they're also human. Donny needed help but I wasn't able to administer it. His hours spent at racetracks and spike bars didn't help either. The influential Dr. Wyman also tried, but his responsibilities too had boundaries.

Donny lost his contract soon after and took a labouring position at Edmonton's nearby country club. Despite his shortcomings though, I remained grateful to him for giving me an industry berth.

Journal Entry #135: Seasons
Dedicated to *Larry Lefko*

The code of the Canadian Professional Golfer's Association:

The term 'golf professional' or 'professional golfer' must be a synonym and pledge of honour, service, and fair dealing. Professional integrity, fidelity to the game of golf, and a sense of great responsibility to employers, employees, manufacturers, golfers and fellow professionals transcend thought of material gain in the motives of the true golf professionals or professional golfers.

After passing my Class "A" exam, I ordered the organizations' plaque. Along with its emblem, were a code and credo ... terms of conduct expected of professionals. I took those words seriously, even though not all my peers were as committed.

Canadian assistants were a unique and varied group, governed by **seasons.** Cousins of the stereotyped cab driver, they could be big or small, loud or quiet and with talent or without. Some were gamblers, hustlers, and playboys while others gentlemen and business-like. In that variety, two characteristics persisted. Egos and love for golf. Those using golf shops as temporary satellites before venturing on tour had the lion's share. Egos stroked by customers mesmerized by that word partnering their name ... professional. And for a while, I too was tangled in the title. Later though, reality replaced vanity.

One had to like the work of an assistant because wages weren't seen as financial coups. Benefits such as driving range use (if one existed), lesson revenues, sale commissions, discounted merchandise, and/or meals, influenced those salaries. The position however, seemed anchored by integrity, weighted by the respect paid us by those admiring what we did. That itself, seemed worthy considering how many average employees in life, then and now, truly embrace their careers. So, while being an assistant lacked the lustre of engineers, lawyers or investment bankers, it did divvy out dignity.

I saw it as an enviable life in a clean, friendly environment, generally populated by decent customers. But like any job ... it's a two-way street where not everything's visible.

Journal Entry #136: The Way They Were (Part 4)

Dedicated to *Neal Connell*

Growing up in my neighbourhood, friends were either next-door or community companions. Soon after, new ones in the golf industry replaced them. Assistants whose futures too, pivoted around the sport. In time and various ways, they all influenced me.

The Bygrave brothers at the south-side Derrick Club appeared like night and day. One, a Wall Street executive, the other a Malibu surfer. Business acclimated, they eventually moved on, becoming successful long time custodians of Alberta's Kananaskis courses.

Big Mike wasn't as fortunate. A long driving, beefy Ukrainian, he had a domineering presence at Riverside. Unexpectedly, he passed away too young after founding the Alberta Assistant's Association. Larry and Jesse were my Mayfair predecessors. The former, dubbed Purpes, was a flamboyant showman flaunting loud paisley slacks while perpetually searching for his next dollar. Jesse, on the other hand, was an accomplished player who remained popular among members. Neal was Edmonton Country Club's long time righthand man. A confirmed gentleman and always enjoyable to golf with, he struggled with the cancer stick.

My friend Derrick was the short blond-haired Brit working out of Red Deer, while Belvedere's Garry was the showman. Finally, there was Ray, a skilled apprentice, who spent a career at the Highlands, succeeding his iconic boss Henry Martell.

Journal Entry #137: The Way They Were (Part 5)

Dedicated to *Colin Craig*

Every Edmonton course had a head professional who advanced godlike images.

The eldest was Henry Martell. The talented Highlands icon had a limp testifying to the fairways he'd stalked over decades. Brian was the fair-skinned, longtime Edmonton Country Club pro whose residual hair colours plagiarized his nickname Copper. He called things as he saw them and, while I'm not sure he took to me, he was a good friend to Donny. Sandy was the Caledonian cog at Riverside, who while talented, struggled with kindness.

The retired Windermere legend Alex Olynyk was succeeded by Bill, a smart upbeat merchandiser from Montréal. Another Bill supervised the east-side Belvedere, alternating between the tour and accommodating his members. Johnny ran the Victoria Muni and was trusted among Edmonton's blue collar set. Older, friendly, and shrewd, he was perpetually retiring.

My eventual boss Gibby, was the well respected Mayfair pro, who skated with ease among the cities' social elite. Kenny was the soft spoken Broadmoor boss who caught me stealing golf in my youth, eventually forgiving me. Finally there was Mike, another of Donny's beverage buddies. As the least accomplished, Sturgeon Valley's head man was the one pro whose job included the challenge of groundskeeping. With no time to practise, he was a nice man whose inabilities never denied him dignity.

Journal Entry #138: It's My Turn

Dedicated to *Henry and Millie Singer*

In spring of '78, while Jackie and her mom planned the wedding, I began the next chapter of my career.

On my first day Gibby familiarized me with the club, completing it with a job description.

The golf shop, as it was called, was a distinct frontier from Glendale. Business was what the word implied. Procrastination didn't exist and members received attention with diligence. All sales were charged with little cash exchanged, while fresh, crisp interior smells originated from rotations of factory fresh merchandise. Stock was accurately priced; brightly displayed, and professionally merchandised.

The members too were distinguished. My father would have quickly labeled them mucky-mucks. But I soon learned for those who inherited wealth, many more were legitimatized in affluence and position.

The second assistant was Randy. A former Riverside Rat, he was a big fellow with a zest toward life. A go-to for sporting stats, he was always smiling and cracking jokes. We enjoyed our time during the next four years and remained friends for decades.

Subsequent days, weeks, and months there were impregnated by vast learning experiences.

I lost my career virginity at Glendale but matured into a club pro at Mayfair.

Journal Entry #139: Too Late to Turn Back Now

Dedicated to *Paul and Helen Fee*

What is it that grooms do the day before their wedding? In Las Vegas, the histories of some are chapters of the unforgotten!

In my case however, the best man and I practised golf at my parent's home. Then, we retired to watch that year's televised Masters, ravishing submarine sandwiches and cider. All in preparation for the rest of my life!

Journal Entry #140: One Tin Soldier

Dedicated to *the Kerrs*

Jackie and I married on April 8, 1978. Spring winds gusted annoyingly that day but they couldn't stop us smiling. And when our vows were exchanged, an exodus of Glendale members quietly captured the ceremonial spirit. Outside they skewered the sky with golf clubs, forming a canopy for us to thread through.

The reception at Glendale was a full house. Jackie's cousin Julian was a professional musician, who then played with the famous Calgary ensemble, Original Caste. Their mega-hit, **"One Tin Soldier,"** became our wedding song when they played live for the guests. It was the coolest festivity I ever attended, enriched more when Gary Player won his third Masters at Augusta then.

Over years, I've spent an extraordinary amount of time developing a golf game which never reached levels I arrogantly felt entitled to. It was a feeling often leaving me miserable. Regardless, reality has always suppressed it, confirming how privileged my life's been everyday since that ceremony.

Journal Entry #141: Mayfair Place
Dedicated to *Curly Currell*

Mayfair's senior personnel were committed to their careers.

Gibby who originated from Saskatchewan, enjoyed the camaraderie of old-timer's hockey. Effervescent, positive and upbeat I rarely saw him down, although occasionally angry. The golf shop was a business to him and I quickly learned a new side to golf's industry. Because the shop applied charges instead of cash to member's accounts, Derek's diligence taught us to account purchases … sooner than later.

Long before hockey star Crosby joined the Pittsburgh Penguins, our course superintendent was Sid-the-Kid. Another prairie product, he too was outgoing with sides of humour. Despite being married though, he was known to occasionally wander roads less travelled. He was also defensive about course maintenance criticisms.

Leo was the club's general manager. A Dutchman with a sliver of accent, he was tall and toothpick thin. An impeccable attire complimented his professional integrity and sharp mind. Leo rarely golfed, preferring to instead supervise from the sport's periphery.

Mayfair's French chef was Caesar. Everyday he clogged the kitchen's slick tile floors with wooden boats. He might have been a natural golfer with such balance?

They were the team I worked with regularly over the next four years.

Journal Entry #142: She's Not in Love
Dedicated to *George Smith*

Golf is a way of life for me!

In my spare time at Glendale, I was consumed with playing tournaments and finding the secret to the golf swing. But during my first year at Mayfair, I began believing golf offered more and could better the person within. Betty Cole was partially responsible for that perspective.

Cole then was one of our nation's preeminent golfers. Playing out of Highlands, she was ranked Canada's finest amateur more than once, compiling numerous international victories.

Describing her in competition though, was like imagining an amazon in battle. Like her tenacious peer Ontario's Marlene Streit, both appeared defiled by Donald Trump's obsession of winning at **any** cost. I had a glimpse of that when Jackie won her first provincial amateur. Cole was in that field and irate at losing to a neophyte from junior ranks. Jackie had surgery before that event and the media cited her convalescence as a winning factor. The article elicited an enraged response from Cole: "If she needed the rest, she shouldn't have been out there. It's tough bananas!"

Then privately, she contacted Jackie a day before the wedding. A divorcée, she insisted Jackie be aware of the misgivings of marriage. I was conflicted hearing that, yet sobered by more rational views. Betty appeared to struggle with happiness … even after decades of success. By contrast, LPGA star Nancy Lopez had also amassed an amazing resume of wins amid similar circumstances. But Lopez had acquired a kinder, less bitter outlook. I measured the differences between the pleasures of playing versus prizewinning. My analysis suggested Cole might have lost her way, forgetting the joy of participation. It was reconfirmed later admiring the compassionate, courteous, and considerate behaviour of Sweden's Annika Sörenstam, who too rebounded from similar setbacks to become an LPGA icon!

Now retired and witness to my wife's endless victories, I'm moved more by the camaraderie Jackie enjoys along with winning. When everything's measured, and the Donald Trumps of the world spout "Winning is everything," I think about golf. I see it now as more than just sport. I see it as an alternative way to live, perhaps superior to religion! I've come to believe that while winning is fun, motivating and an obvious reason to compete … in golf and life, one might be foolish believing it's not overrated.

Journal Entry #143: Just One Look

Dedicated to *Eric and Audrey Thompson*

Jackie would claim destiny and I aren't compatible. I've often joked fate should enroll in fairness classes or vacation more. Case in point ... Costantino Rocca. The charismatic Italian pro had an unsuspecting date with destiny at the 1995 Open. There, at golf's historical altar St. Andrews, Rocca sank an unbelievable seventy-foot final putt for a playoff tie. Then, fate swiftly snatched it back, squandering the title instead.

Nevertheless, despite destiny's consistency, it napped one summer afternoon during the 1978 Provincial Ladies Amateur at Windermere.

Jackie was no longer a junior then. She entered the event opening with a two under score, giving her a three-stroke advantage. It shocked the field, which included ten-time champion Cole, and set the stage for a dramatic final encounter with fate.

I watched them play that afternoon. With one hole left, Jackie continued leading Cole by two. But the hardened matriarch was unrelenting. Windermere's concluding hole was a dogleg left par-five, where Jackie's third finished fifteen feet from the flag. Cole, meanwhile, was on the fringe in two, fifty feet away. Obliging destiny, Cole sank the slippery snake for a spectacular eagle. A statement that ignited the surrounding spectators. My heart plummeted seeing her romp the green and punch the air when plucking her ball from the hole.

Suddenly Jackie was alone and the two putts from fifteen feet became more like fifteen miles. Drilling her approach five feet past the hole, she was ultimately faced with **just one look** from sixty inches to claim her first ladies' title. Maybe fate had turkey for dinner, or a late-night engagement, but whatever the reason, it slept during those moments. For with trembling knees, Jackie rolled the putt in to win! That response to Cole's dramatic swipe, was the defining shot of my wife's future legacy.

Today, destiny and I remain incompatible, leaving me to reconcile that in both golf and life, there appears no clear sense of fairness. Consequently, it's usually best (and civilized) to simply do the best one can and regardless of outcome, roll with the punches.

Journal Entry #144: Bob Wylie (Part 2)
Dedicated to *Justice Neil Primrose*

During lunch break from my Mayfair duties, occasionally I joined members in the men's spike bar.

There, a scorecard mounted on the room's northwest wall attracted my attention. It commemorated the club's course record, a seven under par sixty-three, scored by Calgarian legend, **Bob Wylie**. It detailed the event, date, witnesses, and his scores on each hole. That card wasn't just symbolic of my experiences playing with the veteran years earlier. It was an emblem that captured the attention of many others besides me. An emblem of inspiration. An emblem that fuelled golf passions and energized dreams.

Journal Entry #145: A Beautiful Morning
Dedicated to *Henry Martell*

Henry Martell was the longtime Highlands pro whose snowy hair and chiseled looks bore resemblances to Canadian actor Leslie Nielsen. And when he golfed, he'd hobble to his ball on bowlegs, as if he'd just ridden horse.

But Henry was a seasoned player who competed often, and yet strangely could also be found in the pro shop. His incredible tournament resume and certified teaching credentials testified to puzzling time management. Further, his competitive accomplishments were equally impressive at amateur and professional levels. For example, he not only won provincial and national amateurs, but both professional championships as well!

After Henry retired, he golfed Friday mornings at Mayfair with a group of us assistants. There, he formed a competitive mentorship. He became our role model absent any condescending demeanour. It would have been easy for him to pick apart young pros with cocky attitudes and incompetent swings, but he didn't. And even at his age, Henry's ball flight was pristine, reminding me of the young Spaniard, Ballesteros. Their shapely and stratospheric aeronautics would launch at steep angles until flushed of energy, then drop, as if divined by gravity. They were so mesmerizing, I spent years attempting to replicate them.

Every week, I looked forward to those mornings.

Years later, when I assumed my first head-pro position, I purchased Henry's rustic shop counter. One which had been with him for decades. Its glass top, supported by quarter-sawn oak was clustered with the scars and scratches of golfers, who over years had been served by the Edmonton legend. Later, standing over that very display case too, I also served similar sales to other thirsty golfers.

Journal Entry #146: Checklist Benny

Dedicated to *Benny Van Loon*

Mayfair Benny was the club's ultimate practitioner. As such, he developed a slanted working knowledge of the golf swing from the reserves of range balls he discharged.

Benny owned a successful neon lighting shop. Each day he drove to Mayfair in a white Cadillac garnished by Texan longhorns bonded to its front grill. Older, tall, and thin, Benny had a Dutch name with Asian eyes defying it. His receding hairline, betrayed by black hair dye, was often accessorized on hot days by a stupendous straw hat, accentuating the macabre image. Benny's swing was no less, reminding me of conductor's arms swirling in symphonic performance. With his club soaring high into the back swing, he'd suddenly reverse and swoop downward toward a mandated high finish. A pose resembling a male statue found in a park or famous roundabout. And he'd hold the position longer than needed, as if preening. As entertaining as he was though, Benny too, was a student of the swing.

One day after a lesson, he suggested I could manage swing analyses more efficiently by making check lists when instructing. He recommended having the grip, alignment, backswing, head position, etc, on a page. That way, I could gloss over every characteristic, eliminating irrelevance. "It would be like mechanics use servicing cars," he explained. It seemed logical given the numerous swing tune ups I gave annually. As a result, my lesson routines changed beginning with each student's address position. From there, I weeded through a litany of fundamentals, checking them off as I went. I continued using that blueprint from then on.

Late on Sundays, when Mayfair's parking lot was vacant and the PGA's television broadcast was over, I knew it was only time before I'd see Benny's caddy roll in. He just had to see if he'd discovered the secret.

Journal Entry #147: I'd Like to Get to Know You

Dedicated to *the Aitkens*

Johnny Aitken was head pro at Edmonton's Victoria Golf Course. Located across the North Saskatchewan River from Mayfair, the muni, as it was called, was arguably Western Canada's most active golf centre. Johnny had been there thirty-one years then and was so busy, he never golfed anymore. Something I later identified with.

There was another Johnny Aitken, a Mayfair member, who each morning could be found at the private club's driving range. There, as if part of the foilage camouflaging Edmonton's bustling Groat Road, he'd practise peacefully.

Both men were near the same age, owned similar relaxed demeanours, shared identical names, and—if placed beside each other—might've been considered twins. Each knew of the other but remarkably hadn't met nor were related.

They were different men, separated only by a river, yet magnetically lured and synchronized by golf through the traffic of its mystic aura.

Journal Entry #148: Best That You Can Do

Dedicated to *Jackie Eddy*

One of my earliest Mayfair students was another Jackie, not to be confused with my talented wife. Mayfair Jackie was an entertainment expert, talented chef, and author of bestselling cookbooks.

Often she was a pro-am partner, which was an enjoyable part of a first assistant's job. She was pleasant, eager to become a better golfer, and participated in the club's atmosphere. Also during lessons, she'd offer me tips on navigating about the kitchen. For instance in her first book, the bestselling, *Slicing, Hooking and Cooking,* she included a savoury spaghetti sauce recipe. One which burnt during preparation. She solved the problem by explaining how ketchup is only added later during simmering stages. Her book was so successful, she wrote another entitled, *The Second Slice.* The theme of her work focused on preparing hearty meals for easy entertainment while finding time to golf.

In the coming years, my wife and I prepared our family meals from those editions, including: Baked Devilled Pork Chops, Caesar Salad, Chinese Fried Rice, and Chili Con Carne. Later, when I left Mayfair, she constantly updated me on her golf progress. She was an effervescent lady who I felt had the right club attitude.

Journal Entry #149: Grandpa Walton

Dedicated to *Tom and Shirley Graham*

One bright sunny day returning from lunch, I saw Gibby outside Mayfair's clubhouse talking to **Grandpa Walton**.

I called him that because he resembled actor Will Geer in a popular television series then called, *The Waltons*. Walton was a cantankerous elder who suffered from too much alcohol and a respiratory condition.

Their conversation however, wasn't the typical banter between member and staff. Instead, he was publicly humiliating Gibby in front of an audience, including me. Grandpa was shaking his finger **threateningly**, shouting of the money he'd spent over time in Gibby's shop. His menacing demeanour was suggesting Gibby's time as head pro, might be up sooner than later.

Derek's eyes meanwhile were reduced to slits as he listened in restraint. Bulging veins in his muscular neck though, evidenced contempt toward the foul-mouthed ogre. Only when Grandpa hobbled down and away, did my boss return to work. In my years at Glendale, I never saw anyone rip into Donny, as I'd just witnessed.

I was never admitted to the exchange's origin, but it gripped me. Obviously Gibby disturbed the tyrant. Perhaps Walton had too many gin and tonics that day or detested Gibby flaunting his affluence. Whatever his reason, the incident provided me glimpses into what might lie ahead as a future club pro. In that warning, I recognized how some members could harbour intolerant opinions of staff and how employees should appropriately profile themselves.

Journal Entry #150: Maturity (Part 1)

Dedicated to *Al Pyrch*

To some, manhood may mean fathering children. If so, does that qualify twelve-year-olds in developing countries? Others believe it's one man glaring into the eyes of another without giving ground. If true, how is compromise advanced? If manhood means using fists, does that mean professional hockey players are all men or violent offenders? The answers seem cloudy to me.

I first thought about manhood during a supper invitation from Mayfair Jackie. She and her paediatrician husband invited us to dinner at their home near the museum high above Mayfair.

At first, the evening was casual with drinks, conversation, and an art collection tour. But after her typical four-course meal followed by tea, her husband's tone changed. The physician began slurring his speech from the alcohol. Then, in a way similar to how Grandpa Walton censured Gibby weeks earlier, the doctor surgically cut into me. In front of both wives, he challenged my career choice using gigolo references. He bore in provocatively, accusing me of preying on members and charging exorbitant lesson fees. After finishing and without apology, he vanished to bed without wavering.

During his tirade however, instead of feeling victimized, I strangely saw myself a third-party spectator. I voiced no opinion, finding unknown abilities to listen, rather than be offended. An atypical calm sought out sources for his behaviour. I'd always sensed retaliation in my nature when cornered, but it was far away in those moments.

Was this a layer peeled from the core of my **maturity**? Perhaps, because from then on, my ability to stay even during serious challenges grew within. Ironically, harmless events like negotiating knotted laces, continued haunting me. On the way home though, I was accompanied by a sense of being older without qualification.

Mayfair Jackie kept up her lessons.

Journal Entry #151: Moe Norman (Part 2)

Dedicated to *Moe Norman*

The Alberta Open was contested at Windermere that year. Coincidentally, Jackie won the Alberta Ladies there, months earlier.

The event, part of Canada's then professional tour, included many talented pros such as Canadian legend **Moe Norman.** There was also a newly married young assistant … me.

In the opener, I scored seventy-three and went home thrilled. It tied me with the famous ball striker and chances were we'd be paired next day.

Unfortunately Moe withdrew from injury. Continuing on that day, I was even par playing the seventh when I pulled my approach left and short of the green. It finished on a steep slope above an intimidating water hazard. As I pitched to the nearby green however, my ball nicked a tree root, deflecting it above. Descending, it then added salt to the wound **striking** me. The assault continued when the ball dribbled into the hazard!

Multiple penalty strokes left me with an accumulated score of twelve and seventy-eight total. My final round next day, was even par in the fifty-four-hole event, tying me for tenth with Manitoba's Dan Halldorson.

Many times since I've mediated about that seventh hole. I've sulked wishing fate had been kinder and commuted the harshness of that sentence. If it had, I might have been successful later explaining my failures in competition. Imagining a win there, and how it might have influenced my future is typical of every golfer's folly … knowing how every round's outcome should have been different than reality!

Journal Entry #152: Maturity (Part 2) Summer Rain

Dedicated to *Doug Welliver*

In marriage, where one spouse is famous, relationships get testy. A persuasive number of the world's most famous PGA and LPGA stars attest to that! While my marriage to Jackie didn't share world stages like them, I was the spouse who had to face ego. Egos are part of our profession. And when the opposite gender's involved, it can be fuel for fire.

I'm lucky. I'm part of an envied marriage … literally. Over time, we've loved, cared, and stood up for each other. In that, there's no dispute. But like in golf, occasionally **summer rain** falls and in our partnership it was usually dampened by one reason. Members comparing Jackie's golf game to mine. Jackie played tournaments well. And as a pro, it was perceived I should too. The truth was that I did … but not competitively like her.

My ego became ruptured when particular members began humouring those comparisons. As my career advanced, so did the parallels, consuming me of energy and leading me to question it as ego or perpetrator ignorance? It began that first year at Mayfair.

As newlyweds, Jackie and I were enjoying a life of opportunity. She had wrapped up an incredible junior career and I was carving out our future in the shop. When she won that first provincial amateur though, Jackie was unexplainably thrust into another limelight. One of the club's more cynical members was Mayfair Cal. He began to snipe at me daily with lines like:

"So ... are you getting a lesson from your wife today? Maybe you'll break 80 if you do!" But his tone was always caustic, biting, and accompanied by audiences. I couldn't whine to Gibby or the directors, and confronting members wasn't done. So I swallowed the pill!

But after time, my tolerance weakened and I brought the irritant home. The bickering escalated into arguments before Jackie's tournaments. Her success under those circumstances testified further to her ability. Four decades later, we're still happily married—partially due to some deep digging within. Somehow I arrived at the mature understanding it was better living in a caring relationship than allowing defensive behaviour to deteriorate it. Because Cal wasn't alone. Over decades, I continued deflecting the same burlesque from others using mental veneers. And if readers asked how ... I couldn't answer. Even today in retirement, after Jackie's won more than a quarter of a thousand tournaments, the needling continues. Therefore, I've truly empathized with those well-known stars whose marriages didn't hold. While not famous though, I had the good fortune to not only identify my ego, but harness it.

Journal Entry #153: Do You Know Where You're Going to?

Dedicated to *Roger Carry*

One day into the new job, Jackie and I had one of those disputes. The topic was the same ... grappling with the endless needling from Cal. That particular disagreement was more heated than normal.

On that day, Jackie left work during lunch. I was in bag storage while our support staff were clearing balls from the driving range after a shotgun tournament. A shotgun was an event where the entire field played at the same time, beginning at each of the eighteen tees. When that happened, everyone finished together, resulting in a sudden influx of clubs to clean and replace. With the shop quiet, I kept up until help returned. I was feeling low because of the earlier argument when Jackie suddenly appeared around a corner.

When a woman, particularly a wife, shows up when least expected, sometimes a man's uncertain of the outcome. That moment wasn't different.

"I've just been to the doctor's," she said. "You're going to be a dad!"

Everything we argued about vanished and Cal didn't matter anymore. A rare, hard-to-describe feeling emerged which wasn't unlike our first date again.

Journal Entry #154: Friday on my Mind

Dedicated to *Sandy Shandro*

My marriage and new job led to alternative work arrangements and redefined leisure time. I'd start promptly at six every morning, except Fridays when I practised and played at Mayfair. After, Jackie and I golfed at Glendale until dark.

On one of those evenings, we celebrated my birthday with friends. Life was good and became better at the thirteenth. There on a decadent, double-tiered green and out-of-bounds left, Jackie lofted a stunning shot into the setting western sun. Stunning because from the moment her ball left the clubface and climbed the treeline, every sense in me knew the outcome. It was her first hole-in-one!

Journal Entry #155: Mr. Magoo

Dedicated to *the Robinsons*

Exactly one year to the day Jackie scored that hole-in-one, my father-in-law did the same.

Denzil was the ultimate club member. He wasn't the most accomplished golfer, but always supported the facility with fun along the way … genuine fun. He was the architect of tasteful jokes, the favourite being the empty-beer-glass caper. He preferred mixed settings in the bar with several pitchers of draft beer to detonate the deed. He'd purposely sit next to one of the more spirited women as he sipped his lager. He always finished first, casually replacing the mug closer and closer to the table's edge … directly above her. Finally, when the time was right and there was laughter, he'd drop the mug on the edge, and fake a spill over her. Everyone jumped shrieking. Of course the glass was empty, but she never knew. When realizing they'd all been had, he was affectionately smacked on his bald head.

I often had coffee with Denzil. Stirring his steaming beverage, he relished tapping my knuckles with the hot spoon when I wasn't paying attention.

These entries were written because of him. Denzil was Welsh and the image of cartoon character **Mr. Magoo.** Before relocating to Canada, he was asked to look after his sister's poultry farm. Instead, he thought it more fun golfing. During the derelict round, he jumped a fence to retrieve an out-of-bounds shot and broke his foot. The shite-hit-the-fan later when he fibbed of breaking it in church. The ensuing feud resulted in his sister immigrating to Canada. Denzil and his wife, Mary, were close to her and followed. That's how they arrived in Edmonton and had a daughter, who eventually married this writer.

If golf courses could be better places for members, where authentic humour played part, they would have been prudent taking elocution lessons from him. He would have been the social pro, the Butch Harmon of golf course fun.

Journal Entry #156: Miller Time

Dedicated to *Bruce Collins*

During my industry apprenticeship, occasionally the prosperity of those I served invited questions of true success. The definition became clearer when I met the Miller boys.

The Millers were five young, strapping male siblings who assumed control of their father's heavy equipment sales and rental business. Dominated by physical Cro-Magnon features, they were a clan of natural intimidators, owning large homes in affluent Edmonton areas. Each drove their own colour and make of Mercedes-Benz, the eldest's gold symbolizing his CEO rank. Each day predictably timed, they'd arrive for lunch like a self-imposed team. Gliding into Mayfair's north-side parking lot side by side … they'd alienate themselves from the other members. And it didn't take me long to realize success wasn't always rooted in first impressions. For the lures of attractive women and affluent tastes that forever followed them, began to sniff like … too much cologne.

Journal Entry #157: Fool on the Hill
Dedicated to *Bob Gouin*

Mayfair Pat was retired. He managed a chain of carnival concessions which were so successful, he quit work and joined the club. There, his days were spent in the spike bar, playing lambsy with buddies. Other times, he'd perch himself by the window in the pro shop, grousing on as we worked.

I thought he was a stooge for the directors. It would have been easy for him to subversively extract daily business activities and report back to the powers that were. Pat could talk.

Sometimes however, even his type made life-altering points. When listening to our conversations of work, family or otherwise, he'd join in too, dispensing his own thoughts whether we liked them or not. One of them was: "If you have a problem, deal with it or forget it." It sounded trivial, and yet … sometimes the best sermons were found in uncomplicated logic. That advice lodged with me. For later, as both a head pro and golf course owner, I frequently found myself sorting through weedy problems. The incessant types relevant toward every golfer's enjoyment.

Journal Entry #158: CEO
Dedicated to *Crystal, Eleanor, and Olga*

Successful golf courses are normally weighed by competent management. But at some, that prosperity's measured by female support staff. Labourers whose overlooked capabilities span every golf season. Women whose backbone of service is veiled by daily routine.

Crystal was an attractive German blonde who managed the spike bar for Mayfair's men. She began mid-mornings, serving lunch, coffee, or attending to bar needs. She was the most efficient and trustworthy of anyone in that capacity I worked with.

Eleanor arrived early every morning taking full command of the ladies' dining room. With her, there was always fresh coffee and gossip. Undeniably nosy, she ironically managed the job efficiently—unlike most of that type. For if Eleanor was busy, no one dared interfere, and she could be equally frank with staff and members alike. That was her way and being employed for as long as she was, members not only tolerated but respected her ... and she them.

Olga was a stout Ukrainian who laboured unnoticed in the kitchen. She was a favourite among members and staff though for her sweet dinner buns. And on weekends, she made her famous cinnamon varieties. Garnished in glaze and weeping walnuts, they were unquestionably Edmonton's finest. They were so addictive, members showed up mornings just to take her handiwork home for their java. They even mailed me her baking years later, after I'd moved on.

Usually management dictates the welfare, progress, and success of up and coming young staff members. But the truth at Mayfair seemed then, if you had Crystal, Eleanor, and Olga's respect, your job was secure. And all three, each comfortable in their own unique skin, had the general manager's respect too.

Journal Entry #159: Peter and Lou

Dedicated to *Bill McGregor*

We need to step back from the politics. I think we have to look harder about who we elect. I think we should start, all of us, regardless of what our views are on politics. I think we should look at people that are running for office and put them through the filter. What is their character like and what are their ethics?

--John F. Kelly,
Former Chief of Staff to the
45th President of the United States,
Donald J. Trump.

That was a reference to the former president.

In the golf industry, it was't unusual to serve politicians. Consequently I learned early to avoid conversations about politics with members. That didn't stop a growing curiosity about how and who to vote for though. Conventional hysteria then claimed all politicians were crooked, which I eventually determined was absurd. To learn more about governing, I watched leaders debate in boring televised assemblies under clouds of minimal order and impotent speakers. It became obvious many politicians, unlike other professions, seem unqualified to run for office. (That spoke volumes of Biden's predecessor.) It was also evident that few voters understood campaign platforms and their impact on elections. Consequently, as a young assistant I developed my own primitive opinions about how and who to vote for.

First, I ruled out candidates with egos. Then I dismissed know-it-alls and those with in-your-face behaviour. Whether it was the premier, CEO of a large company, or a union loudmouth, any attitude of arrogance seemed vulgar and misguided. Then I rooted out adulation. Fame wasn't a legitimate reason to mobilize my vote. I was left with a role model who owned **natural abilities to not only lead, but genuinely care for others**! In addition they had to possess a political background, foreseeable vision, intellect, decisiveness, and superb managerial skills.

When sorting through those qualities, I saw the first of them … ironically in a hockey player, one known as the Little M.

The Big M was Frank Mahovlich, a star forward who played years with the NHL's Toronto Maple Leafs. However, the Big M had a younger brother named Peter. One, affectionately known as the Little M. Peter played with many NHL teams, but made his presence known with Montréal. There, he blossomed into one of the league's premier forwards, winning the Stanley Cup four times, eclipsing his sibling's reputation.

One day, he entered the shop and I recognized him immediately. But before I could greet him, he looked down at me, placed his hands casually on the counter and introduced himself first by quietly asking: "Hi, my name's Peter Mahovlich, and I wondered if there was a chance I could play Mayfair today?" *Say what?* I thought. Having served numerous athletes at Glendale and Mayfair, I was never confronted by one that famous being so

humble and genuine. The usual suspects struggled with cocky, immodest behaviour.

While I couldn't testify to the star's other attributes ... his modesty, politeness, and respect for me offered a young assistant pro that first clue when searching for governance.

Journal Entry #160: Black Gold
Dedicated to *Merv Leitch*

During my tenure at Mayfair, one of our province's more intense times took place during contentious oil meetings in Ottawa. There, Prime Minister Pierre Trudeau and his resource's minister Marc Lalonde scuffled with Alberta Premier Peter Lougheed and Merv Leitch. At issue was who held the rights to Alberta's crude.

During lunch hours at the club, every table in the men's spike bar was emotionally charged. Oil patch executives were electrified by the current of each meeting's suspense. Ottawa wanted control of the fuel while Peter and Merv were there protecting those resources, using the controversial notwithstanding clause that overrode the Canadian Charter of Rights and Freedoms.

Both Lougheed and Leitch were club members and amongst the nicest I was pleasured to serve over four decades. Leading with a provincial sense of pride then, they were clapped and cheered on as they strolled up the driveway to lunch in the clubhouse. Branded heroic, their quiet determination and resistance to intimidation was respected by most Albertans then.

Even though I admired Trudeau and felt lucky to have him as a leader, I revered Lougheed.

Journal Entry #161: The Premier
Dedicated to *Premier Peter Lougheed*

One morning outside the shop, I saw my boss talking to the premier. I was thrilled when Derek motioned me over and introduced us. The most noticeable characteristic was his height, as we were eyeball to eyeball. **The premier** had a laidback personality characterized by a monotonous charisma. He appeared almost lazy in speech, yet subtly alert and aware.

I stayed only a minute, not wanting to subvert the welcome. Before leaving though, Gibby indicated Peter, as he liked being called, wanted new grips on his clubs. Examining them, instead of seeing golf's latest, I saw an older, seemingly tired set. They had rusted steel shafts and dry, shiny cowhide handles, remnants of leather past prime. An equally old but expensive canvas bag housed the occupants. I sensed they were sentimental to the owner. We went to the club repair room where he picked out a Golf Pride grip. There and then I began looking after his clubs.

The premier usually golfed in the evenings with his wife. I was impressed how he dealt with so many important provincial, national and worldly figures, yet remembered our names too.

As a taxpayer, I had one complaint about him. Rarely do people enter public life with charisma, knowledge, and persuasive abilities to lead. Lougheed seemed in possession of all those qualities along with a caring disposition. In my opinion, had he chosen to let his name stand nationally, he might have become one of Canada's more astonishing prime ministers. He seemed to have the whole package.

Journal Entry #162: The Publisher

Dedicated to *Mel Hurtig*

One of the club's more charismatic and influential was Mayfair Mel, a book publisher with intense energy levels. We often golfed together and he'd join the judge and I during our Halloween rounds. Mel took an interest in me and when I applied for my first head pro position, he enthusiastically offered to be a reference.

Mel had a genuine connection with golf's culture, publishing books on the subject including one with architect Robert Trent Jones. Mel started book businesses, developed them, and eventually profited from their resale. But his entrepreneurial footprint seemed overshadowed by staunch, magnetic interests in Canadian politics.

Eventually he put his reputation on the line and campaigned for prime minister. As founder and leader of Canada's then National Party, he led with a bold vision seeking to eliminate multinational corporate funding in political campaigns. It wasn't hard to vote for that platform.

Despite those efforts, however, it was short-lived, replaced instead by his publishing *The Canadian Encyclopedia,* possibly the entrepreneur's most enduring legacy.

Journal Entry #163: Walk On By

Dedicated to *Warren Scott*

Mayfair Cal was part of a plumbing supply company. He had a brother named Warren, who was also a club member and supposedly the brains behind their business. He travelled North America promoting their products and playing famous courses I'd read about. He shared those visits as my partner in pro-ams.

One day after a tournament, Warren gave me a pair of his old shoes. He thought they'd be a good fit, being we were similar in height and build. I acted grateful, but inside I thought, "Warren … have you lost your mind?" My spikes were called FootJoy Classics, featuring saddles and leathered soles. His were ancient, shiny, and literally made of rubber. They were thirty years old then and resembled tires on my feet—sleek at best. I accepted his generosity though and put them away until later, donning them during downpours. Oddly enough I kept using them and when I became head pro, the recruitment continued for another twenty-two years.

Later still, we lived on Vancouver Island at a modest little golf course. There the land was soggy in winter and when golfers played in their gumboots, I brought Warren's old cleats out for another fourteen seasons. And finally, like all good things that end, Warren's too bit the dust. I hung them among the branches of a fir by our ninth tee, naming it the tree of lost golf souls. At that time, they were seventy-five years old and had faithfully kept me comfortable and free of moisture for a generation. I thought of Warren every time I passed that tree, along with the phrase, "things happen for reasons."

Journal Entry #164: Sultans of Swing
Dedicated to *Terry Bradburn*

If a reader has spent as much time on driving ranges as the writer, either practising or teaching, they may understand this entry.

Mayfair's driving range was conveniently located downtown and the cities' best then. Consequently, many worldly business executives maintained their games there, hitting balls during lunch hours.

Occasionally, one would show up with a flawless swing diverting attention. It didn't happen often, as ranges tended to be gathering places for pounding balls or socializing. And unfortunately for most golfers, the act of seeing truly gifted athletes was defined solely by a ball's flight pattern.

However, to watch someone deftly wrap both hands around a grip, glide into the plane of a fully rotated backswing … and then in timed precision, drop into the subtle downswing slot, was compelling for what loomed ahead.

Seeing the clubhead's heel delivered ahead of the toe into the impact berth with efficiency and panther-like speed, was electrifying. And when the resistance free movement after execution was supported by weight-transfer with uncommon lower body balance, full extension and an anchored frame … it was candy for the right eye. I understood why Canada's George Knudson stopped practising when Ben Hogan began tuning up.

Journal Entry #165: The Physical Educator
Dedicated to *Dr. Maury Van Vliet*

In 2008, the Swedish Medical University, Karolinska Institutet, published a research paper with the Scandinavian Journal of Medicine and Science in Sports. Their extensive studies proved **golfers who walked when playing**, experienced death rates **40 percent** lower than others. The scientific translation confirmed **five additional years of life expectancy!**

During my sophomore season at Mayfair, the Commonwealth Games came to Edmonton. The cities' largest international sporting event needed someone to organize and oversee it. That person was Dr. Maury Van Vliet, the dean of the university's physical education department. The same who interviewed me earlier when I entered the Institution.

Dr. Van Vliet was an active Mayfair member. He also remembered me as the person who enrolled in his faculty as a teaching pro. I wrote that because later he often visited the course where I eventually became head pro. He'd arrive with an entourage of golfers treating me as a long-lost friend, calling me by name and reminiscing about the campus and Mayfair. It was kind of him being so busy as he was to think of me in such ways.

Dr. Van Vliet passed away in 2001. His legacy insured the universities' department, like the Karolinska Institutet, remained one of the more sought-after faculties of its kind. It was due to the work of scholars like him ... dedicated innovators and catalysts of change ... that physical education advanced beyond the flutter of running and jumping into the scope of legitimized sports medicine.

Journal Entry #166: The Monarch
Dedicated to *Her Majesty Queen Elizabeth II*

The 1978 Commonwealth Games were staged in Edmonton's newly designed stadium. The official ceremonies were held July 15, attracting fifteen thousand spectators. Later, on August 3, her Royal Highness Queen Elizabeth II declared the competition open. There were two thousand athletes from forty-six countries in front of an estimated five hundred million global television viewers.

During the Queen's stay, she visited Mayfair where security was amplified. It was visibly nowhere yet seemingly everywhere. Agents were glimpsed on clubhouse roofs and wandering the golf shop, accessorized with conservative suits and communication devices. They even dabbled in golf conversation from time to time. When she arrived, her majesty was escorted to the main ballroom for customary lunch and tea.

Since her passing, I've speculated how the Commonwealth of Nations might have evolved differently had she formally taken to golf as recreation. Not like the trifle of her uncle, Edward the Eighth, or the fribble of former US President Trump. Instead, I believe had she found the call, her influence on subjects, especially in the world's troubled areas, might have been even greater. Golf, in its basic form before being commercially suffocated, possessed its own unique language that mystifyingly bonded people of varying cultures.

Journal Entry #167: Woman

Dedicated to *Barbara McGregor*

Any reader who knows Jackie can attest to her many attributes. For instance, it's unlikely anyone would challenge her golfing ability. Further, she's a wonderful mother, easily eclipsing me as a father. She's friendly to everyone and possesses laughs and smiles ingratiating her to others. Now she refers to herself as granny, and loves it.

When she was expecting our first child Robert, I was obsessed with understanding golf's history, seeking out old golf books and vintage clubs. I became a local authority when Mayfair members and Edmontonians alike sought my advice for assessing their antiquities.

Normally then, I took January off work. And that winter with Jackie pregnant, we toured the Pacific Northwest, searching for ancestral memorabilia.

When collectors like me sought relics then, they didn't frequent pro shops or courses. Purists of the game scoured old stores, like pawnshops where the authentic finds were. Without today's GPS, I simply looked up addresses and off we went—a determined historian and expectant wife in a not-so-reliable vehicle combing unflattering neighbourhoods in Seattle, Vancouver, and Victoria. Sometimes in my mania, I'd park out front and unforgivingly abandon her in the car. I'd dash in, scavenging each store's inventory. Through it all she always smiled, content I was happy in my pursuits.

In living with this remarkable **woman,** and looking at the numerous times spent like that together, I doubt I'll ever understand what she saw in me,

Journal Entry #168: Victoria

Dedicated to *Laurie Scott*

During that trip, the **Victoria** Golf Club at Oak Bay, was too irresistible to not play.

As history unfolded, the course became iconic in Canadian golf culture. Not because she was allegedly the eldest course west of the Mississippi. And it wasn't because her British influence attracted the countries' most prestigious events or that she was a member of Canada's Register of Historic Sites.

Instead, she was irresistible being a visual respite to those in double-decker buses motoring through Beach Drive. She was irresistible because of her location by the ocean, where spray and wind were part of her essence. She was irresistible being the one Canadian course impregnated with groves of gorse, imported supposedly from Scottish links. Irresistible because her suitors wore plus fours during their seduction and that A. V. Macan designed her seventh green, labeled by Ben Hogan, the world's finest. And she was irresistible because Pebble Beach was a version of her.

But she's special to Jackie too! That's because Victoria hosted the British Columbia Golf Association's centennial in 2004. A year they invited my wife to formally drive a ceremonial shot with a wooden shafted club from its first tee. One meant to symbolically commemorate the organization's advance into the next century!

Journal Entry #169: Dad

Dedicated to *Rob*

On June 5, 1979, Jackie and I became parents to a son. We named him Robert Tyre, after the Georgian amateur, Robert Tyre Jones, Jr. Standing in

Edmonton's Misericordia Hospital, I watched our doctor roll the gurney toward me. Weighing nearly ten pounds, our son appeared infant and old at the same time. My feelings were indescribable then, but as time passed, I explained them as follows.

As a novice parent, I migrated from comfort toward fear, arbitrating whether I was the key to my new family's future. I wouldn't have worried being a renowned physicist whose advice everyone sought. Or being the planet's finest heart surgeon. And I'd have been burden-free being the one person who could snuff out an oil-rig fire. But I wasn't any of them. I was just a golf pro. One oppressed by this sudden parental uncertainty.

Consequently, driven by demons of delusion, I began working harder and longer, fearing job loss. I became a workaholic, labouring hours away from my family at expenses of appearing undevoted … unlike I felt. In the absence of a seemingly stable vocation, my providing livelihood was guided by fearless passions for golf.

That's what it felt like to be a **dad**. And it became my own rationale why some grandparents spent more time with their grandkids. Making up for lost time with their own children.

Journal Entry #170: Eminem

Dedicated to *Freddie Singer*

Long before Roger Cleveland and Bob Vokey designed and manufactured current day golf clubs, there was M and M … McEwan and Morris. Among their peers, they were elite club makers of earlier times.

During winter of 1979, published in the *Golf Collectors* modest bulletin, was an ad auctioning-off a long-nosed play-club. An item discovered during a home renovation in Glasgow, Scotland.

In-the-day, play-clubs were golf's earliest known drivers or one woods. They featured hickory or ash shafts attached to scared wooden heads. Carpenters spliced the heads and shafts together, bonding the oval joints. The heads were long and narrow often with bone splints secured by dowels for protection during impact. The grips were chamois leather and along with the hosels … twined. Today's heads with augered hosels house graphite and steel shafts.

As a novice collector, I'd never participated in an auction, much less one conducted by mail. After submitting a bid though, a telegram later proclaimed I'd won. The prize, which arrived soon after, was a neatly packaged and preserved McEwen play-club. Later, I traded for another similar relic. One made by golf's most famous of the day, Scotland's Tom Morris, Sr.

The shafts of both were between forty and forty-two inches in length. The heads were five inches long, two wide, with clubfaces an inch deep.

In any career, surreal feelings emerge in comparing past and present. Feelings captured by that phrase: "If you want to know what will happen tomorrow, you must know what took place yesterday!"

Journal Entry #171: If I Had a Million Dollars

Dedicated to *Randy Breen*

One of the club's more charismatic and colourful was Mayfair Pep.

Chunky and short, Pep wore wire rimmed glasses which somehow complemented his baldness. A dark green sports jacket and tie consummated the appearance. He'd arrive late each morning joining other retirees for lambsy in the men's spike bar. There he dominated the room with a distinctly drifting, and whiny nasal voice. After lunch, he'd relocate to Mayfair's rectangular putting green, punching putts for hours.

His putting stroke was a series of abbreviated jabs from long distances, always with three balls. At that time of day, the green was vacant and Pep was usually alone, engaged in one-sided conversations with anyone passing.

One day, I sauntered by and he quizzed me, asking, "Howz it goin?" I replied about the challenges of buying our first property. Jackie and I were interested in a condominium then, but finding mortgages was consuming us. Pep said: "Yunno, if you're not having luck, there's always another bank cross the street."

I hadn't thought of that. Like other young couples, we always shopped diligently. However, blinded by loyalty, we never compared lending institutions until Pep volunteered that.

Despite Pep's odd, quirky charm, he was hard to take in large doses. But his suggestion stayed with me, like hard-drive memory. It became vital later when as head pro financing my first going concern.

Journal Entry #172: Traces

Dedicated to *Mike Zolf*

One of the more quirky and unusual who followed Edmonton's golf tournament scene, was known locally as … Isienko!

Think of the movie *Home Alone* and the character played by actor Roberts Blossom. As "Old Man Marley," his portrayal was consistent with Isienko. While some was self-inflicted, the rest were **traces** of folklore and gossip.

Isienko materialized at championships and, regardless of temperature, wore black trench coats and matching fedoras. A dark ensemble that accessorized his bleached facial and timbering frame. Like an incarnate, he'd spectate hauntingly among the trees during play. And as surprisingly as he might suddenly appear, he could as easily vaporize. He was golf's manifestation of the infiltrating spy. Like other golfers, I too felt his ghostly aura. But after, I realized his presence was too consistent to be harmful. Ironically he seemed respectful … infatuated by golf's unique competitive atmosphere.

Looking back at his peculiarities, he was in ways not unlike the original sport itself … enigmatic and esoteric.

Journal Entry #173: The Rifleman

Dedicated to *Peter Sorenson*

One quiet evening, I was working the late shift in solitude. A home game featuring the then Edmonton Eskimos was occupying the city. When that happened, members chartered buses to the game, leaving Mayfair dormant of golfers.

The sun was setting and the air still as I swept outside the shop. It was then a tall, dark suit sauntered up from the parking lot below. As was the custom, I offered him my assistance.

He declined, replying, "No, I'm meeting people here for drinks." His voice too, while recognizable, was indistinguishable. Abruptly, he stopped to inquire where the main lounge was. I humbled a response, feigning recognition. Golf pros are trained to remember names, but that night I was failing. As we idled in the evening's tranquility, girdled by Mayfair's forest green hues, he marvelled, "My ... this is beautiful!" After more ambling minutes, he looked at me with a pause of finality and said, "Thank you ... good night."

It was only when the clubhouse doors swallowed him, I realized he was the famous actor Charlton Heston. He appeared older than movie portrayals.

I felt like that janitor from the movie *Eddie and the Cruisers*. There, in Frank's role played by actor Tom Berenger, he holds a mop, bewildered when first seeing rock star Eddie. I was bound in that same surreal moment, except I had a broom.

Later though, I saw Michael Moore's award-winning documentary, *Bowling for Columbine*. It was a daunting moment acknowledging Heston's staunch leading role with the National Rifle Association. There he appeared morbid, testifying to a darker, more authentic character than the one I spent moments earlier with.

Journal Entry #174: Under My Thumb

Dedicated to *Hon. Bill Haddad*

Peter Pocklington, the bigger-than-life Edmonton entrepreneur, was a member who lived directly above Mayfair. Only minutes from the club's gate, his mansion appeared like a sentry, overlooking the course below.

During that time, he was victimized by a felon who held him, his wife, and two staff hostage in exchange for two million dollars ransom. In the ensuing drama, police resolved it, shooting the perpetrator and wounding Pocklington.

Later, Pocklington disgruntled Edmontonians when, as owner of the NHL Oilers, he traded their star Wayne Gretzky to Los Angeles. I didn't want to see the "Great One" leave Edmonton either, but as is so often said, business is business. In the optics, I couldn't understand the community's ensuing fury. They were dismissive that Pocklington himself engineered the original deal which brought Gretzky and the Stanley Cup to the Oil Capital! And yet as thanks, he was portrayed as cutthroat and ruthless, prompting locals to hang flaming effigies of him in urban hatred.

Gretzky wasn't helpful either, appearing emotionally attached. Until then, I thought of him as a legitimate professional. The kind who was accountable. The kind who should have known trades could be imminent any time.

As for Pocklington, I couldn't account for his personality. But when I saw the hate he endured for simply doing business, in hindsight, I'd have at least given him the benefit of doubt. Especially later when seeing another entrepreneur become a US president. One who began reshaping the American psyche, engaging in obvious hypocrisy, deception, unaccountability, and slander!

Journal Entry #175: The Last Canadian

Dedicated to *Allan Fletcher*

One of golf's most electrifying moments took place in Canada at Toronto's Oakdale Golf and Country Club in 2023. There Abbotsford's Nick Taylor tanked a seventy-two foot putt in a playoff, against an inspired Tommy Fleetwood. It marked the end of a sixty-nine year drought for a Canadian to capture the nation's Open. That moment returned memories of his predecessor, Pat Fletcher.

I've few regrets in my golf life, but among them were opportunities to know more about Fletcher.

One of Mayfair's largest wholesale connections was with a Montréal company named Fletcher Leisure. The father of its founder was Pat Fletcher.

Whether it was because he and Gibby shared Saskatchewan roots or we were a large account, I never knew. Either way, Fletcher routinely visited Mayfair back then and I could have used that time wiser.

Fletcher began his career as a junior in Victoria, before taking assistant jobs at Jasper and Mayfair. Later, after a ten year stint as head pro at Saskatoon's Golf and Country Club he played the tour and won the Open in 1954 at Vancouver's Point Grey. Soon after, he was appointed head pro at North America's oldest venue, Royal Montréal. His career wrapped up watching son Allan develop Fletcher Leisure, a company wholesaling merchandise to pro shops. Finally, he retired back to BC.

Looking back, I exhausted insane opportunities not picking his wealthy golf mine. For instance: What he could have taught me about the golf swing! His experiences playing head-to-head against Ben Hogan. How he managed as Royal Montréal's head professional. Memories winning the Canadian Open. Or the complexities operating one of Canada's largest golf supply houses. He was swarming with information and I naively let him slip through my fingers.

Strangely, curiosity accompanies regret. Given Fletcher's historic biography, what lingered overall with me were his eyebrows. They spiralled skyward flaunting images of Lucifer. A peculiar anecdote when reminiscing about Taylor's predecessor.

Journal Entry #176: A Woman in Love

Dedicated to *Pat and Annabel Bowlen*

During my career, I was often hired by women to teach them how to golf like Jackie.

One of them was Annabel, a young, single, and attractive teacher who ran marathons.

To the surprise of Mayfair's staff Annabel suddenly announced her engagement to a young businessman and club member named Pat Bowlen. Educated in Oklahoma with degrees in business and law, Pat's other affection was college football. After they married, Pat exercised that passion, acquiring part of the NFL's Denver Broncos. The commitment became total later when he and family members bought out the franchise.

Before long he and Annabel left Edmonton, making Denver their new home. It culminated when Bowlen's Broncos won back-to-back Super Bowls in the '90s. I was in the Mile High City during those exciting years playing Cherry Hills Country Club.

The Bowlens became an inspiration to me. Their drive, energy, and self motivation influenced me later when administering my own pro shop.

Journal Entry #177: Dreams Go By

Dedicated to *Dr. Jim Metcalfe*

One day, a man entered the shop to inquire about golfing. Mayfair was a strictly private course, reserved for members, guests, and occasionally visitors. As an assistant, it was my job adhering to those rules.

When he introduced himself, I recognized Harry Chapin, the popular folk recording artist. His music was often heard in coffee shops around North American campuses. I was unaware the singer songwriter golfed, but literally the next day, he was gone … the victim of a traffic collision back in New York.

The fleeting hours between his last shot and that final moment seemed surreal, symbolizing how life unexpectedly and tragically can shift gears.

Journal Entry #178: The Open Champion

Dedicated to *Ken Venturi*

One year, Mayfair brought 1964 US Open Champion and CBS golf analyst Ken Venturi to the club for a private exhibition.

Considering his hands suffered from poor circulation, he still scored even par. A tall man, he was distinguished by neat, silvery hair complementing a pleasant demeanour.

I played ahead of him in a casual round when he introduced himself. With more than an ounce of sincerity, he used the moments to ask about me and my play. Normally, I found famous types like that disingenuous, but Venturi was refreshing for one so immersed in the public eye. It was as if he was one of us.

Consequently, it was no surprise seeing his emotional departure from the network booth twenty years later. On that final telecast, I knew his tears were life's right kind, matched by the genuine commendations extended him by every tour professional. After all, his commentating presence, had been the longest reign of any broadcaster in sport history!

Journal Entry #179: Tired of Toein' the Line

Dedicated to *Betty Metcalfe*

With my new family, there was little time left in workdays to uphold my playing ability. And unfortunately golf was a game demanding constant attention. Adding to that concern, were particular members who demonstrated penchants for imperious boasting. They could be subtly intimidating, bragging of inflated skills that suggested lessons were beneath them. Consequently, a golf pro had to maintain a level of skill for respect. To keep my game sharp, the only solution was quality practise time … a diminishing commodity. It left me caught between a rock and a hard place.

I never let the members know it, but occasionally I grew **tired of toeing the line**.

Journal Entry #180: Woods and Jones (Not Them!)

Dedicated to *Hon. Swede Liden*

Gimmes are concessions on greens taken by players who frankly, are frightened of missing the putt. Mulligans are shots golfers don't count. Neither are part of golf, but like ticks they've historically imbedded themselves within golf's culture. In my opinion, they've eroded the sport and are products of careless course design. Course architecture is a discipline. A science and an art meant to enhance the sport.

Golf is a game. A sport where the playing field's design is integral toward authentic enjoyment. The game's original strategy embraced the same elements we face in everyday living ... rewards, inequities, and penalties. Designers loyal to the game shimmy those characteristics into the sport's original concept of playing each hole in the fewest number of strokes under the adopted rules. By contrast, poorly thought-out courses are climates for recurring triple and quadruple bogeys! Scores that encourage gimmes and mulligans. Professional architects take care to avoid such cancers. Golf wasn't created to crush spirit. It instead offers feasible challenges and rewards honest accomplishments. In that optic I saw architecture as another way golf emulates life!

The first authentic architects who inspired those beliefs were Norman **Woods** and Robert Trent **Jones**, both apprentices of Stanley Thompson. Woods was a Canadian who designed Glendale and Kokanee Springs in the Kootenays of British Columbia. Jones was an American who evolved into the world's most prolific course builder.

From both, I became aware of the responsibility genuine designers shoulder when promoting golf. This was evidenced during my Mayfair years when golf became the rage and numerous courses sprouted up for profit, often compromising the game's integrity ... and its future!

Journal Entry #181: Alexander the Great (Part 2)

Dedicated to *Don Sprague*

The work of Hall of Famer Keith Alexander brought him to Edmonton. Consequently he joined Mayfair, where I enjoyed numerous outings with him. Alexander golfed with customized Kenneth Smith clubs, handmade from scratch. His grips featured twine bound to shafts that aligned hands with clubface angles.

Back then, pros removed rubber handles from shafts through injecting solvent or compressed air. Alexander would persistently ask: "Could you give the seven iron a little squirt ... and move it a smidge right?" I did repairs like that regularly, but with Alexander the process became repetitious. Next time, he requested I relocate it. Then, he'd have me move only certain ones and then a few more, and then reverse them all again. The tweaking continued until he was content. But the finicky nature, while suggesting origins of his success, also exposed insatiable desires.

Alexander began seeing profit in golf and sought to compete on the PGA Champion's Tour. I never felt Keith or his peers had the respect professional golf demanded. Playing any sport for a living was serious business. Alexander nevertheless tried, although unsuccessfully. But I felt greed contaminated a distinguished amateur past.

Journal Entry #182: The Scientist

Dedicated to *Karsten Solheim*

I saw the mind as an endless reservoir of thoughts and ideas. A stockpile of errors, experiments, and exchanges camouflaging information. Then suddenly something would catalyze it, creating clarity.

An example of that took place in Calgary during an Alberta PGA conference. That year, they recruited famous club manufacturer Karsten Solheim to express views on design. Solheim, who pioneered the Ping Golf Club, wasn't just any tooling physiologist. He developed his golf clubs from engineering backgrounds with Ryan Aeronautical, Convair, and General Electric. Manufacturing golf equipment became a passionate distraction.

At the seminar, he lectured on subjects like heel-toe and perimeter designs, swing weight principles and investment casting. The information added to my growing knowledge, which often seemed only a repository for restless facts.

But during those lectures, I was fortunate to sit close to the renowned scientist. I had commanding front row seats for days, where he seemed to magnetize my knowledge. The ultimate results provided me further confidence when teaching and selling equipment.

Journal Entry #183: PGA High (Part 1)
Dedicated to *Jack Biddell*

During the PGA fall business meetings, executives suggested young assistants shoulder responsibility for organizing upcoming conferences. One in particular, Red Deer Larry, intimidated me into accepting the job.

Larry or Purpes as he was called, was a Mayfair predecessor of mine. Golf's version of the impudent Kevin O'Leary. When he pressured me in front of the entire body, what could I do? I took it on, unaware how to administer or operate an educational seminar. It wasn't like now where one simply Googles it. I had five months to prepare. The good news was they scheduled it in Edmonton, where I could work locally.

Journal Entry #184: PGA High (Part 2)
Dedicated to *Bruce Murray*

As the newly appointed chair of our education seminar, my sudden responsibilities included: breeding a budget, lining up locations, thinking up themes, and snaring slick speakers. I chose two topics, combining merchandising with the challenge assistants face when transitioning into head pros.

For location, Mayfair granted me use of their clubhouse.

For the second theme, I recruited an array of talent within Edmonton's accounting, banking, insurance, and legal industries. All were distinguished, high-ranking, and genuinely thrilled to speak before our association. In my merchandising theme I selected Buddy Phillips of Tulsa, Oklahoma, and Eldridge Miles of Dallas, Texas—award-winning pros, renowned for retail savvy.

Immediately before the conference, Miles suffered a heart attack. Fortunately he survived and in a pinch Royal Montréal's Bruce Murray substituted. He couldn't have been better and we remained acquaintances throughout my career.

The seminar was successful, as I stayed within budget, made a profit, and learned it didn't stop there. I was asked to secretary our PGA meetings and administrate the annual Pro-Assistants' Championship.

Journal Entry #185: The Writer
Dedicated to *Lorne Rubenstein*

When compiling golf memorabilia, my areas of interest were historical books and clubs. Items that over time enriched my career knowledge. When I became a member of the *Golf Collectors' Society*, it brought a wealth of global golfers to our mailbox. Golfers sharing similar devotions.

One of those was Canadian golf journalist, Lorne Rubenstein. His career was starting to flourish when he visited Edmonton for the forthcoming Canadian PGA. I met the tall, informed writer then, sharing collecting interests. That same year, he became columnist for Canada's *Globe and Mail* newspaper, as well as *SCOREGolf* magazine's first editor. Eventually he became one of golf's foremost authorities, inducted into both Ontario and Canadian Halls of Fame.

Since then, Lorne has retired and I've read many of the sixteen books he's authored. As an admirer of golf literature, I've also appreciated the works of other quintessentials such as Herbert Warren Wind. But now, from a national perspective, I find it somewhat regal, in a golf sense, acknowledging the gift we Canadians too have contributed.

Journal Entry #186: The Main Event (Part 1)
Dedicated to *David and Robbie Liden*

In the winter of 1980, Mayfair received a surprise visit from our Canadian Tour Commissioner, Dave Zink. Clubhouse staff, greens crew, and us in the shop were startled to learn we'd been selected to host Canada's PGA Championship!

The format had changed, strengthening the field's quality. For instance, the defendant was six time major champion Lee Trevino.

Suspended in speculation, everyone anticipated who the PGA would headline for the upcoming event. We didn't wait long.

Journal Entry #187: Arnies' Army

Dedicated to *Arnold Palmer*

The Canadian PGA rocked the nation's golf community announcing Arnold Palmer would headline its championship that summer!

Soon after, a media day was scheduled at Mayfair. With sizzling anticipation, our staff awaited the arrival of the king's vehicle for a day of introductions, golf, and questions. Her Royal Highness Queen Elizabeth II had lunched in that very room a year earlier. After the sponsors left, Gibby introduced me. Palmer was as charismatic as his reputation. His genuine warmth and sincerity were endorsed by uncommon eye contact.

Palmer's coming to Mayfair was one of the great marketing coups of all time.

Canada was a special place to him. It was at Toronto's Weston, where the king won his first tour event, capturing the 1955 Open. Consequently, twenty-five years after, it was emblematic having Arnold at Mayfair. To lure him, organizers either strategized with persuasive anniversary timing or were plain lucky.

Either way, in my opinion, it remains one of our PGA's most understated achievements. Palmer's endearing and charismatic popularity was so intense, he frankly might have triumphed as a national leader. If that sounds naive, let me ask the reader this. Arnold or Donald Trump? When measuring business acumen, net worth, talent, integrity, and popularity, facts couldn't be more obvious.

Journal Entry #188: Aoki and Arnie

Dedicated to *Isao Aoki*

In June 1980, the US Open was contested in Springfield, New Jersey at famed Baltusrol. As the classic came to a dramatic conclusion, its outcome was clearly between two players. America's legendary Jack Nicklaus and Japan's Isao Aoki, a professional owning the planet's finest short game.

As history books recorded, the latter fell a stroke short. Regardless, the personable Asian glittered the imaginations of global golfers with precision putting during four searing days in the Garden State. It was therefore incredibly fortunate PGA organizers signed Aoki to join Palmer for the championship.

As a Class "A" PGA member, I was included in the field too. I took advantage of that rare opportunity to compete against both and the implausibility of its reoccurrence.

I practised endlessly for months leading up to it and whether I made the cut or not, it was electric just participating. But in silently doing so, I never lost the bearings of my roots, nor the gravity of privilege.

Journal Entry #189: Gary Player (Part 3)

Dedicated to *Dr. Doug and Mary Frew*

On a bright Monday afternoon, the first trickle of spectators spilled about Mayfair's clubhouse prior to the championship. Among them, crept a silver, four-door sedan which halted in front of the shop. From it, dressed in brown shirt and slacks, emerged **Gary Player**!

Player had joined Aoki and Palmer entering the field. The car's owner acquainted us.

Doug Frew was a gynecologist and one of Mayfair's kindest members. He'd been a long-time acquaintance of Players and during the time I served the physician, silently witnessed my admiration of the South African. Aware Player and I had much in common, he ushered the famous golfer past everyone to personally introduce us. Coming face-to-face with my first golf icon was not only humbling, but paralyzing.

My emotions needed little reminding of that moment when typing this decades later.

Journal Entry #190: The Main Event (Part 2)

Dedicated to *Tom Groves*

As the tournament drew near, excitement around Mayfair was energized by anticipation.

We ordered volumes of items bearing the PGA's logo, including men's and ladies' wear, headgear, and souvenirs. Stock to accommodate spectators wanting to see the big-boys golf. Our job was to accelerate normal retailing skills.

Besides being available to work from morning to dark, we were assigned extra duties accentuating regular routines. For instance, I was charged with starting the first tee, arranging storage for competitor's clubs, and assisting the caddie chairman. During the event, long hours flew fast, harmonized by flows of activity. I was drained emotionally and physically each day.

Ironically in that hum, I found endearing moments from new relationships with our own members, golfers we served daily. For instance, the club's president and I worked alongside each other sharing goals and tackling similar challenges. Meeting Palmer was one thing, but labouring with our own employers in such unexpected ways created indelible memories.

If Arnold were here today, I'm confident he'd admit similar associations exist at his annual tour stop in Orlando, Florida.

Journal Entry #191: Gary Player (Part 4)
Dedicated to *Bill Sturgeon*

After the customary pro-am that accompanied the championship, professionals began warming-up for the tournament.

One sunny morning on the first tee, I stood announcing names of those preparing practise rounds. On the nearby putting green were pros from various countries, including Canada's Jim Nelford and New Zealand's Bob Charles, the only southpaw then to have won a major.

As I recorded groups teeing off, **Gary Player** suddenly appeared by a hedge surrounding the green. From there, he called over everyone: "Pat … Pat do you have time for a game today?" Everyone turned and looked at me … and I too, found myself searching. Looking back though, it became obvious he was addressing me. Dazed, my response was silence … when somehow the words, "Ah … yes, that would be great," stumbled out. "Would one o'clock be okay?" He continued. I nodded, almost apologetically. With that and a friendly wave, he abandoned me among the bystanders. I was suddenly vaulted into an unfamiliar place of importance. I knew Dr. Frew was behind it, but kept that to myself.

I continued starting them off with only hours ahead to grapple with what might happen that afternoon.

Journal Entry #192: Gary Player (Part 5)
Dedicated to *Bob Panasik*

The thought of golfing with **Gary Player** was at best a dream come true … at worst a nightmare.

I shared my experience with Jackie, but as exciting as it was, there was doubt to deal with. It would be daunting to play with one of a quartet then in the world, who'd won every major championship. It would have been easy to escape and hide with excuse. Motown singer-songwriter Stevie Wonder supposedly alleged, "Ninety percent of life is showing up."

I believed that, finding it a source of calm as I made my way to the first tee and met my partners.

Paul Villemaire was head pro at the Ladies' Golf Club of Toronto. With his looks and size, he might have been mistaken for a youthful John Daly. Bob Panasik rounded out the foursome. The Windsor, Ontario, native was a seasoned pro who held a rare tournament record. At the tender age of fifteen, he qualified and made the cut at a 1957 tour event! A statistic few Canucks are aware of.

It was one thing golfing with Player, but another in front his crowds. They gathered on both fairway sides, creating an isosceles affect from the tee, widening toward the playing area. Their proximity intimidated me as I prepared an opening tee shot. Fears errant misplays might injure any of the estimated five thousand, jostled with my mind. Fortunately, it never happened.

As the round began, I immersed myself within Player's endearing accent. He was captivating yet relaxing to talk with. After a tee shot on hole three, he laid on the short grass and assumed a fetal position, rocking on his spine. He repeated the exercise throughout. I hoped he'd demonstrate sand shots, which he did from bunkers behind the sixth green. Sand shots were my strength and I truthfully felt his equal, knowing his worldwide reputation. I claim that only from his demonstration then. Within that five-minute show, I could see myself performing identically and possibly better from the hours I'd spent practising. As a putter though, he appeared unequal, sinking numerous from various lengths.

I'd been at Mayfair three years then and stalled in my pursuit of the golf swing. My time instead had been prioritized learning the sport's business aspect. Watching Player that afternoon though, I found another puzzle piece. He employed a wide backswing, a one-piece takeaway utilizing arms, wrists, and shoulders. I taught that fundamental, but his was exaggerated, visually suggesting how he kept pace with peers like Nicklaus, who hit the ball extraordinary distances.

Player learned I was a new father and inquired about my family. I suggested he meet Jackie and watch her swing. "Is she here?" He asked. When I pointed her out behind the gallery ropes, he motioned her over. There, the man in black nodded his approval as Jackie swung his club next to the sea of spectators.

The tournament wasn't all rosy however, as contentions regarding course conditions arose. Player commented on its grooming, prompting the course superintendent to snipe back at the veteran. Player, however, justified his views on the eighteenth. There, he slid a wedge under fairway grass, which was laying down. Lifting it, he exposed four-inch grass lengths; verifying fairways hadn't been verticut. Player apologetically claimed the course wasn't up to tour standards.

Regardless, he'd been a gentleman, scoring an effortless four under sixty-six to my seventy-nine. And as we walked the final fairway toward a mammoth gallery ringing its eighteenth green, I thanked him. During those four hours I was the beneficiary of more than just another snapshot in life's photo album.

Journal Entry #193: Talking in Your Sleep

Dedicated to *Barb Horne*

When the days were over and darkness enveloped Mayfair, I was in the calm of bag storage, minding the competitor's equipment.

They'd all been cleaned and neatly placed in designated slots until morning, where again they'd be summoned for patriotic duty.

In silence, I held the putters of Gary Player and Isao Aoki. Player's was legendary. It was a plain black rectangular blade, chaperoned by balanced weight and a worn rubber pistol grip. Holding the wand, aware of its complicity in winning golf's four majors, I sensed an apparition within.

Earlier that day, I watched Aoki practise putting. His unorthodox style featuring low hand positions, lured his putter's toe high above grass. His bullseye model had mounds of lead tape neatly stacked behind its face. Aoki smoked when practising and the spiral hazes mingled with his squinty eyes. Combined with his stabbing strokes, they were strange effective sights. One's confirming his near deposition of Nicklaus weeks earlier at the US Open.

I carefully replaced the secret weapons, as one would bed horses down for the night. There they continued **talking in their sleep.**

Journal Entry #194: Crocodile Rock

Dedicated to *Jack Newhouse*

Over four decades as a club professional, I served numerous golfers from around the globe. But one of the strangest requests came from New Zealand southpaw, Bob Charles.

Charles was a tall man whose neat, conservative attire was confused by a witty, cynical nature.

I concluded that when he was stalking golf socks in our shop that week. The models we sold then were Lacoste, featuring miniature crocodile logos on their band. Our ensuing conversation evolved into one of the hardest sells ever, confirming Kiwi's don't enjoy parting with the purse. The banter between us, while friendly and funny, went on for thirty minutes. Finally a deal was struck.

He'd buy them but I had to remove the gators. I spent an hour searching for a razor-sharp box knife. One with shearing capacity to shave the infant thread securing each sock's lizard. The former Open champ either didn't like Lacoste, advertising, or was anti-reptilian.

While I never found out, I was rewarded by not only removing his concerns, but the wherewithal from his wallet.

Journal Entry #195: The Mechanic

Dedicated to *Mel Milbrath*

During the tournament, Arnold asked Derek for a professional courtesy. He wanted use of our club repair facilities prior to each round. Gibby instructed me to look after him during those visits. The king's routine was consistent.

Every morning before warm-up, Palmer charged into the shop. My job was to drop what I was doing and escort him to where we fixed clubs.

There he took over. Being son of a professional himself, the king was as proficient in club repair as he was at playing. He began with wedges, individually gripping and waggling them. If not to his liking, it was sentenced to the jaws of the blue vice. There, using lie-adjusting tools he bent the iron's hosel to more likable angles. Even woods weren't immune. They were tweaked up, down, or even sideways if advantageous. The club was then entertained to more waggling before returned to his red-and-white staff bag. He then proceeded to the nine iron and eight, etc. That week while I was starting the first tee, Arnold was five minutes from hitting away when irked suddenly by his driver's leather grip. There, idolized among spectators, he unwound the handle, rewrapping it to his satisfaction.

Spending each day with him, were apprentice moments in club repair.

After that season, the blue vice broke and Gibby retired it. I rescued, re-welded, and extended its odyssey. It came with me much later, when I bolted it to the shop bench at the course I eventually owned. There, when sharpening blades or pounding stubborn bearings from rusted reels, memories of Arnold using that same equipment years earlier minimized the frustrations.

Journal Entry #196: When I Die

Dedicated to *Rick Angus*

During the first round, my tee time was late. Eleventh hour competitors were subject to spike marks on greens, which were fast due to compaction and evaporation. The tournament committee also let roughs grow making approaches to greens … achievements. Grass trapped between ball and clubface grooves during impact, removed backspin. Consequently, shots moved fast and low to the ground, like jack rabbits.

That time of day wasn't the best either, as I'd been up early for work. The round was going good though. Approaching the seventeenth, I needed two birdies for sixty-nine. However, while waiting on the tee, fear wormed its way into my mind, taunting negative thoughts. Like most golfers I fought those feelings, and when they reared themselves, there seemed only one remedy. Aim, swing hard, and hope. My hooked tee shot found trouble resulting in a bogey. On the final hole I repeated, finishing with seventy-three. While disappointed some of Canada's best hadn't scored better either. Next day playing early, I opened with a triple en route to seventy-eight. After that, the field was cut and I missed qualifying by two.

I was out of the event, but Arnold wasn't. At age fifty-one, the king fired a Palmer-of-old sixty-four, ultimately winning! I was thrilled for him, regardless of my performance.

The entire experience though had been memorable, and **when I die**, it'll remain one of many or as said in Latin, *e pluribus unum*.

Journal Entry #197: Stumbling In

Dedicated to *Ralph McManus*

In the spring of '81, after sitting the year out from birthing Robert, Jackie returned to tournament golf. For a small woman, nothing was casual about delivering a ten-pound baby, even by caesarean section. Consequently, she had little energy.

Her debut was Edmonton's City Amateur. Held in the suburb of Sherwood Park, Broadmoor was where I trespassed as a penniless teenager.

Continuing where she left off a year earlier, Jackie scored par, taking a commanding first round lead. She increased it the following day, but tried relinquishing it in round three. Fortunately no one else wanted it either. Ironically, she stumbled in with a two stroke victory, claiming another city amateur.

Journal Entry #198: Four Strong Winds

Dedicated to *Rob and Mona McLennan*

In her comeback, Jackie also played in the Alberta Amateur at Henderson Lake in Lethbridge.

After two rounds, she was four strokes behind Canada's hottest amateur then, Marilyn O'Connor.

In the earlier City Amateur, Jackie's final day high score resulted in a surprise victory. At Lethbridge however, she reversed that with an under-par performance over the wind-swept course, winning by a stroke.

The victory was her second provincial amateur, matching two earlier junior and juvenile crowns. In less than a decade, she'd collected six provincials and seven city championships.

It was her last victory as an Alberta resident.

Journal Entry #199: Down by the Henry Moore

Dedicated to *Derek Gibson*

Compared to my first boss Donny, Derek was a complete contrast.

A committed family man from Prince Albert, Saskatchewan, he entered golf's industry helping pro Peter Semko build Saskatoon's Greenbryre. Later, he became assistant to Jack Kay at Toronto's Rosedale. Kay was also head pro during winter in the Bahamas, consequently Gibby was employed annually. He even had a stand in role during *Thunderball*, the James Bond flick filmed there. After Rosedale, Gibby was appointed head professional at Mayfair, where he stayed over three decades.

Derek was a charismatic entrepreneur whose natural social charm complimented his image as PGA president. However, as an accomplished golfer, it wasn't easy for him breaking par. Like other careers, club pros too have lives to balance and golf extracts toll on that time. With so many responsibilities, Gibby's playing skills were challenged. Something had to give. He was also popular with sales reps but I was unsure if their loyalty was cemented in friendship or the volumes he spent with them.

One of his flaws however, was flaunting success in front of members. They'd often chide about the large car he drove, his dress, holidays in Hawaii and the entertaining at his affluent home. Gibby enjoyed the good life.

As Derek shared his vast industry knowledge, he also allowed me to flourish individually as I advanced toward golf's culture rather than its external attractions. Often, I thought back to when he hired me instead of KayKay. Was my inauguration to circumvent hiring an athlete? Possibly, but I preferred thinking his decision was a compassionate act toward a young assistant needing a break. I spent four years with him concluding he was a people person, good for golf. But sometimes I needed more than glances to find the genuine Saskatchewan homeboy beneath the dash and glitter.

Journal Entry #200: The Manager
Dedicated to *Leo Blindenbach*

Leo Blindenbach was Mayfair's general manager. A Dutch descendant, he brought credibility to the club within Edmonton's business community. His spindly physique and tailored suits, polished an appearance pertinent when overseeing functions such as visits from royalty.

But the impeccable presence was also weaponized by attention to detail. Jackie was responsible for daily bookkeeping entries in the office. Once glancing over her accounting journals, Leo detected an error buried in its volumes. She was amazed how he extracted it so swiftly when passing by. He also led by example. Senior management in any line of work, from bureaucrats to entrepreneurs, often avoid life's unpleasant jobs, resourcing pretexts like division-of-labour or delegation-of-authority for instance. But once during heavy rain, the clubhouse's flat roof accumulated water and a drain required relief. Someone had to climb up and get wet. Despite later looking wringing and wretched, Leo went. That venture, beyond managerial mime along with reliability, promptness, and perseverance set him apart from other managers I worked with.

Later, he also became general manager at Toronto's York Downs and National Golf Clubs. It was surprising he never achieved Canada's highest peer award for performances in club management.

Chapter Three

Autumn

(Journal Entries 201 through 331)

Interviews. Head professional. Kal Lake.
Discovering course architecture. Jackie resumes her playing career.
Businessman. The SS. Times with Jim
Lefevre. World touring. Art and golf.
The game changes.

Journal Entry #201: Vancouver (Part 1)

Dedicated to *Danny Podersky*

In 1980, I began searching for a head professional's position. While hesitant, it seemed necessary to develop the process.

The PGA regularly updated its membership of jobs available. One was at the Richmond Country Club, a prominent eighteen-hole Jewish facility located in the suburbs of **Vancouver**. Unlike others though, Richmond had numerous athletic departments, but needed a new pro for their golf services. I was advised not to apply!

Sales reps detailed grim stories of Richmond's retail woes. Reportedly, many members there were aggressive clothing vendors. Dealers who sold their garments from vehicle trunks within Richmond's parking lot. Back then, it took serious capital to stake one's own shop. For a professional committed to investing thousands, the news wasn't welcoming. But after seeking advice from Edmonton's Jewish business elders, I ventured ahead.

I took weeks preparing the document and was surprised to be shortlisted for an interview. Within days though, I heard the stunning news Richmond's clubhouse burned down. Gossip claimed the flames originated: "From an incandescent light on the second floor, a fluorescent light on the first, or an Israelite in the basement." The news advanced doubt they'd hire quickly, yet follow-up calls indicated otherwise. Long before candidates zoomed for interviews via the internet, club's routinely absorbed applicant travel expenses. Richmond however even shied away subsidizing a taxi. I had to be positive … at least there was an interview and my first at that. I booked a flight to Vancouver.

Journal Entry #202: Vancouver (Part 2)

Dedicated to *Alex Tutschek*

On a brilliant Sunday afternoon, a taxi let me out at the club manager's residence near Richmond's Number 6 Road.

It was an average home used because Richmond's clubhouse went up in flames a week earlier. There I was escorted to a basement entertainment room and grilled by five friendly committee members.

Their questions immediately implicated my impotence. I never thought to immunize myself with answers to potential questions. What was I thinking? The inquiry covered topics like administration, junior instruction, and merchandising. But they were primarily interested in opinions about membership needs during restoration. Then they addressed my own questions … of which I had none. Another miscue! The meeting lasted an hour, whereupon we shook hands and I was ushered out.

At the end of my green attempt to sell myself, I clearly had no credibility. On the flight home though, I proactively wrote out each question, anticipating future encounters. Although my expenses weren't reimbursed, the experience was its own investment. Weeks later, I received a reply from Richmond, confirming success in their search. I was grateful for the outcome which confirmed my prematurity.

I'd be ready for the next audition.

Journal Entry #203: Nanaimo

Dedicated to *Jim Corbett*

Ironically, this was written within the flight terminals of both **Nanaimo** and Vancouver. The same places I flew through in 1980, searching then for that first head pro's job.

Another opportunity became available in Nanaimo on Vancouver Island. I polished a resume, tailoring it to the course requirements. The advert described a busy facility, open all year except Christmas. Even workaholics like me needed more time off than that.

The recruiting committee liked my resume and asked for a meeting.

On interview day, Edmonton was traumatized by a suffocating blizzard. We lived in the northwest community of St. Albert and the airport was on the city's polar end. To get there I crawled west Edmonton's invisible roads in dark early morning hours, peering through battalions of cotton grade snow. Eventually I reached the south side, dodging numerous vehicle casualties. Prairie roads after snowstorms, when temperatures plunged below average, were like classic skating rinks. Finally I arrived at the airport, where security then wasn't intense. My success reaching that first destination under such odds though seemed achieving in itself.

I finally arrived in Vancouver and eventually the island, where I was met by the committee ... descendants of what appeared a fanatic hockey clan. Was I being auditioned by a golf or hockey club? Compared to my previous interview though, the meeting was encouraging. Unfortunately, I didn't own inflated athletic images. Consequently I left believing they'd lean toward a golf pro with hockey credentials. It was confirmed later when they hired the NHL applicant I worked with earlier at Glendale. Hockey jocks can be like cronies to each other, similar to physicians.

In hindsight, their choice was another blessing, for years later I learned the club could be challenging to work for.

Like my morning departure, I returned home in darkness, falling asleep again with my family.

Journal Entry #204: Regina

Dedicated to *Len Harvey*

A third job availed itself that year. Many considered it one of Western Canada's best opportunities. Regina's Wascana was to Saskatchewan what Mayfair was to Alberta ... dignified, old, and respected. I applied for it with deep-down positive feelings.

The Wascana group agreed, shortlisting me soon after. I met with their selection committee there on a cold, grey November afternoon. A prairie day when temperatures implied snow. The job was run down, but they offered an attractive package to the successful applicant. With every question and answer nailed down, my instincts hinted they were genuinely pleased with the presentation. I was treated royally, complete with a realtor chauffeuring me about **Regina.** They were grooming me for what appeared a sure thing. After, I met the outgoing man. Wascana Len was a prairie-seasoned elder with cynical eyes. One's which had witnessed the trauma of numerous bureaucratic wars. Despite looking beyond his years though, he extended me courtesy, absent contempt. He could have easily been less than professional toward an eager young assistant painted in pin stripe. Instead with kindness, he toured me around what had been his work place for years.

Weeks after, I attended the annual golf show where company reps flocked to me, shaking my hand. The grapevine was implying Saskatchewan's top job was mine. No one was more surprised though, when a letter from Regina confirmed otherwise! The blow, while disappointing, taught me to keep an open mind and that nothing should be assumed.

Journal Entry #205: Winnipeg

Dedicated to *Walter Kerr*

The next season, I applied for yet another position. This time, in Manitoba. There on the outskirts of **Winnipeg** was Elmhurst, a private club with a robust membership.

It was a job I fantasized about, rooted from a developing fascination with course design. Surprisingly, Elmhurst was the offspring of golf's legendary architect Donald Ross.

I obsessed why the famous creator from Scotland and based in Massachusetts, wandered Winnipeg's wilderness so long ago. I didn't have answers, but wanted to be part of them. Being club pro there might have been a privilege. My resume was yet again well received and their committee looked after my incidentals. But I had get there first. Jackie and I had recently purchased a home and there was little left to jet across the plains.

Consequently I invested in a return Greyhound ticket to the Western Gateway. During the endless milk-run, my warming companion in the arctic temperatures was the epic novel *Shogun*.

The interview went well until realizing my competition was Paul Villemaire, the John Daly look-alike, who played with Gary Player and I the previous summer. Paul had left the Ladies' Golf Club of Toronto and was seeking the same position. Knowing each other, we dined afterwards, exchanging views. He had an engaging demeanour and deep down I sensed the committee would choose him.

I was back home when the letter arrived soon after. The committee's decision came down to both of us and I ended up second again. While disappointed, it was obvious I was advancing toward to my goal.

Journal Entry #206: Big Yellow Taxi
Dedicated to *Debbie Amirault*

Today, Mayfair's known as the Royal Mayfair. She was chartered in 2005 after hosting Canada's Men's and Women's Opens, as well as our PGA Championship.

Earlier, she owned rare distinctions as one of Stanley Thompson's original descendants. A classic gem having resisted the blemishes of alteration. But while many Canadian courses jealously guarded those Thompson roots, Mayfair unfortunately was destined to be excluded.

Throughout history, golf witnessed outbursts of growth. When I left Mayfair, the sport was again gushing around the globe. Influenced by that spurt, an embodied group of members became intoxicated by the nouveau architecture of Pete Dye. Dye's work then at California's PGA West, foddered Mayfair's renovation, extinguishing Thompson's flame. Those charged with that responsibility, were challenged when seeing what already existed. In frugal strains, they contracted a local to choreograph those changes instead of retaining Dye himself. To me, she was left less. For instance, they bulldozed her tenth, one of the world's finest par-four's, recreating a not so lustrous par-five … which was subsequently mutated again. She emerged clustered with lifeless bunkers, yawning greens and unnatural mounds … reflections of a fashionable footprint. To me it evolved into a pleasant version of mediocrity. To Joni Mitchell's phrase from "**Big Yellow Taxi**," "You don't know what you've got till it's gone!"

Regardless, Mayfair became my next career step, feeding me golf's economic fibre while harvesting my business blueprint. I was seeing the sport through a lens of promotion then as I continued to probe the science of swinging clubs.

Journal Entry #207: Hungry Heart
Dedicated to *George Bulina*

I removed a wedge from the blue vice in our club repair room. It was the same place we fixed our member's equipment and where earlier Arnold Palmer prepped prior to the PGA championship. Beside me stood the senior sales rep for Slazenger Canada.

I was finishing my fourth year then at Mayfair, constantly dreaming of one day becoming head pro. Good opportunities had availed themselves and I'd been considered for them all.

While repairing that club, the straight talking Toronto salesman asked where I'd eventually like to work. Until then, I never gave location much thought. When it came to making a living and relocating, I was a free spirit with a **hungry heart.** Reflectively, I replied, "The Okanagan Valley would be nice." The quaint fruit bearing region surrounding British Columbia's Okanagan Lake seemed endearing.

That's where it began.

Not long after, a position there availed itself. The Kal Lake Golf Club was a semi-private Okanagan course which had a membership, but was also available for public play. They were offering an attractive package for a professional to manage their shop.

Journal Entry #208: What Does It Take?
Dedicated to *Tom and Norah Foord*

When sending out resumes back then ... and even now, their potential has life changing integrity. Intentionally or not, its owner is seizing the day.

Applying for the position of head professional, wasn't unlike other jobs: What? Where? When? And how much? Determine "how much goin' you got," then submit it. Having spent years employed by a boss at a swank urban course, I became familiar with ideal work conditions. And my resume had been successfully reviewed at courses from Winnipeg to Vancouver.

In 1981, many Canadian courses offered head pro positions by contract. Descriptive details in PGA adverts outlined the services required. For example Kal Lake was seeking an applicant to supervise tee times in addition to collecting green fees. They wanted a professional who could manage their driving range, bag storage, instruction program, and power cart fleet. It was all administered through their shop where the pro also retailed equipment. For that, they offered a retainer; a disbursement for providing such services. It was the applicant's responsibility to make up the balance for a livelihood.

Once I gathered the information, I calculated the potential revenues and expenses. The estimate dictated my commitment, should a contract be negotiated.

After modifying it to Kal Lake's requirements, I sent the finished document to then manager, Albert Bibeau.

The wait wasn't long. A phone call came soon after.

I'd seized the day.

Journal Entry #209: The Pro-Am

Dedicated to *Al and Joyce McLennan*

I knew of the Kal Lake course, but had never golfed there. When their manager, Albert Bibeau ... Bert for short, telephoned of my shortlisting, I was initially upbeat, yet cautious from previous outcomes. During the conversation, Bibeau probed my participating in the annual Buzzard pro-am the following week. Buzzard was a blue-collar community outside Edmonton's northeast corner. As former manager of their nine-hole course, he annually returned to partake in its tournament. It was there Bibeau edged his way into the business prior to Kal Lake. While I had no plans to enter ... that quickly changed.

As luck had it our team won, suddenly vaulting me into the spotlight for the assignment.

I sought Bibeau out in the smoky, beer-drinking crowd amid its Legion atmosphere. Five years my senior, he owned a brash street savvy crust, absent managerial polish. As we shook hands, he fired a bullet question,

"Who wrote your resume?" Following the provocative introduction we discussed my upcoming interview. He convinced me an annual net salary of seventy-thousand was foreseeable.

With interest sparked about a long-term career there, I was flown in days later for an all expense paid interview.

Journal Entry #210: Kal Lake

Dedicated to *the Habers*

I arrived in Kelowna where I was met by a volunteer who drove me to the course. When viewed from its industrial road access, Kal Lake's clubhouse was old and cottage like, living out a faintly dignified existence. Inside was full of golfers buzzing over coffees, awaiting frost to lift off greens.

Close by, I saw a long, dark rectangular building resembling an animal shelter ... uninviting at best. With collections of hand and power carts sprinkled outside, I correctly guessed it the pro shop. The club used an innovative approach in their interviewing process. One which included a round of golf with members. As the morning's chill faded and play began, I noticed its atmosphere could never be confused with Mayfair. The **Kal Lake** group were folksy in nature, frosty to those flaunting affluence. In that sense they were refreshing. The course evolved from membership grunt work where capital costs were met when funds availed themselves. The thrifty philosophy confirmed a financial stability, softening initial observations. It was an important aspect when searching for an industry position then.

The wide-open, short course played firm through a valley with a stream bouncing through it. Part of her climbed offering lofty city views, while an irritating railway bisected play ... failing romantic comparisons to Scottish ancestors like Troon.

I shot seventy-six that morning and while hardly worthy, it maintained their interest in me. During the round, I reconnected with a golfer from my past. Fifteen years earlier, Geezy snared the St. Paul Open from my teenage grasp fabricating golf's most spectacular shot. The Legion bartender had relocated to the Okanagan.

With introductions to the club complete and golf finished, I took a breather to prepare for my interview.

Journal Entry #211: The Interview
Dedicated to *Clem and Anne Watson*

The interview took place in a lower level meeting room at a prominent hotel. I was as prepared as ever.

The selection committee was an eclectic group which included the club's captain, a local realtor named Dino Johnstone. Short and lewdly popular among members, he was possessed by a machine gun laugh. Their President, Lyle Pryce, evoked *Back to the Future* memories of mad scientist Christopher Lloyd. Dave Kostecki was a lanky, intimidating accountant who'd previously been a provincial junior champion. Lorne Hilmo played his part as the cynic farmer who mistrusted elected civic officials, while the chair of the meeting was Vice-President Len Loomis. A young moon faced lawyer whose bank of levelheaded questions were balanced by an appropriate sense of humour. Bibeau rounded out the committee as we assembled at a conference table, me at its head.

As the interview unfolded, they examined my career skills, augmenting it with queries about change. The hour-long audition ended on friendly tones.

The following day I returned to the Oil Capital, resuming my duties at the downtown private club. As always, an agonizing period persisted before the dreaded response.

It arrived sooner than expected.

Journal Entry #212: The Professional
Dedicated to *Jean Harris*

Most people remember losing their virginity. Others recall their station during Kennedy's assassination or the events of September eleven.

Similarly, during a 1981 phone call, I became more aware of the term **professional**. It wasn't from any accomplishment, as much as a lack of one.

It occurred a week after the interview by way of a call from Bibeau. When he explained Kal Lake's decision had been close, I felt the daggers of defeat. They had chosen a Vancouver veteran over me.

As our conversation continued however, I emotionally and selfishly steered the exchange toward my dimming future. After hanging up though I unexplainably saw reality in my inner mirror. Like a dowdy apparition, it berated my improper response. Reason accompanied it stinging me with a virtue of etiquette that suggested bad news be accepted positively, responsibly, and … professionally! When later, whipping off my usual letter of thanks to the selection committee, I actually felt better rather than beaten.

Professionalism in the industry can be interpreted various ways. Maybe it's only an ability … like cutting a shot toward a flagstick tucked behind intimidating bunkers. To others, it might be outstanding organizational skills, a mentor passing on life experiences, or impeccable bedside manners. To me though, it's woven within a tapestry of knowledge, empathy, common sense, and integrity.

I wrote this after the thirty-ninth Ryder Cup matches in Chicago, where the golf world witnessed America's shocking defeat to Europe. In their collapse, American players fell far outside any parameter defining professionalism. What wasn't however, were the consoling tributes offered by opposing team captain, José Maria Maria Olazábal!

Journal Entry #213: The Phone Call

Dedicated to *Campbell Leblond and Nancy Mann*

The autumn of 1981 wasn't unlike other fall seasons. On those crisp sunny Alberta mornings, gold and yellow poplar leaves framed fairways painted by frost. It was a time of deliberation after failing again to be selected head professional. Five interviews, five times a bride's maid. I had to weigh the positives though. I enjoyed my job with a good employer at a prominent club in the province. Plus Jackie and I were settling into a new home and expecting another child. While craving my own position, I also realized life was good. It was about to get better!

As was the custom then, after all tournaments were played, our staff began preparing for next season, and the upcoming buying show. By then I was responsible for most of the purchasing. Derek made the ultimate decisions, but most details were relinquished to me and his wife, who ordered the women's wear. I relished visiting every exhibitor's booth with my spreadsheets, flushing out the buys while weighing availability, delivery, and quality.

On the show's last day, I suddenly heard my name broadcast over the intercom … a phone call. It was Bibeau, who'd days earlier delivered the bad news. This time however, he was probing my commitments, asking me to accept the Kal Lake position!

Did I hear that right? He explained the Vancouver pro they'd selected, declined their offer. As runner up among the sixty-two applicants, they picked me. With an unexpected outpour, I exploded into the phone, "Bert … I love you!" While his latent response was suffocating … it didn't matter. I was unexpectedly about to greet my goal!

Journal Entry #214: Head Over Heels

Dedicated to *Dave Morris*

I called Jackie first then Derek, who congratulated me with heartfelt tears.

Kal Lake wanted to fly Jackie and I there to sign a contract. It was an exciting new chapter in our lives.

For the second time within weeks, we buzzed into Kelowna. There, we were met by captain Johnstone, the realtor with the repeating laugh. During the drive, he condemned my predecessors' incompetence, crowing on about Kal Lake's intent to support us. We stayed that evening in a downtown hotel with a large atrium. Next day we met Kal Lake's finance chairman Rob Dalton.

Dalton, who was genuine, friendly, and honest presented us with a three-year contract that spelled out a list of mutual terms and responsibilities.

In the remuneration structure, I'd receive all revenues from bag storage, driving range, merchandise sales, hand and power cart rentals plus lessons. In addition to collecting an attractive retaining fee, Kal Lake allocated twenty-thousand toward improving the existing pro shop. And like many contracts, financial commitments balanced the document. Besides an obligation to all business expenses, I was obligated to purchase my predecessor's equipment and merchandise. I also had to fund new shop stock. It wouldn't be what's today slurred ... chump change. For a young married couple, financing it would be challenging. The contract also spelled out penalties for acting outside agreement fringes.

It was my first contract, and in the overall excitement I was **head over heels**.

Journal Entry #215: The Predecessor

Dedicated to *Ron and Helen Wood*

Chuck Jenzen was my Kal Lake predecessor. During the contract signing, we spent moments with him and his wife. From them, we hoped to learn more about the club's background optics.

Jenzen was a hefty growly type with a grease-monkey appearance, who dressed, talked, and walked not unlike mechanics are often stereotyped. It didn't flatter his image when I saw customers cowering to his manners. In past, rednecks like that usually talked down to smaller types like me, but strangely Jenzen didn't. Despite a gruff exterior and aware he'd soon be jobless, he veiled an air of integrity.

It was equally evident with his wife, who owned a kind, pleasant demeanour. So when she said what he couldn't by endorsing frustrations they'd collected during a decade in business there, it became the first time my thoughts wandered beyond the thrill.

I toured the shop then and its need of disaster assistance wasn't overstated. I may have sensed Jenzen kind-hearted, but there was no mistaking his merchandising skills. On the other hand, perhaps he gave up?

He had an assistant named Curly Bridges, who was considered Jenzen's successor. However, lack of experience failed advancing him. One of

Bibeau's subtle hints though, was to retain him on payroll. I took a wait-and-see attitude with the middle-aged bachelor, hoping he might transition gaps when assessing past methods and meeting new members.

It was only October, and I had until spring before my contract officially began. There would be much to think about and do.

Journal Entry #216: La Isla Bonita

Dedicated to *Garry Biddell*

That autumn prior to the new venture, I celebrated taking three Mayfair members to Portugal for a pro-am.

We jetted out of Edmonton, landing in the Algarve city Faro. There, I experienced my first foreign-speaking country, playing four rounds with my team. Previously I'd toured numerous cobblestoned castles of historic British boroughs. But the seaside village of Albufeira was different. There, I saw the Mediterranean charm of marbled hotel floors, tropical fragrances, and topless beaches. I imagined Isla Bonita like that.

I invited the judge to be one of my partners. On one excursion, we were accosted for speeding while ambling in search of the reputed home of famous British pro Henry Cotton. Our first instinct was to reason with the Guardia Nacional. But the judge silenced us, cautioning we were guests in their country. Bribery and corruption were possibly the norm rather than exception. He persuaded us there en route to cough up the penalty in Portuguese escudos. We gave in—but not before appreciating the customs and freedoms young Canadians back home took for granted.

Journal Entry #217: Henry Cotton

Dedicated to *Bob Manson*

Male fashion on pro tours has always been prevalent. On the PGA's circuit, Rickie Fowler has often blossomed out in pastels from his hat to shoes.. On the European tour, Ian Poulter has been known to dress with flair and style. But before and after World War II was **Henry Cotton**.

And Cotton himself was passed the crown from the effervescent Walter Hagen. Both had impeccable tastes, glamorizing themselves along the way in the company of women. And during that time Cotton imbedded himself in golf's glory winning three Open championships. After his competitive years, he turned to architecture and instruction. In the golf swing, he believed hands played dominate roles and to strengthen them, his radicalized students swung at automobile tires pancaked on grass.

After Cotton retired he designed a Portuguese resort named Penina. I found my way into its main reception area, where impulsively and without expectation, I inquired about the expat. I was astonished when the receptionist directed me to the fourth floor declaring, "Mr. Cotton will receive you there!"

Bewildered, I left the enormous lobby finding another above lavished in swollen settees and towering vegetation.

There I waited. Soon after, an elder flaunting aristocratic flourish, sauntered down the expansive carpeted hallway, escorted by a corgi. Cotton, dressed in flaxen plus fours and hounds's tooth sport jacket was squat and rounder in girth than playing pictures portrayed.

After introducing myself, we mingled the hours away trading golf-swing theories, his resort involvement, and reliving his competitive achievements. His faithful canine all-the-while vigilant.

After saying our goodbyes, I left spellbound by the unforeseen encounter, my pro-am highlight.

Journal Entry #218: Africa

Dedicated to *Bill Thomson*

Most have heard the phrase, "It's a small world."

One of golf's most attractive, yet subtle properties has been uniting and integrating people. For instance players anywhere, thrown together by chance on the first tee, often find common callings. One's forging lasting bonds and friendships. That alone should make the game a passport for a peacekeeping device.

After one of the pro-am rounds, we gathered outside the modest clubhouse at Vale do Lobo golf course. There small groups mingled and lunched in the intimate bar area among beverages, plants, and umbrellas. The judge, pontificating on his round, leaned back thumping the chair behind him. Turning to apologize, he looked straight into the eyes of his former wife's bridesmaid.

Bob's wife had passed away from a brain tumour leaving the judge to care for their two children. The unexpected reunion with a woman he hadn't seen in twenty years, in a place north of **Africa**, was typical of how golf inexplicably pastes people together.

As my career was maturing then, I saw humanity could be like an epoxy … formed by a resin of people and the hardening compound of golf.

Journal Entry #219: Everyone's Gone to the Moon

Dedicated to *Delaine Kardash*

We concluded the pro-am, where I finished only shots behind fellow Canuck Dave Barr. The tournament had been a farewell competition of culture and companionship on the eve of my imminent career change.

Before leaving, we refreshed ourselves in the port of Lisbon, known internationally as Lisboa. There, I failed resisting an eye-catching cappuccino. Within minutes, I felt the physical rummaging which certified Montezuma's Revenge. Previously, I'd beaten the repression by sipping cokes and wine. The altered state however, only previewed my flight home.

On the plane I sat beside a bald, robust Portuguese, slurping alcohol like pop. Fuelled by the one-hundred-proof vodka, his head and lips glistened as he became vulgar to flight staff. Heckling passengers joined in taunting him resulting in an an altercation, with me sandwiched between. Eventually, the pilot and male attendants overpowered and bound him to his seat, curtained off. They were incapable however of silencing his filthy obscenities, brands unheard on any golf course before. His temper escalated, to where the broad three hundred pounder attempted kicking the portals out with his feet. On that black night, mired in delusion, frequent washroom visits and the creature's rage, I hallucinated the glass puncturing and destabilizing the plane, plummeting us toward the steely Atlantic below. I buckled myself in awaiting that final existence until hours later the nightmare ended in Montréal. There, Canada's finest boarded the plane, apprehending the intoxicant.

Journal Entry #220: Golf House
Dedicated to *Lorne Thompson*

Among the challenges of my new duties, were contractual obligations to purchase my predecessor's remaining assets valued at sixty thousand. Consequently we had to sell our home for the twenty-five thousand downpayment.

Christmas holidays prior to the move were spent with Jackie's parents. While there, I checked our home which we'd recently tendered for sale. The outside temperature was minus thirty-five degrees. That day was defined in one macabre moment when opening the front door and seeing my breath inside. With no heat, the furnace too had taken holiday and broken down … freezing the entire house!

Until help arrived, I looked for ways to comfort the building, such as switching on the oven or anything that delivered heat. It was during a time the National Hockey League was merging into Edmonton. I made the best of it watching a televised game and broiling a steak, naive to the looming catastrophe.

Suddenly, the house moved! It literally swayed and I thought earthquake. Moments later, it thankfully subsided. But as in tag team wrestling, was swiftly replaced with the sickening sound of water hemorrhaging from ceilings. A monsoon of water bursting their pipes began irrigating the entire house..

Bundled in my duffel coat, I saw myself participating in some Salvador Dali parody … a milieu of vapors, half-eaten meat, a losing hockey team and emerging floods.

In only weeks we were anticipating our home sold as proceeds toward the new venture.

Journal Entry #221: Starting Over

Dedicated to *Frank Oishi*

After that incident, evidence suggested I was a fatalist.

In the apocalypse of that frozen house which had to be sold immediately, everything appeared insurmountable. It was like we were **starting over**. In the following month, we had to repair the damage, sell the house, move our worldly possessions from one province to another, incorporate, and set up a business in a new community … as well as find a place to live. Not to mention … we were expecting our next child.

Contracting trades like plumbers, dry-wallers, and painters within short time was one thing. Coordinating their schedules was like splitting the atom. Through what seemed a miracle, we not only found, but recruited the labour required to complete the tasks. Only then could we market the home. Selling it too was challenging as our first realtor was as useful as a flat-headed tee. In desperation, we retained the dynamo who sold us our first home, two years earlier. She disposed of it before contractors completed their work. With Jackie pregnant, she remained in Edmonton until the delivery, while I moved our equipment and furniture during a February blizzard. While there, I rented a house and incorporated ourselves through our new lawyer.

All that was accomplished within a month, while continuing to work for Gibby and teaching night classes. I don't believe in cults or conspiracies, but when everything knit together timely before the new venture, I was compelled to admit fatalism existed. It wouldn't be the only time either.

Journal Entry #222: Move on Down the Line

Dedicated to *Ruth Rikley*

It was time to move from Edmonton, a place I'd called home for more than twelve years. I'd leave Jackie for several months to set up our new business in the Okanagan.

That February, the cold was penetrating as I departed in the early morning hours. My relic Datsun was crammed with last-minute strays as I crept through the Oil Capital's slick streets. En route I picked up Jimmy Dow, who'd help drive.

From the prairies, we travelled west on highways aimed at mountainous elevations. There, intimidated by blankets of black ice and raw temperatures, we skittered perilously close to mammoth logging trucks in claustrophobic passes. The taxation continued as we crawled through slippery communities from Hinton to Clearwater. Tolled physically and psychologically, we finally arrived to our motel by a stream near the course.

The next day Sunday was a short respite before diving into work next day, my first on duty as head pro.

Journal Entry #223: Old Time Movie

Dedicated to *Frank Leek*

On that first day, snow lingered on the fairways, as I excitedly yet cautiously edged toward the uncertainties. Before setting about discovering the shop, I had to obtain keys. It was then Bibeau invited us to his home for breakfast.

Bibeau lived in the suburban hills of a nearby hamlet. Driving up, we found him working in his garage and it was then I saw my companion flinch. I'd known Jimmy a dozen years by then and it was uncharacteristic of him. He was the cryptic type in a card game. When the words, "I know him," shot my way, I veered to attention. "From where?" I returned. "Back home" was all Jimmy said, but his tension alarmed me.

Bibeau noticed Jimmy too, acknowledging him by name. The guarded reaction, confirmed uneasy connections between them. Throughout the meal, I felt the silent warning of strain. Perhaps had I been more aware, events wouldn't have taken place as they did, twenty-two years later.

During the ensuing weeks, it didn't take me long to see Bibeau wasn't like other managers I'd worked with. The administrators I knew were suit men who had a bank of terminology that included: business plans, profit margins, and projections. Bibeau instead, was cozy with the club's folksy chutzpa. He shunned ties and sports jackets at work, preferring jeans. Street smart and savvy, he surrounded himself with others like-minded. Self-assured gamblers with brass. Hedonists without creeds, like flies surrounding feces. I was wary of that sort because every course membership had some. But Kal Lake had more, which I found through the lens of time.

We left the drama at Bibeau's table, winding our way back to assess the shop challenges ahead. I never found out what happened between them until decades later. It was just as well. I had enough on my plate.

Journal Entry #224: Stepping Out

Dedicated to *Jim Free*

My first challenge before tackling the shop was acquiring a mortgage. After selling our home to finance the business, we needed thirty-five thousand more. To acquire that, I needed a business' support structure. An accountant, banker, insurer, and lawyer.

Our new attorney Loomis recommended an associate, Dale Clark to be our accountant. They worked in the same building and on that initial day Clark and I were **stepping out**, pounding the streets looking for capital. I was green when he acquainted me about pro forma statements … projections of a companies' future financials based on planned courses of action. A critical process when convincing banks of venture potential. With no business ownership experience, I was insufficient on paper. Nevertheless, I was confident portraying my abilities. I was surprised when the first three banks rebuffed me. But I remembered the advice of Mayfair Pep, who earlier in Edmonton chimed: "If your bank won't help you, there's always another across the street." And he was right as I eventually, ended up at the Royal, where a thin rail reminding me of Keith Alexander took a chance on me. He had everything in place within days and because of that trust, I opened our commercial account with him.

It was his belief in me, which framed the philosophy I adopted from then on. One claiming both parties in any deal should benefit. In other words, a mutual relationship. I learned later, that most who climb into business, unfortunately look out only for themselves. Regardless, I remained faithful to that way of commerce throughout my career. Later still, I was introduced to Marc Larochelle, another club member who owned OKAY INSURANCE. A popular local businessman with an endearing French accent, he became our agent. With support and financing in place, I shifted my focus toward the shop.

Journal Entry #225: Ghost

Dedicated to *Colonel Rogers and Dr. Jack Neilson*

At the start of the movie "**Ghost**," characters sledgehammer through old walls to rejuvenate a vintage building. I needed more than that walking into Kal Lake's pro shop.

The dilapidated structure wasn't vintage either.

Entering the depressingly cold building, every noise echoed despair. With each step taken, dust exploded seeking attention. Shredded carpet, ravaged by histories of metal spike inquisition, exposed cranky floorboards. Pastel-green walls languished behind merchandise caked in soot. Ceiling plywood dared gravity exposing murky trusses, petrified remains, and jeering cobwebs. In one corner, the customer's changing partition was a soiled and torn shower curtain, dangling from rusted reinforcements … gloomy at best. The cash register however appeared authentically classic … a bright spot.

The back shop, where members paid to have their equipment cleaned and stored, was no improvement. Missing only hay and straw, it seemed a repository for bedding livestock. And while there was no bathroom, office, or place to store inventory or fix clubs, it did boast crude running water and bare heat. The entire building appeared no more than plywood and sticks gloating support. If fire had escaped, the remains might have been encouraging.

Besides the opportunity, the other positive were twelve Yamaha power carts … the most useful items purchased in the venture.

With Jimmy's architectural background, he assessed ways to give the shop meaning, while I searched for starting points within the five hundred square foot shanty. My job was to turn it into a pro shop.

With snow remaining on the ground, time remained on my side. But who knew when the white cover might melt, exposing green grass. That wasn't going to be the only problem. I was about to enter the halls of golf course politics.

Journal Entry #226: Empty Garden

Dedicated to *the Bjornsons*

We began resuscitating the dilapidated shop by submitting Jimmy's blueprints, which included a change room, inventory closet, office and washing facilities. Further, Jimmy delivered his drawings with no fee. I felt part of a team, actively participating in a contractual commitment. But I was naive.

When the board met to approve the expansion, they rejected it! I thought they were kidding. Weren't they were serious about upgrading the shop? What happened to their pledges during my interview? A remaining board member I hadn't met was Ron Rudder, a retired tractor salesman. Rudder, who struggled with cynicism, claimed the "new-fangled" plan compromised a garden near the construction site. He remained obstinate and unswayable! The director's decision however, left me floundering. As the newcomer, rocking-the-boat, wasn't in my forecast. But how could I bite my tongue, explaining the developments to my best friend? Further, none of the committee thanked Jimmy for his efforts. In an embarrassing moment, I shared the verdict with him. Fortunately good friendships last.

Their decision however, forced me to swerve in a different direction. It was the first time I saw the miscarriage of commitment. Rudder's opinion changed years later when a new clubhouse was built and his flowerbed was ploughed under. The politics had begun.

Journal Entry #227: Back on the Chain Gang

Dedicated to *Ed Snaychuk*

I had to come up with new plans for the shop. Something fast before the snow melted and golf season was upon me. Time suddenly wasn't my friend.

Kal Lake hired Harry Ham to assist me. Ham was a local contractor and club member, who was challenged by obesity and insecurity. In the beginning, he was helpful, but after work was completed he spent the next two decades criticizing every decision I made. In fact he badgered everyone there. Over time, I realized he joined Kal Lake solely to keep an eye on his partner, an overtly popular server there. Regardless of Ham's criticisms and insecurities though, I couldn't have accomplished the renovations without him.

We purged everything in the shop, keeping only essentials. Carpets, interiors, and ceilings all went. Reusable items were dignified with coats of paint or strokes of varnish. We replaced the floors with attractive commercial carpet after installing wall panels. I took apart the existing counter where my predecessor sold green fees, reassembling it in bag storage for club repairs. It was replaced by that ninety dollar antique purchased from Henry Martel. My inherited cash register resembled a charming, but obsolete 1930s model. The kind drug stores in past rang up soda pop sales. I invested in a modern version to account accurate sales and timely reports. We installed a skylight which brought luminance to the timid shop. Then after displaying antique clubs, decorative plants and curtains, the insides quaintly reinvented themselves.

Finally, to uplift the building's exterior, we hung cedar siding, awnings, and flower boxes coercing friendly, inviting appeals.

With work complete, I remained disappointed how the board casually dismissed Jimmy's work while failing to anticipate future shop needs.

Regardless, there had been progress.

SUMMER PLACE

Journal Entry #228: Key Largo
Dedicated to *Mary Dantzer*

Managing a pro shop back then, included inventorying merchandise to satisfy golfer needs.

When ordering stock, I had to be aware of costs, delivery dates, incentive buying and payment schedules … all part of the terms. Taking over the shop meant going into thirty-five thousand debt. In addition, I ordered merchandise worth seventy-five thousand for the season. In total we owed one hundred and ten thousand. Included among the purchases were bags, balls, clubs, crested soft-wear, shoes, and accessories too numerous mentioning. Was I worried? Was Prime Minister Trudeau French?

As shipments arrived that spring, we'd count and inventory each item. Products then were assigned prices and attractively displayed. It was all based on merchandising I gleaned from Gibby. For instance I'd keystone the software. Software in the golf industry had nothing to do with computers. It was clothing and I'd mark it up one hundred per cent. If shirts cost twenty-five, I'd price them forty-nine. Non-enterprising types might consider that gouging, but most aren't aware of a businesses' liabilities. Expenses are part of retail life. They sprout like unforeseen weeds, adversely and unpredictably affecting bottom lines. Other markups such as hardware or golf clubs for instance were between 25 and 40 percent. Golf professionals like other merchants walked flagsticks when pricing product. I was expected to generate reasonable profits, but the last thing I wanted were members shopping elsewhere due to lavish pricing. Word travelled fast at courses. My goal was to maximize profit, while providing customers fair prices … motivations for perpetual purchasing. Competitive pricing was an underrated skill.

My inherited assistant worked six shifts per week that spring. After his day's work, I continued on, toiling late and attending to other needs like re-spiking shoes, re- gripping clubs, or unpacking deliveries. Some nights I never came home, plodding into hazy twilights with early season pressures dangling over me.

Those chilly dark nights were medicated listening to radio favorites like "**Key Largo**," a refrain reviving the loneliness without family.

Journal Entry #229: The Assistant

Dedicated to *Dick Vickerson*

The first assistant was Curly Bridges. My predecessor, who employed him, cautioned me about his character. However, subtle hints from Bibeau, influenced me to keep him on payroll. Bridges was ten years my senior and primped by an afro. Divorced with a son, he was seeing a local businesswoman, while continually sowing his wild oats. I often caught him peering through the shop windows toward the eighteenth green, wolfishly critiquing the other gender as they bent over retrieving their final shots.

While his knowledge of golf was less, compared to assistants I'd previously known, he could score better than eighty on the modest course. Plus, he possessed a background in sales and in fairness; sold for me what I couldn't myself. Bridges seasoned our new relationship with membership comments such as: "There's Dick … he owns property all over, and'll spend a fortune with us," or "That's Maki, the club's biggest sandbagger!" Golf professionals invariably found ways to assess the personalities of staff and customers alike. While I tried to a fault treating everyone the same, individual opinions regardlessly filtered in, especially when financial credit was factored. Those early impressions were fostered by Bridge's intrusive narratives and my instinctive radar.

Bridges lasted a year with me as his allegiances over that time predictably waned. He drifted off, choosing instead to align himself with the SS. More than I'd have preferred.

Journal Entry #230: Bitsy

Dedicated to *Walt and Jill Keckalo*

The first superintendent I worked with at Kal Lake was **Bitsy**.

Bitsy was an elder, whose eyes aroused images of Kris Kringle. They were narrow and twinkly, anchored by crow's feet from chuckling and insobriety. His short curly hair and rounded shoulders were accentuated by asthmatic grunts when he hobbled the course. As a groundsman, Bitsy was only mildly competent, a result from being his own man and uneasy working with.

But from day one, he greeted me with avuncular respect. Consequently, I became distantly attached to him although we never saw each other socially. At the time, evidence suggested he wouldn't be there long. He'd burned too many bridges and predictably became a casualty of progress. He lasted a couple years more before parting ways, spending remaining moments at the local Legion. While I missed him, it angered me hearing the SS dinning him in his departure. Why couldn't they have been decent to the old man in retirement? It was all I wanted in mine … two decades later!

Journal Entry #231: Leader of the Band

Dedicated to *Mike and Elaine*

There were eight in my first staff including Jackie, who managed our books. While Curly was the first assistant, Darren was my second. In his early twenties, Darren was an aspiring pro I took a chance on. Unfortunately his work continually came up short and team leaders learn early there are only so many times one can go to the well for employees whose efforts are regularly redefined.

I also had four teens cleaning clubs in bag storage. Like the myriad that followed, they all sprouted roots in the industry. Courtenay was attractive with her long dark hair and Irish pedigree. She also tended our front shop and later became a popular local golf instructor. Mickey was the eldest. Lean and dark-haired, he suffered emotional growing pains before turning pro. Jared was blond-haired, lanky, and promising until the following winter when he landed a union job. Sadly, he traded his friendly, youthful zest to become a frowning cynic. Then there was Todd who was a gift to me. Another fair-haired tall teen, he was the quiet silent type, loved by everyone. Finally there was me. Young and naive I was the confident **leader of the band**.

With my team in place, we were set for opening day within the newly renovated shop.

Journal Entry #232: Life in a Northern Town

Dedicated to *Patrick Stel*

On March 20, the course opened on twelve holes. The remaining six were too wet for play.

The first three members I saw then were Clarence Frolick, his partner Julie, and JR. They arrived before me, hoping to be the season's first golfers. JR was disliked by everyone. A short and wiry, tattooed Englishman with an elfish face, his brash tactics and crude humour continually exhausted friendships. On the other hand he was genuine. Frolick was a machinist who was the tall dark and handsome type. My instincts however, claimed he was condescending. He called me his friend over the next two decades, but in the end, proved otherwise. Over time my intuitions were seldom wrong.

The driving range and bag storage also opened that day. As a service, we cleaned, stored, and provided member's clubs ready for play. With more than four hundred customers storing, it furnished us desperately needed capital to pay our merchandise suppliers. I began selling driving range passes also. For up front fees, customers hit unlimited range balls or a bucket per day. Immediately popular, the concept lasted as long as I did.

That first day was spent showing off the new shop, introducing ourselves, and attending to needs. Later that afternoon I met the Zoo, a bizarre collection of commune hippies and rednecks. Their ringleader donned a straw hat with curled edges, like worn by rockabilly Ronnie Hawkins. A dangled leather cardigan completed his attire. After an opening tee shot, he clumped over the first hole's wooden bridge with his bronco boots. On the opposite side, he turned to the clan, opening his vest wide. In a surreal moment he dared them, "Hey yoahl ... nah see if ya ken git me!" The Zoo were a sobering contrast to the premiers and business elders I'd spent my previous years working for.

Customers weren't the only difference. At Mayfair we seldom used tee sheets. Play existed for the pleasure of members and if busy, one of us pros directed first tee traffic like Bangkok patrolmen. At Kal Lake though, we logged play daily to balance green fees. Plus tee times were usually booked by telephone. The frequency we answered that device testified to an exhausting membership vitality.

Toward evening, my walls were tacked in yellow sticky notes. Hasty summonses to follow-up on customer promises such as: re-spiking Tony Selva's shoes, re-gripping Ron Lange's woods, or booking lessons for Ron Nelson. After browsing them, I thought back to the Zoo, who by then were staggering into the clubhouse. I deliberated about the new venture and where **life in a northern town** would eventually lead me.

Journal Entry #233: Stand by Me

Dedicated to *Mike and Faye Latta*

Most golf clubs then had junior programs. One's fostering development of young golfers. Theoretically, they were the future, blueprinting a facility's fate. It wasn't unlike the forest industry, sustaining itself through responsible reforestation.

During that first week open, one of the boys played the front nine in thirty-one strokes ... five under par! Denny was only thirteen. At that age, it was an eye opening diversion from the shop.

Like bees in a hive, I sensed these juniors were different from my previous appointments. And yet while eager, they were only idling, as if waiting for someone to pull-their-trigger.

It seemed opportunistic. At its nucleus was Denny. He was aggressive, brash, and could hit the ball forever. His potential led me to believe he could win the nationals. Each weekend I attended their tournaments, followed their play, and made performance notes. It blossomed into a successful program with rare bouquets of perennial talent.

They became the die cast that I believed could influence Kal Lake's destiny.

Journal Entry #234: Time After Time

Dedicated to *Roxanne Woodman*

Green fees and memberships were the vital nutrients nourishing every course's operating system. They satisfied needs like fuel and labour costs that maintained greens, fairways, fringes, roughs, tees, and bunkers. They paid fertilizer and pest control expenses required when keeping grounds green and free of ravaging insects and disease. They met tolls arising from mechanical breakdowns and replacement parts among arsenals of machinery soldiering typical courses. Ultimately, they were administrative cost quenchers.

My principle obligation was collecting those fees. To that end, we were issued sequentially numbered tickets to account for each fee purchased. Most of those sales were cash sourced before debit cards. In typical transactions, we provided receipts which then were displayed on customer bags, logging corresponding tags. Regular fees, guests, juniors, and twilight rates were balanced daily. The number of golfers had to equal my stub count. I was unsuccessful convincing directors to include an office within the expansion plan. Consequently, my paltry shop became a counting chamber where I tallied reams of numerical receipts. If interrupted, it meant recounts taking even longer. To avoid that, I waited for the last golfers to leave before reconciling. **Time after time,** in darkness, I nervously chaperoned vast sums of cash to their nightly deposits before heading home. With the course's location near city trains, often the dubious walked them till dusk. It wouldn't have taken much for darker varieties to have their way with me. But it never happened.

Journal Entry #235: Guilty

Dedicated to *Spike and Chris Kendy*

Being away from my family was new. The days never felt lonely until arriving home nightly to emptiness.

After two months at Kal Lake, I flew back to Edmonton for the birth of our daughter Janine. Our son Robert was three by then and I was told we had a million dollar family. Both were near ten pounds at delivery … extraordinary given Jackie's delicate frame. After she recovered they joined me, arriving on a sweltering Okanagan day.

In one of my life regrets, Jackie was abandoned with the job of making a home for us. As an only child from a sheltered environment, the immigration was taxing on her and the social climate challenging to penetrate. I complicated it by being self-absorbed developing the business. I assumed roles too familiar with fathers, using claims like, "working-for-us." Like those dads, I was away from home too often. For example, my day off was Sunday. That first year, Vernon's Junior Open was on a weekend, which I managed for the one hundred and fifty entrants. I was continually away on days like that. It emotionally and psychologically scarred Jackie who in convalescing had no one to talk to other than both children, who couldn't!

If readers sense I've neglected writing more of my family, it's from the shame of sacrificing my role as a father and husband. Selfishly driven by those false notions, I consciously abdicated responsibility which ultimately defined me as a parent and partner.

I'm a prisoner of that past and usually, there aren't second chances for fathers like me. But I was one of the luckier ones. I had the understanding of my wife and two amazing people, all whom I admire. In the balance of my life though, painted into a corner, I've carried on a reformation believing it best to be grateful for what I have, rather than what I haven't.

Journal Entry #236: Goodfellas

Dedicated to *Georges Dansereau*

Mayfair's men's nights were like Sunday evenings at an independent living facility. At Kal Lake, it was a Doors concert!

The events began from noon each Wednesday, with crazed competition and social sousing … often with more than two hundred participants. After golf, they retired to the quaint cottage clubhouse with its cement patio littered with plastic orange lawn chairs. There, they ordered beverages and meals, hungrily awaiting prizes.

Men's night was run by the captain, a prized position among directors. Elected from a puree of the frail, and lured by a salacious spotlight, the captain emceed each evening's festivities, prancing like a rock star. Jim Morrison wouldn't have looked out of place. Tensions escalated hourly as the evening partied on. Once all scores were submitted, we'd deliver the prizes amid constant pressures to present them so golfers could retire. But most resisted leaving!

As darkness and imbibing enveloped each night, unusual personal games emerged. The clubhouse's angled roof became a chapter in the betting blood, as wagerers, searching for amusement, threw golf balls above the gables. Rebounding they'd ricochet off cement and onto the adjoining practise green. Those finishing closest to the hole collected the cash. Once after the day was over and I'd left for home, I arrived early next morning finding them still going … chipping balls off the pro shop roof.

During those evenings, I saw the influence alcohol had on attitude. The fuel energized hidden resentment and tempers, tormenting me throughout the summer's toil. The nights were impressive sources of revenue, but I never knew what price I'd be assessed in enemies or surprises.

From my apprenticeship, I learned to avoid drinking excessively with members and instead work in earnest. I was glued to that philosophy, believing it the way of true professionals. Rationalizing members would genuinely appreciate such diligence, I laboured on naively. Instead it strangely infuriated them, forming jealousies. Consequently each men's night showcased new elements of astonishment. A person I thought friendly might suddenly turn without explanation. I wasn't a boy scout nor a snob. I didn't mind having a beverage or even two with them. And each week I golfed with various members, but it never went beyond that. Regardless, many … particularly a group called the SS … felt I was overtly restrained. Kindled by manager Bibeau, the impression was I should have been more socially indulgent than appropriate.

It was during those frenzied evenings of anger, booze, swearing and uneasy laughter, when rumours began smearing my developing reputation. Particular, the revenues I generated.

It was especially testy on evenings of a full moon. It seemed to naturally extract the worst of prejudices.

Journal Entry #237: The SS (Part 1)

Dedicated to *Wayne Kinghorn*

During that first season, I was contacted by Canada's newly published golf magazine *SCORE*. They compiled a list of the nation's top-five newest pros to highlight a special instruction column for an anniversary special. The series to be circulated nationally included me.

It was an unexpected surprise. The one restriction was word limit. I spent time and eventually composed an essay about the relationship between grip and clubface angles. Months went by and then one day, it appeared. It was one of the most memorable days in my budding new position. I anticipated how impressed the board would be, having their club profiled across the country. I found out how naive that was on men's night.

Archie was a new director who owned a city restaurant. A monstrous cartoon memory of him outside his business fronting Main Street testified to a swaggering appearance. Chunky, overweight, and cursed with crude humour, he usually golfed men's nights inebriated.

Late that evening, we finally delivered the prizes. But as we commenced closing, Archie barged into the shop and rumbled toward me. Thrusting the article down on the counter he launched into a blistering dissertation as his hairy belly, peek-a-booed out between his suspenders: "This is your problem! You use words around here no one understands." He continued the dissection jeering: "And you aren't socializing with members either. Don't you realize every woman wants you pinching their behinds once in a while?" The berating went on five more minutes. It was late, I was tired, and the glamour being chosen one of Canada's up and coming young pros vanished. Finally finished, the harrier plundered his way back to the loud night in progress. Previously, when dealing with directors, I'd been accustomed to more civilized and diplomatic means of drubbing. That night instead, I felt beaten and bankrupt. Emotionally swollen, I quietly melted into the parking lot. Arriving home to Jackie, I wept from fatigue and every golf pro's nightmare … knowing I'd aroused an enemy among the board. In reality, I'd been confronted by **the SS**!

Journal Entry #238: The SS (Part 2)
Dedicated to *Everett Olson*

They were called **the SS**, meaning Silent Sect. Supposedly, they were male members of a phantom cult, revelling behind the moniker of some masonic mafioso. While their identities and existence seemed shrouded by speculation, no one disproved the myth either.

Jack Fletcher was supposedly their spiritual head. A retired hockey pro, he had a ten game career with the NHL Montréal Canadians. He retired playing Okanagan senior hockey, using his money to build a local business empire. Fletcher was treated like Don Corleone ... the godfather. But being revered, he was also arrogant and egotistical. Jim Mazurek, or Maki, was a retired realtor from Manitoba. He thrived competing in Calcutta tournaments and was the club's certified sandbagging legend. I respected his mettle for mortgaging his personal property to finance building the back nine holes during the club's emergence.

John and Ron Rudder were siblings who owned a tractor dealership before retiring. Naturally cynical and suspicious, they were probably Levi Strauss's best customers. The SS's bright spot was the sprightly elder Tom Morrison, a retired magazine distributor. He loved to imbibe when playing, implicating a flask as part of his arsenal. Morrison dressed effeminately in pastels including Italian patent leather shoes. Always jocular with grunting laughs, he had the most fun, but only fools wouldn't have thought him shrewd. Bert Proulx was the group's chronic complainer. His tense face appeared spring-loaded, ready to uncoil. I was told he made my predecessor's life hell. Victor Sawatski had purchased the tractor dealership from the Rudders and made a handsome profit reselling it. With a middle name Dean, he was known as V. D. Sawatski. His blonde, voluptuous wife didn't mind the initials though, as long as she was kept.

Another crony was Al Bilko, a local fuel-depot manager. He came across as a tough, wise guy because stories of his wife's infidelity with members was more than gossip. To his credit, he still sponsored a men's event, christening it after himself. It's still played for today. Harry Freshet was the sect's stooge. He'd been a co-founder of Canada's largest independent tire dealership before cashing out. Ian Buick was nervous and temperamental. His brother owned that tire firm and Ian's fuse was so short, his reactions were always unpredictable.

They were the elders!

Like in mafia culture, however, Kal Lake had clusters of middle-agers with avuncular affections for the older, wiser Cosa Nostra. The collection of white- and blue-collar fledglings were the club's nasties. As torches were passed and club members sought directorships, often it were those probates who oozed their way into controlling positions, navigating the club.

There wasn't anything formal about the SS. They were normal philanthropic businessmen, strutting about the valley, griping as much between themselves as with everyone else. At the club, they played cards so late Bibeau just handed them keys to lock up. If they didn't like certain members … their victims eventually quit and golfed elsewhere. I was unsure of my approval rating, but they patronized the shop, which I appreciated. What was said behind closed doors however, was different. I survived because of my work ethic. I was like the eager, young urchin fetching cigarettes or sandwiches for the Don. Except I looked after the prick's golf needs.

Journal Entry #239: The SS (Part 3)

Dedicated to *Alfie and Ester Desnoyer*

My struggles which originated that first season, tragically ended twenty-two years later. Its narrative however, began before I arrived. Over time, the number of pros who revolved through Kal Lake doors was evidence to that. I just lasted longer.

When writing this, two facts mirrored that belief. First, the club fired yet another of its legions. He was one with muscle for the mission. A respected PGA veteran whose integrity, knowledge, and inner stamina challenged the SS. One who wouldn't back down. Second, Europe's Ryder Cup team overtook the Americans in a stunning upset at Chicago's Medinah. Significant in that Medinah was designed by the same vaudeville artist who laid out Kal Lake's initial course back in 1913. Then, Tom Bendelow travelled North America with his wooden stakes. Negotiating with community leaders, he laid out crude courses for the sum of twenty-five dollars. On his transcontinental train trips back then, Kal Lake was one of those encounters. He began there before World War I. Medinah followed in 1924.

During my first season, to understand Kal Lake's history, I trampled hundreds of orchard acres, searching for Bendelow's original site. Finally, using distant mountain profiles from early photographs, I found it below a road, which today shoots skiers up to a popular resort. After several postwar relocations, the course settled in its current location, evolving into an eighteen-holer.

There, swaggering local businessmen were seduced by opportunities of a potential activity lair. The blustery crowd with their swank values differed from conventional club members. Every organization had those types, one's driven by personal gain. At most courses though, they were minorities, never capturing control. At Kal Lake, it was the opposite. That group, **the SS** ... never abdicated. And as generations prospered so too did they.

Journal Entry #240: Gold

Dedicated to *Howie Stevenson*

Golf pros who worked by contract were always subject to membership gossip and jealousy regarding their revenues. Typically, yet ironically, the club wanted a business oriented pro, but not one overtly successful.

My predecessor, Chuck Jenzen joined the club in his forced retirement. One day he privately sought me out with warning. He'd recently golfed with a new member ... a showy realtor, he called Jonesy. Raising an eyebrow, the old pro cautiously confided: "Keep your eyes on Jonesy. He didn't know me, and over beer was bitching about the money you were generating with power cart rentals. He was actually estimating your take!"

The carts were being rented out regularly, but I still had to pay down a thirty-five thousand power cart loan, which wasn't going away soon. Plus there were only a dozen vehicles. The fact Jonesy was assessing revenues, but not expenses was disturbing. I learned the SS were also doing their math.

Before relocating to BC, I had no conscience being profitable. That was due to a seminar I attended in Alberta, where the speaker was the province's most respected golf pro. His belief was: "If your professional's doing well, your golf course will be doing the same!" That comment made sense and consequently I avoided concerns of profiteering. Further, I was always cautious not to gouge customers. If I knew handsome profits could be generated and members benefited fairly, I went for it. It had to be mutual though. Finances also influenced that philosophy. With no pension, we were in debt one hundred and ten thousand, renting accommodation, driving a nearly done Datsun and supporting two children.

Eventually, we were able to afford a home and needless to say, my conscience weighed-in when selecting a realtor!

Journal Entry #241: The Hustler (Self Control)

Dedicated to *the Arkells*

In business, occasionally there were competitors ascribing to and advertising more than reality. Uncertified, they danced-to-their-own-tune, persuasively luring unwary customers. Often described as quacks, they too existed in the golf industry.

Steve Pleye was a well-known pro throughout the Okanagan. Well-known because he nomadically migrated from job to job. Who wouldn't know him? By the time I left Kal Lake, more than two decades later, he'd shuffled through a dozen valley courses. A renegade fanatic of American instructor Jimmy Ballard, Pleye publicly condemned the PGA.

Pleye's methods didn't parallel professionals I'd been accustomed to. And as was his nature my members were solicited for lessons in inappropriate ways.

Like the day, he golfed with three Kal Lake members. After their round, I walked over to use the clubhouse washroom and found him immersed within a teaching demonstration. In normal relationships between hosts and visiting pros, there's usually camaraderie and light banter.

On that occasion though, my greeting was met by only silence as their eyes trailed my route to the restroom. In the following moments, it was unclear what was louder, the sounds swishing the bowl fronting me or the adjacent room's muted voices. Pleye had been promoting himself, a behaviour among pros I was unfamiliar with. And it was only time before the board and SS began gossiping where the membership were taking lessons!

It brewed many uneasy feelings, but I also knew there was little I could do. Openly confronting Pleye, might have only martyred him. Plus, it wasn't right. In the end, I forced myself to mind my own business, inexplicably emerging with insight. In any career profession, one either commits to being the very best they're capable of … or succumb to veins of such bogus showmen.

Soon after Pleye moved on. Decades later he was still roaming.

Journal Entry #242: Fernando's Open

Dedicated to *Mark Longworth*

One of the more unusual events I saw at Kal Lake involved a pig. And one of the most memorable members I served there was Fernando.

Fernando had distinct Mediterranean features including a swarthy complexion and black remaining hair. A robust figure and raven attire coerced images of Italian professional Costantino Rocca. He was possessed by a spontaneous, uneasy laughter which ironically set most at ease despite rumours of a Mafia money laundering history. His mysterious origin was rumoured to be Washington State, where he allegedly nursed underground connections with lavish lumber barons. Other times, he claimed descendance from Spanish royalty.

Fernando seemed friendly enough, and because his numerous assertions included being a former pro, we hit it off. There was no way I was becoming familiar with the strange man though. His bandito image instinctively roused red flags.

During the July long weekend, the club hosted its annual Kal Lake Open accompanied by a meal.

In my second year, Fernando talked Bibeau into hosting a Barcelonian pig roast for the event. A large hole was excavated by the clubhouse, where an obese swine was lowered over embers and covered. Weeks prior to the first round, Fernando sat in his plastic lawn chair, overseeing the roast like an expectant mother.

While the pig baked, hysteria grew daily as members lusted its resurrection.

The tournament dinner was scheduled for five the afternoon of round one. At noon, the animal was finally hoisted and displayed. However, as the beast laid in the searing sun, it was suddenly swarmed by golfers goring, pecking, and devouring it. Within minutes, the carcass was reduced to rind and bone. All the while Fernando, was pumped like a rock star. Meanwhile, forgotten in the feast, were the players who hadn't finished their golf yet. Contestants finishing their rounds without food, angrily vowed never to return.

The following year, the Open received a meagre entry of eight golfers. The tournament was cancelled permanently and organizers asked why?

I knew, and spoke up during the summer board meeting. Instead of addressing the problem though, they shot the messenger!

Meanwhile, Fernando eluded pundits. Maintaining his macabre image, he played a year or two more before eventually vanishing ... possibly from assassination?

Journal Entry #243: Mack the Knife

Dedicated to *Dwayne MacDonald and Sue Carder*

It was once explained: "Out of ten people ... three will like you, three won't, and the rest will be indifferent." Still another said: "In relationships, it's about respect. Deep down, people know where they stand by how they're treated. It's revealed in speech, demeanour, and action."

Both opinions probably held weight and had I been equipped with that life knowledge my second year, it may have been the tool to toggle awkward customer relations. A young pro, fresh in business either learns swiftly or suffers consequences.

A local lawyer became infatuated with golf. He supported the shop and one day asked to use my club repair room. I was embarrassed working out of antiquated facilities. Further, I suffered from hay fever then. That day, the allergies were severe and I politely refused him, offering instead to complete the work later myself. The next day, he shocked me with a stunning phone call. Overnight he researched his purchase history with me and in revenge, vowed never to spend another dime in the shop. Business people become mentally equipped to fend off attacks like that. Not me! His impeachment emotionally scarred me for years. The golf industry was distinct from other retail outlets because pros saw their customers regularly. They're forced into resolving raw emotional issues. Resolve them? I didn't know how! I was distressed every day I saw him, constantly reweighing the infraction. In hindsight, I'd have handled the situation differently, but then my foreseeability was still maturing.

Another member wanted a gift for his wife. He put a set of clubs on hold without paying. Many months passed without seeing him and eventually I concluded he'd decided against the purchase, as occasionally occurs in retail. Consequently, I resold the clubs. Later, his personality took a dramatic turn. He became aloof, taking pokes at me in mixed company. A person picks up on that. Years later, he confirmed it was because of the clubs. I was amazed he'd held a grudge that long. Even after explaining the circumstances, it took years regaining his respect.

Similar incidents began recurring. I was becoming a weary punching bag, collecting impassioned wounds from each licking. Was I too thin-skinned, green-around-the-edges, or lacking business savvy? As the grievances escalated, the SS too inflamed the fodder with gossip. I even began questioning my own respect, especially when looking customers in the eye and taking stands. The weariness impaired my judgment when four tourists visited. I was inexcusably rude to one of the women who was inappropriately dressed. Later, her husband privately reprimanded me for my misdemeanour. And he was right, for it was me who acted inappropriate.

I didn't know where to seek advice for the despair. Young and impaired, I sought answers anywhere I could find them.

It came one day when leaving the clubhouse. There on the cement patio, I saw **Mack the Knife**. Mack was a linesman whose nickname originated from his lean build. Tense, tough and not one to tangle with, he often sat alone outside the clubhouse, smoking and sipping java. On that sunny day, I didn't know if the spirals originated from his cigarette or coffee. But seeing him though, I must have appeared worried, for he unexpectedly encouraged me saying: "It's not you! Don't let them get to you. You're not as bad as you think. You're decent to everyone here and treat them equal. I respect that!"

It's been said respect has to be learned and earned, but I found it instead from that sole encounter. For months after, I desperately clung to that redneck sermon as only wretched find in branches over cliffs.

Amid the social chaos of that turbulent season, Mack's sliver of faith revived me, implicating that golden rule of treating everyone as they would want to be treated.

Journal Entry #244: Lonely too Long

Dedicated to *Bob Bricker, Sr.*

As the season pulsated along, the workload became overwhelming. Only rare moments allowed me to flush out more about the golf swing. One arose from an ironic source.

Schoolteachers joined golf clubs too. There were those in the industry however who saw them as different. First, they left impressions of knowing everything, which were luxuries owned by none. And second, servers working most clubhouse bars affirmed educators were among labour's thriftiest tippers. Golf pros didn't receive tips, at least not formally. Yet, ironically one came from a schoolteacher.

Tom McEvay reminded me of a university lecturer. A high school music instructor, he had grey wavy hair and wire rim glasses sleeping half way down his nose. He was the methodical type who spoke only after thought. One afternoon, we were dissecting the golf swing and he asked if the take-away (start of each swing) began with hands or shoulders? Having earlier discussed that with Open champion Henry Cotton, the Brit convinced me hands started the takeaway. But Tom's question left me curious as I began experimenting on the range. There, initiating rotation from my body instead, I not only saw the natural and time efficiency of core movement, but its relationship to swing plane.

From then on, my shoulders turned the swing. Using analogies, I'd point out to students, "It's the dog that wags the tail, rather than the opposite!" Later, attending the seminars of swing guru David Leadbetter, I included the lower body in that same pivoting. I'd been **lonely too long**, but thanks to an educator was another step closer toward understanding the swing.

Journal Entry #245: Ain't Even Done With the Night

Dedicated to *Ray Miller*

Part of my job entailed golfing with members when I could. As an example I played most men's night with three members ... always different golfers. On one of those evenings I scored my first hole-in-one.

It was calm and the sun was setting when we arrived at the 175-yard seventeenth. My playing partners included a blue-collar telephone employee named Antonio, who reportedly was a violent unionist. Stephan was a brash, fair-haired forestry student who later became a director. A thin-boned, mild mannered senior named Ray rounded out our group. Out of respect, I teed off last. I pushed my six-iron, meaning as a right-hander, it shot right of target ... straight without curving. The ball landed in front of a sand trap guarding the old green then. Exercising rites of a reclusive free spirit though, the sphere broke away and unexpectedly jumped sideways over the bunker. The delinquent persevered a defying mission suddenly ... vanishing! I'd seen holes-in-one before, but not from my clubs. To witness it from a distance, rolling along the green and abruptly vaporizing was surreal. Astonished, I instinctively threw my club in the air ... like Nicklaus did after winning his first Open at St. Andrews.

Journal Entry #246: Capilano

Dedicated to *Zesty*

Each year a life insurance company sponsored a promotional pro-am. Three members qualified, accompanying their pro to the finals at one of British Columbia's premier clubs. One year that venue was Vancouver's famed **Capilano**.

I'd dreamt of playing her for years, but before my practise round, saw a person from my past in the clubhouse. Smartly decked in a black and cardinal tartan sports jacket, his freckles and red, wavy hair returned unsettling memories. Jim Lefevre, the fiery Mayfair manager who admonished me years earlier, had moved on to become Capilano's administrator. I wrestled with thoughts he might recognize me.

Located in the British Properties high above West Vancouver, Capilano's effeminate mounds and fantasizing bunkers seemed born from her creator's erotic imagination. Each hole of the Stanley Thompson classic was distinguished, independent, and pristine framed by towering cedar and Douglas fir. Her subtlest feature however was within her geography, as hilly climbs never felt tiring. The par-five eighteenth was a dramatic finisher, plodding uphill to a plateaued stage. There, golfers felt naked, captured in performance to the delight of viewers from the above Tudor clubhouse.

I golfed that day with one of our qualifiers, a schoolteacher named Norm McCreedie. We didn't like each other too much then. Over time though, a mutual respect developed. Brash, crude and smart, he was an in-your-face Ukrainian mathematics teacher, who relished his beverages. Near the par-three fourth, Capilano's superintendent had fenced off newly seeded ground. McCreedie, who'd been imbibing since teeing off, took a shortcut over the rope. Sinking deep over his shoes, he gorged trails through the moist goop. I looked around, wishing the ground would swallow me. I envisioned Lefevre's apparition suddenly appearing, disparaging McCreedie's behaviour, while abetting me. To quote famous golf broadcaster Henry Longhurst: "I moved silently away lest fate mistake me for an accomplice and in some way give me the hammer too."

Despite McCreedie's questionable etiquette though, he was ironically intelligent. When describing relationships between others, he'd often claim, "Everything comes down to respect." He also borrowed the line, "Say what you mean, and mean what you say."

I left Capilano that day in awe, thwarted none-the-less by recurring notions I hadn't seen the last of Lefevre.

Journal Entry #247: Olympic
Dedicated to *Ed Ouchi*

After Christmas my second year, Jimmy invited me to visit his family in San Francisco. Before leaving, I practised in a nearby town called Lumby, loosening up before next day's play in California.

Snow had crept down the adjacent mountains, but the valley remained clear and pleasant. Directed by a blue highway sign, "Lumby GC," I drove up a lumpy gravel road to the top of a bench. There, December breezes used boughs of fir to sweep the modest octagon clubhouse. Nine-holes existed with sand greens; similar to those I terrorized as a youngster. The club operated by an honour system, meaning no staff … where customers slipped money through a door vent. She was a rough and tumble course with panoramic views of the valley below my feet. On one hole I shanked a shot right of her green, out-of-bounds. Then mesmerized, I saw my result magically conform to ground slope and return back to the green. On the next hole, chiseled from rock cliffs among sheep, a wooden platform cryptically confirmed the teeing area. Positioned out of bounds, golfers teed off there to a putting surface below … in-bounds. Greens were accessorized with cocoa mats linked to chains, used when smoothing surfaces for those who followed.

Before leaving, I looked out toward the surrounding mountains which loomed judicial, ancestral, and paternal. They seemed to be hinting I was earth's sole golfing inhabitant.

It was a complete contrast next day at San Francisco's infamous Olympic Club.

While San Francisco benefited from Tony Bennett charm, **Olympic** owned historic US Open narratives. There in 1955, unknown Jack Fleck denied the unbeatable Ben Hogan an unprecedented fifth championship. It was also where Buffalo Billy Casper stole the same title from Arnold Palmer during the king's stunning 1966 collapse.

The atmosphere was naturally humid and floral with a stagnant Frisco fragrance. I remembered launching long irons into faraway greens, bunkers shaped like the Joker's mouth from Batman fame, and fairways threaded through gnarled cypress and towering eucalyptus.

But the parable of those two days was the blunt distinction separating the humble sand green course from the Open venue by the bay. And in that re-count, my fondest memories always drifted toward the former.

Journal Entry #248: San Francisco (Wear Flowers in Your Hair)

Dedicated to *A. W. Tillinghast*

During that trip I discovered one of my favourite courses, the **San Francisco** Golf Club. Created by American architect A. W. Tillinghast, it embodied aspects of golf I grew to appreciate … shotmaking over brawn. An example being her downhill par-three, seventh.

Short and strategic, it camouflaged misery to the unsuspecting. Whether negotiating the green's tight entry, its wrinkled putting surface, or flanking bunker … one slip and players conceded shots.

Interestingly, the most famous shot there, didn't originate from the tee, green, or any hole-in-one. Further, it wasn't the heritage of Callaway, Ping, or TaylorMade ancestry. Instead, it was triggered by a Belgian .58 caliber pistol on her site in 1859!

Below the tee and right, a small clearing affirms the site of California's last duel. Two politicians of the day, Senator Broderick and David Terry put their opinions of slavery on the line. In the aftermath, Broderick was killed! Terry, then Chief Justice of the Supreme Court was acquitted of murder. As a direct result of ensuing unpopularity, Terry bowed out of politics. The outcome forwarded fights against slavery. With Terry out,

President Abraham Lincoln assigned Stephen Field to the vacancy. The appointment inspired a southern leaning coalition supporting abolitionist movements. California remained part of the union.

If that doesn't move readers beyond historical mumbo-jumbo, consider then ... the United States **with** legal slavery, or **absent** the state of California. Such was the influence of that shot!

Journal Entry #249: Cypress Point
Dedicated to *Jim Langley*

The classic's author Robert Louis Stevenson, supposedly wrote: "The Monterey Peninsula is the most felicitous meeting place between land and sea," meaning pleasant.

Its 17-Mile Drive routed Jimmy and I through immense bonsai forests, where mature cypress were chiseled naturally by wind and rain through time.

Eventually it led us to our destination, Pebble Beach's Cypress Point Club. Harbouring no expectations, we introduced ourselves to pro Jim Langley. Remembering the introductory letter I dispatched weeks earlier, and fully aware Jimmy wasn't an industry colleague, he permitted us to play. Very few golfers I've known have ever accessed Cypress Point, let alone without a member. I'm unsure why Langley comped us except it was the holidays. When he told us to get our gear, it felt like a lottery win.

Cypress Point wasn't any conventional private course. Exclusive in the strictest sense, she was described as celestial and understood then to be the finest offering in golf.

Her human creator, English architect Alister MacKenzie, sculptured her into an existence which continues assaulting time. She was a trio of courses in one. Foremost she was a links, with many holes roving the Pacific's ocean dunes. She was also a spectacular parkland walkabout, lashed by cypress forests. Whether on her links, park or wilderness, I felt privileged just being there, as if guest of some philanthropic golf god.

And if true, that divine one might be responsible for the shot I stole there.

Her second nine began with a modest par-five. My third shot there found the green's backside, where I faced a delicate shot to a pin forty feet beyond. Choosing a sand wedge for the subtle chip, I assumed my address position. But as I thrust down and through the ball, I entered a mental portal in space, where I participated in slow-moving time frames. During impact, I honestly felt the ball rolling up my club's face, seemingly washboarding across each groove.

While the flash was fleeting, the experience seemed as long as ten-seconds. My ball finished eight inches from the hole, but it was the essence of captive cinema which remained with me over time.

I remember every individual hole at Cypress Point, even forty years beyond. Purists claim her eighteenth is weak. To me though, she was the breath recaptured after exhilaration, the summarizing chapter of a page turning novel … or that afterward peace, laying with a lover.

Journal Entry #250: The Coldest Night of the Year

Dedicated to *John and Joan Nakonechny*

When confronted by flesh-eating crocodiles or charging grizzlies, any male would express fear. Probably only fools wouldn't. Yet, why don't males shed their ego admitting fear of other men? Might it explain bullying on school grounds or later in business? I'm one who wasn't ashamed conceding that despair.

He was a club captain who unleashed a reign of terror in my third season.

The job description of captain wasn't always consistent. At some courses, the titles were only symbolic. Others directed appointees to administer club events. Others still, authorized more power than intended. That's what Darren Hearn found out.

Hearn was a stout, intimidating Scottish immigrant who joined Kal Lake soon after I arrived. The son of a bartender, he grew up in Glasgow's savage Gorbal slums. He retired to the Okanagan with his wife and two daughters after making a modest fortune in Vancouver property management.

Through naturally despotic methods though, his influence took root and before long was voted in captain.

After, Hearn charged me with making his daughters golfers. Then after inspecting the club constitution's fine print, he discovered his new post wielded more influence than the president's. He claimed himself Kal Lake's most powerful board member, and took full advantage of it.

Armed with coercion and above average intelligence, Hearn began reinforcing the point daily. Policy meetings became disputes, where often he'd terminate them with levitating eyes of disgust. Then vanishing, he'd leave victims fearful of his comments to others. One such controversy concerned tee times. Tee times were golf appointments customers made through pro shops.

When I arrived at Kal Lake, its calendar was a scattered mess of bookings far into the future. Members could schedule one o'clock everyday for a year if they chose. And if they failed showing, the club absorbed the revenue losses. My resolution was to change the format to forty-eight hour advance booking. I went further, suggesting tourists could reserve ahead to organize their trips. This infuriated Hearn who liked his regular appointments and revoked the idea. It festered into a heated exchange at a hastily called director's meeting. Bibeau didn't help either, siding with the brawny intimidator. Miraculously, the board voted in my proposal. I never forgot the fear when facing him down that cold night.

Hearn never forgot either, and the pressures became enormous teaching his daughters. Fortunately, I took his youngest to the national level.

Thankfully, Hearn wasn't part of the SS, but he tolerated them. Had fate woven a more corrupt cloth however, he might have joined them, accelerating my fate. As luck had it, he antagonized them and they later ousted him, for allegedly pocketing club funds.

I'd been in the industry fifteen years by then, and during that time never felt such fear from another man in golf before. It was only then I recognized that emulsion separating respect from torment. The latter a disgusting fuel bullies depend on when maintaining oppression on school grounds, in business … and even politics!

Journal Entry #251: The Way They Were (Part 6)

Dedicated to *the Blankleys*

The Okanagan's pleasing climate was a refuge for retirees and tourism. Consequently, numerous courses existed from the north down, staffed with pros satisfying the various customers and their needs.

Revelstoke Doug was a man's man, yet ironically the suave kind. I looked forward to our annual inter-clubs in the northern town. Later, he became head pro at Vancouver's affluent Point Grey. Sockeye Bill was the head man at Salmon Arm who toiled exhaustingly there in turbulent times.

I called the silver-haired fox at Kamloops, Klondike Mike. His trademark could have been the perfect part in his hair. I was witness to his rare double eagle at Capilano's opening hole. He was the only pro in the valley who out-lasted me. His local peer at the Robert Trent Jones' Rivershore, was Briar Barry. A fiery redhead whose first love was curling, he'd have relished capturing Canada's top bonspiel, the Briar. Eventually I heard he left the industry, edging toward other ventures.

Swirvin' Irvin was Kelowna's eclectic, heavy smoking pro at the cities' private club. Casting flaunting images of Andy Warhol, he too eventually left, entrepreneuring a local driving range. The charismatic showman at Kelowna's Gallagher's Canyon, was slick Dick. With an effeminate demeanour and George Clooney looks, Dick always got his way. A promotor and acquaintance to affluence, he retired early passing away the same.

The grandaddy was Bob the Kid from Penticton. On the verge of retirement, the paternal pro was a talented amateur prior to entering the ranks.

Whether it was borrowing product, golfing or occasionally picking their brains, I dealt with them all at one time or another. A microcosm of diverse personalities who typically defined our industry.

Journal Entry #252: Eye in the Sky
Dedicated to *Stu Gardner*

During that third year, as anxiety, frustration, and naivety monopolized the moments, I was forced to grow up in the business world. I learned more about myself as I milled among a subversive group of members who wanted me removed. In their eyes, I was a puzzle part without place. Was it was my workaholism, resistance to habituating their peeler bars, or just preferring free time with my family? I didn't know, but in that corrosive climate, a contributing factor was the assistant I'd been coerced to employ. He had too many subtle ties to the SS, forcing me to delicately cut-him-loose. Consequently I hired Stu.

When employing assistants then, I looked for those who could teach, interpret product knowledge, repair clubs, and promote golf in pleasing ways. Stu possessed them all, but I was primarily interested in one particular detail, undeniable loyalty to my family. I needed a pro the SS could trust, but who'd remain committed to me. Stu became my **eye in the sky**, ultimately buying me time.

Journal Entry #253: That's the Way Boys Are
Dedicated to *Taeko*

Stu began in the industry working for the Bygraves at Edmonton's Derrick. He wasn't there long before landing a pro job at an obscure nine-hole prairie course west of the city. The owners later transferred him to their other concern, a driving range near Vancouver. There, in a dead-end career, he reached out to me. I hired him conditionally to be the eyes I couldn't see with.

Stu was extremely handsome and could have doubled as the '60s rock star Johnny Rivers. Several years my junior, he owned eclectic sides to a magnetic personality. While challenged in relationships, he proved none-the-less devoted. So much so, I turned my back on his ardent affair with a young SS member's trophy wife.

His practical jokes became club legend. A customer once asked him about renting a **pull** cart. Stu showed our rentals caravanned outside and feigning concern, pointed to one in the middle claiming: "We only have one left, the rest are **push** carts … you can tell by the number of spokes." He enjoyed gambling, but sadly lost every check he earned. Sadly because he was ironically wise when weighing opportunity.

When Jackie's parents relocated to join us, her dad helped in the shop. There, he and Stu became a pair to reckon with. Vast ages apart, they shared a mischievous nature, guided by the same comedic devil.

And as time passed, tensions settled around the shop. It became critical, for the end of my first three-year contract was near and the directors would deliberate my renewal.

Journal Entry #254: West End Girls

Dedicated to *Fred and Maureen*

In those first three years, there was little social life, even given the course's folksy nature.

But a new couple moved to the valley then and invited us for dinner. That evening, I fell asleep, exhausted. The couple, Fred and Maureen, weren't offended and I knew they'd become friends for life.

Consequently, Jackie and Maureen began golfing together, shedding the awkwardness of fitting into a new community. One afternoon, they wanted to play and the only time was with two young SS members. Stu decided to have fun with the boys, who were starting off. Putting on a straight face, he tested the ego driven candidates asking if they'd tolerate two women joining them. Their eyes and heads rolled skyward. One was a high-profile homebuilder, the other, a not-so-humble lawyer. As both dug in for the upcoming hours of torture, Jackie got over her ball. She launched a shot into the horizon lapping both men's performances. Maureen's went further! Stu's mischievous grin implied the eventual outcome. We watched with humour as the pompous duo screwed themselves into the ground with each desperate shot, striving to mitigate manly losses.

When it was over and they were thrashed, their vain responses were, "rematch!" The many that followed were all predictable.

Journal Entry #255: Uptown Girl

Dedicated to *Anne Newman*

Jackie was an only child. When we moved to the Okanagan, her parents were abruptly abandoned. When they sold out and joined us, we suddenly had built-in sitters freeing Jackie to resume golfing.

Soon after, she competed in the Canadian Women's Amateur at Winnipeg's St. Charles Country Club. While there, she met and played with a teenage sensation named Gail Anderson. Later, Anderson moved to Kelowna, married, and became Gail Graham. There, she and Jackie were reacquainted, competing throughout the valley. In their numerous head-to-head encounters, everyone else played for third, renewing Jackies' competitive spark. It opened a new chapter for Jackie as she began assaulting more tournament records, this time in British Columbia.

Golf, like other athletic endeavours, is a developmental sport accelerated naturally through the physical osmosis of adrenaline from advanced competition.

Journal Entry #256: The Abbey

Dedicated to *Hal Reich*

As club professional, to compete and network with fellow pros, I began attending our national championship. One year, the event was in Toronto where I also visited Canada's new Open venue, Glen Abbey.

The paragon of professional golf, Jack Nicklaus built **the Abbey**. And it was there my artistic impressions of design began articulating themselves. I found myself sorting between the new architecture and turn-of-the-century masterpieces from golf's golden era. And when doing so, my conscience disappointingly rationalized Glen Abbey as not only uninteresting and unmemorable … but sterilized and sanitary. It appeared but a monument built to the maker himself. As the site of our nation's premier golf event, I was anticipating more from golf's greatest campaigner. Were my expectations of the apostle turned architect too critical? Was my posture too demanding of one who commanded million dollar design fees back then? Were my anticipations of another Capilano or Jasper too lofty?

No doubt there are many, and certainly the Golden Bear himself who would defend opposing views. Never-the-less, after censuring Nicklaus's creative merits, I left the Abbey that day guilt-ridden. Decades later however, I exonerated myself when sadly hearing of the Golden Bear's aberrant attempt to influence the 2020 US election … by endorsing Donald Trump!

Journal Entry #257: Moe Norman (Part 3)

Dedicated to *Ed Shewchuk*

The club pro's championship was played at Toronto's historic Mississauga where my playing companion was resident pro, Gar Hamilton, Jr. Hamilton confided **Moe Norman** was cooped up nearby in a Kitchener motel close to another famous Open venue, Westmount.

After the tournament, I drove to Kitchener, hoping to track Moe down and learn more about the swing from golf's quintessential ball striker. I found his hideout but disappointingly not him. I continued on though, golfing Westmount on that hot, humid afternoon. After, I cooled off in their clubhouse finding it somewhat abandoned. It was sometimes like that on weekends at old-established clubs. As I wandered the hallway though, drifts of television lured me to a nearby room.

Peaking into the vacant spike bar, I was U-turning away when sighting a solitary figure cornering the television. Reclined in a plump arm chair, cradling his golf club sat the one and only … Moe Norman. There seemingly urchin, he was lasered into the game show, *Wheel of Fortune*.

I pushed myself into the room, rummaging for excuses to converse. Instead though, acknowledging his hypnotic state, I surrendered to privacy and talked myself out of the invasion. It was the right decision too! Years later I saw that same engaged look on my granddaughter Myelle's face when she watched Elmo on *Sesame Street*.

I quietly exited Westmount's clubhouse and returned to Toronto. All the while though, my mind wandered back to Westmount, musing my own *Wheel of Fortune*. I pondered the outcome had fate instead steered me toward simply joining Norman and watching the game show too? Pat Sajak, Vanna White, Moe and me?

Journal Entry #258: Motor City (Oakland Hills)

Dedicated to *Walt Wills*

In 1985, Okanagan's Dave Barr nearly captured the US Open in Detroit at **Oakland Hills**. There the Kelowna native came within Jimmy Hoffa's shadow of being the first Canuck to win that major. I played the Donald Ross design immediately after.

Driving Telegraph Road there, the '60s **Motor City** hit "My World is Empty," revitalized itself on the radio. The song, performed by the Motown Supremes, fulfilled desires to understand what else drove Detroit beside cars. The refrain finished as I passed the Machus Red Fox Restaurant. The site where the infamous Teamsters boss mysteriously vanished and where I exited toward Oakland Hills.

Inside its white, stately columned clubhouse, their shop staff partnered me with a member claiming to be rock singer, Bob Seger's lawyer. Among my shortcomings, I'm continually challenged dealing with the not-so-humble ... like Biden's predecessor and some pro athletes. The attorney appeared no less brassy.

Later we arrived at the famous par-four sixteenth, a short dogleg right over water. The same place Gary Player lofted a stunning effort over willows to win the '73 PGA.

In dim remaining light, I watched the attorney approach that very green. Using a roundhouse swing, his ball landed near the flag and bounded over.

He was the type who talked and walked while his ball was airborne. I followed with a similar shot, finishing stiff.

As I marked my ball though, the lawyer snapped, "That's my ball!" Caught off guard, I replied, "No, it's a Titleist four." "Yeah," he persisted. "That's my ball!" Clearly we were playing the same number, but unlike him, I knew where his was. However, common sense and civility prevailed. First, I wouldn't be playing there if not for him, and second, staunch defenses to caustic confrontation seemed frivolous.

Compromising instead, I chipped his ball on and made par. We finished in darkness illuminated by a prism of glistening chandeliers peering out between clubhouse columns.

I always wished Barr had won that Open. During my years in the Okanagan I met him occasionally, but knew others who considered him glowering. To me he was misunderstood. Some tour pros looked certain ways when concentrating and playing for mortgages. He was never in my face!

Journal Entry #259: Inverness

Dedicated to *Ab Mills*

God measures men by what they are
Not in what they in wealth possess
This vibrant message chimes afar
The voice of Inverness

—Inverness Club

I left Detroit and headed for Toledo, Ohio. There I visited the Inverness Club for reasons only golf pros might understand.

In 1920, Inverness opened her doors to golf professionals. Prior to that, pros weren't allowed access to clubhouses across North America nor Europe. That changed in Toledo and I was grateful for her part in golf history.

Inverness, also designed by Ross, had a rare friendly poise. Her calming influence was void of the social veneers haunting many country clubs.

Possessing such qualities, while uncompromising duty and obligation, maybe the ultimate recipe every course should strive for.

The same mood penetrated their pro shop. There, I introduced myself to then professional, Don Perne, a man polished by integrity. He was more interested in my little shop back home than my own members were. Touring me around the famous PGA and US Open site, he insured I had range balls for practise and a game arranged. He made a young ideologist feel part of his club, a deportment paralleling Inverness's mission.

Journal Entry #260: Shattered Dreams

Dedicated to *Bob McKenzie*

After year three, my pro shop contract was reviewed. Never before was I subject to such emotional pressure as that first term. And yet in the faith of my commitment, I'd risen to it. I described that to the vice president at a downtown restaurant meeting. There I requested a five-year extension, learning in shock, the board closely voted not renewing! They extended it, but by only a pale two years, which smelled probational. It shattered me, stirring feelings of fatigue and wear.

Dejected, I reflected back to my Edmonton years, cross examining Mayfair's self-made millionaires. The one's who assured me with that frugal advice: "If you work hard, everything turns out for the best." And earlier still, Gary Player echoed that same rhetoric in a personal hand written letter. I was confused! In my diligence righting the wrongs of that decrepit shop, I nearly bankrupted my emotions and family. The meeting concluded with a new agreement rewritten literally upon a restaurant serviette.

Some good news prevailed though. Loomis was appointed club President, while my doctor, Cec Hamilton became the new VP. Hamilton had a genuine interest in both my family and the club. A transplanted Australian, he was supported by down-under vision and clarity. I trusted my doctor, but was cautious of the lawyer. Occasionally he appeared in-my-corner, but then I'd find him atypically schmoozing with the SS.

An attorney rewriting a contract on paper napkins seemed cloudy at best, but it was better than nothing. In the following seasons, I'd come face-to-face with even more challenge and change.

Journal Entry #261: When You're Gone

Dedicated to *Dr. Bryn Jones*

Stu was the human spacer needed to save my career. Somehow he distracted the SS, buying me that two year extension.

I couldn't understand the problem then. In the big picture, our course was prospering since I took over. The shop changes were successful, the club was enjoying historical green fee revenues, its membership doubled, the junior program was envied and the course was extremely busy. Nevertheless, I wasn't satisfying certain members.

Everyday I continued stick-handling around subtle, subversive perils that made shop life edgy. The smutty architects hung out in their shanty off the main clubhouse, gossiping like trolls. Regardless, several events took place that second term which altered Kal Lake's destiny.

Stu applied for his own head pro's job at a neighbouring course and was hired. Soon after, Kal Lake agreed to design a new clubhouse with an updated pro shop. "Things come in threes" is a saying and, sure enough, it was true. Bibeau was lured away to a new venture and resigned! And silently, like helium balloons rise away, so too did years of anguish. My luck would become even better when they sought Bibeau's replacement.

Journal Entry #262: The Mentor (Part 2)

Dedicated to *Charlie and Betty Pierce*

Resumes of candidates for the vacated manager's position poured in daily. The new president asked my opinion about one in particular. As I read the condensed hand written letter, my emotions sank and surged simultaneously.

The author was Jim Lefevre, Capilano's crusty, but capable administrator. The same authoritarian, who publicly scolded me years earlier for playing that extra nine holes at Mayfair. I was terrified reading it, until acknowledging where I was. Lefevre was exactly what Kal Lake needed and I encouraged the president to interview him. As the hours passed that day though, thoughts of Lefevre there as my boss brewed uneasy feelings.

At that same time, Kal Lake hired Harold Ham and Darren Hearn to oversee the new clubhouse construction. Ham was the critical contractor who helped reconstruct the shop years earlier. Hearn was the feisty, later disgraced captain and it was anyone's guess why he was selected.

Meanwhile, the Board invited Lefevre for an interview. Knowing his countrywide reputation, it seemed clear such a meeting would impact my career.

Journal Entry #263: The Mentor (Part 3)

Dedicated to *Jean Kuchel*

Word leaked out Lefevre had applied for the position. As an unknown among the SS, they swiftly began dissecting him. With Bibeau gone, for only ominous reasons, they invested their cancerous confidence in me.

Little Dino sought me out in the shop. A short and balding retiree, he golfed regularly with the SS's more unsavory. I had no personal connection with Lefevre other than the confrontation years earlier. So when Dino lodged his inquisition, I censured his rogue curiosity by keeping my mouth shut.

Later, one cool, cloudy afternoon, Lefevre appeared for his interview wearing a tan suede parka. Ground had been broken and cement foundations poured for the new clubhouse when he wandered into my nearby shop. In the same way one knows a ball hanging on the lip might fall, I sensed Lefevre had reservations about the scruffy little course. It was plainly written on his face, which hadn't changed. He still had freckles and a fair complexion, although his hair was whiter. As he surveyed my humble workplace, I introduced myself reliving the decade-old Mayfair encounter.

He didn't remember. After he left, part of me drowned believing he might withdraw his application. Kal Lake was a distinct frontier from his past.

There were many candidates, but no one in his class.

As a landed Scottish immigrant, he applied for and was awarded an assistant manager's position at Toronto's exclusive Lambton. From there he launched his career as general manager at southern Ontario's St. Catharines. Then he left for a long tenure at Mayfair. After that, his career shifted to North America's oldest golf club, Royal Montréal, where he also chaired the Canadian Open. His final five seasons were spent at Capilano where *SCORE* magazine named him Canada's Manager of the Year. His credentials were flawless. Fearing only the naive would fail retaining him, I quivered anticipating their decision.

The wait wasn't long as they quickly hired him. It became one of Kal Lake's more prudent choices.

Journal Entry #264: Royal Montréal

Dedicated to *Doreen Wallington*

Stu assumed his new head pro position while Lefevre took control of clubhouse construction. Meanwhile I continued working, daily remeasuring my emotions.

At that point in my career, having laboured with a variety of managers, I was suddenly thrust forward working with the cream of the crop. However Lefevre's reputation wasn't all gleaming. He was viewed by pros as a hardliner. What was I in for?

Needing a get away to assess it, Jackie and I took a vacation. We'd been married eight years then with two children and a business, but never celebrated a honeymoon.

We set off for ten days that autumn on a New England golf trip, beginning at the **Royal Montréal** in Québec. Their head pro was Bruce Murray, who years earlier bailed me out during an Alberta seminar. Coincidentally, he worked with Lefevre when both were at the Royal. There, I queried his past working with the venerable veteran. On that moody Montréal morning, Murray reassured me, "Lefevre was the Cadillac of club managers."

Dick Wilson designed Royal Montréal, and at that cool cloudy time of season she appeared radiant among the autumn leaves. As a long, tough tournament test, she was worthy as North America's oldest golf club. But the round was more than culture, colourful scenery, or studying history and design. It was an opportunity to once again golf with Jackie. When dating we often played together, but with children and work, few moments existed anymore.

Before moving onto our next destination Boston, we asked Murray about golfing the infamous Country Club in Brookline. Famous courses were often inaccessible, even for pros. Infrequently, it was whom one knew, and one pro introducing another, occasionally opened doors. After Murray made arrangements through Brookline's manager, we left for Bean Town.

Journal Entry #265: Brookline
Dedicated to *Dr. Rob Ross*

Like the centre of a maze, The Country Club was shrivelled among Brookline's tight, treelined streets. Historically imbedded in golf's memoir, she was the 1913 site where the game shifted laterally in its adolescence. There unexpectedly, America stole the limelight from golf's then theatre, Britain. In a stunning playoff, a young Massachusetts amateur named Francis Ouimet, defeated two British giants, Harry Vardon and Ted Ray.

Seven decades later we arrived there, welcomed by emerald-green fairways and fall's yellow and red leaves. Meanwhile, grey squirrels nimbly gathered food as we drove in oblivious to the awaiting surprise.

The shop was on the lower level of a canary-yellow clubhouse accessorized by gleaming ebony window frames and forest green shutters. Inside, a pro reminiscent of actor Stanley Tucci, glided about in paisley slacks and a soft collar shirt. Introducing ourselves, he volleyed back curtly: "The manager was fired yesterday, so you can't play the course!" That ended the conversation. Without lingering, he trailed away continuing work. Stunned in that surreal moment we fortified ourselves by the counter. Seemingly irritated he returned, pertly adding: "You can't play but if you find a member who'll golf with you … go ahead." Then preening, he vanished again.

The day was approaching a time when full rounds seemed unlikely and there were more squirrels than golfers. Indignant, I said to Jackie: "I'm a golfer of the world and didn't come here to be treated this way … I'm playing!" Redeeming composure, I teed off and strode down the first fairway into a setting sun. Jackie, meanwhile avoided collusion, hugging the tree line. All the while, my thoughts failed to hide contempt for the pro.

Brookline was old and meticulously cared for, pimpled by rock outcrops and character mounds. On the par-four third, a pond where members curled in winter, hid behind her green. Flush with bulrush, its tired cottage seemed a hole where Huck Finn might have hung out. As I explored her famous fairways, replaying Ouimet's performance, I cautiously anticipated The Country Club's cavalry apprehending my once again delinquent behaviour.

But nothing happened.

Brookline may have had one of the more questionable pros, but nothing's ever perfect, even in places firmly entrenched within American golf culture … where it wasn't even a footnote.

Journal Entry #266: Winged Foot (Part 1)

Dedicated to *Willy and Sylvia Leitner*

After that strange day in Boston, we continued through New England toward New York and the infamous Winged Foot Golf Course.

Winged Foot, also designed by Tillinghast, was situated within suburban Mamaroneck. Arriving that evening, we were anticipating accommodations. After all … it was New York. Strangely, in a place having hosted histories of US Open golf, little availed itself. Eventually we discovered Vincent's Motel whose landscape of macabre gargoyles seemed endorsed by an eerie night manager evoking black images of Truman Capote. Among murky shadows separating us, a swollen glass partition and ten-foot protection precinct confirmed a demilitarized zone.

Thirty dollars later, we found our dinky room with its share of insurrections. Enervated, I left Jackie to find food. Nearby, a young gas station attendant with wide eyes beseeched me to find other accommodation: "Ya nad stayin' dere ayuh? A blaguy moidered a wygurl dere lasweek, Okey? Get outa dere! ... Okey?" Edgy, I ventured across the road to an Italian restaurant where a young dark-suited Mediterranean sentried outside. As I approached, his penetrating glare glued to me as only threats insinuate. It was enough.

I returned and rescued Jackie, who was resting casually on the shabby little bed. We left, nervously venturing into the evening's uptown heat amid a swirl of fedoras, shifty jivers, muscle-shirted blacks, and angry motorbikes.

Journal Entry #267: Winged Foot (Part 2)

Dedicated to *Dr. Rich Mori*

Earlier that year, Winged Foot was the US Open site where American Fuzzy Zoeller, in mock surrender, waved a white towel at the Australian Greg Norman.

We found the course without incident, checking in with popular professional, Tom Nieporte. With typical New York swagger, he welcomed us within the unexpected charm of his antiquely furnished shop. He partnered us with a member named Charlie Dalton, an elder who'd recently fallen victim to stroke. Often stuttering with punctuated enunciation, Dalton acquainted us with his Manhattan life as a contractor. As we played the brutally long Gotham layout, he relived his days developing Radio City Music Hall, the Time Life Building, and JFK Airport.

Winged Foot was the most demanding course I'd ever played. Not only was it long, but no picnic once on her roller-coasting greens. Typical putting surfaces might have sarcastically quipped, "You're not quite finished yet!" Our caddie was a tall, seasoned African-American named Curtis, who wore a stetson while claiming to be a grandfather many times over. When Jackie lofted high shots close to pins, his Chuck Berry blarney blurted, "mm ... mm, mai ... mai that lil' wumin, dun hit dem feign wedges."

After, Charlie inquired about our next destination. Learning we were routed through New York's Bronx, he cautioned us to follow him instead. He warned: "That's not where you want to go. If you break down there, you'll be in big trouble!" Remeasuring fear, we followed him via the Cross County Parkway to the George Washington Bridge. There, he abandoned us to navigate our way out of the Big Apple's rush hour clutch.

Among streams of unrelenting vehicles, lightening lane changes and near frequent fatalities, we escaped the squalor fringes of Manhattan. Later that night, we arrived at our sanctuary, Springfield New Jersey. A temporary respite near another Tillinghast thriller, the equally famous Baltusrol.

Journal Entry #268: Baltusrol

Dedicated to *Les and Min Baker*

Tillinghast was called Tilly the Terror, a reference to his playboy reputation. Prior to the great depression he designed a plethora of courses in the northeastern states, Winged Foot and Baltusrol among them.

Baltusrol was where Japanese professional, Isao Aoki nearly dethroned Nicklaus at the 1980 US Open. At Baltusrol, the pro shop was affectionately called *golf house,* and their staff couldn't have been more accommodating. Their level of commitment to members challenged me to advance my own services. But that was where the memories faded.

I determined neither Baltusrol nor Winged Foot possessed what I desired in golf courses. I'd been spoiled earlier playing Tillinghast's west coast classic ... San Francisco Golf Club. I found few similarities between the charming Bay City gem and either Gotham layout. While Baltusrol and Winged Foot were legends in their own rights with hordes of history and scads of stories, for me they represented only gladiatorial domains. Battlegrounds symbolizing a more authentic American aura that suggests arrogance, narcissism, and decadence. A culture proliferating the likes of Donald Trump, yet inspiring authors like Eugene Burdick and William Lederer to pen, *The Ugly American*!

When entertainer Tony Bennett sang, "I left my heart in San Francisco," I had my own interpretation.

Journal Entry #269: Merion

Dedicated to *Jesse Crowe*

> Merion ... I never knew her last name.
>
> —Lee Trevino

The traditions of golf I grew with and felt passionate about began eroding after I played **Merion**. Change and litigation began intimidating the sport. For instance when writing this, a close rule decision regarding the belly putter was challenging golf's community. To understand that, it might be helpful examining Merion.

Merion was located on the outskirts of Pennsylvania's Philadelphia. Ever since discovering golf, she was one course above most others I wanted to play. Was it the famous Peskin photo of Hogan? Her unique flag pole wicker baskets or because we named our son after Bobby Jones, who completed his grand slam there? While uncertain, I remained sure of one thing ... eventually being there.

When arranging our honeymoon, Merion's pro couldn't help me. Half apologetic, he explained: "Look, I just turned down Ken Venturi ... so how can I possibly help you?" If he denied a US Open champion, he surely couldn't accommodate us.

Later, after a plea to a collecting acquaintance, we were in.

We arrived finding Merion quaint, yet extremely private. Storied histories of numerous nationals hosted there, had cemented her within the mortar of golf's lore.

Merion was designed on a paltry one hundred and eleven acres, proving it an ingenious routing. The intricate Hugh Wilson layout, framed by bunkers with seaside shag, was similar to British links I'd explored as a teenager. Exceptionally groomed yet subtly rugged, to me she was defined by her wicker baskets, nesting atop each green's flagpole. Substituting for flags, they abolished advantages of wind direction, suggesting sensual perception when detecting shot strategy. As such, she shunned controversies such as belly putter use, where **leverage over the game** was questionably sought.

Soon after, profound pressures began thrusting themselves upon the game. Historically golf had been lovingly administered by concerned bodies like the Royal and Ancient plus the US Golf Association. But suddenly commerce began elbowing those institutions, challenging their authority, legitimacy, and authenticity. Marketplace madness joined in, suffocating the past and aborting golf's magic with moot proclamations like "make the game more accessible." Strangely, golf's historical spell had never before experienced trouble attracting audiences or maintaining its mystic essence. Consequently to me, it camouflaged the more oppressive intent of **selling more product**!

Over ensuing years, I profited myself from a parade of innovative golf products. But there was no denying the polarizing influence it began wielding on equipment, particularly balls and clubs. Groped by technology, golf began mutating away from a game of strategy and finesse, toward a sport glamorized by a meaty, beastly side … where only vulgar power dominates.

And as a result, in ways great courses like Merion are becoming obsolete, we risk seeing the game plummet too. If not careful, we may witness the elimination of an exceptional way of life!

Journal Entry #270: Somebody's Knockin'

Dedicated to *Bud and Barb Silvester*

Contracts are sacred documents. Whether in business, entertainment, politics, sports, or religion, they're meant to be carefully placed and protected.

My early years at Kal Lake hadn't been the pleasant work environment I'd anticipated, yet subsequent optics revealed a course in rapid change with me at its centre.

With Lefevre overseeing clubhouse construction, it wasn't long before he came knockin'. We talked outside near recently poured concrete where the current shop exists now.

There he inquired about my contract. Stammering, I summarized past arrangements and progress of my two-year extension. Then he stunned me, claiming: "You have no contract! I've been through your file, and there aren't any documents." I was speechless!

Lefevre suggested we talk after work in the club's temporary downtown offices. To get to know him better, Jackie and I had invited Lefevre for a home cooked supper that night. He'd rented an apartment and was on his own.

Later that day I met him and incoming VP Cec Hamilton. The hour-long session evolved into an emotional confession. With both I found muted confidence, when from a prison of despair, early years of festered suppression escaped. I lost my male pride, weeping uncontrollably for minutes in their presence. Lefevre, who had probable contempt for some pros, felt for my well being then, not only as a professional but as a person. I suspect he assessed me in those moments.

That night when he kept his dinner invitation, I sensed an ally. Others might have felt uncomfortable in the aftermath, but he didn't.

We never unearthed my contract among the amateur record keeping he'd inherited! Subsequently Lefevre recommended putting a proper deed together that mutually served both the club and I.

That's when I discovered who the real Lefevre was.

Journal Entry #271: Seven Year Ache

Dedicated to *Don and Celia Merritt*

On the site of its former cottage self, Kal Lake erected its new house for members.

Earlier, a mock effigy had been hung from the building's top floor as a giant bulldozer began demolition. When the quaint old structure splintered apart, many were disappointed until acknowledging its flimsy virtues. Everyone missed it's staidly stone fireplace though, imbedded with the rock initials KLGC.

Conducting business during construction was challenging. That winter, I relocated equipment and merchandise to our home's garage, operating there for months until the clubhouse was operational. Meanwhile, the new building gradually emerged. It was a two-story structure, whose windows faced the course. My new workplace boasted attractive display areas, office, change, and inventory rooms, plus areas for bag storage and club repair. I actually had washrooms and running water. Work became like a *Star Trek* moment … going where no Kal Lake pro had gone before.

As trades people worked about the enhanced shop, occasionally they'd abdicate to other areas. When that happened, Lefevre and I examined the possibilities. Where would counters go? Will the clothing look best here, or there? What about first tee visibility where rounds began? The questions were endless!

After lagging winter months, I merged into the workplace supervising business among weary tradesmen. Opening day was scheduled with the upcoming spring season. The industry became enjoyable again working with Lefevre. I had a partner there for the first time, and it wasn't unusual if we didn't share morning coffee or lunch. It was reminiscent of my early apprentice days where I felt part of a family. With Lefevre, it was the same, except we considered solutions to problems with weight. I was suddenly listened to and those opinions were measured in credibility.

It was clear my early years there were a **seven-year ache**.

Journal Entry #272: At the Zoo

Dedicated to *Warren Larson*

Opening a new clubhouse was one thing. Coordinating it with golf season was another.

As the new facility neared completion, an architect MacGyvered the first tee, eighteenth hole, and new practice greens into the clubhouse perimeter. Also additional space was allocated for my power cart fleet, which had doubled in size.

When christening a new facility on the season's first day … two things could be counted on. Spring's annual golfer enthusiasm and the wide-eyed interest of members seeking what their assessments bought. Consequently, we were consumed with clubhouse tours.

Amidst the excitement, we still accommodated golfers paying for range passes, bag storage fees, and lesson packages which proved overwhelming.

Overwhelming because merchandising, promoting, club repairing, receiving new shipments, and selling green fees also had to be dealt with. Coffee breaks weren't optional. It was an exhausting but good problem, where progress **at the zoo** was rapid.

During this time I hired several assistants who were challenged maintaining the frantic pace of demand. Consequently, I reshaped the staff with a succession of junior graduates who shed their youth and successfully ventured ahead toward the prevailing changes.

Journal Entry #273: George Knudson

Dedicated to *George Knudson*

Canada's often-controversial touring pro **George Knudson**, wrote a teaching manual for our PGA in 1988. It was accompanied by the organization's Junior Development Plan, which I participated in.

Before publishing the work, he crossed the country several times, outlining it in conferences. I had the privilege listening to and querying that body of work then.

Knudson himself owned one of golf's more admired swings. And during those lectures, I absorbed his theory on its more esoteric fundamental: To paraphrase, the golf motion was like being in the eye of a hurricane. One had to be **out of control**, to be **in control**. Years earlier, I saw how divots from a young Seve Ballesteros lingered in air after his swing finished. When listening to Knudson, I sensed a connection between his concept and the Spaniard's technique. It magnified that disparity between **swinging a club** and **hitting a ball**. I'd searched years for that proof and after his seminars, knew the final answer was imminent. Later too, when his book *The Natural Golf Swing* was published, I found many of its basics not unlike those Jackie and I worked on years earlier.

Knudson however, was challenged by absentee bedside manners. At times answering questions, he appeared rude as if not suffering fools. Some of my peers walked out in silent protest, but most were unaware Knudson suffered from lung cancer, which he eventually succumbed to.

I felt his premature passing was a loss for all Canadian golfers.

Journal Entry #274: Too Many Rivers

Dedicated to *John Lent*

Mayfair Randy and I worked together earlier in Edmonton. Eventually he was appointed head pro at a new Kelowna course named Shannon Lake. At that time he and I drove to Vancouver for the Knudson conference.

After the seminar's last day, we left for home. Randy lived up a mountain road in West Kelowna named after the '60s pop singer, Brenda Lee. That evening I approached the community from the connector highway ploughing through fresh snow. But as I drove up Brendalee Road to drop Randy off, astonishingly and unexplainably, her song **"Too Many Rivers"** broadcast over my car radio!

Journal Entry #275: MacArthur Park

Dedicated to *Reg Watson*

Another year, our PGA seminar was held by the harbour front at Vancouver's Pan Pacific Hotel.

Nearby was Stanley Park, which had a par-three course known to be interesting and unusual. And it was!

After the day's meetings, I drove through heavy rain to see it. A sign outside the shop read, "Closed." Inside however, lights invited me to enter and inquire about golfing later. It wasn't staffed by PGA pros then and the brash attendant working the night shift appeared annoyed when seeing me. Before I could inquire, he pointed in agitation toward the outside sign, sneering, "Can't you fuckin' read?" Caught off-guard and too stunned to reply, I left, but not without taking a scorecard.

Returning to my hotel, I re-measured the encounter and plotted a response … to golf later that night, rain or not!

Thinking time to play the short course would be brief; I grabbed some gear and drove west on Georgia Street toward the park. Circling to the back, I found a vacant car park flanked by moss-ravaged cedar fencing. There, below towering Douglas fir, I waited until dark to slip over and play yet another delinquent round. But from out of the gloom, cars began to emerge, parking nearby. Shadows leapt out and in, amid popping umbrellas. Frustrated, I was determined to repel the fluster by out-waiting the flurry. It continued however, seemingly lasting hours. In delusion, I concluded they too were strategizing ways to hop the fence or were sentries patrolling for reprobates like me. Just when I thought they'd never leave ... they emptied the park, leaving me once again alone.

Bundling my clubs, I jumped the hedge and began exploring. The showers maintained their rhythm, while dark veils haunted play. With only my intuition and that soggy scorecard as caddies, I teed off. In the black, unable to see where shots finished, I judged the locations by clubface impacts as only my peers might know. I can tell readers in all honesty, not one ball was lost that surreal night. I even birdied one hole.

Next morning over conference coffees, I shared my adventure with fellow pros who had the last laugh. The cedar rails behind Stanley Park was a local rendezvous for the gay mens community.

Journal Entry #276: My Hearts in the Highlands

Dedicated to *Judy Balcaen*

George Knudson described the route toward the Highland Links as "the highway to heaven," an interpretation that summoned me there. Located on Nova Scotia's Cape Breton Island, the roadway's one of earth's more scenic journeys, known more famously as the Cabot Trail. And as it climbs northward, eventually reaching Ingonish Beach, it welcomes golfing soldiers to the links.

There, along with the Keltic Lodge, I sensed what may have inspired Knudson. The famous inn was Canada's brother to California's Pebble Beach Lodge. Unlike its American sibling however, it was the undeniable product of a Maritime pedigree, standing prominent overlooking an estuary on a rugged and remote hiking peninsula. An extrusion of forest and rock provoking a steely North Atlantic. The ground needed only a golf course which Stanley Thompson complied with in 1939, creating the Highland Links.

In that boreal of salty marshes and stunted pine, Thompson carved out his own precambrian Cypress Point. His numerous groupings of on-site boulders were moulded into irregular mounds forming fairways of lumpy dimensions, somehow complimenting the designer's signature bunkers. The result was a unique public course anyone could afford and enjoy.

She wasn't really a links either, but I couldn't hold that against any course described divine. Had I been shipwrecked there, it might have been a blessing.

I left that day, marinated by Maritime spirit authenticating more of my Canadian culture … or as Knudson christened it … heavenly!

Journal Entry #277: The Living Years

Dedicated to *Ray and Fred Bremner*

In the years I worked with Lefevre, many of my peers weren't complimentary of him. They claimed he didn't like pros and yet I found otherwise.

Lefevre believed pros should make decent salaries, and yet while he was fair, he could just as easily shut down the impetuous. When it came to the new shop, he used my input thoughtfully trusting I had Kal Lake's interests in mind. Also, I didn't have to justify my movements like attending seminars, visiting other clubs, or entering tournaments. He was smart enough to sense abuse of position.

It wasn't that we were always on the same page either. But when we weren't, he treated me individually with voice. And he too had opinions of the SS, often telling them to "go sniff salt." Like me, he didn't satisfy their itch to visit strip bars or drink late, even though he liked a stiff Scotch whisky.

And Jim's wife Barbie was equally special.

She'd been a legal secretary and as sharp as anyone I knew. Positive and upbeat, she personified their home with her elegant cheer. They became our life counsellors … happily seeing each other and discussing family. Lefevre became my friend for the rest of his life.

One year then he was a guest speaker before a PGA conference. I remembered his lecture as old school. But as I sat among my peers and their snickers, I reminded myself how that manager salvaged a dedicated pros career.

Journal Entry #278: Everybody Wants to Rule the World

Dedicated to *Tom Kowal*

Golf unexplainably reveals inner character! For example, it's been said, one can live next to a neighbour and never really **know** them. And yet during a round of golf, their authentic personality always surfaces. Whether they be cunning, kind, or criminal; idealist, egotistical, or ignorant; or fraudulent, petty, or funny ... golf shares that viscera with anyone who's half alert. It may explain why many business executives conduct some of their work on golf courses!

During Lefevre's reign; a popular year-end event called the Horse Race was initiated.

The club acquired a local sponsor and recruited Kal Lake's most talented golfers to participate. It began Saturday with thirteen contestants teeing off together. After each hole one player was eliminated, until eventually two survived. In the event of ties, there were chip offs. My role was referee.

The event proved immensely popular as members flocked to the course, betting on golfers to win, place, or show.

One year, another woman (not Jackie) made it to the finals against a local hot-shot ... a Patrick Swayze look-alike who'd retired from the now defunct World Hockey Association. On the final hole while preparing his tee shot, Swayze's ego took control of him. A blood vessel the size of a snake began squirming down his neck, while beads of sweat betrayed the jock's obsession ... of losing to a woman!

Eventually he won, but later when collecting his cash, I watched him rant on about the event's gender format. It stirred Lefevre to reply in disgust, "I could tell you were a male chauvinist!" A claim prompting the yuppies' pathetic retort, "You bet I am!"

Journal Entry #279: Losing My Religion

Dedicated to *Bob King*

When visiting the United States, I've noticed what appears a chip on the shoulder of African and Black Americans. And it also exists among some of Canada's Indigenous Peoples. I think I understand why even without experiencing their persecution. But I'm not a persecutor nor can I undo history. However, it has compelled me to examine my own career.

During my occupation, I noticed how my own physical traits seemingly betrayed me in disadvantaging ways. First, I'm short in height, which isn't understood by everyone. Second I've been accused of possessing "small man's syndrome," which was always annoying. Third, I never had Denzel Washington's looks. People were never physically attracted to me. Fourth, my voice didn't project, nor did I enunciate like Morgan Freeman. Consequently at risk of appearing indifferent, I've experienced my own forms of discrimination.

A neighbouring course hired a pseudo pro with the charisma and looks of actor Tom Selleck. Selleck chose his vocation by apprenticing via an American golf institution … a place that certified its graduates quickly.

Tall, dark and good-looking, Selleck talked authoritatively with what appeared molecular knowledge, crediting that phrase, "bullshit baffles brains." Settling in, he immediately began courting Kal Lake's affluent business members, playing with them regularly and overstaying his welcome. Convinced he had ulterior motives, I was unsure how to handle it because charisma nor diplomacy weren't part of my arsenal either. And complaining would have only victimized him. Fortunately, Lefevre noticed too and directed me to advise him … "enough was enough!" But as was his nature, Selleck was cavalier, claiming he'd been invited. However, that's how those type perform in business, entertainment, politics or sport. They talk, but they don't walk. Their glitter and glamour is geared toward gain, while the unsuspecting gravitate to their simulations. An ideology that persists in politics suggesting how the GOP were radicalized in 2016 by an incoming president!

Basically, Selleck wanted my job, which was why he golfed at Kal Lake so frequently. And I was ripe picking. Without naturals like strong physical attributes, dramatic voice representation or height ... I was a sitting duck. Most advertising or entertainment executives are likely to confirm that. To get ahead in life, the rest of us depend on diligence, perseverance, sweat and determination. Alternatives can be thorny.

So when seeing minorities with chips on their shoulders, I try putting myself in their shoes while avoiding fanaticism or zealousness. Instead, I attempt to rise above it, and not lose-my-religion.

As for Selleck, he departed for greener pastures. He left his family, abandoned the industry and moved on as those type do, like livestock from one field to another.

Journal Entry #280: Wonderful (LACC)
Dedicated to *Monte and Eleanore Morden*

I was first introduced to the Los Angeles Country Club's general manager, Jim Brewer through an Okanagan vacationer. From that connection, a game was arranged for me in LA.

On game day, I stayed near Sepulveda Boulevard, breakfasting at a nifty '50s diner. There, the Johnny Mathis classic **"Wonderful"** played from a jukebox, inspiring me to carry my clubs to the course. After five kilometres soaking up Tinseltown on that typically cloudless day, my legs wilted upon arriving.

One didn't just stroll into the **LACC** then. They had to submit their name to guards before accessing its fortressed interior. The LACC was extremely private and amongst North America's most valuable real estate, rumoured then over five billion. It was so exclusive that gossip claimed movie stars built homes on her perimeter, hoping to join ... only to be refuted. Once in the foyer, I was instructed to wait for the apotheosized commander.

As LACC's larger-than-life custodian, Brewer had been voted America's number-one club manager. His intimidating manner reminded me of Donald Trump. Although unlike the former president, nothing slipped past Brewer's penetrating glare. He introduced me to club pro Ed Oldfield and with Brewer dictating policy, we were soon playing. I quizzed him why the US Open had never been contested there. He answered, "What could the US Golf Association possibly do for us?" He was unswayable.

As the round progressed, he pointed out monstrous homes planted next to its fairways, including the Playboy mansion, Aaron Spelling's palatial manor, and an estate once owned by film star Douglas Fairbanks. Brewer gushed no secret of resisting Hollywood temptations, painting them with the same brush as adult film.

Ironically though, within a city known for glamour, the George Thomas creation was anything but. The imaginative landscapes of unexpected contours rivalled the world's most impeccable tests of golf.

Brewer was also a historian and after discovering that bond revealed his art anthology in the club's basement offices. There, imprisoned within the nerve centre's walk-in vault, were authentic etchings and works worth more than imaginable. In particular an original painting of Allan Robertson.

Later, in Brewer's office, we sipped homemade chocolate milkshakes and devoured apple pie like I'd never seen. The five-inch high pastry was cut so surgically precise, no crumb dared collapse in front of Brewer. There, I shared desires to play LACC's neighbouring Riviera, sight of the cities' annual Open. An Asian firm recently acquired it and golfing there was proving difficult. Brewer picked up his phone, talked for a minute and I was in … just like that! He added matter-of-factly, "It's who you know in life that counts." The call and pictures of him with numerous US presidents confirmed the conviction. I've never minded know-it-alls, provided they in fact did know it all. And of course, like Trump … most don't. Brewer was different though. He was not only subject aware, but justifiably so. After, I felt my time had been spent in the company of a truly gifted manager. It seemed surreal because I worked for one back home.

It had been … wonderful!

PATRICK LITTLE

Journal Entry #281: Riviera

Dedicated to *Rocky and Carol Rochford*

Amongst the flutter separating efficient golf businesses from others are messages lost in translation. It can happen at any course, where memos from subordinates to managers or opposite, innocently fall through cracks. Clubs minimizing them are where golfers enjoy themselves most.

I had a game arranged at LA's famous **Riviera,** located near the murder site involving football's scandalous O. J. Simpson.

I arrived there finding the appointment misplaced. Meanwhile I waited. Feeling somewhat incarcerated, I wandered the palatial clubhouse, glimpsing memories of Tinseltown's past. Hints of Katharine Hepburn and Howard Hughes mingling with Ben Hogan and Sam Snead, penetrated the mood.

Eventually, their manager apologized, sheepishly presenting me a gold-bound souvenir copy of *Riviera's 50 Years*. Sometimes inconveniences were worth the wait!

The delay resulted in a late time, where I found myself golfing alone, except for one other ... LPGA icon Amy Alcott. Alcott was a member, preparing for the first swing of her upcoming tour. I used the opportunity to observe her from discreet distances. With only two of us on the entire course, it was another surreal moment.

Riviera was bisected by barrancas which siphoned off winter rains, and like LACC, designed by Thomas. I was astonished by his sand trap which literally penetrated her sixth green. Thomas continued his mischief at the short par-four tenth. A mere three hundred yards, it was simple, yet complex. Wide, but tight. Easy and hard. Then I was seduced by magnificent bunkers necklacing her sixteenth green. Finally, Riviera climaxed at eighteen where her fairway demonically sloped left to right. For average golfers, tee shots screwed into its bank were recommended. But when tournament money was on the line, it was a demand.

The mistake made by Riviera's staff was typical of errors made in work places, pro shops not being immune. I came to believe employees making general mistakes created better workplaces. Sometimes however, when their mishaps became repetitious, as head pro I had to learn how to cut them loose.

Journal Entry #282: Fate is the Hunter
Dedicated to *Judy Greig and Todd Stoddard*

When I was first hired, Lyle Pryce was Kal Lake's President and pilot of a single engine Cessna. He'd invite me up to where we'd fly to locations, golf, and return home before evening. Once, we ended up in West Vancouver playing Capilano. An international flight took us to Port Ludlow, Washington while still another veered us into the Caribou, where we golfed the Resort at 108.

The year our new clubhouse became operational, Lyle asked me again … this time to Victoria. He couldn't have asked at a worse time. It was impossible! I was consumed with opening the new clubhouse, an innovative manager, and an exploding golf market. Consequently he asked Stu to go. They left with the young blond-haired assistant Todd, one of my first Kal Lake employees. Eventually they reached Vancouver Island where they played Victoria Golf Club.

The next morning, I arrived at work to find the local airport manager awaiting. It was early in the day for him. With a solemn face he said, "Pryce's plane's missing!"

The previous night it crashed south of Kamloops. Later that day, it was found with no survivors!

The tragedy left devastating scars on Okanagan's golf community. Speculation hinted Pryce wasn't trained in nighttime instrumentation. He'd lost his bearings flying into smoke from forestry slash burnings.

Many years have past, but not the shock. Instead of sorrow though, I've reminisced of the times Stu and Todd spent at our home. I gave Todd winter lessons in our garage, while Stu often stayed with us, helping our children with holiday gingerbread houses. As for Lyle, I remember our junkets over endless forests, yelling above roaring engine drones. But in those reflections, the memories are usually thwarted by author Ernest K. Gann's words: "**Fate is the hunter**!"

Journal Entry #283: Peter Thomson

Dedicated to *Peter Thomson*

Amongst my fellow pros, I enjoyed the friendship of a Kelowna assistant named Bryan Hart.

Hart, worked at an upscale resort called Gallagher's Canyon. One day he asked if I wanted a game with the esteemed Australian professional and five time Open champion, **Peter Thomson**? Was he kidding? As if I had to think twice?

Thomson was visiting Gallagher's at the owner's invitation. Over years, I followed his career as an architect, columnist, commentator and competitor. Highly underrated, particularly in North America, he was charismatic, knowledgeable, talented and visionary within one skin. A consummate gentleman, his relaxed temperament was physically imparted by waves of bloodhound wrinkles lapping his forehead. Only inches taller than me, his swing appeared simple not unlike seen at average courses where its subtlety was lost in visual translation. His small stature supported by a wide stance, complimented a consistent head position throughout. The ensuing compact motion completed a finished product whose playing credentials were difficult debating.

At times later in my career and in retirement, when golf's future appears uncertain and even bleak under the Saudi Arabian LIV cloud, I'd have nominated him in a heartbeat to be the CEO of world golf. He'd have been my trouble shooting choice to not only arbitrate with Greg Norman and his malcontents, but also rescue both the game and professional golf from the restlessness.

Journal Entry #284: The Compliment(s)

Dedicated to *Roberto De Vicenzo*

One of major golf's most regrettable tragedies occurred at the 1968 Masters. There, one of golf's great gentlemen, Roberto De Vicenzo accidentally signed an incorrect scorecard, relinquishing the championship.

When thinking of De Vicenzo though, I prefer remembering him as the '67 Open winner, rather than a misfortune of mistake.

And coincidentally, it was that South American; who left me a compliment I've always treasured.

Jackie and I took time off work to attend the PGA tour's Canadian Seniors Championship. Hosted then by Calgary's Earl Grey, many of golf's great were competing, including Billy Casper, Bob Charles, Sam Snead and Peter Thompson. Further, there were no crowds allowing me access to study their techniques.

There, I saw the distinguished De Vicenzo off by himself, seemingly lonely. He didn't appear like the others. The Argentinean was reasonably tall and broad-shouldered with a head hemmed-in by departing hair. He might have looked like any average tradesman except for his fine European threads.

Knowing he'd won the Open earlier at Royal Liverpool, I brought a scorecard from the English links, hoping he'd autograph it. De Vicenzo took it, but before scribing, squinted the fine script. Then, blending Spanish and broken English he startled me claiming, "You're a professional … aren't you?" Somehow he unearthed that from our brief exchange. But while overwhelmed with that compliment, I also detected gratitude. Perhaps because I acknowledged his accomplishment rather than his accident.

Journal Entry #285: Pinehurst

Dedicated to *Flo and Ken Curtis*

As a professional, I was never fortunate to build my own golf course. At one point though, after discovering passions for design, I considered changing careers midstream. However, flush into my livelihood, with a robust family and business, I deferred instead, remaining a content armchair architect. And in ways one differentiates a performing vehicle from a lemon … I too, over time acquired a discerning eye for courses.

That began during the winter of 1990, when Jackie and I visited the blue-collar golf mecca Myrtle Beach, South Carolina.

There I saw commercial golf from perspectives of art and life. Impressions influenced through visits to numerous fascinating courses.

On that sabbatical we ventured into North Carolina. There, we sought the magnificent Pinehurst Resort and its world-famous Number Two course, the masterpiece of Donald Ross.

Like many, I accepted Ross as the profit of architecture. I'd golfed many of his inspirations, but ironically after playing **Pinehurst,** walked away from descriptions lavishing his other works ... marginalizing them as repetitive, and even boring. For Number Two seemed not only vastly superior, but ingenious, rustic and intricate. Ross had simply, yet cleverly, framed Pinehurst's fairways from forests of pervasive pine. In ways she was similar to St. Andrews with its oceanic presence yet geographically absent salt water. And as Tom Morris, Sr. did at St. Andrews, Ross too pampered Pinehurst. He demonstrated how laying out a course using safe or aggressive lines for new and experienced golfers alike was a complicated formula—binding a planner's knowledge and creativity with a geology at their disposal.

Pinehurst was reasonably long, wide for beginners, and yet provocatively challenging for the seasoned. Provocative as green perimeters were deceptive, functions of her creator's Dornoch origins. And where play into them could be chosen through ground or air strategies. Ross kneaded them using contours that merged into chipping alternatives. It wasn't unusual approaching elevated greens and seeing balls vanish ... rolling off and tumbling below toward easy to find, yet broad chipping basins. Pinehurst was also blessed with a sandy soil that not only appeared a divine growing medium, but was inherently natural among scattered waste areas. Areas complimenting her landscape like aged wine, fortifying Pinehurst's timeless reputation.

Journal Entry #286: Tell Her No (Harbour Town)

Dedicated to *Larry and Lorna Jaschke*

Ever since discovering the game, there were subtle reminders golf was an affluent sport. I accepted that until I played Harbour Town Golf Links.

After leaving Pinehurst, we traveled south, visiting Harbour Town on Hilton Head Island.

While its designer Pete Dye may have been influenced by the links at Prestwick, his reputation seemed moulded at Harbour Town. Having developed several projects earlier, it was in South Carolina partnering with Nicklaus, where both bud into the landscape of building courses. There, I became skewered by notions that sabotaged drooling accolades normally reserved for each's work.

At **Harbour Town,** I sensed both in their zeal, were like two boys with new toys. There I saw unrestrained, impractical use of railway ties among vast unnatural sand traps … crude signals of unbridled maintenance expense. Financial burdens siphoned from one primary source … the green fee golfer!

Somewhere, in a decadent chapter of golfing's history, the sport became shrouded in opulence. Sensing Harbour Town an accomplice to that, I questioned whether Dye and Nicklaus managed their cost due diligence responsibly. Fuelling that impression was what appeared flippant arrogance conveniently stating, "Let the customer pay for it!" A smugness quarterbacking inflated fees.

Those observations led me to believe true architects were best when their creations were not only faithful to golf through form following function, but financially efficient. Essences I didn't see there.

That belief was furthered later by a *Ted Talk*. One featuring Amos Winter, who pioneered a wheelchair that changed thousands of needy lives in poor, remote villages. Guided by desperation, he collaborated art and science in harmony with expense efficiency. Admiring how it affected so many so positively, and for less, I felt similar approaches could also salvage golf's future, while not compromising art nor golf. While I left Harbour

Town disappointed, I was also hopeful architecture might one day mitigate age-old stigmas that golf was only for the wealthy. Because after all, she's lingered for centuries like an itch, reminding us she should be affordable.

Journal Entry #287: Viva La Vida (Long Cove)

Dedicated to *Gloria Irwin*

On that trip, I also began realizing golf course designing wasn't just science, but also art.

Art was supposedly defined as either an applied or fine commodity, described as in the eye of a beholder. And further anything could be converted into art form. To me though art also had to be truthful possessing aesthetic qualities arresting the senses. And amongst mystique and fantasy, it had to be faithful to a subject.

I didn't sense that at Harbour Town. Yet days later, I remeasured Pete Dye's work when playing another of his creations nearby … **Long Cove**. Ironically it had a distilling effect on me.

Admittedly Long Cove still clung to Dye's predictable drama, but it was absent the theatrical tradecraft I harvested from Harbour Town. I was sipping port instead of screech.

Long Cove seemed to be affirming architecture was an applied art. And that genuine architects were artisans, capable of aesthetically extracting their inner selves to life in natural mediums like land art. From that I began to explore the philosophies, ideologies, and skills of golf's golden era designers. Architects whose fierce loyalties to the sport could not only yank surprise from golfers with their art, but not abandon the natural rhythms of nature.

This was all unexplainably revealed when I faced a forced carry at the par-four fifth. Barely three hundred yards, it was a simple dogleg left adjacent one of many streams meandering the course. Fronting and guarding its green however were sentries of playful mounds and pot bunkers. A chastity belt defending a friendly putting surface. It was a risk and reward

voyage occasionally visited by golden era architects like Canada's Charles Blair Macdonald, for instance.

Author Robin Sharma wrote in his book, *The Secret Letters of the Monk who sold his Ferrari,* "What holds us back in life is the invisible architecture of fear." And forced carries challenged golfers to face such fear! There were no options but to fly over the hazards. Choices weren't available. So at that fifth-hole, I found myself staring down that all-or-nothing strategy. One symbolizing death, divorce, or disaster in real time. Events which naturally wavered human spirits and which we're all occasionally faced with in life. There however, I was being allowed safe exploitation of those vulgar thumbprints. And when readying myself to face that fear, I suddenly felt the forces which frisk golfers before such efforts. Forces baiting me to audit my spine. Forces whose scent was verifying whether I was … alive or not. Forces tempting me to taste the authenticating inner truth of who I might be. Ones that not only assessed my comfort zone, but my values of golf and life.

Were these among the emotions (and passions) that subpoenaed golden era designers like Stanley Thompson, Alister MacKenzie, or Tom Simpson? Or extract from the paraphrasing of author James Michener, who supposedly claimed art was a gamble of confrontation? In other words, "go for it!"

That encounter even amplified golf's court of appeal … etiquette and rules … the terms we abide by on golf courses. For example, the rational behind only playing the ball down (or as one finds it).

And in that aroused state, a subtle awareness became not-so-subtle. Golf was explaining life wasn't always going to be fair. But in that measurement, I found myself rebelling against the skin of new golfers whose petty demands of fairness seemed annoying and entitling. Life and golf were instead pestering me toward The Rolling Stones riff, "You can't always get what you want."

And from that day on, I understood that challenges in golf were not only endless, and often prejudicial but they could be negotiated in the face of fear too. And while I left Long Cove with a more deferring respect for Peter Dye, I also sensed how golden era designers ingeniously roadmapped golf and life together in their artistic creations.

Journal Entry #288: Take ... On Me

Dedicated to *the Stephensons*

Golf pros often asked about my junior program's success. Unfortunately, there weren't any secrets and I only had modest connections with the kids.

It began earlier during my sophomore year when I invited the juniors and local media to a clubhouse meeting. Ambitious and confident, I put myself on the line announcing intent to develop Canada's finest junior program. Given the young talent I inherited, a diverse plan seemed obvious.

I wanted swing classes to be more than just swinging. I started a junior day, where youngsters not only played, but were exposed to skill contests. Using my teaching formula of fundamentals and goals, I saw immediate results. For instance, if a student chipped five balls into a circle, I'd encourage them to either chip six in or decrease target sizes. A local educator helped by compiling progress stats. I awarded bag tags for scoring achievements. Tags borrowing belt colours worn in the martial arts. I rehabilitated three club tournaments, distilling them from mundane events into major competitions, each producing record entries. Finally, I scrutinized a handicap system which not only inspired beginners but energized the experienced.

Was it successful? The juniors were the valley's powerhouse, dominating regional tour events. Ten collected zone championships. Sixteen made a living in golf's industry. Seven qualified for the World Junior in San Diego. Over a dozen were awarded golf scholarships to North American universities. One boy twice captured the provincials as did one of our girls. Plus two youths qualified for the prestigious United States Amateur at Oakmont, Pennsylvania. But the most successful story never told was our team who played in the provincials at Prince George. There, they stole the cup from Vancouver, who'd monopolized it for decades.

In the end, my only secret was genuinely caring and maintaining promises to try.

Journal Entry #289: Tender Years

Dedicated to *Scott Mann*

The junior programs success was accentuated by my commitments to their competitive development. Spring swing classes were followed in summer with afternoon playing lessons. Then, when temperatures were blazing, our usually vibrant club was slower. It was a logical time to work on their abilities given their indifference to heat.

During one of those outings, I scored my second hole-in-one. It happened at the then uphill fifth with its rectangular green where I knew the result was close.

The nuance of golf can be partially measured through the anticipation of pleasant surprises after good shots … when outcomes are uncertain. It's like opening Christmas presents. Today however, that aspect of design appears lost. Current day architects have either abandoned or suppressed that playfulness. When I reached the putting surface that day and saw no ball, it joyfully confirmed my hopes.

Decades later though, instead of that ace, I continue remembering the pleasant junior I golfed with that round. He was a physician's son, one of many doctors who were members. For not long after, he was a fatality in a nearby car crash. And while I was never close to him or his family, his memory lingers, reminding me of those **tender years.**

Journal Entry #290: Last Christmas

Dedicated to *Corky and May Correale*

Lefevre had a unique way of celebrating staff Christmas parties. During golf season, our job was to serve the members and directors. Consequently, at the annual staff holiday function, the board in turn served us.

In Lefevre's last year, one of our endearing Italian members volunteered to cater the event. For the main dinner, he prepared and served his popular secret spaghetti-and-meatball formulare. Here, with his permission, is that recipe: Spaghetti and meatballs, Corky's style!

Salsa

Boil olive oil. Sauté garlic and remove residue. Brown meat in oil (you can use varieties ... beef cubes, beef, chicken, short ribs, spareribs, etc.) Add half a chopped onion, 2 cans tomato paste (5.5 ounces), 1 can tomato sauce (13 ounces), 1 can crushed tomatoes (28 ounces), 2 cans water, flavouring spices (oregano, parsley, and sweet basil; avoid over-seasoning), plus salt and pepper to taste. Use a cast-iron pan if available.

Boil and immediately simmer for 2 to 3 hours (lifting lid if too much liquid accumulates). Add meatballs in half-remaining cooking time. (Serves 6.)

Polpette

In a bowl, add 1 pound ground pork, 1 pound ground veal (or lean beef), 2 cloves garlic, 2 tablespoons dried parsley, 1 tablespoon dried oregano, 1/2 tablespoon dried sweet basil, salt and pepper, 1 cup grated Romano cheese (pecorino is best ... **important component!**), 1 cup breadcrumbs, plus 2 eggs. Mix together and form meatballs. Hand-roll meatballs to fortify when later cooked in sauce.

Best served with handmade pasta ... without overcooking! Enjoy the holidays.

Journal Entry #291: If You Leave

Dedicated to *Hamish and Anne Robertson*

I thrived working with Lefevre, finding hidden abilities to work efficiently and seamlessly within inspiration and talent. With my mind restored and re-energized, rounds of golf at the lively course increased even more, in addition to record-high shop sales, and a vital junior program. Industry life was again gratifying ... at least for me.

But it went south again, meaning it ended. Lefevre took me to lunch, claiming he was through.

Originally he accepted the job as a gateway toward retirement, removing himself from enormous pressures of more complex organizations like Capilano. Ironically, he found more stress at Kal Lake.

His departure was due to one particular director; the treasurer called Pot Luck. Pot Luck was one of the SS's most controversial and not the kindest. He made Lefevre's life so miserable, the consummate manager confided the Okanagan course had been the most challenging appointment of his career. A revealing reminder of a resume managing Canada's most demanding workplaces. Over a generation he'd successfully maneuvered around mountains of stress inexplicably finding Kal Lake insurmountable. He said, "He didn't need the aggravation." Who would?

When Lefevre left, I was grateful for his mentorship. He exited, gifting me an emotional stability that claimed the past hadn't originated from immature guilt pinned upon myself. But his departure left me once again vulnerable … for Pot Luck wasn't a pro shop ally either!

Journal Entry #292: Shout

Dedicated to *Judge Gary Weatherill*

Bullies in schoolyards have been known to graduate to the business world and even beyond … to the American presidency!

In the pro shop, I was occasionally assaulted by rumours claiming I generated excessive profits. To mitigate that, Lefevre suggested I make my business books available for him to review annually. Subsequently, he could reassure directors I was reasonably compensated. I abided knowing he could read profit and loss statements intelligently. With Lefevre, it wasn't a problem. When he left, it became one.

A business owner's financials are private. They're windows into the accuracy of a firm's income and expenses for specific periods. Like wills, they aren't intended for casual reading. Soon after Lefevre abdicated, Pot Luck demanded to see my books. I gave in, asking only they be reviewed in the privacy of my office. Pot Luck wasn't having any of that though! He wanted them removed and I remained hesitant because he wasn't reassuring their welfare.

The issue simmered at a board meeting where the club's new president, a young, highly respected lawyer named Travis, smooth-talked me into letting Pot Luck have his way. I respected Travis because he was reasonable, but truthfully any trained eye could have examined those books within minutes.

Pot Luck proved me right. He'd managed a law firm before retiring, and with that background, aggravatingly took months before returning them. He'd bullied his way and it was clear then why Lefevre resigned.

I was never privy to Pot Luck's nickname, although his waistline and cut-throat tactics may have been factors. He had a talent for conflict, best described by the club's then tee time system.

Tee times were premium at Kal Lake because of the course's vitality. With over fifty-five thousand annual rounds played, it was the Okanagan's most bustling facility. Computer software wasn't available then and member's weekend times were manually blind-drawn. Because of demand, prime times were rare. Most members were patient though but if Pot Luck's draw was out five minutes, he'd demand explanations beratingly. Because of his miserable, selfish behaviour, I often sought peace by manipulating times to his advantage. The illegitimate attempts however, only endorsed his bullying further.

Having my financials away from me for so long by one so exasperating, left me helpless and challenged. It wasn't the frame of mind pros needed to efficiently serve their membership. And when Pot Luck finally returned them, he avoided delivering them personally. Instead, he left them with others in his daunting way.

Journal Entry #293: The Graduate

Dedicated to *Bud and Marg Montgomery*

With Lefevre gone, members and staff speculated who'd fill his shoes.

Some approached me, but administering a bustling course required more than knowledge and sound business practise. I was still a year away.

I'd witnessed flounderers in past who accepted jobs exceeding ability. It kindled fraudulent work environments where everyone lost. Besides, I'd have been a prime picking again for the SS. They'd left me alone for the time being.

Pot Luck spearheaded the drive to select Lefevre's successor. His recruit was a young college **graduate** resembling former Canadian Prime Minister Stephen Harper. While not blessed with Lefevre's industry insight, Harper was instead subsidized by the incoming computer age. An evolutionary throng who knew the words, but often struggled singing them. Harper had an ivy league business degree from a junior hockey scholarship. Jim Dow was also an ivy league graduate, but somehow the ink on his diploma seemed drier.

Harper took over during the next half decade, managing by memos, meetings, and meaningful missions often fulfilled. He survived among a dynamic breed of new directors, who guided the club toward even more prosperous changes.

Journal Entry #294: The Perfect Storm

Dedicated to *Bill Taylor*

I've only played two golf holes in my life where each shot was perfect. Prior to that like most golfers, I've had spectacular individual efforts, but never a complete succession of shots on one fairway.

The first time that happened was on a cloudless, desert morning at the Troon Golf Club during a pro-am in Phoenix, Arizona. There on the tee, I readied myself to play the long dogleg left par-five. I used a seven-degree lofted TaylorMade driver with a stiff, steel shaft. Not being a long hitter, I curiously found lower lofts offered me better launch angles for maximum carry and role.

On that occasion, I flushed my drive down the middle, which meant I struck it effortlessly on the clubface centre (known as the sweet spot). In flight, the ball curved in a subtle right to left pattern or draw. The effort went far, clearing a modest rise where then gliding in descent it rolled further than I was normally entitled. Its eventual resting place conveniently hugged her left fairway side making it possible to consider going for the green.

For my second, a fairway metal had to be struck toward an angled putting surface. As my body leaned into the hillside during impact, the ball took off like a missile, scraping a currency note divot from the grass. Drawing in perfectly again toward centre, the bullet kissed the flagstick, ricocheting into a greenside bunker.

Basking in the sand, the ball smirked like a testy teen from a Salinger novel. For my third effort, I aimed toward the upper portion of the two-level putting surface, eighty polarizing feet away from my goal. The flagstick meanwhile, waited on the lower deck, as if anticipating a cue. If I lobbed a shot precisely, the ball might roll out to its first destination, the top edge. From there, synchronized by formulas of direction and speed, it could possibly descend on its own merit and finish close. My effort was struck with surprising skill.

In bunker shots, advanced golfers learn through practise the best clubface angle, desired swing path, and amount of sand to take. Shearing through it, I almost felt the granules commuting over my wedge grooves. The ball fluffed out softly, landing the same. Orbiting with ball bearing efficiency, it then recessed near the contoured crossroads, eyeballing fate. Suddenly, lured by that southern potential … it moved again! Creeping slowly at first and responsive to the arched slope, it miraculously began tracking a collision course on that long-and-winding-road. The shot for an eagle three was far too difficult to imagine success. Yet, it was happening! In fading seconds the ball slowly veered toward the cup's centre and without hesitation, glided down in like spirits do when poured by bartenders.

I would have named that drink **the Perfect Storm**.

Journal Entry #295: Someday

Dedicated to *Herb and Fay Arbuckle*

On our fifteenth wedding anniversary, I surprised Jackie with a trip to Pebble Beach.

I saved a year for that occasion and when the alarm echoed at four o'clock that morning, I was ready. Awaking her gently, I whispered, "Happy anniversary! It's time to get up. We have places to be!" With bags secretly packed ahead and papers in place, I kept her mystified as we sped off toward Kelowna's airport.

Eventually, after reaching Vancouver, we connected to San Francisco and on toward the Monterey Peninsula. There she guessed our destination, the luxurious Pebble Beach Lodge.

That night I coaxed their staff to tape the Masters. There, at one of America's iconic golf resorts, we talked, dined on pizza, and did what couples do on such occasions.

Early next morning, I crept through darkness with my McGregor sand wedge. Stealing about the silhouetted sleepy resort, I conspired with waves that lashed the famous eighteenth fairway until locating the hour-glass shaped seventeenth green. There illuminated by the neighbouring beach club lights, I chipped balls onto the green over the next hour, while surf punched the rocks directly beneath me.

From that exact location, Tom Watson captured golf history, wedging in to defeat Nicklaus for the '82 US Open.

I'm still married to earth's only known angel. And as our time together looks toward five decades, I realize **someday** again there may be another special place to go and another alarm to set … although hopefully it won't be four o'clock in the morning.

Journal Entry #296: Pebble Beach

Dedicated to *Geoff Jell*

Pebble Beach Golf Links ranks among the world's great courses, an opinion I've shied away from. I saw her instead the product of historically slick media, glamorized by cypress, surf, and Crosby's connection (famous entertainer Bing Crosby lived near the thirteenth fairway).

Having written that however, her closing hole represents one of golf's great challenges. Adjacent Pacific swells, its infamous par-five eighteenth, is a classic risk and reward dilemma. One posing choices for golfers during play. Choices where again golf emulates life … where options measure conviction while exploring limitation. For example, among life's endless temptations is the provocative choice facing every culture … the abuse of narcotics!

That aside, I found **Pebble Beach** not unlike many golf courses in the stunning wilderness of my home province British Columbia, Canada. A place where even modest courses appear mind-blowing. Pebble Beach appeared no less! With its metaphoric scenery, I saw it as American camouflage competing against golf's traditional home St. Andrews, Scotland.

On the other hand, the pancakes served in its lodge seemed comparably underrated.

We ordered their signature blueberry flapjacks. And after years of experimentation, I found a recipe close to those we polished off that morning while overlooking that spectacular eighteenth green.

Ingredients:

1 cup sifted white flour (substitute for gluten-free if wished), 3 teaspoons baking powder, 1 teaspoon baking soda, 1 cup sour milk, 1 egg, 1/2 cup freshly cleaned blueberries. (All room temperature.)

Method:

In another bowl, sift baking powder, baking soda, and flour, whisking together. In another bowl, whisk sour homogenized milk plus egg. Have grill hot and ready at 375 degrees.

In the first bowl, scoop a well with the dry mix to hold some milk. Slowly add more to the balance, whisking together until blended. If a little lumpy, it's good. Once batter is poured onto grill, immediately plunk random blueberries. Flip after a few minutes or when multiple bubbles appear. Smear upside with butter. After one minute, flip again and apply more butter.

Remove to warm plates and sift lightly with icing sugar. Blueberry pancakes, Pebble Beach style.

SUMMER PLACE

Journal Entry #297: The PGA Show

Dedicated to *John Halliwell*

In the early '90s, golf's industry grew furiously with new courses built at staggering speeds. Seemingly overnight, woods in one's bag became metal. A company named TaylorMade ushered in the conversion, antiquating laminate and persimmon woods forever. Soft spikes revolutionized golf shoes. That change was so innovative, groundskeepers debating otherwise would be foolhardy. Prior to that, greens were overwhelmed by steel spike damage. When soft spikes became a way of turf life, spike marks died too. Plus distance-measuring devices (DMDs) began pillaging sensual aspects of golf. To maintain knowledge of those and other advancements, I did whatever possible to stay current. That included attending the granddaddy of golf exhibitions, Orlando Florida's PGA Show. I flew there intending to see everything I could.

    The show was colossal in scope, energized by epic human electricity. It attracted pros from across the continent, ordering shop merchandise for their upcoming seasons. Anything golfers desired was there for sale. LPGA stars headlined glittering fashion shows while Greg Norman and Tom Kite communed with the curious. It was so vast, a complete day was needed just to walk its aisles. With no time to talk, I jotted ideas on the fly. Scheduled at January's end before golf season, it lured more than pros too. It magnetized industry leaders and captains of world PGAs for meetings impacting the game. It was golf's glimpse of a Las Vegas schmooze atmosphere, all within Orange County's obese convention centre.

    Two days later exhausted, I made an appointment to golf at Bay Hill, a regular PGA tour stop and Arnold Palmer's winter refuge.

Journal Entry #298: Bay Hill

Dedicated to *Ray Allen*

Being mesmerized within the show's bustle, I didn't foresee the demand for tee times at **Bay Hill.** Located in a nearby suburb, Bay Hill was designed by

Dick Wilson, who built Royal Montréal. Struggling with predictability and redundancy, many holes there featured doglegs skirting passive lakes. And yet despite its flat, uninteresting appearance, Palmer's influence prevailed. At Bay Hill, golf—like its previous owner—possessed a relaxed ambiance which at day's end is what the sport should advance anyway.

Fortunately a time availed itself and there I met Oliver Thompson from Cleveland, Ohio. An accountant-lawyer for the American PGA, he attended the show annually to represent their business interests. Another collector and a student of architecture, we were instantly bonded. He'd played over two thousand different courses, and those discerning views qualified him as panelist for the publication, *Golf*. There, he joined an esoteric group who annually rated the world's top-hundred golf facilities. Over the following years we journeyed together, playing global courses I never expected to see.

Journal Entry #299: First We Take Manhattan

Dedicated to *Stan and Ruth Hoye*

Being a *Golf* magazine contributor, Thompson only recommended courses he'd seen and played. And on that list were a few remnants he was unfamiliar with. Fulfilling due diligence, he set out to appraise them on an around-the-world golf tour, asking me for help.

By then, I'd travelled extensively, playing numerous exotic and interesting courses which unfortunately wasn't inexpensive. They were afforded only through financial caution and also because golf was my business. I could legitimately write off expenses.

But an excursion like that cost seven thousand then which Jackie and I didn't have. However, reasoning it a lifetime work experience, I plotted the off-season trip with a loan.

We took Manhattan first, continuing on to Britain, South Africa, Australia, New Zealand and finally home, rating nineteen courses in twenty-one days. While at times frantic, the trip certified my golf degree further.

Journal Entry #300: Durban

Dedicated to *Stanley*

Our second stop was England, where in drizzle, we rated the links at Rye.

Hours later, we descended into **Durban**, South Africa adolescent to the sudden transition of heat.

At the airport, greeted by a sign scrawled with our names, we were immediately caught within a flux of skin colour. Having grown among a predominately white population, I was immediately devoured by Durban's vast black culture. Our host taxied us through the city's bustle to our next stop near the Indian Ocean, Durban Country Club.

There, I saw the first guarded gates of numerous South African courses. In North America, manned entries usually redirected the nosey. In South Africa it was a definition of crime. Atrocities notarizing South Africa's capital Johannesburg as earth's most dangerous city then!

Inside Durban's clubhouse, we were thrust into the appalling system of apartheid. No subtlety could camouflage Afrikaans contempt toward local Zulu staff.

The course was jungled, punctuated by swollen sand dunes, long ago grassed over. Somersaulting her gentle slopes proved irresistible, citing laughter from my barefoot caddie Stanley.

While Durban was an exacting test of golf, I was romanced instead by panoramic views from lofty tee locations. There, caressed by waves of tropic breezes, I spanned the cities' skyline and Golden Mile beaches bordering a shark-infested ocean. All the while, we were entertained by nimble monkeys, trapezing through trees to hijack our golf balls.

After being whisked through three continents and dinner held in our honour, we passed out in bed, exhausted.

Journal Entry #301: Lost City

Dedicated to *Dick Biggs*

Leaving Durban, we safaried toward the North West Province, visiting one of earth's more extravagant courses, **Lost City**.

Located within shadows of an extinct volcano, it flaunted the marketing ancestry of Disneyland and Las Vegas. Accommodations, casinos, and restaurants were all ornamented by robust sculptures of the animal kingdom's Big Five. There in the glitter, eagerly snapping photos was famous professional Sir Nick Faldo. He was participating in Sun Cities' Million Dollar Tournament, an opulent event symbolized by urinals of gold with ice simulating diamonds. The pro shop elicited *Flintstone* cartoon memories with its boulder interior. The cavernous decor embellishing extravagant attire, was a quantum leap from my modest shop back home.

South Africa's golfing son Gary Player, designed Lost City. Unfortunately, I felt his creative credentials, like Nicklaus, failed to parallel his competitive imprint. Regardless, his par-three thirteenth, seized the environment's more savage side. There and seemingly possessed, was a grisly hazard challenging to ignore. Lurking beside the green, several acres in size was a ten-foot-deep pit shaped in the continent's image. Fortified in concrete, the lair was home to countless carnivorous crocodiles. Later in my round, passing the haunt again, I saw an American filming precariously atop the hazard's arched perimeter! Anticipating a pending outcome, I nervously weighed the dilemma and took the coward's way out … quickening my play in. No degree of empathy saw myself a saviour there!

Journal Entry #302: Royal Adelaide

Dedicated to *Mark McCulla*

I never saw kangaroos at **Royal Adelaide** in Southern Australia. Days earlier however at Lake Karrinyup near Perth, we golfed among colonies of the copper coloured species. I thought then that was how to live my next life. One whose nature's call was mating, sleeping, and hanging around golf courses.

That vanished after the movie *Wake in Fright*. Considered a classic, the Australian flick, coincidentally directed by Canadian Ted Kotcheff, captured decadent down-under lifestyles. The graphic mind-bender, exploiting savage marsupial slaughters on outback hunting rampages, dismembered any after-life kangaroo appeals.

Days later at Royal Adelaide however, my golf education became creatively broader. Designed by Alister MacKenzie, most of the doctor's work had faded over time. Of his lingering traces however, was the eleventh which became my favourite par-four. Despite the changes and uninspiring land, Royal Adelaide ironically evolved into a magnificent links.

She hinted how imagination could influence impassive environments. For during that same time, America's National Golf Foundation intimidated the golf industry using dire demographics. Warning of course shortages for future baby boomers, they issued a course per day construction diet. A forecast that profoundly affected the sport in decades ahead. And considering the flurry of projects that prophecy conspired, creative talent often appeared bankrupt. Convenient alibi's claimed choice land for building courses was obsolete. Yet in those prosperous times, seedlings of inspired architects sprouted. Tom Fazio, Ben Crenshaw, Rod Whitman, and Gil Hanse vitalized weary lands into exhilarating tests of golf. They supported my observations at Royal Adelaide. That endless inventories of surprise lay stockpiled within everyone's imagination. In other words, true art exists in everyone. A percolating natural force that can be drawn upon and applied to our chosen careers, interests, and pursuits.

Journal Entry #303: Royal Melbourne

Dedicated to *Dr. Alister MacKenzie*

Several outstanding—and arguably Australia's best—courses were located on Melbourne's outskirts, an area known as the Sandbelt. Among them were Kingston Heath and **Royal Melbourne**, more of MacKenzie's masterful work.

According to history though, the doctor didn't actually lay out Kingston Heath. Records instead indicate he designed its bunkering, while building Royal Melbourne nearby.

Both were exceptional! While the former could be argued heathland, each owned shares in the planets finest par-threes. They may have also sired the world's most breathtaking sand traps. For not only were they cleverly positioned, but visually stunning. Every hazard appearing sharply cut from ground, as if turf-cutting tools of surgical clarity enhanced their definition. Featuring long capes of grass plunging into deep recesses, their perimeters were striking and sensual. MacKenzie created the essence of waves, rising and receding along shapely shores, absent water and motion.

Their visual strengths schooled me in bunker design. I became partial, believing sand traps like fashion cover women, were capable in scale and shape of influencing commerce. Bunkers could be more than just excavations with sand. They could be artistic and arouse fantasy … tempting and harbouring consumers, influencing a course's economic position.

Where to deploy bunkers is a requisite skill in thoughtful design, but in the aftermath they can also be moulded naturally and aesthetically into their environments. Discovered by only few, such skill continues as an intricate form of creativity, paralleling for example the rare music talents of the Funk Brothers or Wrecking Crew.

Next time readers hear or read descriptions proclaiming a golf course as "great," take time to examine and compare the subject's bunkering. There may be moments of heightened awareness.

Journal Entry #304: New South Wales

Dedicated to *Dr. Terry and Lorna McNamara*

Somewhere I read that "it's a small world." And that occurred to me entering the pro shop at **New South Wales** in Sydney.

There, I noticed manager David Harris speaking without an Aussie accent. Harris introduced himself as a fellow Canuck from … Rosetown, Saskatchewan! While we'd never met, only Canadian prairie originals might have appreciated the fraternal connection.

Harris was overseeing clubhouse renovations there, as US President Clinton was arriving to play the famous venue. Harris wasn't alone there grappling with challenge as the course superintendent too, had his work cut out. Over decades, the land had been overgrown by imported South African ground cover. Peeling back the foliage and exposing its natural dunes was exhausting … and deadly! The dense brush was home to venomous black and brown snakes, which inhabited Eastern coastlines. Our host promptly warned us to use clubs when probing lost balls. The snakebites could be fatal!

Like Royal Melbourne, New South Wales too was designed by MacKenzie. Perched high above rocky bluffs, she boasted panoramic Pacific views, not unlike Pebble Beach. There I saw the integrity of the architect's work. New South Wales was absent his charismatic bunkering. The doctor purportedly discarded his ground shaping wizardry to avoid grandstanding the astonishing seascape. A subtle testament to his environmental convictions.

Regardless, while the views were stunning, I was challenged differentiating between various holes, which appeared repetitious. Bounding up and over large ridges, they eventually swooped down and around toward the legendary penal colony, Botany Bay. Centuries earlier, Britain condemned her convicts to spend their remaining days there. Had it been my incarceration place though and New South Wales a fantasy reform program, any sentence there might have been tolerable.

Journal Entry #305: Paraparaumu

Dedicated to *John and Rosmarie Rachwalski*

Late in my career, austerity renewed memories of my journey's final stop, New Zealand.

Austerity, according to *Longman's Dictionary*: "Is when governments have deliberate policies of reducing the money they spend." During that trip, New Zealand was attempting an economic revival after enormous financial setbacks. A victim of deregulation, high interest rates and the

1987 international recession, it implemented severe cutbacks to survive staggering commercial odds.

We began our travels throughout the countries' North Island, where I golfed a modest nine-holer named Rotorua, or Arikikikapakapa. A geothermal aberration near a dormant volcanic crater, she was rough and scrappy like a punk rocker. Boiling mud pools and geysers perfuming sulphuric scents glared from fairway perimeters. If wayward shots found her mystic hazards, ball scoops were as useful as tattoos, taunting golfers to accept their penalties and move on.

Paraparaumu was another course near Wellington on the west coast. Rated among earth's top hundred then, it tested golfers with irregular fairway mounds, sprinkled by fate using wind and time.

Earlier however, her dunes were framed by mature conifers. They're invisible now! Due to those harsh economics, the club heartbreakingly sold off her timber, exonerating debts to survive. Paraparaumu wasn't immune from Kiwi desperation.

I concluded my round-the-world education admiring Paraparaumu's resolve to resuscitate its financially suffocated course. A noble act to remain viable while maintaining dignity.

When Jackie and I later became custodians of our own golf course, those practises of economizing, making do, and saving became survival prerequisites. That taste of New Zealand golf, uniquely prepared me for those austere measures. Practises that not only saw us stay alive in 2008's Great Recession, but also during the waning lust for golf, which subsequently followed.

Journal Entry #306: The New Course (s)

Dedicated to *Sandy Kurceba*

When first applying for the Kal Lake job, I was motivated knowing the club might relocate. They had considered rebuilding on a nearby site patented for a golf course.

Earlier, I walked its earthy hills amid sagebrush, buffalo grass, rock outcrops, and forests of fir. Numerous natural holes existed, needing only discovery. Golf then was exploding around the globe, including the Okanagan. To capitalize on that, their land owners picked a local contractor and built **a new course**. To me, the real estate was rare, logically inviting a seasoned visionary.

It's been said; some lands beckon golf designers to exploit every potential hole before plucking the best. Such a philosophy might have resulted in a different course than what later emerged.

The resort finally opened on bent-grass fairways, an Okanagan first. Acres of sprawling bunkers and unnaturally spheric mounds, trended others that predictably followed.

Today, while it's enjoyed by many, I continue to arbitrate how modern-day architects such as Ben Crenshaw, Tom Fazio, or even a local Rod Whitman might have treated that same property. A site originally moulded by its natural creator, the original architect!

Journal Entry #307: The Merry Mex

Dedicated to *Lee Trevino*

Lee Trevino, the legendary pro known globally as **the Merry Mex**, participated in an Edmonton exhibition at Glendale. I went back for the brief visit.

Trevino put on several demonstrations that day. One from the tenth tee, the same hole I once birdied from **inside** the pro shop. After Trevino converted several low faded tee shots (which he was famous for), he unexpectedly quipped, "Not bad for a little black kid, huh?" I admired Trevino, but I didn't think his words advanced any remedies for racism. Later that afternoon, watching the Mexican tour Glendale in sixty-four shots, I discovered yet another part of the golf swing. A part television could never deliver. Being close to him, I visibly drafted the role Trevino's left wrist played during impact. It was firm, pronounced, and unwavering, authenticating his clubhead heel leading the toe before impact. It was clearly noticeable via his unusual technique, for unlike Trevino's peers, his feet aimed undeniably left. Normally when addressing the ball, it's customary to align one's clubface through the ball toward target. A body's toes, hips, and shoulders should parallel that vector. But the Mexican's port-side alignment magnified his left wrist movement through impact, like ping-pong players cutting spin to a ball. Trevino did the same using a golf club, resulting in solid contact. The ball's clockwise response was the reason his shots historically arced right (Trevino golfed right-handed).

Journal Entry #308: Sukiyaki (I Look Up as I Walk)

Dedicated to *"Tiny" Ingwersen*

The best compliment of my career came from the lips of Argentinean, Roberto De Vicenzo. It's been said however, where there's sunshine, rain too falls. Therefore I also remember the worst comment.

That memory returned when preparing to leave the Trevino exhibition. I accidentally ran into my old boss Donny whom I hadn't seen him in fifteen years. Together we sat on the grass outside the clubhouse, reminiscing when a moment of magic happened. Some of Glendale's elderly passed by and saw us. Word spread, and it seemed everyone deserted Lee to see Donny and I. Many friendly, smiling faces swarmed us sharing warm, nostalgic times. Then I saw … the gritty pipe fitter!

Griff was still a member. A plumber by trade, he too was watching the clinic. Over years, he'd developed a cozy relationship with Donny, or more accurately, his derelict drinking buddy. Griff, feeling left out disrupted the intimate gathering and dragged Donny away.

Seeing Griff then, revived my most unpleasant moment at Glendale. I was a teen back then beginning my career in the shop when one day he polluted me saying: "You wanna know the difference between you and Donny?" He said intimidatingly, "I'd give Donny the shirt off my back …!" To an impressionable youth, that redneck remark cut deep. And in the following decades, it kept reasserting itself, questioning my worth as a human until eventually it mended into scarred memory.

That afternoon was the last time I saw Donny. He passed away soon after, living as a lonely labourer at Edmonton's Country Club … not always sober.

SUMMER PLACE

Journal Entry #309: Oakmont

Dedicated to *Horace Brownlee*

My fortieth birthday present was a trip to Pittsburgh to play historic Oakmont Country Club.

I flew there via Spokane, Washington. En route I passed Rock Creek in southern British Columbia. There, like an abandoned bride at the altar, the nine-hole Kettle Valley Course awaited me by the road among muted ponderosa. Appearing needy, I accommodated her in the sweltering heat. Absent golfers and staff, I was joined instead by rattlers spectating from fairway perimeters. Snakes and I don't cohabitate and the reptile fears inspired precision shots down each fairway. Later that afternoon … still alive, I left for Pittsburgh.

Next morning, I discovered another heat … the Steel City's humid species. It exhaled in my face as I left the cool, air-conditioned hotel lobby. The muggy temperatures taunted me to change shirts twice that day, but at least **Oakmont** was snake-less.

Oakmont's consummate pro was Bob Ford. Within his intimately furnished shop, Ford was shocked when I shared how many rounds Kal Lake annually turned over. The veteran set me up with caddy Bill Galardi as I began warming up on the practise putter, which doubled as Oakmont's ninth green.

Oakmont's putting surfaces were flagged the fastest on earth, prompting Galardi to launch into a speed demonstration. Motioning to me, he said, "Watch this!" Bending toward the ball, he gently blew at it from a distance. I watched mesmerized as the subtle molecular disturbance caused my ball to begin marching. Galardi had been there since 1927, evidenced by his references to golf bags as sacks. From the beginning, he shared sacred stories with me, including one about a fellow caddie's irate boss. From a bridge joining the first green and second tee, the angry bag toter hurled his employer's equipment far below to the streaming Pennsylvania Turnpike! Needless to say, I treated Galardi right, especially trekking that very trestle.

At Oakmont, putts rolled like lightning on linoleum … but I must have been ready for them sinking an unexpected share. Oakmont reminded me of a longer version of Edmonton's Country Club, except her bunkers appeared artisaned by Salvador Dali. This was no more surreal than at her famous hazard called Church Pews. Oakmont also used special wide-rung rakes for traps. Consequently, balls finished in troughs making bunker play to slippery greens intimidating and unpredictable.

Oakmont was a major league course with a matching history and room for ripping tee shots.

Not long after, I replayed each hole in my mind watching two of our juniors qualifying there during the televised US Amateur.

Journal Entry #310: Memory

Dedicated to *Roy and Vicki Rogers*

In the golf business, pros were occasionally called on to be show people. After all, the sport's ironically considered entertainment too. Club captains were responsible for special events, but sometimes they relied on us to organize those outings, especially nights called "Twilights."

Twilights were nine-hole get-togethers scheduled each month for couples. Along with a theme, supper, and prizes, its purpose stimulated interest and attracted members. One topic we produced was a spoof of Hollywood's Academy Awards. Our script, which followed the format and dialogue of cinema's award ceremony, was timed for after dinner laughs.

In preparation, my staff slicked their hair while dawning black suits, ties, and sunglasses. We even found fake Oscar statues. During the gala, we'd poke fun at our member's numerous idiosyncrasies, such as those with the heaviest golf bags, best laughs, or most outlandish dressers. We'd then follow the Academy's cue listing five nominees. We even acted ... purposely fumbling envelopes while nervously announcing winners. Then amid fun and laughter, we'd award statuettes at the podium.

During those years, we organized similar events. Some included a rubber duck race in the fast-moving creek adjoining the clubhouse. It's been rumoured some of those birds are still found today in a nearby lake. And then we organized Jurassic Golf as a satire of the movie *Jurassic Park* ... playing the course backwards. Each event demanded thought, planning, and time. As memorable as they were though, I always knew showmanship wasn't my strong suit. Deep down, I yearned to own that entertaining bone so many of my peers possessed

Journal Entry #311: Heat Wave

Dedicated to *Mike Pearce*

Everyone from the layperson to royalty has been victim to regret. Hostages to an act or word they wish could have been retrieved. I was hardly exceptional!

One of mine took place during Kal Lake's Wally Motors tournament, an extremely popular event during May's long weekend.

The competition was organized by the SS, chaired by an unpopular retired educator named Jaeger. Once the event was full, our shop began a waiting list. A roster for those wanting to play, but couldn't until cancellations availed themselves. One of those waiting was Hans Wolff, a tall, hard-working German plumbing contractor who could be antagonizing. Jaeger and Wolff despised each other. Eventually Han's name reached the top of the wait list but unknown to him, Jaeger excluded him from the field, shuffling the plumber further down the list. I objected but Jaeger was unrelenting. Wolff however, wasn't anyone's fool and smelled a rat, placing the shop in a delicate position. Smarter pros might have bailed then, but in that weak moment I became the whistleblower, sharing the tournament files with Wolff. In doing so, Jaeger's suspicious financials surfaced. In my eyes, Jaeger got what was deserved, but the SS saw it differently. Instead, they circumvented blame away from its insurgent tournament committee toward the whistleblower. Of course some suspected me, but the only one who really knew was the plumber.

There are times when pros should leave well enough alone and turn the other way. I knew better, but was foolish. Harper made it clear, misjudgments like that couldn't happen twice. He had the motive to orchestrate my dismissal then but thankfully didn't!

Journal Entry #312: The Golden Rules

Dedicated to *Woody and Joyce Woodruff*

When I taught beginner swing classes, I always included messages about golf's "three Rs." Humorously I'd add: "If you want to be known your entire life as a novice golfer … be sure to ignore them!" **R**eplace divots, **R**ake sand traps, and **R**epair ball marks on greens, have been embedded within golf's culture in various languages for decades. They're visible on course signs and scorecards, persisting in hope players acknowledge how exhausting course maintenance is. They've survived in belief **ALL** golfers should perform that trilogy, leaving playing surfaces better than found. Unfortunately, they're often unheeded. Most course owners and managers agree, the constant neglect of those cardinal courtesies remain uphill battles. Ones whose unsavoury origins claim green fees paid absolve customers of thoughtful, considerate behaviour.

One day I had an idea for attracting attention to them. I contacted twelve members for help. Each from various places in the world with their own distinct language. I asked them to translate the three R's into the respective dialects of Arabic, Chinese, French, Hebrew, Hungarian, Italian, Japanese, Korean, Pakistani, Spanish, Swedish, and Ukrainian.

In addition to our weekly club notices, I posted those translations. Unexpectedly they garnered extraordinary attention from our largely English-speaking members who ironically began deciphering golf's most precious code … the three Rs.

Journal Entry #313: Peachtree

Dedicated to *Robert Tyre Jones, Jr.*

Peachtree was one of those extremely private courses, so difficult to access that most golfers abandoned trying.

While attending a Club Car conference in Georgia I was invited to play the reclusive Atlanta course.

Peachtree's historic impact in the world of course design isn't well known. There its inspiration, the legendary Robert Tyre Jones, Jr. relinquished the designing duties to another Jones … Robert Trent. They were different men with similar names, each playing vast roles within the vignettes of golf.

Consequently, Peachtree kick-started Trent Jone's voracious architectural career.

Peachtree's first and second holes were great openers. The first was a short dogleg right par-four, while the second a unique par-five. It bent the same direction but with two fairways near the green where golfers could choose the most advantageous angle to approach from. I saw value in courses starting with doglegs right as most golfers are right-handed and slice the ball. It was an early form of subtle forgiveness in a typical four-hour round of challenges.

The intrinsic red Georgian soil was a unique and fertile growing medium, however I found the rest of the course uninspiring. I was captivated rather by its original civil-war clubhouse, a tasteful brick mansion previously commandeered by Union General William Sherman. On its veranda, were authentic expressions of Deep South golf … stout and white wooden rocking chairs. The kind good, ol' Republicans rocked in after golf, tawkin' suthern and tradin' storiz. The kind daddys teetered in when decreeing younguns to vote obediently, rather than intelligently or objectively.

In that iconic *Gone with the Wind* setting, I questioned which direction the wind of golf's industry might have blown, had Tyre Jones retained Alister MacKenzie at Peachtree … instead of Trent Jones … like he did at his masterpiece down the road, Augusta National?

Journal Entry #314: A Letter to Hank Haney

Dedicated to *Bob and Flo Whiting*

Dear Mr. Haney:

The following is true.

One of my members here in Canada had a brother, a Tennessee club pro who golfed Kal Lake when vacationing. As a result, the pro and I became friendly. Aware of my interest in architecture and the world's top hundred courses, he invited me to visit him in the Deep South and play the Honors Course, near Chattanooga. The veteran knew a member there who extended us invitations.

The host was a young, burly type who looked like his name should have been Bubba. He was working on his tour card then and eventually became successful. Unfortunately he didn't last, turning toward a more stable career … broadcasting. He became a commentator for a new television network devoted to golf.

When we played the Honors Course that day, Tiger Woods had recently competed there in the US Amateur. Like many, I was fascinated by the rising, young star and asked the big man his impressions. Suddenly his southern hospitality vaporized. Drilling me with a venomous glare, he delivered a vulgar lecture, spitting out, "He ain't nuthin' but a nigga!" I hadn't spent much time in the southern states and only read of the Ku Klux Klan and their toxic racial hatred. But at that moment I was mired within it.

So Hank, after reading your book *The Big Miss* and absorbing your comments about Tiger, I was moved to write you about that incident decades ago. Personally, I'm unsure whether Tiger lost his own rare opportunity as the ultimate role model. On the other hand, having witnessed first hand what he no doubt experienced frequently … maybe someone else lost something as well?

Sincerely, Patrick

Journal Entry #315: Beautiful Life

Dedicated to *Muriel Wynn*

One of my more memorable golf experiences took place during two consecutive weeks in the '90s.

Week one: I flew to Prince Edward Island to watch Jackie participate in the Canadian Amateur at Mill River, a wedge shot from where singer,

Stompin' Tom Connors hailed from. There Jackie introduced me to Canadian legend Marlene Streit and LPGA favourite Lorie Kane. Jackie was among the favorites finishing second a year earlier. In the opening round, when her ball found trees, her exuberant young caddie picked it up, innocent of the rules. The ensuing four shot-double penalty shook up Jackie forcing me to take over the caddie reins. She didn't win, but deep down I knew that incident influenced her performance.

Week two: Days later in Alberta, our son Robert who'd developed into a superb competitor himself, played in his first National Amateur at Glendale. There I caddied for him also.

Our daughter Janine then was developing her own career as an Equine Canada Certified Coach for Dressage horses and riders. A third week with her would have been a complete dream-come-true, but I settled for two out of three. It was a rare occasion caddying for both my wife and son in the nationals, only days apart in different provinces of the country.

Journal Entry #316: Albatross

Dedicated to *Carol McKergow*

I pulled my tee shot left among a trio of elms on Kal Lake's par-five eighth hole. My playing partner was an influential local who owned Canada's largest independent tire dealership. He stood beside me as I negotiated a low hook around the obstacles to the green. For that second effort, I trusted my persimmon Tommy Armour four-wood of the day. What followed was a flushed, fast-moving low draw which curved around the foliage, landed quick, and then with topspin scampered up the fairway. We watched it ascend the gentle slope, unexpectedly jump on, and then suddenly clunk against the flagstick … hanging on the lip.

That was as close as I came to a double eagle. Also known as an **albatross,** it's three under par on a single hole and much rarer than an ace. I once sank my second on a 460-yard par-four, but as they say, "Close, but no cigar, Chico," because par-fives then were a minimum 470 yards. However I did witness an albatross during the National Club Pros tournament at

Capilano. I remembered that day ... the one when Canada mourned the NHL trade of hockey star Gretzky.

It was understandable why an entire nation was enveloped within the furor that followed. Now however, it seems frivolous for when writing this, we Canadians traded away possibly the most powerful agent on earth ... with minimal fanfare. And worse, most Canucks were apathetic!

Mark Carney was lured to the world's monetary capital, the United Kingdom. There, he was appointed the Bank of England's Governor, an assignment that began July 1, 2013. That was because Britain's Chancellor of the Exchequer felt the Northwest Territory product was earth's most qualified candidate—a testimony to Carney's financial talent navigating Canada through the Great Recession. As Governor of Banks then, Carney's decisions saved each and every Canadian untold amounts of hard-earned cash. But Canucks will never know how much, nor will they care until Carney scores fifty goals in thirty-nine games or double eagles the fourteenth at St. Andrews!

Journal Entry #317: The Record

Dedicated to *Dan Dally*

Accompanying the title of club professional are expectations of playing abilities. Skills blurring a public's perception of golf professionals versus professional golfers.

As written earlier, the former are responsible for growing golf. They oversee each facilities' day-to-day operations which include managing, merchandising, teaching, repairing equipment and administering events. The latter's the tournament player, recognized in media. Their performances are exceptional because their business is playing golf. That doesn't mean club pros are incapable. But to be blunt, their forte is business.

Nevertheless, club pros aren't respected if their talent fades, regardless how extensive their responsibilities may be! Therefore maintaining a respectable game while overseeing business requires additional time and focus.

I resolved that over decades setting modest season goals. Each year within frantic schedules, I practised just enough to break seventy, which usually was two to four under par. It didn't matter if those round(s) were sixty-six or sixty-nine, but that was my benchmark.

One year, I scored a five under thirty-one on the front nine, which included a three putt. I followed it with a two under thirty-four on the back, rendering me the official course record sixty-five. That stood for a dozen years, before one of my junior graduates on the PGA tour, returned home scoring sixty-one.

It was my only course record; unlike Jackie who has them all over the province. But I was grateful to have one and for as long as it stood.

Journal Entry #318: Girls Just Want to Have Fun

Dedicated to *Bob and Joanne Bradley*

Gradually, as our children outgrew parental supervision, Jackie began competing again provincially. British Columbia's competition was strong but so was she when the Amateur was played in nearby Salmon Arm. There, she outdistanced the field except a friend from Alberta. Marilyn O'Conner was the reigning Canadian champion and clipped Jackie by a stroke.

Two years later at Vancouver's Shaughnessy, Jackie contested again. This time tying New Zealand's top amateur Lynnette Brooky, a powerful teen who later became a touring pro. Among a squad of spectators, they went into sudden death. With our son Robert caddying, Jackie lofted her third shot stiff for a winning birdie.

That evening in the clubhouse, a television sports channel broadcasted the win. Suddenly the crammed spike bar erupted into cheers unlike anything seen or heard there before. Even the SS celebrated!

Journal Entry #319: Have I Told You Lately?

Dedicated to *Dodie Corner*

When I was appointed head pro, Kal Lake had no history of significant competitions. I felt more seasoned tournaments would increase revenues and promote the club. Consequently early in my tenure, I used that opportunity to influence the course into hosting more provincially sanctioned events.

Finally twenty-two years later it became reality. It required scheduling the course years in advance, taking advantage of cancelled opportunities, and selling possibilities to directors. Often members weren't eager to share their course for such occasions. But it was an ironic posture, given their desires for prosperity. Promoting ladies' competitions seemed easier, so we began by hosting the Senior Women's Provincial. That was followed by the Junior Ladies. Finally we were selected to host British Columbia's Amateur.

Jackie was defending champion that tension filled week as she performed in front of members. She led from start to finish with Robert caddying again.

I was never more proud of being club pro as then. It seemed every past emotional obstacle had been worth it. I thought I'd reached a career pinnacle. That was before Jackie and I invested in retirement!

Journal Entry #320: On the Dark Side

Dedicated to *Bob Roy*

For reasons which aren't clear, lawyers haven't always enjoyed flattering images in the public eye. Perhaps the legal essence of lawyer-client privilege isn't as readily understood as a physician's hippocratic oath?

Also it's been suggested, bad things happen when motive, means, and opportunity exist. Later when I lost my job, investing in retirement appeared to root such a motive.

Its origins began at an obscure, nine-hole Okanagan resort which flew under popularities' radar. Located ten kilometres off the main highway near Penticton, it was just far enough to eliminate large slices of golfers unwilling to negotiate its narrow, winding entry. Shackled by mountains, she had a secluded yet luring appeal. Alongside her a tasteful housing development mingled with gentle ponderosa.

The clubhouse was a West Coast post-and-beam design with modest accommodations and an inviting swimming pool.

It was in that paradise the Lefevre's made their home. Jackie and I often called upon them, breaking away from Kal Lake's hectic shop routine.

During one of those visits, they shared the course's vision of developing additional lots. New purchasers could choose a home site and benefit with lifetime golf memberships. That was our inspiration to invest in future retirement. We selected a treed lot offering panoramic views of the course below. Our lawyer handled the legalities.

Soon after, someone else saw the opportunity. After our deal closed, the development sold to a Vancouver barrister, one with an unsavoury past! Lefevre urged us to immediately withdraw the investment, which we assumed was in-trust.

Coincidentally our own lawyer changed jobs then, transferring his clients to the firm's newest partner, a young Italian named Flavio Corlazzoli.

After numerous failed calls to the new developer, we recruited Corlazzoli to reclaim the investment. Days trickled into weeks, which dripped into months and frustration mounted from Corlazzoli's silence, mobilizing Lefevre to get involved. My old boss discreetly couriered the original paperwork to us, proving the new owner illegally removed our funds from trust. Suddenly, we were in the driver's seat.

Lefevre went further, arranging an awkward meeting with the swindler at a Penticton restaurant. Instead though, I was unexpectedly met by the principle's underbelly trouble-shooter … an intimidating Afrikaans. During the cool, tense time, he weaponized the moments with provocation and intimidation until reluctantly returning our investment. The rendezvous suggested what the underworld's dark side might appear like.

While we relinquished the retirement dream, we settled for our original investment. However it didn't end there!

Corlazzoli stunned us submitting an invoice for expenses. In the aftermath of that harrowing restaurant encounter, I was in no mood to pay for uncompleted work. And that stance probably nudged my eventual demise!

Journal Entry #321: Trouble!

Dedicated to *Barry and Pixie Fifer*

With the retirement deal over, we dodged several bullets, beginning with the return of our investment. Plus I left unscathed, after successfully negotiating with the mysterious restaurant man whose license might have read, out-of-work mercenary.

Months later however, The Law Society of British Columbia unexpectedly knocked at our door. They were investigating the development's main principle who had siphoned our trust funds. In deposition, I detailed the lot purchase which unfortunately included the role of our local lawyer. Was it coincidental he joined Kal Lake immediately after? Did my statement have a bearing on what happened later at the course? Did I inadvertently put a second nail in my coffin, unaware of the looming **trouble**?

Journal Entry #322: Eyes Without a Face

Dedicated to *Gary Strom*

Earlier as a young assistant, Mayfair's millionaires massaged me with the virtues of working hard. And by the mid-'90s a list of achievements corroborated that.

Jackie won the British Columbia Amateur two consecutive years. Another student won the Provincial Senior Women's twice as well. Plus two of our juniors won their respective provincials, multiple times.

Then our PGA presented me with their junior development award.

In addition, I was twice voted Best Professional by readers of a popular glossy, Okanagan tourist guide.

Accolades like that, normally should have made any work climate comfortable. But it wasn't! Something wasn't right! Any pro with intuition knows when a work environment isn't. The SS were up to something. There were **eyes without a face.**

Journal Entry #323: The Prime Minister

Dedicated to *Dr. David and Sandra Harder*

When Lefevre was manager, Kal Lake entered a silent metamorphosis which progressively penetrated the business community. In addition, British Columbia completed the Coquihalla Highway linking the Okanagan to BC's Lower Mainland. Together they redefined the little folksy course into a bustling club with more annual rounds played than other valley courses.

The reformation was joined by three visionary presidents. Cec Hamilton, spearheaded an architect's long-range development plan as well as a new clubhouse. With the legal direction of Travis Wotherspoon, the club's constitution was updated. He and successor George Pell, negotiated the sale of Kal Lake's vacant land to acquire more useful property that advanced the course's character.

In that decade of prosperity Kal Lake climbed the rungs toward industrial integrity becoming efficient and profitable. Within that dawn of enrichment, we even hosted Canada's **Prime Minister,** the Right Honourable Jean Chrétien.

Not everyone shared that campaign however!

Journal Entry #324: Good Thing (Where Have You Gone?)

Dedicated to *Don and Mary Matheson*

The course changes successfully accommodated the lusting masses who flocked to the valley. Tourists fuelled by the planet's popularity toward golf then.

The three presidents' shifting those gears needed a fresh face to sustain the progress. Kevin Wright was the logical successor. Wright retired to the Okanagan with his Maritime wife after a career with a world renown plumbing chain. With a sharp acumen for business, he would have become an astonishing leader. But the club's progress wasn't shared by everyone!

Bitsy, Jr. detested Kal Lake's futuristic ambitions. His dad was Bitsy, the frazzled course superintendent I met fifteen years earlier. Bitsy, Jr. had left long before and returned home to settle. Cunning, crafty and trained in community politics, he assumed a governing position in a nearby hamlet. Growing up with his dad as a descendant among the SS, he craved the club's past, rather than its liberal lean. Armed with an arsenal of how golf courses should operate, a fickle five-handicap, and a loathing for the new regime … he too ran for president.

At the annual general meeting, where new board members were voted in, Wright lost the presidency to the politician. The winner campaigned on the SS's shifty strategies and tasteless tactics. They turned their back on bankers, developers, and lawyers for the all too familiar cynics, whiners, and complainers.

Wright, mortified by how he'd been smeared, quit and joined another course. Things wouldn't be the same. In the blink of a vote, the club's **good thing** vanished, receding toward previously regressive times.

I too should have been aware. My instincts and mind were elsewhere pushing the buttons of business. I didn't see the ocean for the water!

Journal Entry #325: Mercy Mercy Me

Dedicated to *Herb Willms*

Over four decades I worked with many talented superintendents. Gatekeepers who supervised each course's maintenance routine. Steadfast gardeners who confronted endless natural challenges while tolerating the whims of golfers. Diplomats who constantly justified agronomic practises while keeping pace with fluctuating budgets and effervescent technology. All effecting the war on earth's greenhouse gas emissions!

Not all superintendents were that devoted, however.

Kal Lake weathered several changes in ground's management, until eventually settling on one known as Chemical Ali. Originally from Ontario, he eagerly joined the staff with his silky persuasive demeanour. It wasn't long before the essence of his expertise exposed itself. It began with his addictive use of the edgy herbicide Roundup, manufactured by the corporate monster Monsanto. Ali sprayed the chemical around every individual tree, converting the green grass brown. Experts in the business claimed: "Roundup was safe. When applied to the plant leaf, it stayed within the organism, killing only the life form as far as the root." Supposedly, it didn't contaminate surrounding soils. However, I never believed anything that powerful, could be so reliable. It partnered that phrase, "If it looks too good to be true, it probably isn't."

Next, women wearing shorts complained of skin rashes, indicting Ali's pesticide assaults. In response, Ali inflamed their insinuations, convicting them casualties of personal diets and sunblock choices. Their aggravation was antagonized further when seeing his crew protecting themselves from the fumes and foams they bombed the course with daily.

Then one by one, greens began dying, fatalities of fertilizer burn. I'd studied agronomy and knew the potency of misapplications. Most fertilizers had to be immediately irrigated in to avoid burning plants. Failures ran high risks resulting in dead greens which then were closed months for reseeding and recovery.

As summer progressed, so did the number of temporary greens, impacting Kal Lake's revenues and reputation. Ali sliced into the budget further imploring various golf associations for lavish remedies. I was certain he'd burnt the greens, but no one asked my opinion. And my replies wouldn't have been flattering anyway. Our relationship was strained as the appalling conditions made the shop targets of caustic customer complaints. Unfortunately the directors procrastinated dealing with Ali's aloof, arrogant posture. It was heartbreaking to witness the withering of previous prosperity.

Reckless behavior by staff impacts the lives of golfers who pay dues and green fees to keep courses economically viable. It also impugns the efforts of other dedicated employees. Chemical Ali finally lost his job, but in the aftermath never acknowledged accountability. He continued on at other courses with his silky style. A behaviour any American citizen with an **honest conscience** would have acknowledged following the 2016 election.

Journal Entry #326: Augusta National (Part 1)

Dedicated to *Dessey and Tripp*

Among my cherished memories of St. Andrews was the weather. It was always perfect, as if ordained for my visits. It was the same at Augusta.

In 1994, I was invited to play the world's hottest golf ticket, **Augusta National** Golf Club. The National, as it's referred to, is in Augusta, Georgia, and home to the famous Masters Tournament.

I never admitted the source of that rare invite because of promises to respect anonymity. But it included the perk of bringing a guest so I asked Jackie. The all day occasion was arranged in advance and one week prior to that season's championship.

As we edged closer to our date, the southeastern states were tormented by tornadoes. Amid the turbulence, we flew into Atlanta without incident. With weather forecasts equally grim ahead, lightning intensified it, persisting among hovering clouds.

Stationed in our La Quinta Hotel room, speculations about our lengthy journey to a place we'd long dreamt of playing, only finding we couldn't consumed us. Adding to doubt, the National was readying for that years Masters with exhaustive final week preparations.

Strangely twenty-four hours from our appointment, the climate disobeyed barometric orders and broke. Next morning in sunshine, we loaded our gear for the hundred kilometre trip. But common sense nagged us with questions like: "Was there too much course damage? Would they simply close it and apologize?"

The conditions prevailed however, accompanied by a reassuring voice on our hotel phone saying: "Welcome to Augusta. When you reach the guard gate, tell them you're my guest. We'll see you then."

A day later on our flight home, gloom drew in yet again like curtains closing after stage performances. When our plane drilled through dark clouds, the familiar rocking resumed, as tornadoes swirled in for encores.

Like at St. Andrews, the golf gods seemingly rescinded previous edicts and blew away the madness just for us.

Journal Entry #327: Augusta National (Part 2)

Dedicated to *Kurby*

Some cities are acknowledged by their street names. For instance, Toronto has Bay Street. London has Carnaby and in Paris it's the Champs-Elysées. At Augusta, Georgia, it's Washington Road ... where the entrance to **Augusta National** Golf Club is located.

The drive from Augusta's main gate through a canopy of magnolias is a wondrous experience. Emerging from it, we were met in the parking lot by a member who'd never hosted a female guest there before. There was no women's locker room then forcing Jackie to change in the ladies' washroom.

On the other hand I was escorted to the ground-level men's locker room. Modest in size it was enriched by dark brown, wooden lockers etched in membership names. In awe, I changed my shoes in a luxurious leather chair distinguished by divisions of glossy tacks.

We began our odyssey at the driving range, practising off exquisite turf. Our irons surgically peeled through ground which surrendered irresistibly. A squad of suited caddies idled nearby, exchanging respectful comments about Jackie's' swing. After arming up, we followed our host past green and white gabled cabins to the nine-hole pitch and putt course below. He touted its charm claiming many members visited exclusively to play just the little course.

Ahead of us, a team of twelve workers laboured meticulously, priming and trimming the grounds as women preparing for dates. Moving from hole to hole in uniform precision, they swarmed with legendary efficiency. Lingering impressions suggested regimented routine. Consequently the course was immaculate. Vibrant emerald playing surfaces and brick pine straw tapestried about two glimmering lakes flanked by towering loblolly.

After, in the clubhouse, with its undeniable casual pace decreed by elegant southern dining, we lunched on cornbread buns, toasted bacon-and-tomato sandwiches, and cream-of-chicken soup.

The host punctuated our numerous questions with answers unlocking the National's past including seldom publicized membership admissions. Afterward, we toured the upstairs Crow's Nest, library, and champion's locker room. Displays included the club Gene Sarazen used recording his famous 1935 double eagle, as well as Bobby Jone's original 1930 grand slam equipment ... individually preserved and authenticated by weight. Lower-level walls were checkered with original artwork of club founders Bob Jones, Clifford Roberts, and former POTUS Eisenhower. Most members lived elsewhere, but when visiting their names were listed in the main foyer for networking.

Following the tour, we tackled Augusta's long course. There heaving terrain undetected by media, we outlasted putting greens that challenged the pace of porcelain.

Their gleaming speeds suggested playing strategies of distance control when approaching greens ... and abilities to execute the same. Therefore to score well, one had to **stay below the hole.** That meant positioning shots where putts to uphill pin locations were most advantageous. For that exclusive reason, I admired the National. The caddies were the most efficient and knowledgeable I'd ever seen. Polite and coached socially, they allowed guests first input toward each shot's strategy. It was mandatory employing them and ours was Chris ... number forty-nine.

I flushed an opening drive and eventually arrived at the final hole, bunkering my approach. From there I blasted to seven feet finishing with par. In between were sixteen holes of ebbs and flows. Regardless one couldn't help feeling exhilarated each step of the idyllic four-hour journey.

The National is a masterpiece of evolution. Its conceptual design is classic ... hard to birdie, yet easy bogeying. The thirteenth, a dogleg left par-five, is arguably the world's finest hole. A drawn tee shot for right-handers is rewarded by an equally challenging fade to a defiant green. Many courses, particularly American, attempt emulating Augusta with perpetual capital. It doesn't take much accomplishing that, but recreating its ambiance is improbable. There's that saying … "Less is more." Augusta National seems partial to that philosophic asset … yet anchored by mountains of money, imbedded history, and a coveted essence conceived from the soul of golf.

To my knowledge, there is no other place then … or now like it!

Journal Entry #328: Billy Billy Went A Walkin'

Dedicated to *Mike Whalen*

Kal Lake entered a downward spiral after Wright was defeated. Soon after, Harper called it quits too, moving onto a new venture in Vancouver. Then the board procrastinated dealing with Chemical Ali. Their next mistake wasn't hiring Manager Mike, but neglecting to bind him in contract.

Mike was another professional club manager. Placid in nature and smart, he was committed and capable. Dressing with managerial swagger, he evoked images of confidence wearing tailored suits and shoes as glossy as anyone enlisted. Single and elderly, he worked out religiously, while leading with direction and informed staff meetings, which in short time led to our bond of respect. As a result, he encouraged me to move forward into club management, believing in my ability to breach the next level.

Soon after however Mike went walking. He took advantage of a Vancouver opportunity, claiming Kal Lake "dragged their feet" putting a contract together. As protection, he went elsewhere.

Once again, Kal Lake went looking for a new administrator.

Journal Entry #329: Constant Craving (Pine Valley)

Dedicated to *Dale Krebs*

It is all very well to punish a bad stroke, but the right of eternal punishment should be reserved for a higher tribunal.

—Bernard Darwin

In October 1995 I flew into Newark, New Jersey, seeing Manhattan's twin towers for the last time. After a short drive to the isolated hamlet Clementon, I stayed and played the devil's home course ... **Pine Valley**!

I loved almost every moment there. Near Atlantic City, she was a wicked layout serpentined among long ago sand dunes and pines. Using deception and intimidation, Pine Valley subverted minds by taunting prey with natural diversions that camouflaged generous fairways. Like blackberry barbs that prick skin, she humbled the impetuous, punishing wayward shots without conscience. And deadly? Eerie sand traps of casket dimensions often interred victims, while a sphincter-like pot bunker fronting her tenth green was aptly named, the Devil's Asshole! Her par-three, fifth of 223 yards was referred to as "the hole where only god made three." I was one of the luckier ones, but readers shouldn't draw religious parallels. On that same hole, playing television's *Shell's Wonderful World of Golf*, former US Open Champion Gene Littler scored thirteen.

I golfed uncharacteristically well there that perfect autumn day, surprising my host who claimed few play the Valley under eighty their first time ... even tour pros.

The clubhouse was no less! Supposedly real men hung out within its main vestibule. Those engaging in lewd humour, swearing, and obnoxious farting. I pictured them hoisting drink under the lordly fresco of course founder, George Crump. Beyond that male bastion was the dining room where jackets and ties ordained them gentlemen.

At lunch I downed the signature favourite ... sherry flavoured turtle soup. At dinner, there was rack of lamb with too much wine. After, my vino and I explored the upstairs hall, examining historical trivia abounding one of earth's more intriguing courses. Later still, I found my evening's accommodation, the presidential cottage normally reserved for American leaders. Amid glowing hallucination in darkness, I migrated out toward the adjacent fourth hole. There under stars I reflected back to the pines and sand of the primitive two-hole course of my origins.

I had one reservation at Pine Valley. Patronizing their shop next day, I accompanied an Asian customer completing a large purchase. When offering his credit card, the assistant sneered at him: "We don't take plastic here!" His spiteful tone reminded me how comparably polite my staff were back home.

That aside, Pine Valley remains another mistress, condemning this apostle to mortal spells of **constant craving.**

Journal Entry #330: House of Cards

Dedicated to *Ted and Mavis Strother*

Watching the television series ***House of Cards***, brought back grim memories of another unusual course. Unusual because the Burning Tree Club then, may have been the most inaccessible to play anywhere.

Located in Bethesda, Maryland, she's a stone throw from Washington DC, where I golfed the US Open site, Congressional Country Club. There I met legendary teacher Bill Strausbaugh who introduced me to Burning Tree's distinguished pro, past PGA President Max Elbin. Through that connection, I was allowed rare access to the convoluted enclave.

Burning Tree was given its name because of a deciduous variety whose top leaves matured red in fall, citing flaming appearances.

Inside the clubhouse, colourful flags of various countries whose ambassadors were members, rainbowed the rafters. Also featured were displays of golf clubs hung in perpetuity ... cudgels donated by every US President. In the Spike Bar, a famous cartoonist's caricatures of congressional leaders stamped walls, while another room lionized more gripping features. Discreet and sacred, the chamber was designed to accommodate former POTUS Eisenhower. Constructed with private door and telephone, it permitted the general convenient course access, while conducting business.

Burning Tree's membership was exclusive to almost every former US president. But it was chilling to hear Max detail how Burning Tree excluded one past leader for membership ... Bill Clinton. Close to retirement, the veteran shared the inside skinny. Burning Tree was an all-male bastion and Elbin's members felt Clinton's spouse Hillary **ran** the White House. It was eye-opening! Why Clinton? A scholar with histories of philanthropy and sincere passions for golf? It didn't make sense. Perhaps the former Commander in Chief dodged a bullet though. Especially knowing the 2016 republican in name only, who probably did get the nod.

While grateful for the experience, once was enough! The veil of tension couldn't hide a metastasized Washington bureaucracy ... as fictionalized in the **House of Cards.**

Journal Entry #331: The Secret

Dedicated to *Dr. Nicholas Rety*

In earlier journal entries I wrote of two surreal experiences during separate British trips. Experiences defying explanation.

A third occurred in our shop.

In a 1953 *Golf Digest* article, Ben Hogan reportedly revealed the golf swing secret. It was followed by hypes of media attention with golfers debating the blueprint's existence. Earlier Hogan suggested, "The secret is in the dirt," which I felt was the real answer.

But on July 25, 1997, a day after my birthday ... the Texan died. I wrote his obituary in the shop.

The counter where we served our membership was constructed at a ninety-degree angle. On its outside corner I positioned a white board for rotating messages which kept golfers abreast of club events. Finishing the eulogy, I walked away to reread it. I always wanted member's perspective when interpreting those signs. That moment was different.

Instead of seeing what was written, I saw an image. A headless apparition holding a club simulating a right-handed swing in an abbreviated follow through. But the image's bent **left** elbow visually suggested it was unified in movement ... with the **right elbow** and wrists. Hogan wrote two instructional books, *Power Golf* and *Five Lessons*. In each, were subtle after-impact swing differences. In the former, Hogan was plagued by an uncontrollable hook. In book two though, his after-impact left elbow position appears perpendicular, and more importantly ... pointing down! A follow-through that not only mirrored his backswing plane, but foreshadowed his right elbow's influence on squareness at impact!

It was a sudden and brief vision—or fantasy—that unexpectedly gave me transparency. For ironically, it capsuled years of experiments ultimately revealing the golf swing to be … compact, symmetric, and utilizing minimal joint use. An analogy suggesting the simple opening and shutting of a door.

This entry doesn't claim to be Hogan's algorithm. Regardless, much like the last page of a novel's turned or a plane lands, my search ended for the golf swing that day. I taught with newfound confidence while finding significant advances in my own efforts. First, trajectories were higher from increased ball rotations. Second, impact moments between ball and clubface were closer to sweet spots and highly charged. Third, each shot was significantly more accurate.

Historically, planet earth has been riddled with secrets and conspiracies. Myths of monsters, disappearances, and methodologies have mystified the masses like QAnon. Unlike them however, that day I exited the ranks joining orders of the less persecuted.

Chapter Four

Winter

(Journal Entries 332 through 399)

The Ryder Cup. Junior Johnson and the President. Expropriation. Returning to work as an employee. Chevy. The squeeze and the sting. Firing and forced eviction. Lawsuit. It ends. We buy a golf course.

Journal Entry #332: The Circle is Small

Dedicated to *Charlie Brown*

When Manager Mike left Kal Lake, the circle became small. I was alone again and the weariness from adversarial clashes returned. As the club's longtime professional then, one would have thought I'd have risen above the paranoia. I found myself again working among board members who not only failed to lock Mike into a binding contract, but allowed Chemical Ali to continue altering the positive work gained during the club's previous dozen years. And as usual, new directors continued to be influenced by the SS.

It was in that environment, the job for general manager once more became open. Through the grapevine, I learned Ali was licking his chops for the position. It wasn't reassuring.

At that pinnacle of my career, I assessed the situation warily.

The course was plagued by temporary greens, tarnishing a recent lustrous image. The one responsible was applying for the job. While I wasn't interested in the position, I couldn't see glowing futures working for the alternative either. Consequently I entered the race with purpose.

I submitted my own resume, strategizing the board might look at both of us and hire neither.

On the last day for submissions, I left my application on Rosa Klebb's clean, uncluttered desk. It vanished!

Journal Entry #333: Rosa Klebb

Dedicated to *George and Nancy Richardson*

Among seldom seen working relationships at courses, are those between club pros and office staff.

In every club's daily survival, administrative employees play integral roles. Anything relative to a course's business accounts such as payables and receivables plus answering phones fall within their job description. They also coordinate in-house communications between course superintendents, managers, and club pros. For environments to be meaningful and enjoyable for customers and members, pro shop and office staff must work together.

Rosa Klebb was Kal Lake's long time secretary. A short and stout Slovakian, she was a bookkeeper with a technical title. Struggling with public relations, she often appeared rude to members although reliability and numerical competence repeatedly compensated her job. Our working relationship was cooperative for years, but went south one day during the 1997 holidays.

That Christmas, I took Rosa to lunch as I annually did, a modest expression of gratitude for her seasonal hard work. During our meal however, she emotionally confided a chapter from her personal past. But in that moment of strain, she strangely arraigned me as an accomplice to her anguish. Consequently in one of life's ironic twists, she began an endless chiding campaign toward me.

The relationship soured from then on. It became an achievement collaborating with her at work. Her constant berating and scolding became insufferable. And as time passed, her behavior merged with other accelerants, igniting fuels of misery around the shop.

Journal Entry #334: The Way They Were (Part 7)

Dedicated to *Wynne Steel*

Dedicated pros avoid sharing inside optics of their club's membership. Especially when many contributed to one's eventual retirement. Nevertheless, only glossing over grains of the good, bad, and ugly among Kal Lake's more colourful, would hardly satisfy curiosity.

Some of the Good

Jack and Jimmy supported the club endlessly. An elderly husband and wife, they were genuinely kind. Jack was compassionate and wise, while Jimmie's demeanour and smile weren't unlike my Jackie's.

Vi was a veterinarian's wife whose laugh and crinkly smile hoisted others out of depression. She was always bouncing around, effervescent, and humourous.

Cec was my doctor, who eventually became Kal Lake's President. A charismatic and visionary Australian, he ironically couldn't convert his cricket bat swing into a golf equivalent.

Fred and Maureen became dear friends from the moment we met. They remained loyal to us over four decades.

The Waynes were decent members of the SS. One was a robust middle-ager with an equally good heart. A fast thinker with snappy quips, he took over marketing a large independent tire firm. The other was the perennial auctioneer at every Kal Lake Calcutta.

Clem and Anne found longevity as members. As Kal Lake's first manager, he suffered miserably working for the SS. Despite a victim, he maintained his dignity, eventually becoming recognized as an honorary life member. She was a loyal wife whose candidness accentuated thoughtful humour.

Wynne's floral talents annually beautified the course. Another honorary life member, she possessed a sharp mind, never allowing anyone to escape with toxic behaviour. She golfed well into her nineties and remained a lifelong friend to Jackie and I.

Hamish and George were two peas-in-a-pod who became close friends and mentors. While not part of the SS, they functioned seamlessly among them. Both served as directors, reminding me of *Sesame Street's* Bert and Ernie.

Bob's endearing qualities were decency and compassion. A redneck trucker, he loved life and was comfortable in any walk. A stabilizing force among the SS, his untimely passing influenced Kal Lake's descent into decadence.

Patrick was among my first club cleaners. Polite, honest and a pleasure being around, he later became a physician.

Jesse graduated into the golf industry from our junior program. His engaging, personable disposition was accented by rare blends of enthusiasm and friendliness.

John became my assistant in the '90s. A genuinely good person with career challenges, I was fortunate to have him on staff.

The Toms were smart, clean-cut types who worked for me in the shop. One became a National Hockey League referee, the other graduated from Indiana's Notre Dame with honours in law.

Some of the Not-So-Good

Tommaso's strained voice claimed knowledge of everything, yet the lanky southpaw's continual search for the next dollar, always fell short. He made my life edgy, soliciting directors behind closed doors to hire a taller pro.

Donaldo played pro ball for Saskatchewan in the Canadian Football League. The hefty veteran bullied club regulars with his intimidating presence.

Raimondo was challenged by an annoying repetitive laugh. His reputation as a gossiping realtor was overshadowed by his spouses numerous reputed affairs.

Arturo was a union peon, constantly followed by whispers alleging he vandalized management vehicles during arbitration. His volatile Italian heritage ancestered a vulgar sense of humour.

Giovanni wasn't the club's most positive member, nor the sharpest tool in the shed. I was challenged continually by the realtor's constant pro shop criticisms.

I was grateful Arsenio retired from law enforcement. There were doubts any civilian ever got a fair shake from the obese ogre. He considered himself a closet comedian, but even closet comedians know the statute of limitations for publicly humiliating a spouse!

Cosimo was another retired law enforcer. A former captain, he was the sole person during my entire career to author a letter of complaint about me. He was an ally of Junior Johnson's.

The Others …

Jaeger was not only extraordinarily cheap but barbaric. A short, retired educator, he always volunteered, but only to accessorize his own portfolio.

Roland had talent for golf with his abbreviated backswing. As a unionist however, the short man wasn't someone to be met in the dark. In another life, he might have been Jimmy Hoffa.

Pot Luck had managed a law firm. The temperamental critic made life extremely challenging for staff and management alike.

Duthie was another intimidating lawman who stalked the course daily with the morning crowd. One of Junior Johnson's spies, he wasn't the type you wanted to be pulled over by for traffic violations.

Finally there was Bruno, the logging equipment salesman. The vilest member I ever served would delightfully recount the marmots he slaughtered on course with his titanium slingshot. He owned the club's soapbox, speaking his mind at anyone's expense. He would have been among the fiercest radicals of Donald Trump's base ... and in full force during the insurrection.

Journal Entry #335: There is an End

Dedicated to *John Newlove*

> May your hands always be busy
> May your feet always be swift
> May you have a strong foundation
> When the winds of changes shift
>
> --Bob Dylan

When Dylan wrote those words in 1973, they reminded me of that day when applications closed for the manager's position!

The season was only months away and rumours whispered I was the frontrunner or offered the job. Neither were true, but they persisted. Regardless, I had applied. I'd never been a club manager but knew the prerequisites. I'd worked with ten in past and had my own qualifications. Having successfully managed my own company for almost two decades then, I knew the business thoroughly and had supervised dozens of employees.

That day however, everything in my world changed. In the same way Americans awoke in shock following the 2016 presidential election, that morning wasn't different. I had gone upstairs to find Gunter, the club's German chef. Passing the kitchen's walk-in freezer, I suddenly saw Rosa Klebb introducing the facilities to none other than ... Junior Johnson!

I froze as my emotions plummeted toward the tiled floor below!

Journal Entry #336: Cherry Hills
Dedicated to *Carole Williams*

I wanted to play **Cherry Hills** for one reason ... Arnold Palmer!

It was at Cherry Hills in Colorado's mile-high Denver where the king's legend originated. A final sixty-five during the 1960 US Open there, cemented his win and subsequent place in golf history. An assault inspired after he drove the par-four opening hole. Later on that same tee in the Centennial State's cool fall sunshine, I wanted to measure myself while embracing the essence of his achievement.

My attempt was right and shorter; confirming latent suspicions ... there was more to Palmer than charisma and sex appeal.

Arnold wasn't the only beneficiary of a memorable tee shot there though. Coincidentally Cherry Hills was where I too commandeered the most perfect drive of my career.

The sixteenth at the William Flynn designed layout was a downhill par-four, subtly doglegging right. That afternoon I was intending a high cut shot with the driver. One meant to start left of the fairway centre. From there, I hoped it would drift slightly right, finishing in middle where I anticipated my next effort. My execution was perfect and the impact flush as I watched it taxi to its final location. As of this writing, I'm still waiting another as memorable.

Knowing what shots are required in given situations means one thing. Executing them's another, leading to what defines the **perfect** golf shot. To me classic, peerless efforts require first, unconsciously swinging the club as desired. Second, solid contact. Third, sending the ball toward its designated target. And fourth, settling into that exact final location. Even the world's best fail that prescription persistently. They might have the line but not the location, the solid connect, or other combinations but rarely all four synchronized. There's another optic to the perfect shot though, one of different context from Robert Frost's, *The Road Not Taken*.

Since human existence, sex has dominated procreation. Cresting that has been the sensation of climax or orgasm. Of this there seems little denial. Debatably it's a common thread guiding human relationships. The physical release is pleasurable, arguably a reprieve from anxiety. But a similar emancipation exists when perfect golf shots are struck! In those rare moments of impact that sensation penetrates the clubhead following the hosel up the shaft toward the grip. There it continues flowing from our fingertips onward, satisfying pleasure centres of the mind. That fleeting liberation strangely and persistently lures golfers back to play unlike any other sport. It also acts to naturally disarm the intense stresses accumulated from everyday life!

Journal Entry #337: Harvest Moon (Sand Hills)

Dedicated to *Ben Crenshaw and Bill Coore*

Until I played **Sand Hills**, I wasn't familiar with minimalist creativity as articulated in course architecture. It was a flavour defined by one minimalist designer as, "A derivative of nature first and man second."

I realized Sand Hills had the very essence which had stimulated my senses as a young teenage pro traveling about Britain.

Sand Hills was a product of the prosperous '90s, arising from barren eskers near Mullen, Nebraska. She was the creation of pro golfer turned architect Ben Crenshaw and partner Bill Coore. To find her, I drove from North Platte after a commuter flight from Denver accompanied by O. J. Simpson's lawyer, F. Lee Bailey. The drive was an hour of boredom with little to see except sandy scrub hills, Black Angus cattle, and sky. Absent buildings, people and trees, the landscape possessed a stark, desolate nature. I could barely imagine what her creators speculated on their own maiden visit.

Amid the terrain though, I saw numerous indigenous holes ready to be discovered. The difficulty creating Sand Hills must have been selecting her best eighteen from the hundreds already born there. In short time she became classic, verified by one of my earliest mentors Scotty McGregor, who claimed Sand Hills … Scottish … a compliment as good as Crenshaw and Coore would ever receive.

Near the practise putting green was a quaint gazebo, affectionately named after Crenshaw. I sat there in silence on my last night, gazing down and out at the course. Staring back, was an inland Caledonian links, ironically characterized by a culture of cowboys, lassoes, and steers, harmonizing beneath the **harvest moon**.

Journal Entry #338: Field of Dreams (Prairie Dunes)

Dedicated to *Brian and Jean Harvey*

Leaving Sand Hills, I faced a dilemma. Being close to the Kansas State line, I knew the famous farmland course Prairie Dunes was nearby. I could either return home or submit to temptation. One claiming I'd be resisting fate. So, as my daughter's tattoo cites *carpe diem* … I seized the day and went.

Prairie Dunes was designed by Perry Maxwell. Located in the agricultural hub of Hutchinson, Kansas it was pinioned within hectares of farmland, reminiscent of the baseball fantasy **Field of Dreams**. There among friendly, strong community members, I met their club professional, who significantly influenced my career then.

During my later years at Kal Lake, I began feeling out-of-place within golf's industry. During the economic boom, new courses began emerging throughout the valley, many with lustrous, upscale images, staffed by nouveau pros. One's xeroxed as tourist concierges rather than golf leaders … prodigals with clean hands. At the same time, club pros were being salaried rather than contracted or retailing their own shop. The shifting roles toward industrial grey areas seemed unsettling. Over time I'd evolved into both a manager and labourer, capable of engaging seamlessly among white and blue collars alike. Cleaning clubs, helping customers place equipment on power carts, or retrieving range buckets never bothered me. I paid employees to carry out those tasks but I also valued the feedback. Golf's new managers however, appeared more acclimated toward getting their name out there or networking. Their appearance as schmoozers didn't parallel peers I'd grown knowing. And the analogue of schmoozer and slacker seemed clear.

In that cloudy environment, with career uncertainty raining upon me, I met Charles Craig, Prairie Dune's tireless pro.

There, at one of golf's more highly respected courses, was another like me. Craig too always appeared busy. He seemed physically everywhere at any time while simultaneously soldiering the shop's front lines.

His ambitiousness reinforced my identity and the uncertainty faded. If modern-day pros were evolving into this ambivalent entity, so be it. I'd carry on my way.

There was something big-league that defined Prairie Dunes and yet it remained subtle, peaceful and comfortably subservient to its agricultural backbone. Content among meadows of sunflower, hardy grass, and yucca it engendered senses of Tom Watson and mom's apple pie.

I left there believing that sometimes, seizing the day was the right choice.

Journal Entry #339: When Smokey Sings

Dedicated to *Dr. Ivan Reed*

Another contributing factor to my eventual demise was changing lawyers. More accurately, they were shuffled around for us. After our long time lawyer resigned from his firm, he left us his replacement ... Corlazzoli.

Later, we retained the Italian to recover our investment from a corrupt development. I questioned his fee following that, refusing to pay legal bills for work, which in fact I completed. Hard feelings followed.

After that Corlazzoli joined Kal Lake's membership. Soon after, he became a director and then vice president, my ultimate superior. And during my final years, he was Kal Lake's shoo-in president! Possibly because of his legal promotion counselling the glossy corporate entity ... OKAY TIRE.

I wrote this from the Cuban resort Ocean Varadero El Patriarca, which in Spanish means patriarch. And that's what Dick Buick was to British Columbia. Throughout the province, he was affectionately known as Mr. OKAY TIRE, owner of Canada's largest independent dealership. He was to the Okanagan what Smokey Robinson was to Motown.

Buick and I got along famously, but he did with everyone. He annually spent a small fortune with the shop, was always funny, seemingly wise, and yet undeniably absentminded. For instance, on two separate occasions involving different members, Buick actually drove their cars home from the club ... believing both vehicles his! In another chapter he backed a power cart into the creek behind the shop. That was the way he was and yet everybody loved him. But for decades he'd also been a **made** member of the SS. So when Flavio was named OKAY TIRE's new legal tech, it made Corlazzoli untouchable and Kal Lake's next acclimated president!

And inexplicably, it was Corlazzoli along with his predecessor Bitsy, Jr. who hired Junior Johnson.

Journal Entry #340: More Than This

Dedicated to *Joanne Bannister*

Acknowledging Johnson as the new manager wasn't unlike the world's stunned response to a newly elected 2016 American president! But something whispered to me Johnson was headhunted before the application deadline. That's because a phone call weeks earlier, warned me he was a candidate. Knowing his reputation though, I ignored it.

The geriatric had garnered a questionable notoriety. Years earlier he applied to be my assistant. Like Bibeau, he too hailed from Buzzard. There he struggled managing his mother's bridal wear store before moving on to used car sales. When that also failed he relocated to British Columbia finding golf industry work. Like a checkerboard piece, he jumped from course to course, eventually turning pro. Ultimately he became known as a dubious card-carrying member of the PGA. A reputation spawned by alleged rumours he'd been investigated by the organization. Was it true? I didn't know. Golf pros gossip through grapevines too, but it wasn't reassuring.

My reason for concern was Johnson's bond with Bibeau. They were buddies … birds-of-a-feather. Had they not been grafted in Buzzard, they could have been the lads from television's *The Dukes of Hazzard*. Both were free spirits, the gambling, schmoozing kind. Like former President Trump they were guided by what appeared contempt for moral rule. Sly and coy, they used charismatic and psychological tradecraft to lure pigeons into murky webs.

I knew Johnson well enough to be aware Kal Lake might have made another miscalculation. One paralleling that 2016 American election. Similar to the Grand Old Parties' insurgence then, Corlazzoli and Bitsy, Jr. seemed to be finessing their own subtle strategies at Kal Lake. If they handpicked the new manager, given his past, it wasn't difficult questioning why? Were they serious? Was the GOP serious? There had to be **more than this**.

It became natural to query: "If the board wanted a golf pro as manager … what were the reasons I wasn't considered? And what happened to my resume?" Hiring a professional for the position might have been a strategically sound business decision. But only if the selection committee understood the labour pool's chain of command. In other words, hiring one pro to oversee another required an accurate job description. I pondered whether Kal Lake would even think of that let alone exercise it.

A heavy feeling like a shot put began anchoring in my stomach and I felt Corlazzoli was responsible. At the time, I was comfortable in my long-term contract's final years, but when that concluded what would the future hold? The best I could do then was work hard, go with the flow, and hope … like average Democrats did after that election!

Journal Entry #341: Seminole

Dedicated to *Brian and Rita Usher*

Serious golfers would almost do anything to play **Seminole**!

Seminole was another creation of Donald Ross. In fact, a nearby road is dedicated to him. Harnessed to the Atlantic in West Palm Beach Florida, the gated enclave thrived in seclusion and affluence between two parallel sand drifts.

On the day I played, my opportunity appeared doubtful as rain obliviously fell. I stood impatient under an outside canopied bar watching others sipping coffees and snipping crackers smothered in Wisconsin cheese. Calming swells lapping beaches yards away from the Spanish clubhouse softened my outlook. The salty air was so close; it pleasantly misted my face. Then suddenly, the rain subsided.

At first, Seminole didn't seem of championship quality, yet nostalgic airs persisted. Ones reminding visitors Hogan himself annually prepared there for the Masters. Lingering impressions alleged he might appear from the locker room any moment to tune up. No golf club could buy that flavour.

Compared to Floridian peers known for flatter, more dreary landscapes, Seminole's barreling dunes were used advantageously in her routing. Straightforward and palm-tree defined, her short distances from greens to tees encouraged fast play. And as if attempting to keep pace with Augusta National she was exquisitely groomed. Finally, Ross sculptured Seminole into a thinker's course. Trading wits with ocean winds whipping her drifts, the architect converted his assets into a tasteful design that played unsuspecting lengths.

My coveted theft there was a modest yet memorable birdie at her punishing par-four sixth. A rare heist for Hogan purportedly claimed it the world's best golf hole.

Journal Entry #342: The Roman Coliseum

Dedicated to *John Gay*

To me, the Tournament Player's Course in Jacksonville, Florida, was a stern, stiff, and strenuous test of golf. Contemptuously long and narrow, she was predictably unforgiving. Her greens were fast with cruel undulations and, like former President Trump, in-your-face. She wasn't for me.

Regardless, she was home to PGA Tour competitors and their annual event known as The Players Championship.

At one time club pros and touring players were governed under one roof, the Professional Golfer's Association (PGA). Led by a young Nicklaus, the players revolted and migrated away. They became the Tournament Players Division. Joe Dey, Jr. became its first commissioner. Deane Beman succeeded him. From that latter appointment, collaborating with Pete Dye, the Players'Course and championship were spawned. Its birth however, seemed but a bid to instantly levitate her among golf's majors: the British Open, Masters, PGA, and US Open. Or an act to hijack the PGA? Lacking historical gravity, it appeared the corporate rendition of millennials groping entitlement without equity.

And following its inception, those sentiments provoked my passions further. At the Players, I saw pros transition from golfers to gladiators. An opinion fortified from annually watching the savage dramas unfold at the par-three island hole seventeenth. A modern-day **Roman Coliseum** where the loud, fuelled by alcohol and intimidation, stir cravings for blood.

I didn't play my best there, for as they say, "different horses for different courses." However in my despair, I parred that seventeenth. And each year, during the television spectacle, I offer it to the wretched ones on that home stretch. The weary, and ragged. The abdicated scrounging pars and pleading for clemency like those back in time, begging for lives.

Since then, my passions have been cross-examined further by the question, "Is this **really** golf's destiny?"

Journal Entry #343: Call of the Wild

Dedicated to *John and Shirley Desimone*

During Johnson's initial days at work, preliminary meetings advanced my opinion of him. He described a Machiavellian method he once used to exterminate young hoods from the bridal store his mother owned. A recipe that would have failed any justice system. It was my first experience labouring with an employer who thrived next to life's underbelly.

On the other hand, club managers who'd previously shaped my career were industry polished ... Bibeau the exception. And after Johnson's appointment, Bibeau returned to join his buddy ... like one of those unwanted relatives.

The managerial mentors of my past employed business buzzwords such as: "community involvement, employee relations, or fiscal management policies." Bibeau and Johnson's lingo however could have been torn from Trump's Twitter tirades. A flippant **call of the wild** slurring, "We don't get mad, we get even!"

Journal Entry #344: Goldilocks
Dedicated to *Bob McCallum*

Johnson distinguished himself early with the SS, firing Chemical Ali!

When one of our most beloved members died of cancer, she believed that it was from Ali's persistent pesticide applications. However his fearless denials and cavalier manner finally caught up with him, and to Johnson's credit, he let the rebel go. Was it because of that or his job description entailed cleaning house?

As a result, Junior hired **Goldilocks**. It became one of the more eccentric managerial-superintendent relationships I witnessed.

Goldie and I got along well. That was because we were both committed, hard working, and professional. Short also, he grew long blond locks contrasted by a colossal Caribbean tan. Steel-toe work boots, heavy wool socks, and cargo shorts accentuated the gold trinkets clustering him. Reminders he was either wealthy or a moonlighting drug dealer. Regardless Goldie could grow grass ... and kept our members alive doing it.

Goldie and Johnson's relationship however was bizarre. It may have been because Goldie was the opposite of a Trump-like buffoon. Unlike Goldie, Junior never worked hard, preferring to golf and schmooze instead. Johnson's image wasn't held in high esteem, unlike Goldie who became sectional president. Goldie was alert, young, and in touch with staff using Motorola walkie-talkies. Junior was older than sixty, acting thirty, and rarely connected with staff. Still like most Republicans who clung to

Trump, Goldie treated Johnson like a macabre mentor, but with undeniable slivers of contempt. Clearly Junior was no role model but regardless, Goldie aligned himself with the monger as if owing covert favours from shifty pasts.

Either way, despite what took place in following years, I was grateful for the improved course conditions. Goldie returned it to a playable venue and for that, I was appreciative of Johnson.

Journal Entry #345: Miss Chatelaine (Morfontaine)

Dedicated to *Tom Simpson*

> Just a smile, just a smile
> Hold me captive, just a while
>
> —K. D. Lang, Ben Mink

I have mistresses around the world. They've all seduced me with names like Merion, Jasper, and Augusta. But **Morfontaine** didn't even have to tempt me. There was only one reason the sandy, pine-infested layout near Paris could make me unhappy … not playing her!

Morfontaine was relatively unknown, an impression suggesting it was intended. Perhaps the French more than other cultures understood the philosophy, too much of a good thing spoils?

The clubhouse with its vintage French charm, resembled a country domicile of stone, indistinct and farm-like. There was no pro shop. And only members could buy their modest stock of V-neck sweaters, soft collar shirts, or balls … inventoried within a cupboard. Its provincially furnished clubhouse served strong coffee, while baguettes were baked on site … produce to be guillotined for. As I relaxed on the building's slabbed patio, enjoying a tomato salad worth dying for, the course baited me with rustic ambiance.

Tom Simpson designed Morfontaine. Most golfers are unfamiliar with the architect because his reputation's vaulted within archives of time. Fantasy might have marked him a mutation of Zorro and Walter Hagen.

Simpson would arrive on site with his silver Rolls Royce, resplendent in cloak and beret. There he'd lash out with creative comments like, "Golf holes must never be what they look!" Philosophies hinting erotic parallels between golf and sex.

The course featured forced carries over yards of heather where sandy footpaths snaked their way through the same. Blankets of fern flanked bunkers and greens, while indiscriminate boulders penetrated air from soils of birth. And like Seminole, her routing was outrageously perfect. Compared to current-day courses, distances from greens to tees were close, encouraging leisurely yet fast play. Adding to her seduction was that France continued as a country unknown for golf, identified instead by food, history, language and of course wine. But yet there, inveigling and isolated was Morfontaine … uncompromising in her place among golf's great playgrounds. Another worldly lover.

Journal Entry #346: The Cup

Dedicated to *Ron Lyons*

Golf's famous tournament, the Ryder Cup, was a competitive team extravaganza matching the United State's finest pros against European counterparts.

In 1997, it received a turbo boost of publicity when Spain's Valderrama was awarded the coveted site. I was offered accommodation nearby at no charge so I gratefully accepted. Having never visited Spain, I was latinized by Seve Ballesteros, and his apostles José Maria Olazábal and Miguel Ángel Jiménez. Swashbuckling conquistadors whose radiant passions too, were devoted to golf.

The Ryder Cup was a kaleidoscopic view of big time sport mottled by legions of hungry fans, savvy media and gaudy jet setters idling to be seen. The mass hypnosis and euphoric cheering were blended in a cultural magic bullet whose electronic pulse was ignited by riveting human energy. Even moments after arriving, I felt I could do nothing, yet be circuited along its current.

Ballesteros was the European *comandante* while the bespectacled Texan, Tom Kite captained America. One calculating, daring, and effervescent.

The other … a confederate. Everyone sensed a European victory. And in the aftermath, I stood feet away from Seve as he hoisted **the cup** on the steps of Valderrama's mammoth Mediterranean clubhouse. He was accompanied by roars reaching decibels I'd never heard on courses before or since. They pulsated the air while the ground quaked, products of incitement. And while immersed within that hysteria, it was clear these too were among the sounds of golf I yearned for each day.

Journal Entry #347: The Truck Driver

Dedicated to *Bob Kilborn*

Bob drove commercial trucks for a living. Normally accustomed to long hauls, he stayed closer to routes near home as retirement beckoned. A redneck with a past confirming a life lived full, he owned a laid back personality which seemed content with golf, beer, and cigarettes.

As a member, Bob golfed in blue jeans while others wore the sport's latest gear. He avoided rumours that festered many golf communities, deterring them instead with subtle, non-confrontational opinions that held weight. Friendly, funny, and likable, he was genuine but no one's fool. However Bob was also the unpolished gem among the SS … their stabilizer. That may have been why he and I were friendly.

When Bob suddenly passed before his time, the twine binding the SS loosened. Consequently Kal Lake began slowly unravelling toward previously unsavoury times. Workdays became like an oven whose heat by day's end siphoned off my energy. It was approaching a time when renegotiating my next contract. A time I began noticing the peculiar looks certain members began extending me. Members, I'd faithfully served the previous decades. Any aware professional can sense the like. Eyes reveal truth.

For instance, one of Bob's closest acquaintances was an accountant. One I enjoyed a pleasant, prosperous arrangement with. Unexpectedly, he began picking at the most minor of pro shop flaws. His easy-going manner was replaced with a campaign of sharp sarcastic taunts lasered at me. Another member was Lyle Pryce's spouse. Pryce was the former president who passed earlier in the plane crash. Over that same time, his wife and I shared a congenial business relationship. But she too inadvertently changed, developing a crusty disposition. A never-seen-before demeanour.

Two things became evident. Bob's departure shifted the membership equilibrium, diverting the organization's destiny. And second like the American GOPs undeniable Third Reich devotion to Trump, many members suddenly too had the ear and growing confidence of Johnson.

Journal Entry #348: The Galloping Gourmet

Dedicated to *Reiner Langenhan*

Gunter was Kal Lake's popular German chef. Personable, proficient and profitable, Gunter had two flaws: He loved his beer and detested Johnson.

As efficient as Gunter was, he suffocated during Johnson's impromptu and exhausting staff meetings. Like me Gunter made minutes count and was geared toward service and business. Unfortunately Gunter liked a pint when counting inventory, graft from a Rhineland pedigree. A habit that didn't suit Junior nor his new bartender, Pee Wee Corrigan. Corrigan was like many Johnson recruits … young, entitled, and only stalking a career.

Pee Wee and Junior antagonized Gunter by taking away his beer. This proved challenging to Gunter since Johnson's rookies did whatever they pleased. Why couldn't Gunter?

Unknown to Gunter, however, Johnson and Corrigan covertly filmed the chef with a delinquent ale. That precipitated Gunter's dismissal, suggesting there was more to Junior's hiring than met the eye. He hired a flighty saloonkeeper while firing a committed and profitable chef.

Was Johnson a hit man or a respected troubleshooter? Like former President Trump, he was cutting loose anyone disliking the glow of his tan or part in his hair.

Unknown to the members however, Gunter's firing took tolls on his marriage. Junior went further, contaminating the chef's search for alternative industry employment. Was I next?

Journal Entry #349: Borderline

Dedicated to *Norm May*

Soon after taking over, Johnson solicited me to mentor him in the PGA.

By then I was still a Class "A" professional in good standing. It took time and effort maintaining that category. I had to stay current, participate, and cultivate images consistent with organization standards.

As manager, however, Johnson's job was to administrate Kal Lake's bustling clubhouse. But Junior was also a pro, part of an obscure rank known then as the "F" class. A designation that circumvented usual membership routes. Consequently for Johnson to maintain that affiliation, rules dictated he had to work under me. Being older though, Junior's ego had the final say. That's when I saw how he could squeeze a situation.

I wasn't comfortable with what seemed an inquisition. It wasn't only a conflict of interest but I had no budget. I acquiesced however, believing his fantasies would vanish once the PGA confirmed the gossip from his past. But they didn't! They refused to cooperate with my inquiry claiming it violated his privacy. By avoiding my queries, they chose sides and indifferently, weren't on mine. I was looking for due diligence. After all, who wanted staff who could tarnish the PGA's reputation or mine? The ones who could satisfy that question … weren't forthcoming.

Further Johnson was mingling with the SS like a wolfish investment advisor. If I declined his advances, he'd have spread false rumours, like Trump's fake-news propaganda. The SS would've labelled me uncooperative. Astonishingly I found myself in unfamiliar territory … on the **borderline,** hemmed into a corner. Without options, I gave in! And like that, Junior had carte blanche into my shop's intimate business affairs.

I felt abandoned by the PGA and my confidence began to wane again. While I continued my membership, I began retreating from the organization and their competitions.

Journal Entry #350: A Reason in Dornoch

Dedicated to *Herbert Warren Wind*

In his passionate treatise *A Season in Dornoch,* author Lorne Rubenstein refers to the writer Herbert Warren Wind who wrote: "No golfer has completed their education until they have played and studied Royal Dornoch."

For that reason I was obligated to visit the Scottish seaside resort. The place where Donald Ross was raised and apprenticed, prior to his life's pursuit as an architect.

I was astonished learning Dornoch was situated on the same latitude as Juneau, Alaska, fifty-eight degrees from the North Pole. Throughout the links, elevated greens were framed by natural dunes and graceful valleys as gorse glittered her landscape. Following our round that sunny golden leafed afternoon, Jackie and I wandered the town, pub hopped, and visited Ross's humble home.

I had developed opinions that Ross's work was overrated even knowing he'd created some of golf's sacred temples like Pinehurst and Seminole. But while I continued admiring the works of Stanley Thompson, Alister MacKenzie, and Tom Simpson, I began recognizing Ross's inspirations too impacted golf in ways I earlier failed to understand.

For after playing Dornoch, it was evident his inspirations powerfully influenced golf's short-game techniques. If any one designer played a role in the livelihood of those who taught the art of chipping and pitching, there could be little dispute it was Ross.

Journal Entry #351: Brother Love's Travelling Salvation Show

Dedicated to *Max Voets*

The relationship between Johnson and myself ruptured after I hesitatingly extended him pro shop teaching privileges.

With his foot-in-the-door, Junior began eliciting fact-less Trump-like claims, subtlety inferring I was insecure with him instructing on site.

Frankly, I was confident in any golf environment. I couldn't play like Jack Nicklaus but I could talk intelligently about the game with him or most anyone. Plus I was comfortable with my own teaching. With more business than needed I never advertised for students. I'd been schooled by the best including David Leadbetter, Butch Harmon, and Dave Pelz. I was also learned from classic instructors like Paul Runyan, Henry Cotton, and Bill Strausbaugh, all whom I'd personally met and discussed theory with. Consequently I never felt challenged by Johnson's outdated conventions.

Regardless grievances grew when Junior's presence became persistently pesky. I began questioning whether all club managers of my past were wrong and Johnson right, especially when he neglected his own managerial matters. In addition, I didn't employ Johnson, which was a PGA bylaw infraction. Last and most important, Junior's intrusion was unfair to my three assistants who were trying to carve out careers. They needed those lessons for experience and revenue.

But he didn't stop there!

Guided by what appeared false senses of avuncular endearment, he became their self-appointed mentor. Ignoring my staff relationships, he moved in as cancer does to body cells.

I'd developed effective work habits through peer guidance. But Johnson didn't see it the same. He was older but far less experienced. So instead, using age and ego as batons, he extorted superiority. And when it was soon evident his behaviour was undermining my business plans, I felt needs to act.

On the cusp of renegotiating my new contract and in mounting frustration, I broached the directors. Surprisingly, like the GOP supported Trump, they backed Johnson. Something wasn't right because the solution seemed simple. Junior should have been reacquainted with his job description. With the entire clubhouse to manage, his shop obsessions were inappropriate, especially considering Kal Lake's problems then. Plus his blossoming fraternity with the SS was inflaming the issue. He became their poster boy and when they wanted anything regardless of fiscal probability, he got it for them. And like Trump's march into madness or Brother

Love's Travelling Salvation Show, Junior's train too gathered speed ... with no one in control!

Journal Entry #352: Y2K

Dedicated to *Dr. Shirley Godbehere*

The year 2000 imposed itself upon a restless world. Fear suppressed optimism as computer geeks supposedly miscalculated binomials. Nervous projections anticipated private enterprise, governments, and the public would be shut down in final moments. Generators, survival devices, and provisions were ruthlessly appropriated to persevere plausible disaster.

In the hysteria, there was little I could contribute toward solutions. Consequently, on December 31 that year, I self-authorized myself Kal Lake's last golfer of the century and millennium.

To realize that, I altered equipment and changed my apparel. I dawned mukluk boots, a ski jacket, and attached fluorescent feathers to orange Titleist golf balls. Then with my clubs, I ventured out toward the six-inch snowy fairways. There, I remained until dark insuring my historic place. Even with the outerwear and frosty hands, I scored two legitimate pars when my ball found the clearings I'd shovelled at frozen pin positions.

After the exhausting eighteen-hole odyssey, I celebrated with Champagne.

Later, as clocks threatened to doom the planet, I focused on another achievement. Overlooking the lake outside our home, I teed up that same Titleist for the time change and final assault.

When the second-hand approached midnight, Jackie filmed me driving the sphere toward the silvery waters below. In that final second, it penetrated both time frames.

Days later, watching television's newborn Golf Channel, I was astonished seeing commentator Peter Kessler describing his same event in Florida.

Earth endured **Y2K** with no repercussions. In that relief, I emerged as the Okanagan's last golfing centurion and millennial. As well, my midnight shot became forever locked within the vaults of golf eternity.

Journal Entry #353: Ballybunion

Dedicated to *Ken and Lil Nistor*

As a young Glendale assistant, I often enjoyed coffee with old Tom Megan. An accomplished player, he could spin golf balls in wind there as no other could. It was that gritty immigrant who first stirred my curiosity about the links of Ireland. He spoke reverently while admonishing courses like **Ballybunion,** Lahinch, or Ross's Point were infested with spirits other than good. And those myths always circled back to Ballybunion.

Three decades later Jackie and I arrived there and played … or I did. With gales over seventy kilometres per hour, Jackie found it impossible standing let alone swinging.

Ironically Ballybunion began next to a cemetery, suggesting a ward of interred victims. The first six holes seemed foreplay to a wild side. And Oscar Wilde she appeared, as one could be forgiven feeling engaged in the Irish playwright's work. Amid the turbulence, I often felt as paper might, when tossed within tempests. Immense gusts continually used my carry bag as wings; vaulting me up with each step braved. The fury continued as I attacked her par-four eleventh. There I was assaulted by venomous spits of lager-shaded ocean foam. Was it devil's drool or delusions of art imitating life? On the beach below I heard an enraged wind's commentary. Like hordes of hissing serpents their convulsions suggested Satan himself was present. Adding to the ghoul … large, anthracitic ravens strutted her fairways and long grassy knolls, impaired.

On that day, Ballybunion played a seven-club wind, which meant adding that many club distances to one's normal yardage. With my scorecard apprised of numbers well above par, I felt molested yet strangely rejuvenated.

Tom Megan is no longer with us but my ordeal verified every moment he described, as in the mind of Oscar Wilde.

Journal Entry #354: Swinley Forest
Dedicated to *Roy Murray*

Jackie and I were nearing end of a short British golf trip. Before the return flight home however, I had one final wish.

Nearing London we drove into the tony horse racing community Ascot. There at its thoroughbred racetrack, I sought a souvenir for our daughter Janine whose life revolves around horses. Unfortunately the facility was undergoing renovations. Continuing through the affluent suburb we found the inland course **Swinley Forest** minutes away.

Rain plundered our chances of play however, persuading Jackie to remain in the comfort of our accommodation.

Veering on however I sought out professional Bob Parker in the brick Edwardian clubhouse. It was late and the course appeared lonely when Parker gave me the green light. I dashed to the tee aware a daylight finish was plausible.

Swinley Forest was strangely unknown, even among golf's most ardent. But from my opening shot, evidence claimed it extraordinary. Designed by Englishman Harry Colt, I sensed subtle expressions of Stanley Thompson's work occasionally peeking back at me.

As I approached her first green, a dog bounced out from behind pursued by a figure clad in outerwear. My paranoid mind assumed he was the club's secretary, readying to query my presence. Shrouded in grey mists, drizzle, and a rain hat, he turned toward me exposing a familiar youthful face. My surprise was halted by the embarrassment that follows forgetting a name. Sparing me, he offered a glancing nod while continuing to apprehend the animal.

I too plodded along in the wet paradise, navigating about the forested fairways. Hours into the round, a dazzle of fireworks crackled, splitting the night. The celebration for Guy Fawkes Day, seemed to originate from nearby Windsor Castle. It was then the reality of whom I'd seen earlier accosted me.

Had it really been former Prince Andrew?

Swinley Forest was a compact challenging course banked by firs and floored by sandy soil. Crafted bunkers were framed by heather, while its rustic landscape advanced sibling notions of nearby Sunningdale. Both seemingly products of nature.

Afterwards in the continuing darkness, I echoed my way through the empty clubhouse parking lot. There I took surreal wonder with me … as my own souvenir.

Journal Entry #355: Slap Shot
Dedicated to *Betty Clarke*

I don't want readers to think I disliked Johnson. I had no reasons other than industry rumours to judge him or his thwarted NHL past.

But admittedly, a weariness from his constant gloating began to emerge endorsing an indisputable lack of respect for him as manager. Comparing predecessors, it was absurd adapting to his primitive style in a rapidly shifting marketplace.

As months passed, working with him seemed not unlike Democrats shackled to Trump's trifle. Often Junior appeared late or unprepared for staff meetings. Pro shop budgets arrived disputed by misspellings, sentences ambiguous interpreting, and elementary addition errors. Subordinates suggesting grammar and math lessons to brawny ex-jocks is delicate. In addition he golfed daily … literally. Misconceptions of management golfing regularly plague our industry. Being on-course is invaluable for membership feedback, but only the careless overindulged. Occasionally I'd find his mental trails … scribbles of my work performances carelessly scrunched between cushions of our shop's couch … where he sat and loitered long after I'd left.

No, it had nothing to do with disliking him. Instead, it was the prevailing subversive mood which led to the self inquiry: "If Johnson golfed daily, regularly misplaced notes, mismanaged staff meetings, and lacked elementary calculation and grammar skills … why was he hired, and who'd commit such recruiting errors?"

Then again, one only had to look at that 2016 US election!

Journal Entry #356: 2001, A Green-Fee Odyssey

Dedicated to *Joe O'Hearn*

Another challenge faced me in 2001 when Johnson obsessed over green-fee categories. Normally then, we sold four rates: Regulars, Guests, Juniors, and Twilights (late day). Johnson became paranoid the organization wasn't tapping into more income sources. Consequently he began crusading for more customers. Normally a sound strategy, it was vain then given our return to high-volume sales. Regardless, shooting from the hip, he fabricated twenty-nine additional revenue streams. It became an inefficient, time-consuming nightmare, impacting my shop's thin labour budget. The daily thirty-minutes of green-fee balancing tripled in the absence of technology.

At that same time, computers became indispensable tools when researching customer spending. Golf courses were rapidly gulping them up to grow revenues. Even I purchased a powerful laptop to ease running my own business affairs. However, Johnson's resistance to the digital age prevailed.

When I approached the directors, they responded again like typical Republicans to Trump. That's when Junior began inferring I was a non-team player!

Journal Entry #357: Still the Same

Dedicated to *Jeannie Steele*

During the 1990s Jackie celebrated back-to-back BC Amateur victories. Near the decade's end however she disappointingly withdrew from formal competition.

Her dream was to represent Canada internationally. However after successfully qualifying, she was instead brushed over by the selection committee. Even when contending at the British Amateur, she was overlooked and labelled past prime!

Despite the setback however, she was **still the same,** winning the BC's again in the new millennium! And in the years following, she went on to collect even more impressive victories. Amid constant irony, she'd steamroll over competitors, winning or placing in most events entered. Locally she became known as, "Jackie ... who else?" Weighing a mere hundred pounds, her deceptive attributes made her unexpectedly yet certifiably one of Canada's finest amateurs then. She was amazing in that prime.

Journal Entry #358: Bandon Dude
Dedicated to *Mike Keiser*

If readers asked me to name who in the golf world I'd pick in my dream foursome, some of the names might be predictable. One might not.

First, I'd start with my family. But after that, choices might be challenging. I would choose from amongst the following: Tom Morris, Sr., Bobby Jones, Jr., Tom Watson, Mickey Wright, Harvey Penick, Marion Hollins, Alister MacKenzie, Nancy Lopez, Ben Hogan, Lorena Ochoa, or Annika Sörenstam.

But I might also include Mike Keiser!

Mike who?

I admire Keiser because of his dream. Not since Canadian Charles Blair Macdonald blazed onto the American golf scene in the early twentieth century, has anyone dreamt, paid for, and delivered a series of authentic golf links like Keiser has. While fortunate in business to have executed it, Keiser gave North American public golfers Bandon Dunes and partnered building the Cabot Links.

Golf hungry patrons fantasizing of traveling abroad to play Britain's great links, but couldn't ... need look no further. As a voice whispered in the movie, *Field of Dreams,* "Build it and they will come," so did Keiser when developing links in Bandon, Oregon, and Inverness, Nova Scotia. There reviving spirits from golf's golden era, he birthed more of the game's legacies on lands littered with nature's dunes. His endeavour, seemingly born from embryonic passions, appears to have subtly inspired a re-examination of North American golf.

Journal Entry #359: 1984 (Johnny Get Angry)

Dedicated to *Pat Wheatley*

Johnson had already dismissed Kal Lake's chef using covert filming. Following that, one of our members took me aside, offering a warning.

Our shop butted up to a corridor leading into the clubhouse. One evening she turned into the hallway to find a board member in a crouched position, peering into the shop. Intently focused, he was secretly scribbling notes of the night assistant on duty. When confronted, the crimson faced director scurried off.

I didn't understand it. My staff were skilled golfers and off-season curlers who seemed capable, energetic, and trustworthy. That wasn't my opinion. It was confirmed by statistics compiled before Johnson's arrival. A comprehensive membership survey, awarded us service scores of ninety-four per cent compared to the clubhouse and grounds, rated less than sixty. Further, a trendy tourist magazine voted us among the valley's best pro shops.

Unfortunately publications and surveys meant little to Johnson.

After hearing about the stakeout, rather than get angry there was only one recourse ... address the board directly. But at that same time a fly appeared in the ointment! Junior had begun smearing me as a non-team-player. Any challenge or criticism by me, would have leveraged the allegation fanning disloyalty flames. Plus I couldn't sound espionage alarms. Who'd believe it? I decided to keep my eyes open and mouth shut. It was only the beginning though, as George Orwell's **1984**, classic seemed real ... at a golf course of all places!

Journal Entry #360: Anywhere but Here

Dedicated to *Ken Holmberg*

At Glendale, the first manager I worked with introduced me to the industry. At Mayfair, fertile years with management were spent within a bustling Wall Street environment.

When I became head pro, I laboured with Canada's finest manager who became a friend and mentor. That was followed by others too who ran Kal Lake competently and business-like. Even during my travels, I profited firsthand from extraordinary administrators. Among them, the infamous colonel who leveraged Scotland's Muirfield with an iron fist and the number-one-ranked manager at the impeccable Los Angeles Country Club.

But after three career decades, I was suddenly thrust into a working relationship with the unknown.

There was no measuring stick to probe Johnson. There weren't seminars for golf pros in deception, deceit, or duplicity. Consequently, within growing desperation and grim suspicion I sought answers from fellow peers—ones with industry esteem.

The responses were identical. Be wary. Take notes, keep accurate records, and synchronize dates!

For the first time in my career, I thought **anywhere but here**.

Journal Entry #361: Batteries not Included

Dedicated to *Paul Geier*

My largest source of shop revenue was realized from rented power carts.

To maintain and protect that income, I was diligent in their maintenance, especially at season's end.

Among those routines were the removal and upkeep of batteries. This included cleaning exteriors, eliminating corrosion, and adding distilled water to cells. Finally in that annual nursing, I administered trickle charges as they hibernated until spring when recalled again for active duty. That regimentation continued for more than twenty years.

Once Christmas sales were over, I took January off, spending time with family. The following spring when reopening the shop however, all my previous efforts began corroding.

I discovered a foreign flux emerging from each battery cell. I rechecked, recleaned, and recharged them all again, finding nothing else amiss. When the course opened however, one by one each cart died stranding golfers in mid-rounds. Initially, I dismissed the batteries as defective, but they were all inconsistent in age and manufacture. Batteries had life spans and from experience I knew the expiry signs. This was different!

The result was a five-thousand-dollar battery replacement bill, which excluded customer grief. Something had failed in my absence that winter. Something I didn't grasp then.

Journal Entry #362: Tired Out!

Dedicated to *Vi Harrison*

After that incident, I became one of OKAY TIRE's best customers.

By then I'd accumulated thirty power carts to service our members. And each year, as was the nature, mechanical repairs were necessities. Our revenues didn't justify employing maintenance technicians therefore my staff and I repaired them in-house, meaning we did the work. Among the challenges were flat tires. Golf courses were places where lost machine parts or innocents like golf tees, occasionally punctured inner tubes.

Typical remedies required removing the wheel, sending it to OKAY TIRE for repair, and finally reinstalling it. The cost … twenty-five dollars. Over twenty years, we averaged four flats per season.

During the new millennium though, tire repairs unexpectedly spiked to an unprecedented eighty-two in seven months. Eighty-two replacements in one season compared to sixty the previous two decades! Plus each invoice inflated from twenty-five to eighty. Explanations were dismissed as, "Costs of doing business."

Later that summer I discovered a clipped valve stem ... and then another ... and then more! During evenings unknown forces were entering the cart compound and deliberately biting off tube stems with crimping tools. It was a subtle, methodical campaign intended to be frustrating.

By year's end, there was little left but to lick our financial wounds. Our annual tire expenses however, increased from one hundred dollars to seven thousand, deflating our budget's bottomline further.

Journal Entry #363: Still of the Night

Dedicated to *Thelma Trickett*

After two inexplicable incidents of vandalism, I wondered what was next? Or whether I was delusional? Time didn't wait long replying.

Early one morning, I arrived at work to economic disaster. Our entire power cart fleet had been destroyed!

In the **still of the night**, six vandals silently entered Kal Lake's property, solely intending to demolish each vehicle. Our largest source of income was suddenly crushed. In acts of deliberate and premeditated savage behaviour, the carts were rammed at full speed into mature trees and then as encores, submersed within the seasonal high creek bed. Normally our carts were secured by electric cable. But the club deactivated it during construction the previous day.

Curiously several carts remained in the enclosure appearing undamaged. Unfortunately the felons used flat-end screwdrivers to rupture their ignitions. With corrupt starters, they looked functional but were useless. In the remains of the day, though, my assistants and I performed minor miracles. Using spartan electric and mechanical skills along with desperation and hope, we removed and replaced mangled ignitions from drowned vehicles. Unbelievably, we revived the remaining carts. To average mechanics, our excitement might have appeared juvenile but to us, still in shock, it was amazing. Furthermore, during the following month until receiving insured relief, not one customer went without power cart service. Every day required scrupulous tee-time bookings, diligent cart assignments, and constant maintenance. Very few noticed how extraordinary my staff was in that trying time.

In other years, like many courses, I was ravaged by random acts of vandalism, but never to such extent. That particular incident was calculated! Regardless two vandals dropped their wallets identifying themselves. Naively, I believed prosecution would be undisputed. But for weeks their identities remained shrouded by the Young Offenders Act. During ensuing court cases, the delinquents were released with minor amends for their deed. It was a wake-up call probing my anguish and accountability. Disillusioned I believed our members would rally behind the pro shop. In the end however, confined to a desolate courtroom, I faced the reality of a lonely business victim without support!

The economic and psychological tolls were severe. In the aftermath, reeking retribution, I was endlessly reminded of that famous Confucius warning: "When embarking on journeys of revenge … dig two graves." For in that climate of vengeance, I miscalculated the next step.

Journal Entry #364: It Always Happens This Way!

Dedicated to *Bob and Georgie Grierson*

"I will put an end to this, once and for all," he said. His voice was clear and without feeling. That was all he said and started to walk out. "How?" He turned and answered. "I will stop the motor of the world."
Then he walked out.

—Ayn Rand, from *Atlas Shrugged*

I became my own architect. Not for designing any great golf course, but for creating what led to my eventual downfall. I can blame, defend what took place or like here, document the deed. But in the end it was me who asked for the meeting!

During that year of sabotage along with normal season stress, I was suffocating, hence vulnerable. In desperation I asked to meet Johnson.

Having sat through the loneliness of that deserted courtroom, I agonized in conclusion that future torment could be absorbed more efficiently through an organization rather than a single individual. Hence, I wanted Johnson's reaction to a proposal of Kal Lake incorporating the shop. That way, by becoming a salaried pro, I was signalling directions the industry was shifting toward anyway.

A day later after reconsideration, I requested it be rescinded. I was too late!

The reader has to understand Johnson. He rarely took my advice. And in his Trump-like molasses stroll, never appeared more active than yeast at best. But all that changed following our first meeting. Like the speed of a gazelle, he leapt into action. Within a day, he'd met board members and initiated plans to acquire the shop!

His mysterious rapid speed was speculating I'd somehow delivered ammunition to a weapon aimed at me.

Journal Entry #365: Hazy Shade of Winter

Dedicated to *Norm and Melanie Korol*

On a November evening soon after, one of the most painful days in my career took place in the clubhouse.

Earlier that day, Johnson summoned me to a late afternoon meeting with Corlazzoli.

In Canada, winter twilights begin early and darkness looms quick. That night was typical as medieval clouds gathered with a penetrating cold, threatening the year's first snow.

The staff were sent home early and a grim hue eyeing a drab coffee table made the clubhouse a lonely, gloomy, and interrogating place to meet. The interior's chilly, barn-like ambiance intensified the speculation. Huddled in overcoats among dispassionate echoes, the collaborators eagerly apprised me of the board's latest decision … to expropriate the shop! It would become effective in a year, after my contract ended.

In situations like that however, what I assumed might normally follow were commitments cementing an already long-term association. Especially with retirement looming. Instead though, I was dangled but a condescending carrot suggesting only possibilities. I was to make a proposal to them without reassurances, guarantees, or promises for my families' welfare. They were wielding a veiled surmise of where I **might** fit in to the future. It wasn't a welcome-back meeting!

I left shivering in my cold car, feeling stabbed and bleeding paranoia. What I suspected since Johnson's appointment was clearly gaining traction.

I pasted positive spins on the grim development to my family. Inside, though, remembering chef Gunter, I sensed my golf life in early stages of unravel! I had several months to prepare a presentation in what appeared next-victim reality. But their enthusiasm for its submission already seemed slim at best. Looking back it would have been more civilized to either end the relationship then or set up parameters for a new working union. They did neither.

An often heard word on the links of Scotland is shite, and that's what it smelled like.

Journal Entry #366: Stay

Dedicated to *John Hocken*

Despite the emotional burden, my upbeat submission outlined two strategies.

First I suggested maintaining the current system. The second was joining the organization as a salaried employee whose job description paralleled peers of neighbouring courses. Up until then I'd taken an ineptly run pro shop and converted it to one of consistently thriving revenues. Strict budgeting, attention to purchasing, and consistent customer service resulted in us paying off both the business and our home. Consequently Jackie and I were in early stages of retirement planning.

Assuming a negotiating stance, I began optimistically in hopes of a modest settlement. I suggested sixty thousand with benefits. Literally hours later, the board shot back with thirty thousand. The chilly retort reconfirmed my suspicions. They didn't want me back!

Their response however incited the membership, who'd purposely been kept in-the-dark. They were beginning to see what I'd experienced since Johnson's recruitment. Consequently they confronted Corlazzoli about my staying. It was about to become worse!

Journal Entry #367: Sounds of Silence

Dedicated to *Sandra and Ken Larsen*

What followed were a series of lonely negotiations which were intimidating, patronizing, and unfriendly.

As the tension-filled summer simmered on, eventually Corlazzoli succumbed to the membership's mind. Reluctantly he increased the proposed salary from thirty to fifty thousand, but oddly commuted the term to but a provisional year. It seemed more probational than promising and I wasn't privy to the nucleus of their foil. Then like fog, the plot thickened.

Our accountant's job was to determine the value of our business assets during acquisition. Assets obligated through contract to be purchased from us during the hostile takeover. But in the discussion's **sounds of silence** he uncovered a conflict of interest. Corlazzoli (our lawyer) was acting as legal counsel for Kal Lake also!

Journal Entry #368: Dreamboat Annie

Dedicated to *Murray Koroluk*

In that final contract year I was lucky to salvage any sanity. It had been an another busy season toothached by tense hardball negotiations spearheaded by Johnson and our former lawyer. Further, my future role in their murky agenda remained clouded in speculation.

Among numerous meetings, we wrangled to determine the shop's equipment value.

Meanwhile at that same time an acquaintance from our past resurfaced.

The judge, aware of our situation, offered us a temporary respite to escape the anxiety. He'd rented a home at the Hawaiian golf resort Princeville on Kauai and invited us to stay there. All we had to do was find passage.

It became one of our most needy holidays, briefly suppressing the persecution.

While there however Johnson quietly allowed auctioneers access to our assets without permission. Consequently Kal Lake did their due diligence underhandedly rather than mutually. It was another blow beneath the belt, rupturing the relationship further.

Meanwhile Jackie and I relaxed ... fools in paradise!

Journal Entry #369: Don't Get Me Wrong!

Dedicated to *Tom and Brenda Fletcher*

To work out the final settlements, I met with the club's treasurer, a short, squat banker known as Seinfeld George. George was the twin image of George Costanza from the television sitcom, *Seinfeld*. With George, I reluctantly agreed by handshake to accept the club's unconditional terms. Reluctantly because the amounts weren't mutually determined. Unconditional because their interpretation of value subsequently differed from mine and became non-negotiable.

Later that day, I had an appointment with my new lawyer. An active club member himself, he naturally inquired how the talks were progressing. He too felt the directors were ... as he put it, "a distasteful bunch." When I mentioned the handshake agreement, he suggested the appropriate way was, "putting it in writing."

Consequently, I asked Rosa Klebb to hold off issuing a cheque until I saw George later, when we could legally paper it.

The next morning wasn't what I expected!

I arrived at George's office to find him seething and aggressive ... a level of anger suggesting physical altercation. Younger people today might have texted, "WTF?" George had been misinformed and believed I backed out of the agreement, which hadn't happened. Regardless, he wasn't hearing my side. I'd learned over decades that directors were usually reasonable. But George appeared emotionally out of control, and had it wrong. Thankfully one his employees intervened, otherwise the outcome might have differed.

Not only was it the closest I experienced to physical engagement with a club member, but it was the last thing I needed, another challenge from the board.

Journal Entry #370: Born too Late
Dedicated to *Carmen Lafontaine*

"Be yourself!" That's what I'd always heard. Whether it was from books, mentors, movies, parents, or teachers. I knew the words, but never acknowledged their true meaning until I turned fifty.

Nearing the end of my contract, the directors would soon oversee the shop with Johnson taking over. Junior, who wasn't qualified as a manager, compared to the many I'd worked with, was gifted instead with a massaging persuasiveness. The kind seen in used car lots. Since his appointment, he'd successfully converted the opinions of many loyal members and directors.

Desperate, I imagined two could play that game. Fight fire with fire. There was a pro-am where I selected three board members for my team. Ones who seemed sensible, unbiased, and could think for themselves. During the two-day tournament, I sought to reacquaint them with my own managerial skills.

After the event however, nothing was accomplished! While the opportunities to sway them were endless, I found it wasn't in me. Maybe I was **born too late**, but the reality was, I had no stomach to be anyone but myself! I didn't have the silver tongue of sales nor was I one out to get another. And there was no gratification subverting a situation toward a biased outcome. It just wasn't in me!

There's a saying from Dr. Seuss paraphrased as follows: "Why try to fit in, when you were born like everyone else to be unique." At age fifty, I learned to respect myself and accept who I really was.

Journal Entry #371: Apache
Dedicated to *Pete Bender*

My long-term contract ended when the new millennium began. I then handed over the shop to Johnson and re-entered the ranks of the salaried, continuing on as head pro ... or so I believed.

Just prior to that, the course remained open on frozen ground. A time when one of the Okanagan's more carefree assistants began appearing frequently, golfing with his young pals. Twenty years earlier, Chevy briefly worked for me and was part of my junior program. At the behest of his father then, I gave him a job cleaning clubs, despite no room on staff. His father was the kind, gentle type and I couldn't resist. Chevy however wasn't like the elder. An Indigenous member of the Tseshaht First Nation, Chevy was a free spirit who soft pedalled potential.

After leaving Kal Lake, he entered the industry elsewhere. He became an assistant, migrating from course to course moulding a career reputation that lived on the fringes of loafing, joking, and other diversions.

Most professionals when visiting other facilities avoid over-staying their welcome. That fall however Chevy golfed daily, becoming pesky. I brought it to Johnson's attention who brushed it off. When Chevy's presence became persistent and Junior continued glossing over it, I smelled a rat.

Unknown to me, I was about to become Kal Lake's puppet head pro—and not working under Johnson either. That reality was confirmed days into the New Year, when Junior made the astonishing announcement Chevy would become pro shop manager ... and my new boss! The only outcome more absurd was the election later of Donald Trump. I was never asked nor consulted about Chevy's appointment, querying my role in the new set-up.

And from that start, Chevy and Junior began collaborating conspicuously out of my sight. I'd already endured two years with Junior, and knew the type of administrator he was. Chevy, on the other hand would never have been my choice as an assistant, let alone shop manager. Numerous industry rumours insinuated the fun-loving, happy-go-lucky pro was somewhere between two winks and a shrug! It seemed everyone except the board were aware of it. His new assignment was my staggering reintroduction to the salaried world.

It was evident I was under their microscope. Consequently, I had to suck it up because behind the scenes, I continued being slandered a non-team player. The question remained why?

Journal Entry #372: Disclosure
Dedicated to *Harold and Judy Rourke*

Early one morning then, our son phoned and in disbelief said: "Dad, turn on the TV, you won't believe what's goin' on!" We arose to witness New York's Twin Towers plunging from Gotham's skyline. The attack and aftermath survived as a surreal memory, staying with me like Kennedy's assassination, a tragedy coinciding with the year my golf journey began. And ironically, 9/11 became the low point in that golf life. A time spent abused and bullied at a workplace that I'd built and made a living at for decades.

While the news testified to Manhattan's terror, Johnson and his new staff took over the shop. I wasn't in control anymore and, from its infancy, torment seemed part of the menu. Using subtle subversive strategies, emotional leverage was immediately applied to inspire my resignation.

There was a movie released then titled *Disclosure,* based on Michael Crichton's bestselling novel. The corporate drama, starring Michael Douglas and Demi Moore involved sexual politics and, aside from its erotic content, possessed a plot closely paralleling my experiences with Junior and Chevy.

As shop manager, Chevy was effervescent and upbeat yet manipulable. Characteristics mingling within a job description that included hiring staff, merchandising golf product, setting up point-of-sale computer programs, as well as administering tournaments. And with each change, results implicated Chevy in over his head.

I stayed on as head professional, relegated to the job of inventory control, permitted to teach only in times outside assigned hours. It became demeaning, cutthroat, and void of compassion. But as time went on, I warily honed my skills of grovelling. I was determined to work within their web and play by their rituals. My goal became to survive without being snagged within the scales of their underbelly.

Journal Entry #373: The Wrecking Crew
Dedicated to *Paul Toovey*

Kal Lake then was operating for the first time without a contracted professional. Consequently they were obligated to convince its membership that the buy-out decision had been sound. Staffing should have been part of the blueprint.

Previously I hired trustworthy employees who were not only golf savvy, but pleasant being around. It was a simple formula. Chevy, on the other hand, recruited a different detail.

Among them was an acquaintance of Chevy's. Red wasn't a golfer but an in-your-face know-it-all. Crowing an acumen for haute couture, he could typically talk the talk but not walk the walk. The club paid Red well even though I never saw him sell anything. That was inconsistent however with his upstairs bar bill which soared over two thousand. The members unknowingly absorbed the loss.

Then, to sell product, Chevy hired Miss T and A. While the alluring blonde also had no golf background, she did fulfill Chevy's spoken desire for tits-and-ass merchandising. Unfortunately, she never sold as much as Chevy boasted. And while there were more men in the shop, most were peeping rather than purchasing.

Chevy hired another sidekick to supervise bag storage services. A big man, flaunting the intimidating image of heavyweight fighter Mike Tyson. Tyson was a member of a biker gang, chaptered throughout Canada. It wasn't long before their strains began showing up in our back shop. Ones who ran in other circles and different times of night. Bag storage became a haunt for hushed conversations in secluded corners with Tyson. It didn't take a genius to know the topic. It was Tyson's job to open the bag room each morning. Often I arrived hearing his slurred voice from local bars on the telephone answering machine. Decreeing his sabbatical for the day, he'd frequently leave us short staffed. Then, the quality of care we'd conscientiously shown to our members' equipment in the past vaporized ... as did their clubs. During the twenty years I operated the shop, I never had a theft. But in one month alone, under Tyson's watch, three members' sets mysteriously vanished. Consequently Kal Lake awoke to insurance nightmares and loss of long-established credibility. I urged Johnson to dismiss Tyson. He reluctantly complied, then quietly rehired him on my days off.

And of course there was Chevy. Throughout the new season's first half, he was the same happy-go-lucky quipster ... charming everyone. He had rare skills of making promises, not keeping them, yet never losing customer confidence. I envied the flimsy talent, for when he constantly forgot orders or tee-time requests, his customers, like Trump's base, laughed along with him and remained loyal. But those whose needs went unsatisfied, sought me out, multiplying weary workloads.

Clouded, I began questioning who our members were becoming. Kal Lake was robust with prominent white-collar professionals. Surely they noticed the trickle of grifters infesting the shop? Were they blind ... or just apathetic?

Absent answers, I then questioned myself! Maybe it was me who was naive, blind-sided instead by my own passions?

Journal Entry #374: If I Had a Hammer

Dedicated to *the Clancys*

When I wrote this, Canada's then-Prime Minister Stephen Harper was quoted in response to the tragic death of Nova Scotia teen, Rehtaeh Parsons. He said: "Bullying to me has a kind of connotation ... of kids misbehaving. What we are dealing with in some of these circumstances is simply criminal activity."

In my new position, bullying partnered the conversion. As Johnson and Chevy set about rebranding the shop's twenty-year image into Walmart strains, they also smeared any efforts I made when acquiescing to their demands.

For instance, a senior member wanted to purchase a newly marketed set of clubs. Hybrids were emerging then as the-must-have product. Crosses between irons and metal woods, they possessed muscle of the latter and control of the former. The elder member was uncertain about them and asked if I'd play a quick nine with him for advice. I was scheduled in the shop that morning, but it was an irresistible opportunity to promote the club's nouveau image and help in equipment decisions. It was a normal practise among pros, usually resulting in sales. I arrived back after the quick round and successfully made the transaction. But I also found a stony letter from Junior awaiting. Memos like that began following me routinely. Chevy made a formal complaint, claiming, "I abandoned my post." Regardless of intent, I was convicted.

Another member wanted to buy a hot TaylorMade driver. She was a talented competitor who trusted my experience and knowledge above other staff. Consequently, she too asked me for five minutes of driving-range advice. Knowing it was quiet in the shop, I spent time with her as well, selling the club in the process. A new subordinate, however, made another chilly complaint. Those were typical examples of the sordid methodology used in my persecutions. Persecutions featuring employees coached into authoring accusations through twisting my movements. Copies then were placed in my mail along with a hidden file bearing my name.

In life's bigger picture, job intimidation could never be confused with Rehtaeh Parsons' death. My oppression was only work related, yet significant in my life. It was employee bullying of an extreme yet subtle nature intended to extort my resignation. But in the face of that workplace tyranny, it failed to extinguish my immunity.

Journal Entry #375: Boogie Nights

Dedicated to *Dennis Yano*

Over years, I shared numerous duties with various captains, but none were like Dougie Greers. Nicknamed Dirk Diggler, a porn-star character from the film "**Boogie Nights**," Greers began conspiring with Johnson and Chevy … collectively becoming Kal Lake's great triumvirate.

As captain, Greers took over club functions including men's nights.

He and Chevy directed the weekly games and in the speed of a shanked shot, the frothy evenings slipped from soirees to Sodom and Gomorrah. While most men enjoyed the overall fiesta, they were also too fuelled up to be aware what was happening.

In past there was always pressure on men's night. It was challenging to complete tournament scoring and deliver prizes for men who couldn't stay. Timing was paramount. Chevy found that out and was overwhelmed by the two hundred golfers. To accelerate those nights, he'd flip coins to decide winners, rather than scoring and handicapping. Competitors weren't aware, and his laughing response to my concerns were "They're plastered. They'll never know."

Chevy and Greers presented the prizes. It was a job Chevy loved, leveraging him rock-star status to the lathered-up crowd. As a result, more important details were neglected. For instance, some mornings I arrived to find stacks of cash lounging on counters from the previous evening's take. Another night the jumbo deuce jackpot vanished, forcing Chevy into a frenzy. Its mysterious loss was shrouded by the captain's shadowy slush fund. When closing, it was Chevy's job to lock up. Often security phoned our home late notifying us again the shop had been left open with Chevy's keys dangling from the lock … inviting the unwanted.

Greers on the other hand, was a married man who reputedly never lost touch with the club's female servers. During those nights, they felt more than his eyes, as the charismatic captain revisited paradise. "I never promised anyone I was a saint," Greers boasted to naive teenage club cleaners. After the evening's action, he'd chauffeur them about town, trolling for more pleasure. The club had a conference room used for business seminars. When elected captain, Greers swiftly ended that side of the organization's revenues. He converted the large room into a gaming sanctuary with a pool table and disturbing sound system that rapidly elicited after-hour adult activities.

Each week, under alcoholic inertia, the indiscretions spun further out of control. Being under constant scrutiny, I was powerless curbing it. Speaking out would have only amplified their views of me as a non-team-player, accelerating my impeachment.

Overall it might be cozy for readers to dismiss it all as ramblings of a spurned head pro. And to some degree such assertions might appear true, except there weren't dossiers kept on others, as there was me. A collection to be levied at some opportune moment. For suddenly ... it became clear! Chevy had sometime or somewhere been illicitly promised the designation he coveted ... head professional!

Journal Entry #376: Things Have Changed

Dedicated to *Hon. Doug and Betty Wetmore*

My career was deviating dramatically. No longer was I free to do as I chose, which was understandable. But other things were changing also. Some were good, while most lacked business strategy. It became an uncomfortable environment where I sensed new employees wanted me out ... or was I fantasizing? Days were challenged differentiating fact from fiction. I worked outside transparent political barriers, continually stressed among unfriendly forces while subjected to error.

As the veteran, I was defenseless ... embarrassed knowing everyone knew everything, except me.

Then as the season progressed, like winning lotto tickets, others discreetly confirmed my anguish—members with moral compasses and mirrored credibility. Maybe I wasn't delusional? Perhaps proof existed in paranoia?

Thelma was a successful, retired businesswoman who joined the club. She'd been a member of a neighbouring course where Johnson had worked prior to joining Kal Lake. Thelma became a Kal Lake member because her best friend was. One day she confided to her companion about grandstanding she overheard years earlier at her other course. There, she recalled Junior bragging to pals that he was leaving ... quitting to become Kal Lake's manager. He'd been specifically hired "to get rid of me!" Thelma didn't know who I was then, and the conversation meant little until she joined Kal Lake. She passed it onto her friend, who relayed it to me during a lesson.

Thelma didn't know Louise. Louise was a city realtor and another student. One day during a lesson, she shared a bizarre conversation heard earlier outside the ladies' locker room.

The room was located on the clubhouse's lower level. Often the doors were kept open allowing breezes to cool its interior. On that occasion, Louise was inside changing shoes when overhearing Johnson outside, convening with shop staff. The trouper was mutinying me, coercing them to take orders only from Chevy. The furtive encounter away from prying eyes and ears was meant to undermine my remaining authority. His sermon incensed her and, out of loyalty, she confided in me.

The stories of Thelma and Louise among others, confirmed a collection of experiences since Johnson's arrival. For instance perceptions of equipment sabotage, the sway of membership opinions, and the suspicious midnight destruction of power carts. After both women's testimonials, a cold collage began to form challenging my neurosis. Perhaps I wasn't phobic?

After three decades in the industry, I'd attended numerous seminars. I'd accumulated five years post-secondary education. As a father, husband, and businessman, I also enjoyed a healthy rapport among peers. Regardless, none of that prepared me to confront and oppose this type of oppression. And any outlandish claims might have alienated my closest supporting members. Because after all ... who'd believe such fables at a golf club? But could anyone have realistically imagined the 2016 US election either?

Journal Entry #377: Uncle Norm's Cabin (Part 1)

Dedicated to *Paul and Jackie Sullivan*

Spiteful assaults made each workday miserable and humiliating, while frequent lies invaded my integrity. It became traumatic on our family too. Further, I didn't earn as much as accustomed. Previously, as a business owner I lived an affordable lifestyle. But then as an employee the new income influenced needs to moonlight.

An interest in renovating homes and reselling for profit appealed to me then. I had saved a modest amount and ventured forward to invest in my first property, a neglected log home. Quaint and well made, the house nestled peacefully within a twenty-acre forest. I sensed its potential but didn't know where to start other than submitting an offer.

It was accepted and I instantly became a minor league land baron.

Journal Entry #378: Uncle Norm's Cabin (Part 2)

Dedicated to *Norm Metheral*

Omnia causa fiunt! The English translation is "everything happens for a reason."

Norm was a new club member, who moved to the Okanagan and took up golf. After some lessons, we became friends and pro-am partners. In one conversation we discussed how to restore the log house I'd purchased. Norm said, "I'll give you a hand." That's how it became **Uncle Norm's cabin**.

And when not challenged in that abhorrent pro shop, we'd travel to the country and renovate the chalet among the Okanagan's gold fall leaves, brilliant winter snows, and searing summer heat.

Norm possessed a variety of building skills and attempted passing them onto me. As a pro, my trade tools were lie and loft machines, cash registers, fitting carts, and profit detectors. My new equipment was different and indispensable later as a golf course owner. Norm taught me bench- and skill-saw uses, building material basics, and measuring accurately before cutting. Reading levels and identifying various nails and screws became mandatory. It wasn't just knowledge and technique either. It was often a classroom where I majored in emotional development.

One cold December near darkness, I was working alone among an underbelly of footings, installing a crude vapour barrier. Squirming and crawling, I felt the exposed earth's hostility against my outerwear. As seconds passed, uncertainties of encountering a bear or wolverine den entered my mind. My only weapons were a flashlight and staple gun. Feet became inches in my bid to sync up the confining sheet. Hours into the claustrophobia, my clothing suddenly snagged, wedging me in.

A death-defining aura, as if I'd disturbed evil, fuelled the panic. In that near frozen state, cave-exploring fears insinuated that the massive timber might collapse upon me. Delusion partnered the despair suggesting my flashlight batteries and me would expire and never be seen again. But during those hours of frigid immobility, reason unexplainably ousted the dread from my mind ... and I released myself. Fears like that identified distress I hadn't met before. Deficiencies that demanded attention when later tackling the challenges of owning a golf course.

And in that later role, when Jackie and I took possession of a modest course on Vancouver Island, most of the jobs encountered weren't related to marketing, teaching, or merchandising. Instead they enlisted the endless trade and emotional skills that stemmed from those experiences at Uncle Norm's cabin.

So while inexplicable, I've found events in my life happened via reason.

Journal Entry #379: Djobi, Djoba (El Saler)

Dedicated to *Ray and Rita Foisy*

When Norm retired from Air Canada, the Ryder Cup was being contested at Valderrama in Spain. He desperately wanted to travel there and golf, so we made a pact. If I arranged a game for him there, he'd look after my plane fare. With each wanting to fulfill the other's wishes, we left for Spain.

Before arriving at Valderrama, I booked us to golf another Spanish course. While not as well known, **El Saler** was one of Spain's few links courses.

El Saler wasn't the beneficiary of usual accolades lavished upon the world's top hundred courses. Newbies to golf left there with false expectations of eye candy, unparalleled course grooming, and unconditional fairness. But El Saler wasn't like Valderrama, whose owner assaulted her with vast unlimited resources. El Saler instead was not only a links, but an affordable public course shaped from subtle pined slopes shared with the city of Valencia. Initially, I was attracted to her through passions for links golf. But then I discovered she wasn't counterfeit. She flourished in the spirit and soul bred from her designer, early Spanish sensation, Javier Arana. Arana wasn't a recognized name either. Absent architectural portfolios and engineering degrees, he relied instead upon devout understandings of golf ... blood from a decorated amateur past. Working solo, Arana forged his craft under Tom Simpson's mentorship.

El Saler horseshoed herself around the Paradores Hotel, where we were seduced by a glimmering Mediterranean lapping nearby shores.

A smaller, par-three course there was niched out among umbrella pines fronting the hotel. That evening after an unfurling drive from Madrid, Norm and I introduced our clubs to the modest layout before our round. Sipping sangria, we golfed casually in the fading Hispanic sunset when one of my tee shots found the cup for my third hole-in-one. An unexpected moment for a golfing Gipsy King.

Journal Entry #380: Mas Que Nada

Dedicated to *Diane Nohr*

Where there are greens, there is peace.

—David Plotz

Jackie and I relaxed on Kal Lake's clubhouse balcony, pondering how to celebrate my fiftieth birthday. A member joining us had worked as a lab technician in the Yukon city of Whitehorse. Humorously, she proposed a trip there. On the spur of that, some cider, and urges to live life ... we went.

Since then, I've criss-crossed Canada, golfing from Whitehorse to Winnipeg and Haida Gwaii to Halifax. It's a massive country and in every place I played enthusiasm existed for a game hampered by winter setback. Canada's also a peaceful country, not at war with others. American journalist David Plotz makes a compelling argument that countries where golf is popular never fight other golfing nations. He charges war is founded on violence, cheating, and crushing your rival. I believe he's right! Geographic comparisons might support that.

For instance, golfers in South Korea aim their clubfaces at flags, while North Korean's aim ballistic missiles at countries. Moroccans shoot for pars while neighbouring Algerians shoot each other. Peaceful Thailanders love their golf, while outcast Myanmar love their military. The Dominican Republic is rife with courses, while neighbouring Haiti is rife with strife. Taiwanese bankroll golf course development while China suffocates it. Scandinavians bomb drives, while Russians bomb Ukrainians.

And I'll edge further, suggesting that ideology roots the anger, aggression, and adversarial behaviour of Donald Trump who, as Commander in Chief, solely led his own country to the brink of domestic warfare. The former president's adopted Roy Cohn doctrine of never apologizing, admitting blame, and attacking clearly present not only danger to civilization, but to the game of golf … for, as is so well known, Trump also … unfortunately golfs!

Take for example his relationship within the Saudi Arabian backed LIV formula.

The potential for golf to root in Saudi Arabia and the Middle East, reducing histories of warfare, should represent a symbolic olive branch toward overdue peace. Yet ironically, LIV's CEO and Trump nemesis Greg Norman has waded in, creating instead a polar effect. For no golfer today can dispute the result of his white-shark inquisition … provocatively steering golf ironically … and sadly toward conflict. War if you will!

Journal Entry #381: No Matter What Shape

Dedicated to *Ann Samuel*

Art critics have suggested that: "If you're successful in one creative world … best to leave it at that!" Celebrity art for example. Art in the form of paintings by the famous like Bob Dylan, Sir Paul McCartney, or Johnny Depp. Works whose efforts haven't bled into their more eminent depths. Yet such art has been known to debatably sell for inflated fees. Late in my career, I saw the golf world challenged by a similar vain.

The discipline of golf course design became diluted when famous pros shucked their shots to become arm-chair architects, often with results disarming the sport's compass. In the wake of their careers and flattered by myopic disciples, Nicklaus, Palmer, and Player forged these audacious new paths, challenging artisans from golf's golden era of architecture. To me however, their interpretations of scale and shape failed to capture the glory from their competitive years. Instead they appear as summons from profiteering developers seeking rushed returns on investment.

I did see sunshine among the clouds though. When Masters Champion Crenshaw was lured toward that same domain his artistic responses appeared not only sensual, subtle, and scintillating … but tempered by a genuine golf philosophy coupled with early twentieth century design principles.

Admittedly however, while my observations then and now appear conservative and rejections of the new, they've remained respectful of each past champion's playing credentials. But they've also found an appetite for respected art critics like Robert Hughes, who might have frankly snapped: "The shock where the famous can claim any mantle of success, **no matter what shape** and get away with it, is frankly … a piss off!" Consequently, when comparing amateur architecture to yesteryear's golden-era greats … like MacKenzie and Macdonald, Thompson and Simpson, or Raynor and Ross … one might be able to sense the gravity of that phrase, "Art is the receipt of pain!"

Journal Entry #382: The Sting

Dedicated to *Bill Schenk*

When Chevy was promised the title head pro, the board didn't anticipate the volume of members advocating for me. Their pledge to him went on-hold for a year.

Until then I was assigned the job of inventory control and sequestered to Greer's pleasure room where more than just billiards were played. I laboured daily in that asylum, counting, pricing, and inventorying new merchandise before it could be sold.

Midway through that first season, several shipments arrived from Callaway and TaylorMade. During the processing, I sensed they'd been tampered with. Invoice recounts confirmed missing items, but no one confessed ... including Junior. But as I left him to file theft reports, he raced after me. It must be understood paint dried faster than Johnson normally moved. Acting like a long-lost pal, he discreetly shouldered me toward a locked cabinet in the pleasure room. Nervously he fumbled opening it, revealing the embezzlement. He claimed in panic that Greers was "just having fun!"

Later that day Greers apologized too, but instead of sincerity I sensed a plea coerced from unknown sources. The morning's behaviour of both hustlers was a silent warning.

I realized how exploitable I was. Inventory losses were my responsibility. I was a patsy awaiting oversight accountability. A pigeon whose shortfalls possessed dismissal value.

It was clear, they were serious about removing me. Everyday I had to stay alert, walking on broken glass!

Journal Entry #383: Stay Loose
Dedicated to *Stu and Barb Robertson*

My inventory control assignment was also because Junior didn't share my marketing intuition. And yet over decades I'd demonstrated proven ways to sell. I merchandised using skills acquired from my apprenticeship, seminars, mentors and famous courses like Pebble Beach and Pinehurst, whose pro shops I'd studied. In addition, I hired knowledgeable staff whose similar devotion, enthusiasm, and passion inspired sales. That was my marketing philosophy. Johnson instead leaned toward Walmart methodology. I could have employed those means too but felt committed to Kal Lake. I chose cleaner, small-business-like approaches based on reliability and trust. Sound fake? Perhaps ... but as stated earlier, I believed in the code of my profession.

That was why Junior recruited Chevy ... because he could talk the talk. But Chevy couldn't walk the walk! So his marketing asset was a curvy adolescent with no golf pedigree. He called her Miss T and A ... or tits and ass. Most women today—and even then—would have been offended, but the alluring one he hired then didn't seem to mind, confirming what's been said of some blondes.

One hot weekend, T and A was working the late shift, and wanted to retire early for a date. With only few players remaining on the course, only fools would have believed a mad rush impending. Seeing no reason to keep her and with Chevy absent and partying at the lake, I made a common sense decision. To minimize drains on payroll I sent her home. Chevy was informed and returned to the course enraged. In front of an audience he berated me, anticipating my resignation. As a fifty-year-old veteran though, shamed and publicly censured by the young inebriant, I sensed a compelling need then to **stay loose**.

Under Johnson's direction and Chevy's tits-and-ass merchandising, the shop succumbed to epic financial losses!

Journal Entry #384: Fork in the Road

Dedicated to *Dave and Barb Greenan*

When you come to a fork in the road, take it!

—Yogi Berra

In their pro-shop conquest, the directors reached their own **fork in the road**. By mid-season, enormous losses and dissension demanded immediate solutions.

Corlazzoli found one and summoned me to a downtown restaurant to discuss it. Initially, I believed his strategy was to reinstate me and straighten the mess out. Instead, he outlined a new plan which included Chevy and I along with one of my previous assistants. Keeping Chevy seemed ironic, as the happy-go-lucky pro had already slaughtered the shop's credibility. Plus the young assistant they chose struggled with personal issues. It was well known. Yet both were hand-picked by Johnson, who continued controlling policy and procedure.

To me, the new fabrication appeared worse than their first. Nevertheless to keep working I maintained a team spirit of staying positive.

Clearly, the president's meeting was meant only to unveil more of Johnson's folly. When facing that fork in the road, the board might have been wiser asking Yogi, rather than Junior.

Journal Entry #385: Someone Like You

Dedicated to *Jack and Bonnie Ellett*

The Corlazzoli-Johnson solution proved late and desperate. Junior and Chevy had squandered too many club resources resulting in numerous failures, disillusioned members, and apathetic staff. Consequently Corlazzoli convened a second downtown restaurant meeting. There, he laid out another blueprint for next season. This time however, he wanted me completely in charge. But there was still that glaring three-letter word … **b-u-t**. It was to be another one-year sentence labouring on with Johnson and remarkably still-absent authority.

By now readers surely realize Junior, also a golf pro, was the most challenging club manager I'd crossed paths with. I felt what many global victims found later, when Trump became leader of the free world. For like the former president, Junior too struggled with a vast ego, seedy street smarts, and fraudulent popularity. He'd been there three years by then and only someone other than me understood why. So when Corlazzoli insisted I continue on with the burly bureaucrat, I not only had to resolve staying positive, but find means to oversee business without control.

In other words things hadn't changed. I was back in charge … but not really. In hindsight, I could have quit but truthfully I was passionate about my work—just not the conditions. And ideas of resigning seemed like giving up which I never considered.

Raising one eyebrow, Corlazzoli concluded the luncheon smirking, "We need **someone like you!**"

Journal Entry #386: Count Me In

Dedicated to *Don and Joyce Wiseman*

Flavio put me back in charge and even though reporting to Johnson remained a condition, I returned profitability to the shop! I balanced budgets, sharpened service, coddled caution, and stopped the squandering. We ended the year back in black. Nevertheless, one concern lingered … inventory!

With my new responsibilities, I continued overseeing stock control. The issue was a shortage of Titleist ProV1 balls, the market's most popular then. My physical count was less compared to printouts.

Two problems persisted. The first was Kal Lake's new point of sales program. Many upscale courses were using multi-variable software systems. Junior and Seinfeld George however acquired a cheaper alternative without a track record. An example of its shortcomings were golf balls.

Before stock entered inventory, computers produced labelled SKU numbers which attached to merchandise. Counter scanners read them during sales … adding or subtracting merchandise from disc memory. Because ball boxes were too numerous labelling, they instead were shipped with generic codes. The new program however, failed recognizing them! Circumventing that we keyed individual sleeves into inventory manually. When sold in high volumes, as balls were, inaccuracies surfaced. The more serious dilemma was Chevy. Johnson's protege distributed inventory keys to every staff member including young, newly hired back-shop help. The result was significant shortages before locks could be changed. Plus in that climate, I couldn't indict anyone.

At year's end, the board was pleased with the improved figures and service. But it wasn't enough! They continued singing inventory shortfalls to incite doubt.

I was mobilized to a third and final meeting with the lawyer at a local Boston Pizza. There in an ultimatum, he called-for-me to present solutions at a special board meeting. Before leaving the restaurant though, I used the moment to apprise Corlazzoli of Greers' stock removal, a desperate attempt to portray the distorted environment that had evolved. However as he slurped his soup, the president's eyes revealed only indifference.

In the upcoming showdown, how would I ever convert the board's tainted opinions? It would have been like a Democrat flogging the obvious to Trump's Republican base.

Journal Entry #387: Peacekeeper
Dedicated to *Beth Harmata*

A week later, I presented my solutions.

During my rehearsals at home, an uneasiness hinted this might be my last supper.

My original draft was a no-hold-back twenty-five point submission detailing everything I'd worked with and documented the previous three years. Being lengthy, I instead condensed it to four points on more positive notes.

I inferred their numerous problems were rooted in mismanagement. He too attended. Being face-to-face with Johnson among his partisans, proved to be the most daunting moment of my career. To steer us out of the disaster, I suggested retaking control of the shop. This included new staff of my choice, more accurate point of sale systems, multiple terminals, and strict policy and procedure manuals. After investing in damage control, I'd re-define and re-image the shop.

After the presentation, Greers attacked me like a Republican pit bull … shooting from the quip. Director Ivan Salenko joined in, barking no remedies. It was clear my efforts were futile. Facts meant nothing and their enduring loyalties to Johnson were unwavering.

The presentation was a somatic adventure, abetted by chills that lingered regardless of room temperature. Aside from that I was calm.

Corlazzoli concluded the meeting, stating, "They'd get back to me later."

I ushered my way out pursued by the question. Did a similar plight inspire Canadian singer Paul Anka to compose his classic, "My Way?"

PATRICK LITTLE

Journal Entry #388: Black Day in October (Part 1)

Dedicated to *Dennis and Cody Edwards*

Jimmy knew what was coming before I did!

Thirty years earlier, he'd entered my life when I began forging this career. That Saturday though he just lounged in the shop, grimly staring out the windows.

He'd been visiting and was killing time before flying back to Edmonton later that day. I was keeping him company and working, while waiting for a noon appointment with Corlazzoli.

Corlazzoli wasn't a friend, had only recently entered my life, and was about to decimate that career. He arrived promptly although not usually. As a young, about-town lawyer he normally draped himself in striped suits, like those sold in Europe. That day though, he breezed in sporting athletic shorts and an angled ball cap with a flipped gangsta brim.

After introducing the president to Jimmy, I led him to my office.

Shutting the door, I faded into my burgundy recliner when the Italian came to his point. "You're done!" he said! "What?" I questioned. "You're done!" he repeated. "I tried saving you, but you did yourself in with your presentation." He was referring to my recent meeting where I faced down eight board dissidents.

Moments of disorientation followed as my eyes drifted toward the office window. Across the stream from the shop, I saw my young student Cody warming up for his lesson that followed the meeting. How could I ever compose myself when teaching him? I murmured in a barely audible whisper to no one, "Oh man ... I've never been fired before!" I sensed the lawyer fidgety and, as if compelled to answer my thoughts, he muttered: "You've got to get a lawyer and sue the club, but you can't have Cavanaugh!" Paul Cavanaugh was also a club member and a well-known attorney specifically trained in employment law.

From within this sudden shock, I heard Corlazzoli continue: "You may not feel comfortable coming into work for the next while ..." The club wasn't sailing in calm financial waters then, and all along they'd been clear ... I was strictly a one-year contractor. Consequently I interpreted his words as a warning dressed in subtle counsel ... live up to the terms of your contract! Submissively I replied, "You can count on me. I'll fulfill my obligations."

After Corlazzoli conveniently vanished, Jimmy left also. Meanwhile, I attended to my young student on the range. It was the most challenging lesson of my career. I stood disarmed behind the tall, good-looking sixteen-year-old, watching him loft fades toward distant targets. My thoughts volleyed between the lesson and the meeting, distracted by what felt like thick blood sunburning the inside of my skull from the top down.

Over the years, even though I'd dismissed my own share of subordinates, to be personally fired seemed life-altering. You see my past there had been much more than just a job. It had been my way of life, one conceived half a century earlier when swinging that first golf club.

Throughout the lesson, hopes this was a depraved dream kept flickering in my mind.

Journal Entry #389: Black Day in October (Part 2)

Dedicated to *Jack and Jimmy Wills*

That night feeling demoralized, I shared the outcome with my family. I didn't remember much except a need to remain calm. A clear head might finger a future.

My next challenge though was to focus on the following day. The first of my remaining time left looking after the needs of my members and guests. One mandating a cheerful, smiling disposition while camouflaging the wounds within. The ultimate sacrifice of a golf pro.

At that late time of year, with daylight in short supply and early morning frosts, the club decided on midday shotgun starts. I began preparing early with only sheer help from a young girl they'd recently hired. We had to be ready for players who'd literally invade the shop prior to tee-off. It was a routine I'd adopted in past to minimize unforeseen events arising in each golfer's day.

Dew had to be towelled off motorized carts before mounting them with bags. Driving range baskets were filled with balls while member's clubs were pulled from storage and placed on hand carts. It all happened before assisting customers at front counters with their charges and cash sales. We were a humming club and normally I was aided by two assistants. But for unknown reasons that day, Junior hadn't scheduled either in for work. Knowing I'd soon by jobless was one thing, but managing a hectic shotgun virtually solo was another.

After ... in the cool fall evening ... when every set had been cleaned, each cart washed and parked, and every golfer had deserted the club ... I arrived home. I was too exhausted and emotionally stained to contemplate what would happen next day.

Journal Entry #390: Black Day in October (Part 3)

Dedicated to *Tim Ouellette*

After those first two days, the trauma remained anchored within. I had to rise above it though. That's what professionals did. On day three, by ten o'clock, all the shotgun's prep work was finished when Chevy finally moseyed in. It was often his way ... arriving after work was complete ... glowing with a double-double Tim Horton's coffee. As he entered the shop that particular morning, though, his naturally frivolous banter suddenly vaporized upon seeing me.

There was no "Good morning" or "Hi, how are you?" Instead I was met with a cold, spiteful glare accompanied by a blunt and demanding, "What are you doing here?" Taken back, I replied, "Good morning ... working ... why, what's up?" Chevy's response was a huffy retreat out the same door. That didn't surprise me. As a schmoozer, his departure left me thinking he'd simply begun his daily routine.

Later, Corlazzoli phoned asking if I'd reconsidered? My initial reaction led me to believe I hadn't been terminated. After all ... what kind of answer was he expecting? Reconsidered what? He replied, "About coming into work." I reconfirmed my commitment from our meeting days earlier.

I wasn't an employee, but a contractor. I thought his question was to again ensure I'd honour the framework of our agreement. In today's work-world such thinking's outdated, nevertheless those were my thoughts then. Besides, no one specifically said otherwise and I'd laboured the previous two days uninterrupted.

That same morning, a friend phoned asking me to lunch. Chevy eavesdropped on that call, which accounts for what followed.

Returning, I saw a lady attempting to buy a shirt. No one was assisting her. It was when I asked if she needed help, a fragment of hell broke loose.

I'll tell readers what happened next, however, let me share two earlier events that influenced those moments.

Years before, I'd been in Johannesburg, South Africa. Jo'burg as it's called, was then the world's most dangerous city. Sitting in a bus there, outside a downtown hotel, I saw a young black man with an unkempt afro loitering near the open door. His eyes possessed a barbaric, savage look—one of terror I'd never seen in others. He was hinting of vehicle invasion and, while it never happened, the daunting appearance haunted me for years after.

The second incident occurred more recently when Greers suspiciously relocated merchandise. Foolishly, I never spoke about it until a week earlier, when with my back against the wall, reported it to Corlazzoli.

Anyway ... as I began assisting that lady with her purchase, we were disturbed by a commotion from behind. Turning, I saw Greers and board member Ivan Salenko storming into the shop. They were literally lunging toward me. Greers had the same look in his eyes I'd seen in Jo'burg, which instantly aroused fear. He reinforced it, barking in sharp, piercing tones, "We want to see you outside ... now!" He emphasized the words "outside" and "now." Shaking, I replied, "Why? What ... what's goin' on?" Greers led and the cadaverous climate continued when Salenko followed. Something wasn't right. We patrolled through the shop, past my office, and into the corridor. I was certain Corlazzoli admonished Greers about the theft. I envisioned the enraged captain taking it out on me with a fistfight outside ... revenge for tattling. Greers was that type. But as the mad man reached the hallway, he inexplicably turned left into the building's belly, rather than outside. I was relieved because I'm not a fighter and Greers was much larger.

However, the fear was quickly accompanied by incarceration. It was militant and Salenko's physical Gestapo image didn't help. I was being led, guarded, and followed to avoid escape. *From what?* I silently and nervously questioned. Marching down the hallway, Greers stopped at his pleasure room. As he fumbled keys to open the door, he stated as commandos snap to prisoners: "You won't leave when you're told to, and that's why this is happening!" The tension remained thick as they appeared to be imprisoning me in the pleasure room. Warily I cried back, "This isn't the way business is done!" After finally breaching the lock, he motioned me inside, snarling, "This is exactly how it's done!"

As my body physically quivered, I crept inside. There, on the billiard table in solitary confinement, a mountain of personal possessions were strewn about. The disarray was a collection of golf equipment accumulated over two decades of pro shop life. "If this isn't out of here by four today, we'll throw it to the street," Greers sneered. Terrified, I broke away from the two board vipers toward the table, stuttering, "What tha … wha … where's the inventory?" Overwhelmed, I reeled behind the cluster, grabbing a hickory-shafted golf club for protection. Frantic, I stammered in defense: "I need time to find a truck … I … I … need to make phone calls!" Then I saw a breath in their frenzy when Salenko asked Greers, "Is he allowed to make a call?" Unexplainably, it became clear … I was being forcibly evicted from the workplace … not imprisoned! Salenko had asked if I was permitted to make a call … from a public place!

I almost laughed. Instead, I shook away the terror and put my club down. Gathering myself, I walked back to Salenko. Looking him in the eye I stated, "I expected better of you than this." The dumpy banker with Hitler's mustache returned my look without expression. As my stare shifted toward Greers though, I continued, "But I expected this from you!" Then I walked out. They followed me like two hyenas stalking prey. On the way, I passed a shocked and teary-eyed club member who'd witnessed the entire assault.

Outside lumbering toward my car, I felt my breathing constricted. Lightheaded and dizzy, I was invaded by chills from the warm afternoon sunshine. I was shivering but it wasn't cold. I questioned why no one asked me to leave or confiscated my shop keys? Of all the valley pros I was probably the most submissive. It made no sense, especially knowing the pettiness they'd subjected me to in past. I would have left peacefully than endure all that. And yet, knowing them as I did, it was their way.

It wasn't over!

Journal Entry #391: What Becomes of the Brokenhearted?

Dedicated to *Janine*

I was in a feeble state during the short drive home.

Arriving, I phoned Jackie at her work, detailing the events. The conversation was emotional as the club was a dominant part of our lives. Coincidentally our daughter was home at that time. I didn't realize she was in the background listening intently!

Janine isn't a person to cross, but she isn't a bully either. Gifted and smart, she's the type who instinctually speaks up for victims of moral miscues. So before I became aware, she had left and driven to the club, undetected.

Straying in through the main clubhouse doors, she stumbled upon a small party in progress. Being reclusive and not among the golfing set, no one there knew her. Leaning against a nearby trophy case, she watched ... appalled and stunned. Unwittingly, she'd wandered into a mire of warrior club members clustered in jubilation. The warmongers were lauding and reliving the conquest of evicting their club pro. Among the gibes she heard were, "He never knew what hit him!" Another chimed in, "And he thought he was going to retire here, huh!" Still, another confirmed, "He never knew we had a pool table until today!" It was all accessorized with laughter fuelled by draft beer anointing the despicable celebration.

When she returned and replayed the final chapter, I felt gutted knowing how cruel they'd been. A strain of unforgiveness seethed within me.

Above all the rumours and stories which later surfaced, none were more devastating than what she'd witnessed.

From the time I swung my first golf club until then, I truthfully never missed the thrill. In that way, I wasn't unlike Moe Norman or Mickey Wright. But at that moment I instead felt sacrificed by golf, accompanied by desolation and a lonely question. Was the carnage of my career that day the pinnacle of those four decades of such intense passion?

Journal Entry #392: Why Do All Good Things Come to an End?

Dedicated to *Ken Friesen*

Days after, my family and I returned with a vehicle to remove what remained of me from the pleasure room. My business documents, communications, and letters on the computer hard drive were also annulled. They erased me, discontinuing my existence there! As well, many personal effects conveniently vanished too.

The club's bizarre behaviour was notarized further by how they purged their own booking orders.

In their zeal they cleared my desk, which included the shop's valuable spring orders, collected weeks earlier at the buying show. Consequently I was accused of destroying them, which of course didn't happen. It took hours to sort through and find that which they'd banished themselves.

In the following days, directors were inundated with protests. Their newly elected treasurer abdicated, submitting a strongly worded letter of dissent. Streams of emails, letters, and phone calls flowed with outrage. Expressions of anger and resentment assaulted the club, while compassion and reassurance converged on our home. Assorted groups huddled vigilantly about the community. The annual membership meeting, one normally attended by eighty sleepy souls, bulged to life with more than four hundred demanding answers. Their efforts were met by the terse legal retort, "No comment!"

The board even contaminated our only glimpse of good news. By then, Jackie was a provincial legend. Only days after, Golf Canada appointed her Team Captain for the New Zealand Commonwealth Games. In a cavalier moment, the directors sent her a good-luck card … as if nothing happened.

Our shock was still maturing days later when I drove her to the Kelowna Airport. There, weighing the previous decades, we emotionally measured the future upon her return.

That night she left for Auckland supported only by the strength of our relationship.

Journal Entry #393: Say it Right

Dedicated to *Fred and Anne Dickinson*

Corlazzoli meanwhile was overwhelmed from bickering, finger-pointing members and fallout from his board's barbaric eviction methods. As well, there were emails, letters, and phone calls of rage to deal with. He had to end it!

The solution turned up right under his nose. He found it among the traditional tools of trained lawyers. Using Kal Lake's monthly newsletter, he published a plea, appeasing the anger.

Earlier he and the directors cited inventory inconsistency as reason for my dismissal. Cunningly, they reworded the account, strategically referring to it as **inaccurate record keeping**. That revision extinguished the fury.

Soon after, a club member and retired RCMP officer urged I defend myself. He claimed, "The newsletter implied theft!"

While Corlazzoli's shady report may have harboured the message, there seemed to be no disputing its origin. Only one person possessed that handiwork. It wasn't sufficient removing me from Kal Lake. Johnson wanted more. Using deception, he stick-handled the blame, distorting the board's sordid image of bad guys ... into suddenly good guys.

That's when Lefevre phoned me.

Journal Entry #394: The Haig

Dedicated to *Sig and Marg Arndt*

Losing my job and being accused of theft wasn't how I saw my career pinnacling.

Both Lefevre and my long time friend the judge, advised me to take legal action. I'd never participated in a lawsuit before, but knew it could be bitter. Plus I sensed Johnson and the board saw me as emotionally impotent to pursue matters in court. What kind of lawyer would I need anyway, and who? I knew many over the years, but the fraternal valley was tight and word travelled fast. Selecting locals didn't promise confidentiality. Consequently, I sought outside the region. However, I didn't know where to begin the search until Lefevre forwarded a name. That's how I met Liam Hagen ... **the Haig**.

Journal Entry #395: The Verdict (Part 4)

Dedicated to *Gary and Sandi Huston*

Anyone who thinks lawsuits are fun, needs their sense of humour reexamined.

By definition, they're proceedings in a courtroom airing disputes between two organizations or people.

It became clear I had to sue Kal Lake. The persuasive phrasing they used in their membership bulletin that defended my dismissal ... suggested theft. On the other hand, my side hadn't been amplified, leaving me defenseless.

After the newsletter was distributed, Liam Hagen phoned me, introducing himself. In our exchange I provided him a synopsis and with little hesitation he took the case.

Hagen was sharp, conventional, and a quick study. A longtime litigator and past Capilano president, he'd represented other Vancouver pros in past. Our relationship lasted the length of the suit, which was several years. Time was a steady stream of emails, faxes, letters, and phone calls that verified facts and reconciled timelines in weaponizing a strategy.

On the other hand, Kal Lake's legal defense appeared like GOP radicals ... antagonizing, negative, and distorting. Hagen however, remained diligent using accuracy and authenticity to ambush their accusations. Like Donald Trump's administration, it was a reality check of truth's integrity within adult culture.

In addition, Hagen suffered from health challenges. He was often sharp with me, while short with them. During that time, several club members nuzzled me to drop the suit. I had no options at that point though. One in particular was prominent club member Dick Buick, who spent an afternoon appealing to me. By then however I was too committed.

After years of volleyed information, a mediated discovery date was scheduled. If it hadn't resolved there, it would have been sent to court. During discovery, I learned the value facts play when supporting claims. In one exchange, their lawyer hurled a harsh indictment across the table toward me. Being passionately aware of the evidence however, I deflected it. Had I not been quick, however, it might have altered the legal mood.

We won the suit and Hagen negotiated a settlement through us. One condition specified outcomes couldn't be published. Before the settlement, though, we requested atonement for the accusation of theft. During discovery, Corlazzoli downplayed his wording's intent, prompting the mediator to sigh: "Oh come on Flavio ... it was so obvious!" Eventually, the club insensitively plodded on with its promise, apologizing by newsletter.

In the aftermath, I was vindicated further when they awarded the head-pro position to Chevy. Despite the enormous talent applying for the position from across Canada, they instead bestowed it upon the one who'd made such a mess of it all. I'd been right all along. Within a year though, he too was dismissed and passed away soon after.

I was grateful for Hagen's work. I didn't mind his fee. It's safe suggesting in a fifty- dollar settlement that the lawyer is entitled to twenty-four of it.

Lawsuits though, aren't unlike relentless toothaches, except they loiter in the loins of mind rather than mouth. No one wins and even the compensated are left with lingering bank accounts of emotional trauma.

Journal Entry #396: Homeward Bound

Dedicated to *Barry Ensor*

I had come around full circle. Decades earlier I was a teenager without work, contemplating a future. I returned back to that place in life, but older. There weren't many opportunities either. I searched for head pro and management positions, but unlike other career times, opportunities seemed stifled.

One in particular was a head professional's appointment at Campbell River on Vancouver Island. Storey Creek Golf Course then was one of Canada's top-fifty facilities and shortlisted me for the job.

Jackie and I drove there in a blinding blizzard. Unlike the province's interior, the Island was victimized by different winter storms. There, Pacific fronts delivered wads of heavy, wet snow which made driving slick and dangerous. Eventually we arrived at the seaside community and enjoyed a successful interview until later learning they awarded it to a young touring pro.

Homeward bound, we visited the mill town of Port Alberni where for the first time, saw a golf course for sale. Owners of the Hollies were asking a million for the nine holer, which included land, clubhouse, inventories, equipment, goodwill, and living facilities.

I found other courses for sale on the internet prompting the idea of buying a job. I focused on contemporary golfers and diminishing leisure times. Shorter courses seemed futuristic.

Later we returned to Port where we met the owners, arranged a formal business tour and assessed it more thoroughly.

Journal Entry #397: Holly

Dedicated to *Jason Pley*

In buying a golf course, we narrowed our search down to two. In addition to the Hollies, another was offered in the Okanagan where sellers wanted a million and a half. Both facilities had living accommodations above the clubhouse and were efficient mom-and-pop operations. Because it suited our budget, we revisited the Hollies.

Before placing offers to buy property, our way arriving at due diligence was listing positives and negatives. The former had to substantially outweigh the latter. From that and a thorough financial scrubbing, Hollies appeared like a sincere going concern. As well, Jackie had an outgoing nature dealing with the public ... always positive in any industry. Consequently we submitted an offer, subject to financing.

Our proposal was met by a hostile rejection, but a week later we reconnected settling for a mutual amount.

In qualifying for a commercial mortgage (which differs from residential), we had to liquidate our possessions. Earlier, I wrote how some events in our lives came together easily, as if preordained. Sorting and selling our assets, while finding accommodation for Jackie's parents then, which normally would have proven insurmountably challenging in short time ... turned out simple. It all appeared predestined.

We were about to become golf course owners!

Journal Entry #398: Good Night and Good Luck!

Dedicated to *Preban Rasmussen*

One of the most amazing accomplishments in our golf lives didn't take place on a golf course, but after buying one. To finance purchasing the Hollies, we had to liquidate our assets and convert the capital in short time. We packed a home we'd lived in for two decades, finalized real estate details, contracted movers and found living accommodation for Jackie's parents. We closed one company, opened another, and began prepping a business in another part of the province. It was all framed in a portal of time viewing the upcoming golf season. Unbelievably, we pulled it off within weeks.

When the moment of departure arrived, Jackie and I heartbreakingly left our close-knit family. Overwhelmed in that emotion, we crammed two cars and left the Okanagan for the west coast with our loyal Pomeranian, Tiger. We refuged with Liam Hagen in West Vancouver, scouring final details of the offer to purchase Hollies.

Next morning in sunshine we set off for Port Alberni to begin our new adventure. To reach the island, we boarded an ocean ferry coincidentally named, *The Queen of Alberni*. We adopted the subtle sign as good luck for our future ahead.

Journal Entry #399: Somewhere Over the Rainbow/What a Wonderful World

Dedicated to *Koichi and Sacheko Masuda*

Later that day in sunshine, we arrived in Port Alberni. There we were greeted by the owners busying themselves with last-minute details and looking after golfers.

After the brief visit, we left to begin the arduous tasks demanded in ownership transition. They included signing endless deed papers, setting up local business accounts, adjusting utility information and scheduling locksmiths. We also needed to hire an accountant, insurer, and local lawyer. Later that day we'd officially sign off and begin the new venture.

While we were at the bank though ... the owners dropped a sudden bombshell, calling the deal off!

By then, our home in the Okanagan had sold. We'd left our family while movers were in transit delivering our possessions. We initiated business ownership changes, hired a lawyer to legalize the transfer and upon hearing the news, were literally preparing mortgage papers. Suddenly, it was being whisked away by obstinate landlords wanting out!

We returned, finding them unyielding, stubborn, and unwilling to commit. Jackie and I left stunned. That was our introduction to the fishing, mill town.

There was a hockey tournament in the city then, and every accommodation was reserved. We searched endlessly for an overnight room until finally locating a pokey end-unit at an inn on Redford Street.

There, huddled in the cold compressed room not much larger than a closet ... we found ourselves homeless! In disbelief, we combed the past for reasons. I'd lost a longtime job contentiously, split a close family, sold our assets and used the proceeds to purchase a golf course ... only to find it fading away. That night, we continually asked ourselves why?

The answers seemed shrouded within the still and lonely mists of Port Alberni.

The End

Epilogue

Journal Entry #400: Don't Dream It's Over

Dedicated to *Phil and Laurelee Edgell*

In the end, answers eventually materialized, exonerating the despair.

And when acknowledging them, I became aware of my own shortcomings as a professional. I saw myself a victim of arrogance. Arrogance petulantly demanding logic and reason behind our unjust treatment. I failed to see an essence of golf which I'd shared with students over decades.

I'd missed the bigger picture!

It was all simple. Life ... like golf ... wasn't always going to play fair.

Why did I overlook the similarities that existed between moments of birth, for instance, or when teeing up that first golf ball? Similarities claiming impartiality didn't exist beyond those seconds. I didn't have answers until foolishly realizing that fairness wasn't a factor. I had personally come face-to-face with the reality that life wasn't always going to be equitable nor compensatory.

And from the same well, where true friends arise in adversity, came that parting shot in my search for parity. Attitude! The kind found when dealing with each day's endless challenges ... whether in golf or life. The kind moulded from past choices. Like jealous choices when questioning harshness and its allotment. Empathetic choices when inflicting physical, mental, financial, spiritual, or emotional pain. Guilty choices when leaving environments lesser than before. Or angry choices provoked by the Donald Trump types claiming, "Winning was everything."

Those kind!

But fortunately next day, the owner's accountant mended fences by mediating an agreement. But even then, they stung us for half the reconciliation bill. However at the end of that day, we signed papers and became owners of a golf course. There, over the next fourteen years, Jackie and I operated that sliver of heaven.

Following that, we sold Hollies and retired. Jackie was inducted into golf's various halls of fame and I—as Picasso supposedly did—completed my own career circle, returning to what inspired that pilgrimage … golfing!

And occasionally in those rounds, I've found myself seemingly nudged by past mentors, scrutinizing my sabbatical from these **summer places**. At first, there weren't answers. But then, like spring's golf course grass that suddenly turns green, meanings sprouted.

First, paraphrasing Michelle Obama, golf didn't change me. She revealed who I was. Second, in her **original form** golf continues to be the world's healthiest and finest sport. And, like life, nothing should be expected from her except hopes and dreams.

And finally, I realized that, as a **purist** and endangered species of the game's past whose passions remain intrepid despite change, I should be grateful. Indebt for being chosen as a modest companion to golf in her own much longer journey.

Summer Place Jukebox

Dedicated to *Brian Dayholos*

Journal	Song	Artist	Composer(s)/Lyricist(s)
#3	Keep Searchin'	Del Shannon	Shannon
#4	Summer Place	Percy Faith	Max Steiner
#5	Cherish	The Association	Terry Kirkman
#7	Time of the Season	The Zombies	Rod Argent
#9	See You in September	The Happenings	Edwards/Wayne
#10	Downtown	Petula Clark	Tony Hatch
#11	I'll Be Doggone	Marvin Gaye	Moore/Robinson/Tarplin
#14	Riders On The Storm	The Doors	Densmore/Krieger Manzarek/Morrison
#15	Soul Coaxing	Raymond Lefèvre	Lefevre/Polnareff
#16	The Rain, the Park, and Other Things	The Cowsills	Duboff/Kornfeld
#17	Dream	Roy Orbison	Johnny Mercer
#18	Out of Time	The Rollingstones	Jagger/Richards
#20	Ten Pound Note	Steel River	Jay Telfer
#22	I Go To Pieces	Peter and Gordon	Del Shannon

#25	Snowbird	Anne Murray	Gene MacLellan
#28	A Horse With No Name	America	Bunnell/Freeze/Jackson
#29	California Dreamin'	The Mamas and Papas	Phillips/Phillips
#30	Reflections of My Life	Marmalade	Campbell/Ford
#31	In My Father's Footsteps	Terry Jacks	Mandel/Sachs
#32	Pipeline	The Chantays	Carman/Spikard
#33	Crystal Blue Persuasion	Tommy James and the Shondells	James/Gray/Vale
#34	Moon River	Henry Mancini	Mancini/Mercer
#35	Pretty Lady	Lighthouse	Skip Prokop
#36	My World is Empty	The Supremes	Holland/Dozier/Holland
#37	Angel Baby	Rosie and the Originals	Rosie Hamlin
#38	Odds and Ends	Dionne Warwick	Bacharach/David
#39	Band on the Run	Wings	Paul McCartney and Wings
#41	Sunny Afternoon	The Kinks	Ray Davies
#42	Mr. Bojangles	Nitty Gritty Dirt Band	Jerry Jeff Walker
#43	One Fine Morning	Lighthouse	Skip Prokop
#45	Tapestry	Carole King	King
#47	Tiny Dancer	Elton John	John/Taupin
#48	Concrete and Clay	Eddie Rambeau	Moeller/Parker
#49	Elusive Butterfly	Bob Lind	Lind
#50	Duke of Earl	Gene Chandler	Chandler/Edwards/Williams
#56	You've Got a Friend	James Taylor	Carole King
#57	Raindrops	Dee Clark	Clark
#58	Softly, as I Leave	Frank Sinatra	De Vita/Shaper

#59	Rainy Days and Mondays	The Carpenters	Nichols/Williams
#66	Little Things	Bobby Goldsboro	Goldsboro
#67	Land of Make Believe	Bucks Fizz	Hill/Sinfield
#68	Vincent	Don McLean	McLean
#74	On the Border	Al Stewart	Stewart
#81	Killing Me Softly	Roberta Flack	Fox/Gimbel
#82	C Moon	Wings	McCartney/McCartney
#85	Admiral Halsey	Wings	McCartney/McCartney
#86	Dunrobin's Gone	Brave Belt	Allan/Ericson
#87	Daniel	Elton John	John/Taupin
#91	Beyond the Clouds	The Poppy Family	Terry Jacks
#93	Yesterday Once More	The Carpenters	Bettis/Carpenter/Carpenter
#94	Superstar	The Carpenters	Bramlett/Bramlett/Russell
#95	Doctor My Eyes	Jackson Browne	Browne
#98	Educating Rita Theme	David Hentschel	Hentschel
#101	Night Moves	Bob Seger	Seger
#102	Whiter Shade of Pale	Procol Harum	Brooker/Fisher
#104	I Saw the Light	Todd Rundgren	Rundgren
#107	Alone in the Ring	Bill Conti	Conti
#109	If You Could Read My Mind	Gordon Lightfoot	Lightfoot
#110	These Eyes	The Guess Who	Bachman/Cummings
#111	Philadelphia Morning	Bill Conti	Conti
#112	The Year of the Cat	Al Stewart	Stewart/Wood
#113	Girl Don't Come	Sandie Shaw	Chris Andrews
#116	Heaven Must Have Sent You	The Elgins	Holland/Dozier/Holland
#117	First Date	Bill Conti	Conti

#118	The Lovin' Sound	Ian and Sylvia	Fricker/Tyson
#123	Space Oddity	David Bowie	Bowie
#124	Summer Wine	Nancy Sinatra	Lee Hazlewood
#127	Stoney End	Barbra Streisand	Laura Nyro
#128	Exodus	Ferrante and Teicher	Ernest Gold
#129	Funeral for a Friend	Elton John	John/Taupin
#130	Strange Magic	Electric Light Orchestra	Jeff Lynne
#131	Jackie Wilson Said	Van Morrison	Morrison
#132	Summer Song	Chad and Jeremy	Metcalfe/Noble/Stuart
#133	Where Have All the Flowers Gone	Johnny Rivers	Pete Seeger
#134	Gypsy	Fleetwood Mac	Stevie Nicks
#135	Seasons	Bob McBride	McBride
#136	The Way We Were	Barbra Streisand	Bergman/Bergman/Hamlisch
#138	It's My Turn	Diana Ross	Masser/Sager
#139	Too Late to Turn Back Now	Cornelius Brothers and Sister Rose	Cornelius/Otis/Reynolds/Williams
#140	One Tin Soldier	Original Caste	Lambert/Potter
#142	She's Not in Love	Kim Stockwood	Stockwood
#143	Just One Look	Doris Troy	Carroll/Troy
#145	A Beautiful Morning	The Rascals	Brigati/Cavaliere
#147	I'd Like to Get to Know You	Spanky and Our Gang	Stuart Scharf
#148	Best That You Can Do	Christopher Cross	Allen/Bacharach/Cross/Bayer Sager
#152	Summer Rain	Johnny Rivers	James Hendricks
#153	Do You Know Where You're Going to?	Diana Ross	Goffin/Masser
#154	Friday On My Mind	The Easybeats	Vanda/Young

#157	Fool On the Hill	Sérgio Mendes and Brasil '66	Lennon/McCartney/Mitchell
#159	Peter and Lou	Valdy	Craig Wood
#163	Walk On By	Dionne Warwick	Bacharach/David
#164	Sultans of Swing	Dire Straits	Mark Knopfler
#167	Woman	John Lennon	Lennon
#171	If I Had a Million Dollars	The Barenaked Ladies	Page/Robertson
#172	Traces	The Classics IV	Buie/Cobb/Gordy
#174	Under My Thumb	The Rolling Stones	Jagger/Richards
#176	Woman in Love	Barbra Streisand	Gibb/Gibb
#177	Dreams Go By	Harry Chapin	Chapin
#179	Tired of Toein' the Line	Rocky Burnette	Burnette/Coleman
#193	Talking in Your Sleep	The Romantics	Canler/Palmar/Skill
#194	Crocodile Rock	Elton John	John/Taupin
#196	When I Die	Motherlode	Kennedy/Smith
#198	Four Strong Winds	Neil Young	Ian Tyson
#199	Down by the Henry Moore	Murray McLauchlan	McLauchlan
#207	Hungry Heart	Bruce Springsteen	Springsteen
#208	What Does it Take?	Jr. Walker and the All Stars	Bristol/Bullock/Fuqua
#214	Head Over Heels	Tears for Fears	Orzabal/Smith
#216	La Isla Bonita	Madonna	Gaitsch/Leonard/Madonna
#218	Africa	Toto	Paich/Porcaro
#219	Everyone's Gone to the Moon	Jonathan King	King
#221	Starting Over	John Lennon	Lennon
#222	Move on Down the Line	Roy Orbison	Orbison

#223	Old Time Movie	Lisa Hartt Band	Rayburn Blake
#224	Steppin' Out	Joe Jackson	Jackson
#226	Empty Garden	Elton John	John/Taupin
#227	Back on the Chain Gang	The Pretenders	Chrissie Hynde
#228	Key Largo	Bertie Higgins	Higgins/Limbo
#231	Leader of the Band	Dan Fogelberg	Fogelberg
#232	Life in a Northern Town	The Dream Academy	Gabriel/Laird-Clowes
#233	Stand by Me	Ben E. King	King/Leiber/Marino/Stoller
#234	Time After Time	Cyndi Lauper	Everhart/Hyman/Lauper
#235	Guilty	Barbra Streisand and Barry Gibb	Gibb/Gibb/Gibb
#240	Gold	John Stewart	Stewart
#241	Self Control	Laura Branigan	Bigazzi/Piccolo/Riefoli
#243	Mack the Knife	Bobby Darin	Brecht/Weill
#244	Lonely Too Long	The Rascals	Brigati/Cavaliere
#245	Ain't Even Done With the Night	John Mellencamp	Mellencamp
#248	San Francisco	Scott McKenzie	John Phillips
#250	The Coldest Night of the Year	Bruce Cockburn	Cockburn
#252	Eye in the Sky	Alan Parsons Project	Parsons/Woolfson
#253	That's the Way Boys Are	Lesley Gore	Barkan/Raleigh
#254	West End Girls	Pet Shop Boys	Lowe/Tennant
#255	Uptown Girl	Billy Joel	Joel
#260	Shattered Dreams	Johnny Hates Jazz	Clark Datchler
#261	When You're Gone	The Cranberries	Dolores O'Riordan
#270	Somebodies Knockin'	Terri Gibbs	Gillespie/Penney
#271	Seven Year Ache	Rosanne Cash	Cash

SUMMER PLACE

#272	At the Zoo	Simon and Garfunkel	Paul Simon
#275	MacArthur Park	Richard Harris	Jimmy Webb
#276	My Heart's in the Highlands	The Barra MacNeils	Robert Burns
#277	The Living Years	Mike and the Mechanics	Robertson/Rutherford
#278	Everybody Wants to Rule the World	Tears for Fears	Hughes/Orzabal/Stanley
#279	Losing My Religion	R.E.M.	Berry/Buck/Mills/Stipe
#280	Wonderful! Wonderful!	Johnny Mathis	Edwards/Raleigh
#286	Tell Her No	The Zombies	Rod Argent
#287	Viva La Vida	Coldplay	Buckland/Berryman/Champion/Martin
#288	Take On Me	A-ha	Furuholmen/Harket/Waaktaar-Savoy
#289	Tender Years	John Cafferty and Beaver Brown Band	Cafferty
#290	Last Christmas	Wham	George Michael
#291	If You Leave	Orchestral Manoeuvres in the Dark	Cooper/Humphreys/McCluskey
#292	Shout	Tears for Fears	Orzabal/Stanley
#295	Someday	Sugar Ray	Kahne/Ray
#299	First We Take Manhattan	Jennifer Warnes	Leonard Cohen
#308	Sukiyaki	Kyu Sakamoto	Nakamura/Rokusuke Ei
#310	Memory	Barbra Streisand	Eliot/Nunn/Webber
#311	Heat Wave	Martha and the Vandallas	Holland/Dozier/Holland
#315	Beautiful Life	Ace of Base	Ballard/Berggren/
#318	Girls Just Want to Have Fun	Cyndi Lauper	Robert Hazard
#319	Have I Told You Lately	Van Morrison	Morrison

#320	On the Dark Side	John Cafferty and Beaver Brown Band	Cafferty
#321	Trouble	Lindsey Buckingham	Buckingham
#322	Eyes Without a Face	Billy Idol	Idol/Stevens
#324	Good thing (Where Have You Gone?)	Fine Young Cannibals	Gift/Steele
#325	Mercy Mercy Me	Marvin Gaye	Gaye
#328	Billy, Billy Went A Walkin'	The Beau-Marks	Frechette/Hutchinson/Tailleur
#329	Constant Craving	K.D. Lang	Lang/Mink
#332	The Circle is Small	Gordon Lightfoot	Lightfoot
#335	There is an End	Holly Golightly	Fox/Keeler/Lawrence
#337	Harvest Moon	Neil Young	Young
#339	When Smokey Sings	ABC	Fry/White
#340	More Than This	Roxy Music	Bryan Ferry
#345	Miss Chatelaine	K. D. Lang	Lang/Mink
#349	Borderline	Madonna	Reggie Lucas
#351	Brother Love's Travelling Salvation Show	Neil Diamond	Diamond
#357	Still the Same	Bob Seger	Seger
#359	Johnny Get Angry	Joanie Summers	David/Edwards
#360	Anywhere But Here	K. D. Lang	Lang/Nowels
#363	Still of the Night	The Five Satins	Fred Parris
#364	It Always Happens This Way	Toulouse	Mitchell/Thurston
#365	Hazy Shade of Winter	Simon and Garfunkel	Paul Simon
#366	Stay	Jackson Browne	Paul/Williams/Wonder
#367	Sounds of Silence	Simon and Garfunkel	Paul Simon

#368	Dreamboat Annie	Heart	Wilson/Wilson
#369	Don't Get Me Wrong	The Pretenders	Chrissie Hynde
#370	Born Too Late	The Poni-Tails	Strouse/Tobias
#371	Apache	The Shadows	Jerry Lordan
#374	If I Had a Hammer	Trini Lopez	Seeger/Hays
#376	Things Have Changed	Bob Dylan	Dylan
#379	Djobi Djoba	The Gipsy Kings	Baliardo/Baliardo/Bouchikhi Reyes/Reyes/Reyes
#380	Mas Que Nada	Sérgio Mendes and Brasil '66	Jorge Ben Jor
#381	No Matter What Shape	The T-Bones	Granville Alexander Burland
#383	Stay Loose	Gordon Lightfoot	Lightfoot
#385	Someone Like You	Van Morrison	Morrison
#386	Count Me In	Gary Lewis and the Playboys	Glen D. Hardin
#387	Peacekeeper	Fleetwood Mac	Lindsey Buckingham
#391	What Becomes of the Brokenhearted?	Jimmy Ruffin	Weatherspoon/Riser/Dean
#392	Why Do All Good Things Come to an End	Nelly Furtado	Danja/Furtado/Martin Timbaland
#393	Say It Right	Nelly Furtado	Danja/Furtado/Timbaland
#396	Homeward Bound	Simon and Garfunkel	Paul Simon
#397	Holly	Terry Jacks	Jacks
#399	Somewhere Over the Rainbow/What a Wonderful World	Israel Kamakawiwo'ole	Arlen/Harburg`Thiele/Weiss
#400	Don't Dream It's Over	Crowded House	Neil Finn

Author's Blurbs: The Sounds of Golf

Dedicated to: *Rob Longeuay*

Golf has its own music. Remove your ear pods and sharpen your senses. The sport's own melodies might filter in. Rhythms and percussion like the following:

1. The ripples of a flag's fabric fluttering in wind.
2. The muffled thud following a ball's descent when punching ground.
3. The hydraulic engagement of a mower's cutting unit.
4. The inherent shrill from each golfer yelling "Fore!"
5. The pin-ball echo when a ball drops into a cup.
6. The exclusive flavour of each course's natural bird calls.
7. The cannon crack of tee shots reverberating about a course.
8. The uniform shearing of grass from razor sharp mower reels.
9. The unison clanking from a bag of irons with each step taken.
10. The sounds of silence prior to each golf shot.

In more recent times, those melodies have been breached. New golfers now suppress golf's very soul, accessorizing their on course equipment with mobile devices blaring rap and punk to grunge and heavy metal.

An acquaintance was once asked by a golfing partner whether he minded some music on the course. The acquaintance replied, "Yes, I do mind!" "I don't bring my golf clubs to the discothèque ..."

Are we witnessing the end of golf as a sport or an installment of the inane?

Printed in the USA
CPSIA information can be obtained
at www.ICGtesting.com
JSHW080757070923
47970JS00005B/102